◼ Application Software Manual

Using:

WordPerfect® 5.1
Lotus® 1-2-3®, Release 2.2
dBASE III PLUS®
dBASE IV®
VP-Expert® 3.0, Educational Version

Meredith Flynn
Steven L. Mandell

West Publishing Company
St. Paul   New York   Los Angeles   San Francisco

WordPerfect® is the registered trademark of the WordPerfect Corporation.

Lotus®, 1-2-3® are the registered trademarks of the Lotus Development Corporation.

dBASE®, dBASE III PLUS®, dBASE IV® are the registered tradmarks of Ashton-Tate Corporation.

VP-Expert® is the registered trademark of WordTech Systems, Inc.

IBM® is the registered trademark of International Business Machines Corporation.

MS-DOS® is the registered trademark of Microsoft Corporation.

WEST'S COMMITMENT TO THE ENVIRONMENT

In 1906, West Publishing Company began recycling materials left over from the production of books. This began a tradition of efficient and responsible use of resources. Today, up to 95% of our legal books and 70% of our college texts are printed on recycled, acid-free stock. West also recycles nearly 22 million pounds of scrap paper annually—the equivalent of 181,717 trees. Since the 1960s, West has devised ways to capture and recycle waste inks, solvents, oils, and vapors created in the printing process. We also recycle plastics of all kinds, wood, glass, corrugated cardboard, and batteries, and have eliminated the use of styrofoam book packaging. We at West are proud of the longevity and the scope of our commitment to our environment.

Production, Prepress, Printing and Binding by West Publishing Company.

Contents

❏ CHAPTER 7: MORE dBASE III PLUS FEATURES   235

❏ CHAPTER 8: INTRODUCTION TO dBASE IV   265

❑ CHAPTER 9: MORE dBASE IV FEATURES   311

❏ CHAPTER 12: DESKTOP PUBLISHING WITH WORDPERFECT 5.1   397

Preface

The purpose of this **Application Software Manual** is to teach students how to use the most popular professional software currently available for IBM/MS-DOS computers.

The book begins by providing an interactive introduction to the IBM/MS-DOS operating system. The remaining chapters instruct students on how to operate WordPerfect 5.1, Lotus 1-2-3, release 2.2, dBASE III PLUS, dBASE IV, and VP-Expert. Two chapters are devoted to each program. The book concludes with an extra chapter on WordPerfect 5.1. This final chapter introduces the concept of desktop publishing software and explains how to use the desktop publishing features in WordPerfect 5.1. The chapters take students step-by-step through the basic features of the program. Hands-on exercises follow each explanation of a software feature. These exercises provide students an opportunity to immediately use the feature just explained. Exercises, Problems and Challenges complete each chapter. These exercises progress in their level of difficulty. The Problems all involve manipulating files included on the Student File Disk that accompanies this book. A command summary is also found at the end of each chapter. Each command summary provides a quick reference to all the commands covered in that chapter.

The chapters have all been written assuming the user has a hard disk system. Difference Boxes have been included to accommodate those users with floppy disk drive systems. In chapters 2, 3 and 12, Difference Boxes have been included to accommodate those users who have WordPerfect 5.0 rather than 5.1.

In addition to the Student File Disk, this book comes with the Educational Version of VP-Expert 3.0. VP-Expert is an expert system development tool that allows the user to build an expert system.

This manual was designed to accompany Steven Mandell's *Computers and Information Processing: Concepts and Applications*, 6th edition. It can be used independently of this text, however. This manual is appropriate for any learning environment where the purpose is to have students quickly using the fundamental functions of popular application software programs.

CHAPTER 1

Introduction to Personal Computers and DOS

OUTLINE

❏ INTRODUCTION

Microcomputers that use the IBM Personal Computer DOS or MS-DOS operating system are among the most popular computers today. These microcomputers are both powerful and inexpensive enough for small businesses to use for word processing, financial management, bookkeeping, billing, and professional-looking document preparation. Large businesses are also buying these types of microcomputers to link to mainframe computer systems. Employees can use these microcomputers independently for tasks that do not require the power of a mainframe but can connect to the mainframe for tasks that require greater processing power. The employees can also access data stored on the mainframe system through the communication lines that connect the mainframe and microcomputer. This type of data processing solution keeps a business's data in one central location, thus facilitating data integrity by reducing the number of places where the same piece of data must be maintained.

The IBM Personal Computer operating system was developed by Microsoft Corporation for the IBM PC microcomputer, which was introduced in August of 1981. Since that time, the IBM Personal Computer/MS-DOS operating system has been revised and enhanced and is currently used on microcomputers built by a number of different manufacturers including IBM, Compaq, Tandy, Epson, AT&T, Texas Instruments, NCR, Dell, Northgate, and CompuAdd. Microcomputers running the IBM Personal Computer /MS-DOS operating system are also very popular in schools and homes. A wide variety of software is available for educational, recreational, and home-management purposes.

❏ HARDWARE

Standard pieces of equipment are needed in order to run software on an IBM or MS-DOS microcomputer. The primary piece of hardware is the system unit which holds the computer itself and one or more disk drives. A monitor and a keyboard also are needed. A printer is needed to print paper copies of your work.

Microcomputers running the IBM Personal Computer/MS-DOS operating system typically contain a minimum of 512 kilobytes (K) or 640K of memory. The amount of memory a computer can handle is important because each program requires a specific amount of memory. The software package lists the amount of memory needed. More memory can be added by installing additional memory chips or expansion boards containing memory. In some cases additional memory of up to 16 Mb (megabytes) can be added.

The Monitor

The monitor displays output on a screen that is similar to a television screen. An IBM PC or MS-DOS microcomputer usually is equipped with a monochrome or color monitor. A monochrome monitor displays a single color on a black or gray background. In some cases, color monitors require that a special circuit board be installed in the computer. The type of monitor depends on the purposes for which the computer will be used.

The Cursor. The cursor indicates where text will appear as it is typed. The cursor for many programs is a tiny horizontal bar. As you type, the cursor moves ahead of each typed character that appears on the screen. When the computer is first started, the cursor appears next to the A> or the C> prompt.

The Keyboard

Except for the placement of some specific keys, the keyboards used on IBM and MS-DOS microcomputers are very similar. The keyboard used on the original IBM PC contained 83 keys. Many of the IBM or MS-DOS computers sold today come with keyboards that contain 102 keys. In either case, the keyboard contains letter and number keys, function keys, and a numeric keypad. The letter and number keys work the same as a typewriter's keys. Pressing <Shift> with a letter key produces a capital letter. Pressing <Shift> with a number or special character key produces the character shown on the top half of the key. When any key is held down, the character is repeated until the key is released. Because of this feature, be sure that you press keys just long enough for the character to appear on the screen or for the computer to receive the command.

On the left side or at the very top of the keyboard is a set of ten or twelve numbered function keys. These function keys have the letter F followed by a number printed on them. The function that each key performs is determined by the software being used.

The keyboard has a numeric keypad on the right side, similar to a calculator's keypad, which also is used for editing purposes. When <Num Lock> (located in the top row of keys) is on, the keypad can be used to enter the numbers 0-9.

Arrow keys used to position the cursor are often located within the numeric keypad. They can be used to move the cursor up, down, to the left, or to the right on the screen when <Num Lock> is off. The left arrow key is the same key as the 4, the right arrow key is the same key as the 6, the up arrow key is the same key as the 8, and the down arrow key is the same key as the 2. If you make a typing mistake, these keys help you move the cursor to it. Then you can correct the mistake. Mistakes also can be corrected by moving the cursor to the left using <Backspace> which is located in the top row of keys and marked with an arrow pointing left. Pressing <Backspace> deletes the character to the left of the cursor.

The key marked with the symbol, ⏎ located just to the left of the numeric keypad, is referred to as either <Enter> or <Return>. It moves the cursor down to the beginning of the next line.

The Disk Drive

The hardware device that reads a disk or diskette is called a disk drive. Disk drives allow programs and other data to be stored so that the computer can process it again later. When two floppy disk drives are used, one drive is called drive A and the other is called drive B. If the floppy disk drives are side-by-side, the drive on the left is usually drive A; if the drives are on top of each other, the drive on top is usually drive A. If the system has one floppy disk drive and one hard disk drive, the floppy drive is usually drive A and the hard drive is usually drive C.

Floppy disk drives that are sold for today's IBM and MS-DOS computers come in two sizes and four capacities. A 5¼-inch floppy diskette is made of a soft flexible cover and the diskette can hold either 360K or 1.2 Mb of data. A 3½-inch floppy diskette is made of a hard inflexible cover and can hold either 720K or 1.4 Mb of data (see Figure 1-1). 5¼-inch diskettes that hold 1.2 Mb of data and 3½-inch diskettes that hold 1.4 Mb of data are called high density disks. These diskettes can only be read by high density disk drives.

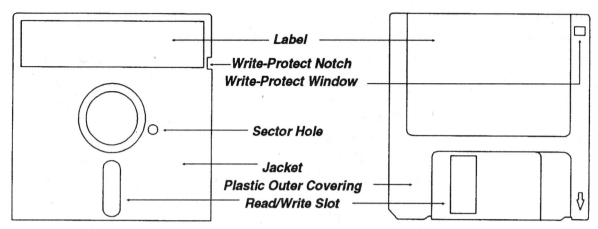

FIGURE 1-1a 5 1/4" Floppy Diskette   FIGURE 1-1b 3 1/2" Floppy Diskette

❏ CARING FOR YOUR COMPUTER

Taking good care of a personal computer will help keep it working properly. The computer should be set on a sturdy desk or table. The room should be clean and dry, but not too dry. When the humidity in a room is very low, static electricity may be created, which can destroy the data stored on floppy diskettes. Extreme heat and cold also may harm the computer. Keep the machine away from direct sunlight. Keep hardware away from heating ducts and air conditioners.

Eating and drinking should be avoided near the computer. Crumbs and spilled drinks can make the keyboard keys stick. Dust and dirt from the air can harm the keyboard or cause static. It is a good idea to keep the computer and hardware devices covered with antistatic covers when they are not being used.

When the computer is on, be careful not to move it or jolt it, including the desk or table where it is placed. If the electrical plug is disconnected accidentally, data that has not been recorded on a disk is lost forever.

Your computer is only as reliable as the data storage medium. Floppy disks always should be handled with care. Never touch the exposed surface of the diskette. Hold diskettes by their labels. Floppy diskettes can be ruined by extreme temperatures, dust, and eraser crumbs. For example, diskettes should not be left in a car when it is hot or cold outside. Avoid setting diskettes near magnets, telephones, or television sets. Magnets and electrical devices can destroy data stored on disks.

Always prepare the diskette label before affixing it to the diskette. If you must write on a label that is already on the diskette, use a felt-tip or nylon-tip marker and press very lightly. Pressure caused by writing on the label with a pencil or ballpoint pen may destroy the data stored on the disk.

Do not bend the diskette. Store diskettes, in their paper envelopes, in an upright position to avoid warping. Diskette storage boxes are available for this purpose.

Common sense is the key to proper computer care. Keep the equipment clean and away from harmful conditions.

           Chapter 1: Introduction to Personal Computers and DOS

Before you can use software with a personal computer, you need to know how to load it. To load a program means to put it into the computer's memory. The method used to load software differs from one package to another, so you should read the directions accompanying the software.

Most software packages require that some type of operating system software be loaded first. IBM PC DOS is the operating system sold with IBM microcomputers; MS-DOS is sold for use with IBM-compatible microcomputers (clones). An operating system consists of programs that allow the computer to manage itself. Disk operating system (DOS) is a name given to an operating system that resides on a disk. One of the programs in a DOS, for example, governs the transfer of data to and from disks.

The directions in this chapter assume that you are using a computer with one floppy disk drive and one hard disk drive. Directions for computers with two floppy diskette drives are provided in Difference Boxes.

To start the computer, turn on both the power and the monitor switches. Depending on the type of computer you are using, the power to the system unit will be located on the front or the right side of the unit itself. Power switches for the monitors are typically on the front or right side of the monitor. The disk drive makes a whirring noise as it reads the disk. Most computers with hard disks have been set up so that they automatically display the time and date for you. However, some systems require you to enter the time and date yourself. If this is the case, the system will prompt you to enter these values. Type in the date, press <Enter> and then type in the time and press <Enter>. Follow the format for the date and time shown on the screen. The time is entered using a 24-hour clock. For example, the following would be entered for 1:30 p.m., October 23, 1992:

```
Current date is Tue 1-01-1980
Enter new date (mm-dd-yy): 10-23-92
Current time is  8:28:53.62p
Enter new time: 13:30
```

A screen similar to the following appears:

```
Microsoft(R) MS-DOS(R) Version 4.01
          (C)Copyright Microsoft Corp 1981-1988

C>_
```

The symbol C> is called the system prompt. This prompt indicates that the computer is waiting for your next command. The letter C means that the C drive (the hard drive) is currently being accessed. Files stored on the hard drive can now be used. If you wish to access a disk in drive A, type A: at the C> system prompt and press <Enter>. The system prompt changes to A>, indicating that drive A is currently being accessed.

Difference Box: Starting a Computer with Two Floppy Diskette Drives
Insert the DOS disk in drive A and turn on the computer. Turn on both the power and the monitor switches. The computer whirs for a few seconds. When prompted to do so, type in the date and press <Enter>. Next, type in the time and press <Enter>. Use the format for the date and time as shown on the screen. When entering the time, remember the computer usually uses a 24-hour clock. The A prompt (A>) will appear. You are now ready to use the system.

❑ IBM PC and MS-DOS Conventions

Each operating system has certain conventions that must be followed by the users and by the programs that interact with the files stored on the computer system. The sections that follow describe conventions used by IBM PC DOS and MS-DOS to manage the files stored on the computer system. Conventions related specifically to naming files, managing directories, and specifying the location of files are discussed.

Files

Within the IBM PC DOS and MS-DOS operating systems, there are two basic types of files—executable files and data files. Executable files include both program files and DOS batch files. Program files are directly understandable by the microprocessor and are the result of translating (or compiling) a source code program. Batch files, in contrast, are interpreted by the operating system as they are run. Both of these types of files ask the operating system to execute commands required to perform specific tasks.

Data files contain data that can be manipulated by a program. Data files can take on many different forms. For example, one data file may contain employee data records. Another may contain a letter written using a word processor.

Each file that is stored on a diskette or hard disk must have a unique name. The name of a file consists of two parts, the file name and the file name extension. The file name and file name extension are separated by a period (.). The name SAMPLE.FIL, for example, has a file name of SAMPLE and a file name extension of FIL. A name does not require a file name extension, but it is often helpful in providing an indication of what is contained within a particular file. For example, files with a file name extension of EXE or COM represent executable program files, and files with a BAT extension represent batch files.

A name can be one to eleven characters long. A maximum of eight characters can be used for the file name, and a maximum of three characters can be used for the file name extension. The set of valid file name characters includes A-Z, a-z, 0-9, $, %, ', -, @, {, }, ~, _, ', !, #, (,), and &. When using MS-DOS file commands, a valid file name must be included within the command.

Directories

As a way to keep files better organized and separated on both floppy diskettes and hard disks, IBM PC DOS and MS-DOS allow for the creation of directories. Directories can be compared to file folders. For example, all the information pertaining to employee Smith can be kept in a file folder labeled Smith; information pertaining to employee Jones can be kept in a file folder labeled Jones. If the information is kept on a floppy diskette instead of in file folders, there can be one directory labeled Smith and another labeled Jones. All the information (files) required for employee Smith would be stored in the directory Smith, and all the information required for employee Jones would be stored in the Jones directory.

There are two types of directories that can be created. The first is a root directory. The root directory is created by default when a floppy diskette or hard disk is formatted, and there can be only one root directory per disk. In addition, a root directory is fixed in size and is stored in a fixed location on the disk. The size of the root directory will vary depending on the type of disk being used. A double-sided, double-density (360 K capacity) floppy diskette, for example, can contain up to 112 files and/or directories.

The other type of directory is known as a subdirectory. A subdirectory is created as an extension to the root directory. See Figure 1-2 for a graphic representation of a root directory and its subdirectories. A

Chapter 1: Introduction to Personal Computers and DOS

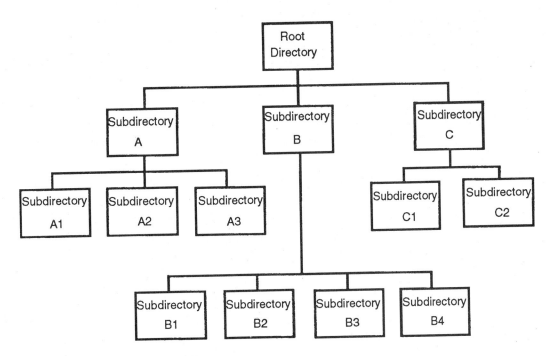

FIGURE 1-2 A Root Directory and Subdirectories

subdirectory can grow to be any size and is stored anywhere on the disk. The directory that you are currently in is referred to as the working directory.

Again, directories simply give the user the ability to better organize and separate files that are being stored on floppy diskettes and hard disks. Commands that create and remove directories, show the user a list of the files in a directory, and move from one directory to another are discussed in the section headed Directory Commands.

Paths

A path is a way in which a user can tell the operating system where a specific file is located. IBM PC DOS and MS-DOS use path names in much the same way that file names are used. File names combined with path names form what is sometimes referred to as a fully qualified file name. The backslash character (\) is used to separate path names from file names. For example, if there was a file named SAMPLE.DAT in the directory XYZ on drive A, the fully qualified file name for SAMPLE.DAT would be:

```
A:\XYZ\SAMPLE.DAT
```

By using a fully qualified file name, the user has explicitly told the operating system where a particular file is located. As mentioned previously, the directory that you are currently in is the working directory. If a command requiring a file name is used and the file name that is provided does not contain a path name, the working directory is assumed to be the path name and the operating system acts accordingly. In the example given above, if the user was in the XYZ directory on drive A, the working directory within the operating system would be set to the following:

```
A:\XYZ
```

Therefore, for any command requiring a path name, the operating system would add A:\XYZ\ to the beginning of the file name supplied by the user. Path names are used in many of the examples provided in the following sections.

❏ DISK OPERATING SYSTEM COMMANDS

As noted earlier, an operating system consists of a number of programs that control the functions of the computer system. In addition, an operating system also provides commands that allow a user of the system to direct the computer in performing certain operations. For example, the user may want to initialize, or format, a diskette so that it can be used to store programs and data. The operating system, therefore, must provide the user with some way of formatting a diskette. In the case of the IBM PC DOS and MS-DOS operating systems, the FORMAT command is used to initialize or format a diskette. The FORMAT command is provided as part of the operating system that comes with a personal computer. The following sections discuss some of the commonly used IBM PC and MS-DOS commands.

Initializing a Diskette

Before a new disk can be used for storing programs and data, it must be formatted or initialized. Formatting prepares the disk so that data and programs can be stored on it. When a used disk is reformatted, the contents of the disk are erased so that the disk can be used for new data and programs. Never format a disk with data stored on it unless you are sure you no longer need the data.

The way data are stored on a disk depends on the operating system being used. Disk manufacturers produce standardized disks that can be used by a wide variety of computers using a number of different operating systems. The blank disk must be customized for the particular computer and operating system being used. Formatting a disk is the process that prepares the disk to be used with a particular computer and operating system.

Difference Box: Formatting a Disk Using Two Floppy Diskette Drives
The DOS disk should be in drive A. The disk to be formatted should be in drive B. Type A: and press <Enter> to make sure drive A is the drive being accessed. The A> system prompt should be on the screen. Type FORMAT B: and press <Enter>.

     YOUR TURN

The exercises used in this chapter assume you are working on an IBM PC or MS-DOS computer that has a hard disk (drive C) and a floppy diskette drive (drive A). The exercises also assume that the computer system will boot from the C drive and that to begin the exercises you are positioned in the directory on the C drive where the DOS command files are located.

1. Turn on the computer and monitor to boot the system.
2. When the system prompt C> appears, type the following command:

    FORMAT A:

Press <Enter> . Typing the letter A tells the computer that the blank diskette is in drive A.

3. The following message appears:

```
Insert new diskette for drive A:
and strike ENTER when ready . . .
```

Insert the blank diskette in drive A and close the drive door. Then press <Enter>. Once the FORMAT program is done formatting the blank diskette, you should see the following message:

```
FORMAT COMPLETE
```

Information on how much storage space is available on the diskette is also displayed. Remember, never remove a diskette while the light on the diskette drive is still on.

4. The system asks if you need to format another diskette. Press N and then press <Enter>.

Directory Commands

The IBM PC DOS and MS-DOS directory commands can be used to create a new subdirectory, remove (delete) an existing subdirectory, change your working directory, and display the list of files in a directory.

MKDIR. The MKDIR command is used to create a subdirectory. The MKDIR command can be shortened to just the letters MD.

RMDIR. The command RMDIR is used to remove an existing subdirectory. The RMDIR command can also be shortened to just the letters RD. For example, the commands RMDIR DOS or RD DOS would delete a subdirectory named DOS.

CHDIR. The command CHDIR is used to change from one working directory to another. The CHDIR command can also be shortened to just the letters CD.

 YOUR TURN

---

1. At the C> prompt, type the command:

```
A:
```

Press <Enter>. This command allows you to switch from drive C to drive A.

2. Make sure the newly formatted diskette is in drive A. The A> prompt should be on the screen. Type the following command:

Type: MD DOS
Press <Enter>

You have now created a new subdirectory named DOS.

Type: CD DOS
Press <Enter>

You have now changed your working directory from the root directory to the DOS subdirectory on drive A.

Difference Box: Making a Directory Using a Computer with Two Floppy Diskette Drives
The DOS disk should be in drive A and the formatted disk should be in drive B. At the A> prompt, type the command B: and press <Enter>. The B> prompt should be on the screen. Type the command MD DOS and press <Enter>. You have created a subdirectory named DOS on the disk in drive B.

---

3. The PROMPT command can be used to modify the DOS command prompt.

> Type: `PROMPT $P$G`
>
> Press <Enter>

Note that the prompt has changed from A> to A:\DOS>. The $P used with the prompt command tells the DOS operating system to include the working directory as part of the prompt displayed to the user. The $G portion of the command indicates to DOS that the > character should be displayed at the end of the prompt. Consult your operating system manual for additional ways of modifying the DOS prompt.

Movement from one directory to another is easy if you understand how to tell the operating system where you want to go. Please refer to Figure 1-3 and consider the following example. The user is currently in the directory A:\LEVEL_1\XYZ and would like to go to the directory A:\LEVEL_1\ABC. As you can see in Figure 1-3, if the user were to move to this directory one step at a time, he or she would have to move up one directory level and then down into the ABC directory. However, the move from the first directory to the second directory can also be done with the following command:

> `CD A:\LEVEL_1\ABC`

In addition to explicitly telling the operating system what directory you would like to go to, there are a number of shorthand identifiers that can also be used. The command CD .., for example, changes the

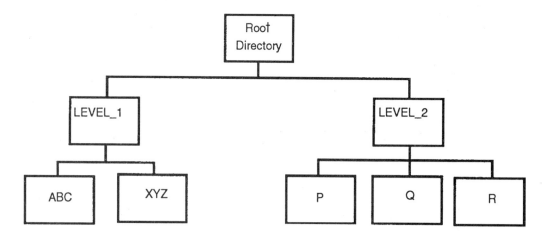

FIGURE 1-3 Moving from One Directory to Another

Chapter 1: Introduction to Personal Computers and DOS

working directory to the directory immediately above the directory you are currently in. The command CD\ changes the working directory to the root directory of the current disk drive. In addition, if the directory is on the current disk drive, there is no need to specify the disk drive letter as part of the path name. In the example above, using the command CD\LEVEL_1\ABC would have been the same as using the command CD A:\LEVEL_1\ABC.

DIR. The DIR command is used to display the list of files in a subdirectory. The command DIR DOS would display a list of files in the DOS subdirectory. The command DIR B:\ would display a list of files in the root directory of drive B.

 YOUR TURN

1. You should still see the prompt A:\DOS> on the screen. You are going to use the DIR command.

> Type: DIR
>
> Press <Enter>

2. Your screen should contain information similar to the following:

```
Volume in drive A has no label
Directory of A:\DOS
.          <DIR>      12-27-90 9:45p
..         <DIR>      12-27-90 9:45p
      2 File(s)      729088 bytes free
```

Two files are listed and they are both shown with <DIR>. These are markers used by the system. The single period to the left of the first <DIR> indicates the previous directory, or the main directory. The two periods to the left of the second <DIR> indicates the current directory, or in this case the DOS directory. Since there are currently no files in the subdirectory, there are no file names listed.

File Commands

IBM PC DOS and MS-DOS file commands allow a user to perform operations on files that are stored on diskettes or hard disk drives. With file commands, a user can copy a file from one place to another, change the file's name, delete (or erase) a file, display a file's contents on the screen, or print a file. These commands can be used to operate on a single file or on multiple files with a single command. For example, if a user wants to copy five files with similar names from a hard disk to a floppy diskette, it is possible to accomplish this with a single command.

COPY. The COPY command is used to copy one or more files from one place to another. For example, the COPY command can be used to copy a file from one floppy diskette to another, from a floppy diskette to a hard disk, from a hard disk to a floppy diskette, from multiple files into one file, and from the display screen into a file.

YOUR TURN

---

1. You are going to use the COPY command. Your formatted working diskette should be in drive A.

      Type: `COPY C:FORMAT.COM A:`

      Press <Enter>

The COPY command requires a source file name and a destination file name in order to work properly. If there is no destination file name specified, the name of the destination file will be the same as the source file. You copied the file FORMAT.COM from the working directory on drive C to the working directory on drive A.

2. You are going to check to make sure the file was copied.

      Type: `DIR`

      Press <Enter>

Your screen should contain information similar to the following:

```
Volume in drive A has no label
Directory of A:\DOS
.           <DIR>        12-27-90  9:45p
..          <DIR>        12-27-90  9:45p
FORMAT.COM           22875 11-15-89 12:00p
        3 File(s)          705536 bytes free
```

Since you copied the file FORMAT.COM from the hard disk to the formatted diskette, there is now one file in the DOS directory.

The COPY command can be used in many different ways to accomplish many different tasks. For example, the command

    `COPY A:FILE1.DAT C:`

will copy the file FILE1.DAT from the working directory of the floppy diskette in drive A to the working directory on hard disk drive C. The command

    `COPY A:FILE1.DAT D:\TEST`

will copy the file FILE1.DAT from the working directory on floppy diskette drive A to hard disk drive D and the directory named TEST. The command

    `COPY C:\FILE2.DAT A:`

will copy the file FILE2.DAT from the root directory on hard disk drive C to the working directory on drive A. The command

```
COPY C:FILE2.DAT A:\XYZ
```

will copy the file FILE2.DAT from the working directory on hard disk drive C to the XYZ directory on floppy diskette drive A. The command

```
COPY FILE1.DAT FILE2.DAT
```

will copy the contents of the file FILE1.DAT into another file of the name FILE2.DAT. A word of caution should be noted, however. If the file FILE2.DAT already exists, the contents of FILE1.DAT will be written over top of FILE2.DAT, destroying its original contents. If the file FILE2.DAT does not exist, the operating system will create a new file by that name.

The command

```
COPY FILE1.DAT + FILE2.DAT + FILE3.DAT FILES123.DAT
```

will copy the contents of FILE1.DAT, and FILE2.DAT, and FILE3.DAT into one file named FILES123.DAT. The three files will be joined together in the order specified in the COPY command. Again, note that if the file FILES123.DAT existed prior to issuing the command shown, its contents will be destroyed when the new contents are written to the file.

The command

```
COPY CON TESTFILE
```

will copy everything typed on the display screen after the command is issued into a file named TESTFILE. In order to stop entry to the file and save its contents, press the <F6> key and then press the <Enter> key. The source file name CON is an MS-DOS reserved name that indicates input is coming from the display screen (or console) rather than from another file.

 YOUR TURN

---

1. Change directories from the DOS subdirectory on drive A to the root directory by entering the following command and pressing <Enter>.

```
CD\
```

2. You are in the root directory.

Type: `COPY CON AUTOEXEC.BAT`
Press <Enter>
Type: `DATE`
Press <Enter>
Type: `TIME`
Press <Enter>
Type: `PROMPT $P$G`
Press <Enter>
Press the <F6> key

Press <Enter>

You have created a file named AUTOEXEC.BAT in the root directory of drive A.

3. Now you want to verify that the file is in the root directory:

Type: `DIR`

Press <Enter>

The information displayed on your screen should look similar to the following:

```
Volume in drive A has no label
Volume Serial Number is 2858-468E
Directory of A:\DOS
DOS          <DIR>      12-27-90  9:45p
AUTOEXEC BAT        23  12-30-90  9:40P
        2 File(s)         631808 bytes free
```

DEL. The DEL command is used to delete (or erase) a file from a disk. For example, the command

`DEL FILE1.DAT`

would delete the file FILE1.DAT from the working directory. The command

`DEL C:\DATA\EMPLOYEE.DAT`

would delete the file EMPLOYEE.DAT from the directory DATA on drive C.

REN. The REN (rename) command is used to change a file's name from one name to another. For example, the command

`REN FILE1.DAT FILE100.DAT`

would change the name of FILE1.DAT to FILE100.DAT. The command

`REN A:\XYZ\TESTFILE TEST`

would rename the file TESTFILE on drive A in the directory XYZ to TEST.

TYPE. The command TYPE can be used to display a file's contents on the display screen. For example, the command

`TYPE FILE1.DAT`

will display the contents of the file FILE1.DAT on the display screen. If the file exceeds a screen in length, the MORE operation can be used to display the file's contents one screen at a time. The command

`TYPE FILE1.DAT | MORE`

would cause the display of the file to pause after each screen full of information is displayed. The display will continue when you press any key on the keyboard.

PRINT. The command PRINT is used to send the contents of a file to a printer. The command

`PRINT FILE1.DAT`

will send the contents of FILE1.DAT to the printer, where a hard copy of the file will be created.

YOUR TURN

---

1. Enter the following command in order to display the contents of the file AUTOEXEC.BAT:

```
TYPE AUTOEXEC.BAT
```

Press <Enter>.

Using Wildcard Characters

The IBM PC DOS and MS-DOS operating systems also allow you to use what are known as wildcard characters when issuing commands that require file names. These wildcard characters allow one character or a number of characters of a file name to be treated in a generic fashion. The two wildcard characters used in IBM PC DOS and MS-DOS are the question mark (?) and the asterisk (*). When a question mark is used in a file name or file name extension, it means that any valid file name character can occupy that position or any of the remaining positions within a file name.

For example, the command

```
DIR FILE?.DAT
```

will list those files that begin with the letters F, I, L, E and then have any other character in the position following the E. In the example given, the files listed must also have a file name extension of DAT. The command

```
DIR *.DAT
```

will list all files with a file name extension of DAT.

Wildcard characters can also be used in any of the other file commands already discussed. For example, if you wanted to copy all files with a WKS file name extension from diskette drive A to hard disk drive C, you could issue the command

```
COPY A:*.WKS C:
```

This command would copy all the files in drive A's working directory with a file name extension of WKS to the working directory on drive C. The wildcard feature can be very powerful. Caution should be exercised when using wildcards. You must be certain of the result of a command issued with wildcards. The command DEL *.*, for example, would most likely produce very undesirable results. It will delete all the files in the working directory. Therefore, exercise extreme caution when issuing commands with wildcard characters in the file names.

Other Useful DOS Commands

There are many DOS commands that can be very useful. Because of the number of these commands and the many different ways to use these commands, all of them cannot be covered here. Reviewing a DOS manual will provide a basic understanding of the types of commands available and their capabilities. The remainder of this section discusses the IBM PC DOS and MS-DOS commands to copy the DOS system files onto a disk, check the version number of DOS your computer system is using, check for errors on a disk, and copy the entire contents of one diskette to another.

VER. The VER command can be used to determine what version of IBM PC DOS or MS-DOS is currently being used by your computer.

 YOUR TURN

---

1. You are going to experiment using the VER command. The C> system prompt should be on your screen.

>Type: VER
>Press <Enter>

A message similar to the following should appear.

>MS-DOS Version 4.01

2. Now try using the CHKDSK command.

>Type: CHKDSK A:
>Press <Enter>

3. Information similar to the following should be displayed.

```
730112 bytes total disk space
 71680 bytes in 2 hidden files
  1024 bytes in 1 directory
 23552 bytes in 1 user files
633856 bytes available on disk

  1024 bytes in each allocation unit
   713 total allocation units on disk
   619 available allocation units on disk
655360 total bytes memory
577264 bytes free
```

The information displayed includes information on the total number of bytes available on the disk, the total size and number of directories, the total size and number of files you have created on your disk, and the total number of bytes available for use on the disk. The last two lines of information printed by the CHKDSK command indicate the total size (in bytes) of your computer's memory and the total amount of memory that is available for use by programs that you run.

DISKCOPY. The DISKCOPY command is used to copy the entire contents of one diskette to another diskette. You should make copies of the diskettes that hold your files and programs as a precaution in case the originals are damaged or lost. Keep these backup diskettes in a place where they will not be damaged, and update them each time you update the original files or programs.

 YOUR TURN

---

1. To complete this exercise, you need a second blank, formatted diskette. You are going to copy the contents of the disk in drive A to the second blank formatted diskette.

Type: DISKCOPY A:

Press <Enter>

The DISKCOPY program will tell you when to switch diskettes during the copy process. The Source disk is the diskette being copied. The Target disk is the backup disk or the diskette onto which the files are being copied.

2. After the DISKCOPY program is done copying the source diskette's contents onto the destination diskette, the following message appears:

COPY ANOTHER (Y/N)?

Press N

3. Now check to see if the DISKCOPY process worked correctly.

Type: DISKCOMP A:

Press <Enter>

If the two diskettes are not identical, an error message will be displayed by the DISKCOMP program.

❏ DOS 5.0

As software programs improve, they are given a new version number. If the change is major, the version number increases by a whole number. If the change is minor, the decimal portion of the number changes by 1. IBM PC DOS and MS-DOS have been greatly improved since their introduction as DOS version 1.0. The newest DOS release is DOS 5.0.

Starting with DOS 4.0, Microsoft introduced the DOS Shell. The DOS Shell is a graphics-based interface between DOS and the user that makes DOS more user-friendly. Instead of having to type in a DOS command at a system prompt, the user can make a selection from a pull-down menu using a mouse. The user no longer must memorize the exact format of each command.

Computers that use MS-DOS 5.0 can be set up so that the MS-DOS Shell automatically appears on the screen when the system is started. However, if your computer uses MS-DOS 5.0 and does not automatically start up the shell, you can start it manually. Make certain that you are in the subdirectory containing the program DOSSHELL.COM and type DOSSHELL. Press <Enter>. A screen similar to Figure 1-4 appears. This shell allows you to access different drives and perform functions such as listing the names of the files in a particular directory, copying a disk, or printing a file.

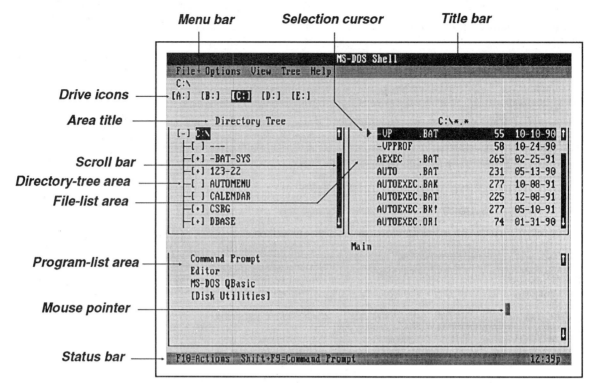

Menu bar   Selection cursor   Title bar

Drive icons

Area title

Scroll bar
Directory-tree area
File-list area

Program-list area

Mouse pointer

Status bar

FIGURE 1-4 The MS-DOS 5.0 Shell

The Shell Window

As you can see from Figure 1-4, each part of the Shell window displays different information. The upper-left corner of the window contains the drive icons (symbols). On systems with one floppy drive and one hard drive, the floppy drive is usually called drive A and the hard drive is usually drive C. When a particular icon is selected, that drive becomes the current drive. In Figure 1-4, drive C is the current drive.

The area in the middle-left portion of the window is the directory tree. This area shows how the directories on the current drive are structured. Whenever you select a directory tree or a drive icon, the Tree menu appears on the menu bar. The Tree menu allows you to determine what level of the directory structure you wish to view. For example, you may wish to see only the names of the files in the current directory or the names of the files in this directory plus all the files in any of its subdirectories. The files in the selected area will then appear in the file-list area, which is to the right of the directory tree. The program-list area appears below the directory tree. The "Main group" is always displayed in the program list. The "Main group" includes two programs that you can start from the MS-DOS Shell. One of the programs is QBASIC which is a program that reads instructions written in the Basic computer language and interprets them into executable computer code. The other is called the MS-DOS Editor, which is a special editor that can be used to type in text and save it in files.

Using the Shell

Before you can use a particular area of the shell, you must select it. On a monochrome monitor, the selected area has a small arrow to the left of one of the items in that area. On a color monitor, the selected area changes color. Press the tab key to move from one area to the next until the desired area is selected. Use <Shift><Tab> if you wish to reverse the direction in which you are going. You can also use a mouse with the shell. Simply position the mouse pointer in the area you wish to select and click.

After you are in the desired area, use the up and down arrow keys to select the item you want. For example, if you are in the Drive Icons area and wish to switch from drive C to drive A, simply press the left arrow key two times. Alternately, use the mouse to position the mouse pointer on [A:] and click. The file-list area (refer to Figure 1-4) will now contain the names of the files on the disk in drive A.

If you wish to go to the command prompt, select Command Prompt from the Program-list area. The system prompt will then appear.

Using the Menus

The menus are listed across the top of the window. To open a specific menu, press <Alt> and then the menu's first letter. The menu commands are then listed. For example, press <Alt><H> to acess the Help menu. The menu now opens and the screen shown in Figure 1-5 appears. The Help menu can help explain how to use the shell and various MS-DOS commands. If the Help menu is opened, press <I> to see the Help index. To close a menu without executing a command, press <Esc>.

You can also use a mouse to open menus and select commands. Position the mouse pointer on the menu name and click. The menu opens. Then move the pointer to the desired command and click again. The command will be executed. To close the menu without executing a command, click the mouse button anywhere outside the menu bar.

The File menu, in particular, is especially useful. It is shown in Figure 1-6 and allows you to perform many tasks, such as opening a file, copying a file from one place to another, running a program, and leaving the MS-DOS Shell to go to the command-line prompt. When you execute one of these commands, a dialog box appears. A dialog box asks you to enter information concerning the task to be performed. For example

FIGURE 1-5 The Help Menu

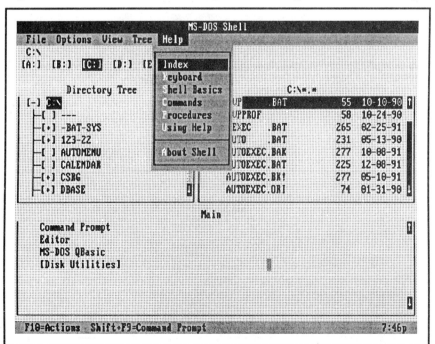

to copy a file named FILE1.DAT first access the drive containing the file and select that file's name in the file-list area. If you want to copy a file from the hard disk to the floppy disk in drive A, enter <Alt>, <F>, <C>. Enter the name of the drive or subdirectory where you want the file copied and press <Enter>.

Other useful file menu commands are Delete, which allows you to erase a file from a disk, and Rename, which allows you to change the name of a file.

Formatting a Disk

All disks must be formatted before they can be used on a computer. Formatting prepares the disk to have files stored on it. To format a disk, move down to the program-list area, use the down arrow key to select [Disk Utilities] and press <Enter>. The Disk Utilities are shown at the bottom of Figure 1-7. Choose format and press <Enter>. The Format dialog box appears. Drive A is always entered as the default drive to format. If necessary, you can enter a different drive letter. Press <Enter>. The following appears on the screen:

```
Insert new diskette for drive A:
and press ENTER when ready...
```

Follow the instructions. The system will respond with these messages:

```
Checking existing disk format.
Saving UNFORMAT information.
Verifying 360K
Format complete.
```

When the formatting is done, you will be allowed to give the disk a name. This name can be used to identify the disk's contents. For example, you might name a disk to contain classroom assignments as follows:

```
Volume label (11 characters, ENTER for none)? ASSIGNMENTS
```

FIGURE 1-6 The File Menu

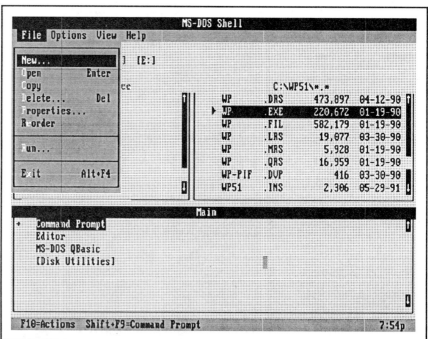

FIGURE 1-7 Disk
Utilities

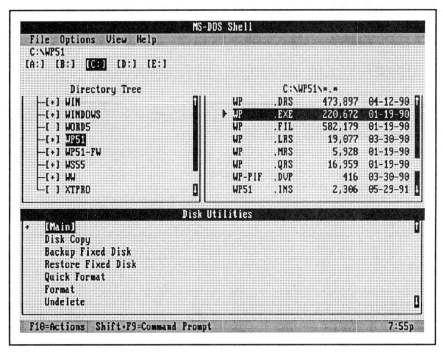

When done, press <Y> if you have more disks to format or <N> if you are done. If you press <N>, you will be returned to the shell.

YOUR TURN

In order to complete this exercise, you need to have MS-DOS 5.0. You are going to format a disk using the MS-DOS Shell.

1. The MS-DOS Shell should be on your screen. If necessary, type DOSSHELL at the C> prompt to access the MS-DOS Shell.

Press <Tab> until the Disk Utilities area is selected

Press the down arrow until **Format** is selected

Press <Enter>

2. The Format dialog box appears. Drive A is already entered as the drive to format.

Press <Enter>

The following prompt appears:

```
Insert new diskette for drive A
and press ENTER when ready...
```

Place a blank disk in drive A.

Press <Enter>

3. When the formatting is complete you are asked if you want to give the disk a volume label. Type a name if you want the disk to have a label and press <Enter>. Just press <Enter> if you do not want a label.

4. The prompt `Format another (Y/N)?` appears.

Press N

You have finished with these Your Turn Exercises. Take your disk out of drive A and store it carefully. Turn off the computer and monitor.

❏ SUMMARY POINTS

■ The IBM PC DOS and MS-DOS microcomputers are popular with businesses for performing routine tasks and for linking with larger computers. They are also popular in homes and schools for a variety of educational, recreational, and home-management purposes.

■ The standard parts of an MS-DOS microcomputer are the system unit, monitor, and keyboard. The system unit holds the computer itself and the disk drive(s).

■ The letter and number keys on a microcomputer work the same as a typewriter's keys. Computer-specific keys let you move the cursor and perform other functions by entering keystroke commands.

■ In a system with two floppy disk drives, the drives are called drive A and drive B. A hard disk drive is usually called drive C.

■ The best place for a computer is on a sturdy desk or table in a clean, dry room. Keep food, dust, and dirt away from equipment and disks, and avoid creating static electricity around the equipment.

■ Computer equipment should be kept out of direct sunlight, and away from heating ducts and air conditioning units.

■ Floppy diskettes should be handled with care so they will remain reliable storage devices. Store them vertically in their envelopes, away from heat or cold.

■ Programs are loaded into the computer's memory in several ways. If operating system files are on the disk, you can insert it into the disk drive and turn on the computer. Otherwise the operating system software must be loaded first.

■ The operating system contains the programs that control the computer. Disk operating system (DOS) programs reside on a disk and are loaded from the disk drive.

■ There are two types of files in the IBM PC DOS and MS-DOS operating system—executable files and data files. Executable files are directly understandable by the microprocessor and are the result of translating a source code program. Batch files contain operating system commands that are interpreted by the operating system as the batch file is run. Data files contain data that can be manipulated by a program.

■ Names of files in the IBM PC DOS and MS-DOS operating systems consist of the file name and the file name extension. A maximum of eight characters can be used for the file name; a maximum of three characters can be used for the file name extension. The set of valid file name characters includes A-Z, a-z, 0-9, $, %, ', -, @, {, }, ~, _, ', !, #, (,), and &.

■ Directories are a way to keep files better organized and separated on both floppy diskettes and hard disks. There are two types of directories: a root directory and a subdirectory.

■ The directory that you are currently in is called the working directory.

■ Paths are used to tell the operating system exactly where a file is located on the computer system. The backslash character (\) is used to separate path names from file names.

■ Formatting a disk prepares it so that data and programs can be stored on it according to the specifications of the operating system.

■ MKDIR or (MD) is used to create a subdirectory, RMDIR (or RD) is used to remove a directory and CHDIR (or CD) is used to change from one directory to another.

■ The PROMPT command is used to change how the prompt that is displayed to the user looks.

■ The DIR command is used to display the list of files in a particular directory.

■ The COPY command is used to copy files from one location to another, the DEL command is used to delete (or erase) a file, and the REN (rename) command is used to change a file's name from one name to another. The TYPE command is used to display a file's contents on the display screen and the PRINT command is used to send the contents of a file to a printer.

■ Wildcard characters are used to treat file names in a generic fashion. The two wildcard characters used in IBM PC and MS-DOS are the question mark (?) and the asterisk (*).

■ The VER command can be used to determine what version of IBM PC DOS or MS-DOS is currently being used by your computer.

■ The DISKCOPY command is used to copy the entire contents of one diskette to another diskette.

■ The DOS Shell, which was introduced with DOS 4.0, is a graphics-based interface between DOS and the user. The purpose of the shell is to make DOS easier to use.

■ The directory tree in the Shell window shows how the directories on the current drive are structured.

■ The DOS Shell includes menus that can be accessed by pressing <Alt> and the menu's first letter or by using a mouse.

❏ COMMAND SUMMARY

DOS Command	Function
CD *or* CHDIR	Allows you to change to a different directory or subdirectory on the same drive. Type `cd\subdir1\subdir2...` and press <Enter>, where `\subdir1` is the name of the first-level directory, `\subdir2` is the name of the second-level directory, and so on.
COPY	Allows you to copy files, either individually or in groups using wildcards, from one disk or directory to another. Also allows you to make a backup copy of a file in the same directory if the new file's name or extension is different from the original one. Type `copy d:oldfile.ext d:newfile.ext` and press <Enter> where `d` is the drive, `oldfile.ext` is the full name and extension of the original file, and `newfile.ext` is the full name and extension of the duplicate file. If you are copying from one subdirectory to another, you must use full path names.

DOS Command	Function
DEL	Allows you to delete either a single file or a group of files using wildcards. To delete a file, type `del filename.ext` and press <Enter>, where `filename.ext` is the name of the file you want to delete.
DIR	Allows you to display the contents of a directory. To display the contents of the current directory, just type `dir` and press <Enter> to make the directory listing pause, type `dir/P` and press <Enter>. To display a wide listing of the contents of the directory, type `dir/W` and press <Enter>. You can use wildcards to limit the files that will be displayed, and path names to display the contents in another directory.
DISKCOPY	Allows you to make an exact duplicate of a disk (and all files on it), using either a single disk drive or two identical disk drives. To use DISKCOPY on a system with two floppy disk drives, you must first place the DOS disk in the default drive. Type `diskcopy d:` and press <Enter> to make a copy of a disk using a single drive where d is the drive containing the disk you wish to copy. Or type `diskcopy a: b:` and press <Enter> to copy the contents of the disk in drive A to the disk in drive B.
FORMAT	Allows you to prepare new disks for use in your computer. To use FORMAT on a system with two floppy disk drives, you must first place the DOS disk in the default drive. Then type `format d:` and press <Enter> where d is the drive containing the disk you wish to format.
MD *or* MKDIR	Allows you to make a new subdirectory on the current drive. To create a new directory, type `md\subdir\newdir` and press <Enter> where `\newdir` is the name of the new subdirectory and `\subdir` represents the full subdirectory path.
PRINT	Allows you to send the contents of a file to a printer. To send a file to a printer, type `print filename.ext` where filename.ext is the file you want to print.
RD *or* RMDIR	Allows you to remove a subdirectory from the current drive. In order to be removed, a subdirectory must be completely empty. Also, the subdirectory to be removed cannot be the default directory. To remove a subdirectory, type `rd\subdir` and press <Enter>, where `\subdir` is the full path name of the subdirectory to be removed.
REN	Allows you to change a file's name from one name to another. To change a file name, type `ren oldfile.ext newfile.ext` and press <Enter> where `oldfile.ext` is the original name of the file and `newfile.ext` is the new name you want to give to the file. If you are renaming a file in a subdirectory, you must use full path names.

DOS Command	Function
TYPE	Allows you to display a file's contents on the monitor. To display the contents of a file, type `type filename.ext` where `filename.ext` is the name of the file you want to display. To pause the display after each screen full of information is displayed, type `type filename.ext	more`.
VER	Allows you to determine what version of IBM PC DOS or MS-DOS is currently being used by the computer. Type `ver` to check the DOS version.

❏ DOS EXERCISES

1. In this exercise you are going to create a subdirectory called HOMEWORK. You could save all your homework assignments in this subdirectory. You will need your formatted data disk. You will also need a DOS disk if you are using a computer with two floppy disk drives. Turn on the computer and monitor. Type the current date and time if you are prompted for them. The system prompt C> should be displayed on the screen. Place the formatted disk in drive A. You want the default drive to be drive A.

> Type: `a:`
> Press <Enter>

The system prompt A> should be displayed on the screen.

> Type: `md \homework`
> Press <Enter>

Now check to make sure that the subdirectory has been created by listing the files.

> Type: `dir`
> Press <Enter>

The HOMEWORK directory should be displayed with the word <DIR> after it. This is DOS's way of indicating that this is a subdirectory rather than a file.

2. Now you are going to change to the HOMEWORK subdirectory. Drive A should still be the default drive.

> Type: `cd\homework`
> Press <Enter>

Now list the files.

> Type: `dir`
> Press <Enter>

the current subdirectory name is listed. The two items listed below it and labeled <DIR> are special files that DOS creates in each subdirectory to help in file management. You cannot edit or delete them.

3. Next, you will return to the root directory.

> Type: `cd\`
> Press <Enter>

You have returned to the root directory.

1. To complete this exercise, you need the Student File Disk. If you are working on a system with two floppy disk drives, you also need the DOS disk. Turn on the computer and monitor. Type the current date and time if you are prompted for them. The system prompt C> should be displayed on the screen. Place the Student File Disk in drive A.

> Type: `dir a:`
> Press <Enter>

A list of the files on the Student File Disk appears. The first column contains the file name, and the second column contains the extension. The file size is in the middle column of the directory. The fourth and fifth columns indicate the date and time the file was last saved. At the bottom of the screen is the number of files on the disk and the amount of space left on the disk.

2. Now you want to display the entire directory on the screen at one time.

> Type: `dir /w a:`
> Press <Enter>

The entire directory appears on the screen. Notice that all that is displayed about a file in this wide directory is its name and extension. Individual file sizes, dates, and times are not displayed. However, the total number of files and the amount of space remaining on the disk are displayed.

3. There is a file on the Student File Disk called DELETE.ME. You are going to delete this file. To make sure the file you want to delete is on the disk, you will display a list of all files that have names beginning with the letter *d*.

> Type: `dir a:d*.*`
> Press <Enter>

The file DELETE.ME should be displayed on the disk. Now you will delete the file.

> Type: `del a:delete.me`
> Press <Enter>

To make sure that the file has been deleted, relist the files with names beginning with *d*.

> Type: `dir a:d*.*`
> Press <Enter>

The DELETE.ME file should not appear.

4. Now you want to make a copy of a file called JUNK. You want to copy it on the same disk, but with another name. You want to name the new file JUNK.2.

> Type: `copy a:JUNK a:JUNK.2`
> Press <Enter>

When the drive light goes out, the file is copied. The message "1 file(s) copied" appears on the screen. List the files.

> Type: `dir a:junk.*`
> Press <Enter>

Both JUNK and JUNK.2 should be listed on the screen. Notice the size, date, and time of the two files are the same.

CHAPTER 2

Introduction to WordPerfect 5.1

OUTLINE

❑ INTRODUCTION

Of all the application software available, programs written to perform a specific task, word processors meet the largest variety of users' needs. Word processors not only are a useful tool for more users than any other application program; they also are the easiest application software programs to learn. This chapter introduces word processing. It provides instructions on how to get started using WordPerfect, one of the more popular word processing packages on the market today.

❑ GUIDE TO WORDPERFECT

The remainder of this chapter focuses on how to use WordPerfect 5.1. Difference Boxes are included for WordPerfect 5.0. WordPerfect is a full-featured word processing program that is extremely powerful, yet easy to use. Some of the directions for using WordPerfect vary depending on whether the computer has two floppy disk drives or a hard disk drive. The directions in this chapter are written for computers with a hard disk drive. Difference Boxes are also included for running WordPerfect 5.0 on a computer system with two floppy disk drives.

Each of the following sections introduces one or more features of WordPerfect. At the end of each section there is a hands-on activity marked with the symbol **Your Turn**. Do not try the hands-on activity until after you have carefully read the section preceding it.

This chapter refers to the key marked ⏎ as <Enter>. Throughout the chapter, when instructed to press <Enter>, press the key marked ⏎. WordPerfect uses the ten function keys that are either on the left side of the keyboard or at the top of the keyboard to activate most of its features. The function keys are labeled F1 through F10. Some keyboards also include F11 and F12 function keys. A template is provided with the software to place around the function keys at the left or on top of the function keys at the top of the keyboard. The template lists the four functions each key activates. Each key's functions are activated by pressing the key alone or at the same time <Alt>, <Shift>, or <Ctrl> is pressed. The template's functions are color coded to indicate whether the key is pressed alone or with one of the other keys:

Black   Press the indicated function key only.

Blue   Hold down <Alt> and press the indicated function key.

Green   Hold down <Shift> and press the indicated function key.

Red   Hold down the <Ctrl> key and press the indicated function key.

A few other keys are important in using WordPerfect. <Num Lock> is used to control the ten-key numerical keypad on the right side of the keyboard. If <Num Lock> is pressed once, the keypad is used for writing numbers to the screen. If not pressed, or pressed twice, it allows the keypad to be used for controlling the cursor. <Backspace> allows mistakes to be erased by backing the cursor over them. The CANCEL function, which is activated by pressing <F1>, allows a feature to be canceled after it has been called up. It can also restore text that has been accidentally deleted.

The following symbols and typefaces appear throughout the chapter. This is what they mean:

Save Document?   The information in boldface indicates prompts that appear on the screen asking you to enter information.

Press <Enter>   The angle brackets (< >) are used to signify a specific key on the keyboard. Press the key whose name is enclosed by the angle brackets.

Press <Alt>-<F4>	If a hyphen appears between two keys, it means the keys have to be pressed together. Hold down the first key while tapping the second key once. In this example, the user would hold down <Alt> while pressing <F4> once.
EXIT	All capital letters indicate the name of a command.
Type: Resume	Typewriter font indicates text that is to be entered into a document.

Getting Started with WordPerfect

To use WordPerfect on a hard disk drive, the program will first have to be installed on the hard drive. Follow these steps to access WordPerfect from a hard drive on which it has been installed.

1. Turn on the computer and monitor. A prompt may appear asking you to enter the date. If it does, type the current date using numbers and hyphens, for example 11-15-92. Press <Enter>.

2. A prompt may appear asking you to enter the time. If it does, you can either press <Enter> to bypass this prompt, or you can enter the time using a 24-hour format. For example, enter 16:30:00 if it is 4:30 p.m. Press <Enter> after entering the time.

3. When the system prompt C> appears on the screen, type cd\ and the name of the directory in which WordPerfect is stored on the hard drive. For example, if the program is stored in a directory named WP51, type cd\wp51 and press <Enter>.

4. The system prompt C> appears. Type wp and press <Enter>. A blank document window appears.

Difference Box: Starting WordPerfect 5.0

The steps for starting WordPerfect 5.0 are the same as for WordPerfect 5.1 except for the location of where the program is stored. The program may be stored in a directory named WP50. If it is, at the C> prompt, type cd\wp50 and press <Enter>. Type wp and press <Enter>.

If you are using WordPerfect 5.0 on a computer with two floppy disk drives, you need a DOS disk, WordPerfect Program Disk 1, WordPerfect Program Disk 2 and your data disk to start the program. Follow these steps to start WordPerfect 5.0 on a computer system with two floppy disk drives.

1. Place the DOS disk in drive A. Place the data disk in drive B. Close the disk drive doors. Turn on the computer and monitor.

2. A prompt appears asking you to enter the date. Enter the current date using numbers and hyphens, for example, 11-15-92. Press <Enter>.

3. A prompt appears asking you to enter the time. You can either press <Enter> to bypass this prompt, or you can enter the time using a 24-hour format. For example, enter 16:30:00 if it is 4:30 p.m. Press <Enter> after entering the time.

4. When the system prompt A> appears on the screen, take the DOS disk out of drive A. Place the WordPerfect Program Disk 1 into drive A. Close the disk drive door. Type b: and press <Enter>. The system prompt B> appears on the screen. Type a:wp and press <Enter>.

5. After a moment the message **Insert diskette labeled "WordPerfect 2" and press any key** appears at the bottom of the screen. Take the WordPerfect Program Disk 1 out of drive A. Place the WordPerfect Program Disk 2 into drive A. Close the disk drive door. Press any key.

When WordPerfect has been started properly, a blank document window appears on the screen. If the message **Are other copies of WordPerfect running? (Y/N)** appears, press N for no. This message appears if the program was improperly ended the last time it was used.

YOUR TURN

In this exercise, you are going to start the computer and access the WordPerfect 5.1 program. This exercise assumes the WordPerfect program is stored in a directory named wp51. If WordPerfect 5.1 is stored in a different directory in the computer you are using, ask your instructor for directions.

1. Turn on the computer and monitor.

2. If a prompt appears asking you to enter the date, type today's date using numbers and hyphens. For example, if the date is September 28, 1992 you would do the following:

> Type: `09-28-92`
>
> Press <Enter>

If a prompt appears asking you to enter the time, either press <Enter> or enter the time in a 24-hour format and press <Enter>.

3. The system prompt C> should appear on the screen.

> Type: `cd\wp51`
>
> Press <Enter>

The system prompt C> should appear on the screen again.

> Type: `wp`
>
> Press <Enter>

Your screen should look like Figure 2-1. This is WordPerfect's text window. You have completed this Your Turn exercise. Leave the text window on your screen so that you can refer to it while reading the following section.

The Text Window

Each time WordPerfect is started, a blank screen appears with a blinking cursor in the upper-left corner. The status line is in the lower-right corner (refer to Figure 2-1). The status line displays the number of the document and the cursor's location. The number following Pg is the page number in the document where the cursor is currently located. The number following Ln measures the cursor's location from the top of the page in inches. The number following Pos measures the cursor's location from the left margin in inches.

The remainder of the screen is often referred to as the text window. The text window displays the words as they are typed. All editing of a document takes place in the text window, which can contain twenty-four lines of text. When you type a document that is longer than twenty-four lines, the lines at the beginning of the document scroll off the top of the screen to make room for any additional lines.

The cursor, a blinking line, is in the text window. The cursor indicates where the next character will appear when entered. Once a document has been given a name and saved, the document name appears in the lower-left corner of the text window.

**FIGURE 2-1 WordPerfect's
Text Window**

                                                                    Doc 1 Pg 1 Ln 1" Pos 1"

Getting Help with WordPerfect

WordPerfect includes a useful on-line Help option that provides the user with information on any of WordPerfect's operations. To get help, press <F3>. The <F3> key is marked Help in black on the template. After pressing <F3> the help screen with the following message appears: **Press any letter to get an alphabetical list of features. Press any function key to get information about the use of that key.**

To get more information about a specific function, press the function key that activates that particular function. Information about that function appears on the screen. Pressing a different function key brings up information on that function key. To get an index of all the features included in the Help function, press any key. When you are ready to return to the document, press <Space Bar> or <Enter>.

Difference Box: Using the Help Option with WordPerfect 5.0 on a Computer with Two Floppy Disk Drives

If you are using WordPerfect 5.0 on a computer with two floppy disk drives, the following message appears at the bottom of the screen when you press <F3> to access the Help option:

WPHELP.FIL not found. Insert the diskette and press drive letter:

When this message appears, take the WordPerfect 5.0 Program Disk 2 out of drive A. Place the WordPerfect Program Disk 1 into drive A. Close the disk drive door. Press a. When you have finished using the Help function, replace the WordPerfect 5.0 Program Disk 1 in drive A with the WordPerfect 5.0 Program Disk 2.

Exiting from WordPerfect

To exit from WordPerfect, press <F7> for EXIT. The prompt **Save document? Yes (No)** appears in the lower-left corner of the screen. Press <Enter> to save the document. You do not have to enter Y for Yes because the program's default setting is Yes. If you do not want to save the document before leaving it, enter N for No.

The prompt **Document to be saved** appears next. Enter a name for the document. It is helpful to give your files names that will remind you of their contents. A file name can be up to eight characters long. A file name can include letters, numbers, underscores, hyphens, and the special symbols:

! @ # $ (> { }

An optional extension can be used following the file name. The extension can have from one to three characters with no spaces, and is separated from the file name by a period.

After naming a file the prompt **Exit WP? No (Yes)** appears. If you want to exit from WordPerfect, press Y for yes. When the system prompt appears, you can take the diskettes out of the disk drives and turn off the computer and monitor.

 YOUR TURN

The text window should be on your screen. In this exercise you are going to practice using WordPerfect's Help function and exiting from the program.

1. A blinking cursor should be in the upper-left corner of your screen and the WordPerfect status line should be in the lower right corner.

Press <F3> for HELP

The help screen appears. Now you can get help with any of WordPerfect's functions.

Press <F1O> for SAVE

A help screen appears with information about saving a document. Read the screen.

Press <F7> for EXIT

A help screen appears with information about exiting a document. Read the screen. Access the help screen for any other function you would like to learn more about.

2. You are now ready to exit from WordPerfect. Since you did not enter anything, you are not going to save the document.

Press the Space Bar to exit from the help screens

Press <F7> for EXIT

The prompt **Save document? Yes (No)** appears at the bottom of the screen.

Enter: N

The prompt **Exit wp?** appears at the bottom of this screen.

Enter: Y

When the system prompt appears on the screen, you know you have exited from the Word-Perfect program. When the system prompt returns to the screen, you can take your data disk out of the disk drive and turn off the computer and monitor.

The files created with WordPerfect are similar to files in a file cabinet. Each file is a unit of storage. Files can be used to store memos, letters, and term papers. For example, when a memo or letter is completed, that file is given a specific name and is saved on a disk. Once saved, that file can be retrieved in order to revise, edit, or print its contents.

Entering Text

Each time WordPerfect is started, a blank text window appears with the blinking cursor in the upper-left corner. The status line is in the lower right hand corner. The text window displays the words as they are typed.

When entering text, you need to use both uppercase and lowercase letters. If the letters are all capitals when you begin typing, press <Caps Lock>. Letters should appear in both uppercase and lowercase. Pressing <Caps Lock> again produces all capital letters.When <Caps Lock> is on, the letters POS in the lower-right corner of the screen are all capital letters.

<Enter> does not need to be pressed when the end of a line is reached. WordPerfect has a feature called word wrap, which automatically moves a word to the beginning of the next line if it crosses the right margin. Press <Enter> only if you want to start a new line. For example, press <Enter> to end a line before it reaches the right margin or to insert a blank line.

Features such as margins, tabs, and spacing are set automatically according to WordPerfect's default settings. These settings can be changed easily or a document can be entered using all the default settings.

Setting the Default Directory

The default directory is where WordPerfect will automatically store and retrieve files unless the user overrides this directory and instructs the program to do otherwise. It is important to set WordPerfect's default directory to the drive containing the data disk onto which you will be saving all the files you create. To set the default directory, first press <F5> for LIST FILES. The current directory is displayed at the bottom-left corner of the screen. The prompt **Type = to change default Dir** appears at the bottom-right corner of the screen. Press = (the equal sign). The prompt **New directory =** appears at the lower-left corner of the screen. Type the letter of the drive where your data disk is located followed by a colon. If you are using a hard drive, your data disk may be in drive A. If this is the case, you would type a: and press <Enter>. If you are using a system with two floppy disk drives, you would type b: and press <Enter>. It is important that you check the location of the default directory at the start of every session on the computer. If you do not check the default directory, you may end up saving your files on the wrong disk.

Saving a Document

There are two ways to save a document using WordPerfect. One way allows you to save the document and continue working on it. That is, you do not exit from the current document after saving it. The other method saves the document and either clears the screen so you can begin work on a different document or exits you from the WordPerfect program.

To save a document and continue working on it, press <F10> for SAVE. The prompt **Document to be saved** appears at the bottom of the screen. If this is the first time the document has been saved, there is no file name entered next to the prompt. Enter a file name and press <Enter>. The document is saved and remains on the screen. If the file has previously been saved, a file name appears next to the prompt. You do not have to enter the file name again. Simply press <Enter>. The prompt **Replace** followed by the file name appears. Pressing Y for Yes saves the latest version of the document under the file name listed next to the **Replace** prompt. Pressing N for No gives you the opportunity to save the latest version of the document under a new file name. After pressing N, enter the new file name and press <Enter>. You should get into the habit of saving your work using this method every ten minutes or so. That way if anything unexpected happens, such as the electricity going off, you will not lose all of your work.

The second method for saving a file both saves the document and exits from that document. To use this method press <F7> for EXIT. The prompt **Save document?** appears. Press <Enter>. The prompt **Document to be saved** appears. If this is the first time the file has been saved, no file name appears next to this prompt. Enter a file name and press <Enter>. If the file has previously been saved, a file name already appears next to the prompt. If this is the file name to be used for the document, simply press <Enter>. The prompt **Replace** followed by the file name appears. Pressing Y for Yes saves the document under the file name listed next to the **Replace** prompt. Pressing N for No gives you the opportunity to give the document a new file name. After pressing N, enter the new file name and press <Enter>. The prompt **Exit WP?** appears. If you want to continue using WordPerfect, press <Enter> to accept the default setting of No. If you want to exit the program, enter Y for Yes.

Backing Up a File on a Disk

The importance of backing up a file on a disk cannot be stressed enough. It you have backup copies of your files, you are spared having to retype a file from scratch if something happens to the original file. One way of making backup copies of files using WordPerfect is to retrieve the file to be copied and press <F10> for SAVE. The prompt **Document to be saved** appears with the current name of the document entered next to the prompt. Enter a new name for the file and press <Enter>. The document is then saved on your disk twice—once under the original file name and once under the new file name just entered.

YOUR TURN

In this exercise you are going to start WordPerfect on the computer and enter a letter.

1. Turn on the computer and monitor.

2. If a prompt appears asking you to enter the date, type today's date using numbers and hyphens. For example, if the date is September 28, 1992 you would do the following:

> Type: 09-28-92
>
> Press <Enter>

If a prompt appears asking you to enter the time, either press <Enter> or enter the time in a 24-hour format and press <Enter>.

3. The system prompt C> should appear on the screen.

> Type: cd\wp51

Press <Enter>

The system prompt C> should appear on the screen again.

Enter: wp

Press <Enter>

The text window should appear on your screen. Place a formatted disk in drive A. You will store the letter you create on this disk. Check the location of the default directory by doing the following:

Press <F5> for LIST FILES

If **Dir C:\WP51** appears in the lower left-corner of the screen, you should change the default drive to A. Follow these directions to change the default drive to A:

Press = (the equal sign)

The prompt **New directory =** appears in the lower-left corner of the screen.

Enter: a:

Press <Enter>

Press <Esc>

4. Before typing the letter, you are going to activate the FLUSH RIGHT and DATE functions. Remember that functions are activated through the combined use of the ten function keys and <Ctrl>, <Shift>, and <Alt>. Use the color-coded function key template to find the proper combination. In this case, FLUSH RIGHT appears in blue beside the <F6> key and DATE/OUTLINE appears in green beside the <F5> key.

Press <Alt>-<F6> for FLUSH RIGHT

The cursor jumps to the right side of the screen.

Press <Shift>-<F5> for DATE/OUTLINE

At the bottom of the screen a menu appears with numbered choices for the DATE/OUTLINE function. You want to select the first option for Date Text, which is number 1.

Type: 1

The date is automatically inserted, flush with the right margin. (Note: If you bypassed setting the date when starting the computer with DOS, the date will read January 1, 1980.)

5. Enter the rest of the letter as follows:

Press <Enter> four times

Type: Joy Langston

Press <Enter>

Type: 4332 University Road

Press <Enter>

Type: St. Louis, Missouri 63155

Press <Enter> two times

Type: Dear Ms. Langston,

Press <Enter> two times

Type the body of the letter as follows. Remember, do not press <Enter> until you reach the end of an entire paragraph. The ending of your lines on the computer screen will not be the same as they appear here on the page.

As your advisor, I want to help you in any way possible with your job hunt. Since graduation is only six short months away, I'm sure finding a job is a top priority for you right now. I just received some information from the placement service office that I would like to pass along to you. I think this information will help you in your job-search efforts.

Press <Enter> two times

Continue typing the letter as follows:

The placement service is sponsoring a series of seminars designed to help upcoming graduates locate potential employers, write cover letters and resumes, and improve interviewing skills. There is no cost for attending this seminar, but if you plan to attend, you must register with the placement office no later than Monday, February 17. These seminars will be divided up according to majors. The seminar for Accounting majors is scheduled for Saturday, February 22. I have enclosed a tenative schedule of events.

Press <Enter> two times

Continue typing the letter as follows:

I hope you plan to attend this seminar. I think it will be well worth your time.

Press <Enter> two times

Continue typing as follows:

Sincerely,

Press <Enter> four times

Continue typing as follows:

Professor Herbert Moser

Press <Enter> two times

Continue typing as follows:

Enclosure

When you have finished, your screen should look like Figure 2-2.

6. You are now ready to save the letter.

Press <F7> for EXIT

The prompt **Save Document** appears at the bottom of the screen.

Press <Enter>

The prompt **Document to be saved** appears at the bottom of the screen.

> Type: SEMINAR
>
> Press <Enter>

After a moment the prompt **Exit WP?** appears. You are ready to exit from the WordPerfect program.

> Type: Y for YES

When the system prompt appears at the bottom of the screen, take your disk out of the disk drive and turn off the computer and monitor. You have completed this Your Turn exercise.

Retrieving a Document

To edit a document that already exists, activate the RETRIEVE command by pressing <Shift> and <F1O>. The prompt **Document to be retrieved** appears. Type the name of the document that is to be edited, and press <Enter>. If there is a file that corresponds to the name entered, the document appears on the screen, ready to be edited.

If you do not remember the name of the document you want to retrieve, activate the LIST FILES command by pressing <F5>. The prompt **Dir A:** appears in the lower-left corner of the screen. Press <Enter> to get the listing of the files in Directory A, which contains your data disk. Use the up, down, right, and left arrow keys to highlight the name of the file to be retrieved. To retrieve the highlighted file, enter 1. The desired file appears on the screen.

FIGURE 2-2 Entering Text

```
some information from the placement service office that I would
like to pass along to you.  I think this information will help you
in your job-search efforts.

The placement service is sponsoring a series of seminars designed
to help upcoming graduates locate potential employers, write cover
letters and resumes, and improve interviewing skills.  There is no
cost for attending this seminar, but if you plan to attend, you
must register with the placement office no later than Monday,
February 17.  These seminars will be divided up according to
majors.  The seminar for Accounting majors is scheduled for
Saturday, February 22.  I have enclosed a tenative schedule of
events.

I hope you plan to attend this seminar.  I think it will be well
worth your time.

Sincerely,



Professor Herbert Moser

Enclosure
                                           Doc 1 Pg 1 Ln 7" Pos 1.9"
```

YOUR TURN

In this exercise you are going to retrieve the SEMINAR file.

1. Start WordPerfect. A blank text window should be on your screen. First, check to make sure the default directory is set correctly by doing the following:

> Press <F5> for LIST FILES

Look at the drive letter next to Dir in the lower left corner of the screen. If it is not the drive where your data disk is located, enter an equal sign and then enter the drive letter of that drive followed by a colon and press <Enter> and press <Esc>. If it is correct, simply press <Enter>.

2. Now you are ready to retrieve the SEMINAR file.

> Press <F5> for LIST FILES
>
> Press <Enter>

Your screen should look like Figure 2-3. This screen lists all the files saved on your data disk. You need to move the highlighting to the SEMINAR file.

> Press the down arrow key once

The SEMINAR file should now be highlighted. Notice the menu at the bottom of the screen. This menu lists all the options available to perform on the SEMINAR document. You want to retrieve the document, which is option 1.

> Enter: 1

The beginning of the SEMINAR file should appear in the text window.

3. You have completed this Your Turn exercise. You can either exit from the WordPerfect program by pressing <F7> for EXIT, N at the **Save document** prompt, and Y at the **Exit WP?** prompt, or you can leave the file on the screen while you read through the following sections. The SEMINAR file will be used in the next Your Turn exercise.

❏ EDITING A DOCUMENT

Now that a document has been saved on a disk, it can be edited. The text editing function of a word processor enables the user to enter and edit text. The most fundamental aspect of this function is the word processor's ability to accept and store the text that is typed in at the keyboard. Without this ability, all the other functions and procedures would be useless.

Text editing also includes the ability of the word processor to insert and delete characters, words, lines, paragraphs, and larger blocks of text. The insert and delete modes are two of the most often used text editing features. The text editing features of most word processors, including WordPerfect, also allow blocks of text to be moved and copied. These features make it easier to rearrange and retype documents.

FIGURE 2-3 Retrieving a File

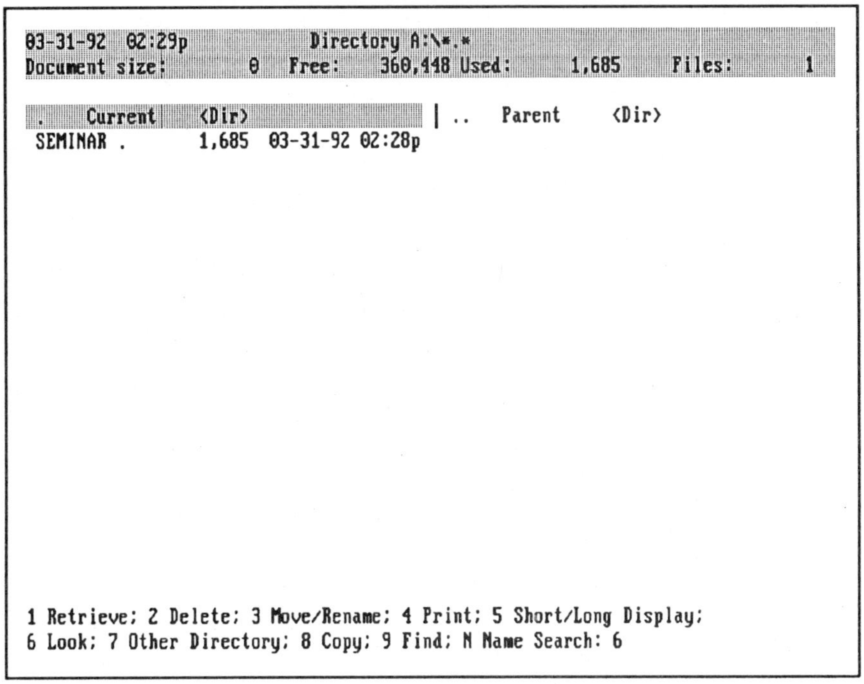

```
03-31-92  02:29p            Directory A:\*.*
Document size:        0  Free:      360,448 Used:        1,685     Files:         1

    .   Current   <Dir>                      |  ..    Parent     <Dir>
    SEMINAR .        1,685  03-31-92 02:28p
```

```
1 Retrieve; 2 Delete; 3 Move/Rename; 4 Print; 5 Short/Long Display;
6 Look; 7 Other Directory; 8 Copy; 9 Find; N Name Search: 6
```

Moving the Cursor

Before starting to work on a document, you need to be able to control the position of the cursor. The cursor is controlled by the arrow keys. On some keyboards these arrow keys are in the numeric keypad on the right side of the keyboard. On others, the arrow keys are separate from the numeric keypad and are in a group by themselves in the lower-right corner of the keyboard. The down arrow key moves the cursor one line down. The up arrow key moves the cursor one line up. The left arrow key moves the cursor one position to the left. The right arrow key moves the cursor one position to the right. If the arrow keys are located in the numeric keypad, <Num Lock> must be off in order to move the cursor. If the numbers 2, 4, 6, 8 appear on the screen when you are trying to move the cursor, then <Num Lock> is on. Press it once to turn it off, and use <Backspace> to delete the numbers. The cursor can also be moved word by word or page by page through the document. Table 2-1 summarizes the cursor commands.

Selecting Blocks of Text

Manipulating a document a character at a time is extremely slow when working with large blocks of text. To help speed operations, WordPerfect includes a block operation feature. This feature defines a block of text—which can be a word, sentence, paragraph, or page—and then either deletes it, copies, it or moves it elsewhere in the document.

When a block of text is selected, it appears highlighted on the screen. To select text to be blocked, press <Alt>-<F4> for BLOCK. The words **Block on** start flashing in the lower-left corner of the screen. Use the up, down, right, and left arrow keys to highlight the text to be blocked.

Deleting Text

There are several ways to delete text from a WordPerfect document. The most efficient method depends on the text to be removed and the user's typing preference.

Pressing <Backspace> moves the cursor one space to the left, removing the character from that position. This includes spaces as text. If you hold <Backspace> down, it continues to remove characters until it is released. Pressing <Del> removes the character above the cursor. <Del> can also be used in conjunction with the block feature. After a portion of text has been selected and is highlighted, press <Del>. The prompt **Delete block** appears in the lower left corner of the screen. Enter Y for yes, and all the text that was highlighted is deleted.

If text is deleted by accident, pressing <F1> for the CANCEL command enables you to undo the deletions. Text that has been selected as a block and deleted with the <Del> key is placed in a temporary storage location. After pressing <F1>, the text that was deleted reappears on the screen and the menu listing undelete options appears at the bottom of the screen. Pressing 1 for **Restore** restores the deleted text back to the document. Pressing 2 for **Previous Deletion** displays the previous block of text that was deleted. If you wish to restore that deletion, press <Enter>. Only the last two blocks of text that were deleted can be restored with the CANCEL command. To cancel the CANCEL command, press <Esc>.

TABLE 2-1 Commands for Moving the Cursor

Keys	Description
<Left arrow>	Moves the cursor one character to the left
<Right arrow>	Moves the cursor one character to the right
<Ctrl>-<Right arrow>	Moves the cursor one word to the right
<Ctrl>-<Left arrow>	Moves the cursor one word to the left
<End>	Moves the cursor to the end of a line
<Home>-<Left arrow>	Moves the cursor to the beginning of a line
<Home>-<Right arrow>	Moves the cursor to the end of a line
<Home> <Home>-<Left arrow>	Moves the cursor to the left edge of the screen
<Home> <Home>-<Right arrow>	Moves the cursor to the right edge of the screen
<Up arrow>	Moves the cursor up one line
<Down arrow>	Moves the cursor down one line
<Home>-<Up arrow>	Move the cursor to the top of the screen
<Home>-<Down arrow>	Moves the cursor to the bottom of the screen
<Ctrl> <Home>-<Up arrow>	Moves the cursor to the top of the current page
<Ctrl> <Home>-<Down arrow>	Moves the cursor to the bottom of the current page
<PgUp>	Moves the cursor to the top of the previous page
<PgDn>	Moves the cursor to the top of the next page
<Home> <Home>-<Up arrow>	Moves the cursor to the beginning of the document
<Home> <Home>-<Down arrow>	Moves the cursor to the end of the document
<Ctrl> <Home> #	Moves the cursor to the page number entered
<Esc> # <Up arrow>	Moves the cursor up the number of lines entered
<Esc> # <Down arrow>	Moves the cursor down the number of lines entered

Chapter 2: Introduction to WordPerfect 5.1

<Ins> can be used for replacing text. If <Ins> is pressed once, the word **Typeover** appears in the lower-left corner of the screen and the overtype mode is on. When WordPerfect is in the overtype mode, text can be changed by typing over the characters above the cursor. For example, if the cursor is under the d in "The dog ran up the street" and **Typeover** appears on the screen, typing *cat* produces the sentence, "The cat ran up the street." Typing *elephant,* however, results in the sentence "The elephantup the street." For one word to replace another, the two must have the same number of letters. Usually it is not efficient to work with the overtype feature on, because important information could easily be written over. Pressing <Ins> again puts WordPerfect back into the insert mode.

 YOUR TURN

In this exercise you are going to practice moving the cursor and deleting text.

1. Start with the SEMINAR file on your screen. If necessary, start the WordPerfect program and retrieve the SEMINAR file from your data disk. If you need help retrieving documents, refer to "Retrieving a Document" earlier in this chapter.

> Press <Home> <Home>-<Up arrow>

The cursor is now at the very beginning of the document. Notice that in the lower-right corner of the screen it says Doc 1 Pg 1 Ln 1 " Pos 1 ".

> Press <Down arrow> ten times

The cursor should now be on the A in the first word of the first sentence.

> Press <End>

The cursor jumps to the very end of the first line of the letter.

> Press <Home>-<Down arrow>

The cursor jumps to the bottom of the window.

> Press <Home> <Home>-<Down arrow>

The cursor moves to the end of the document.

> Press <Esc>

The prompt **Repeat value = 8** appears at the left corner of the screen.

> Type: 15
>
> Press <Up arrow>

The cursor moves up fifteen lines.

2. So far you have only moved the cursor up and down vertically in the document. Next practice moving horizontally across a line.

> Press <Ctrl>-<Left arrow>

The cursor moves left one word.

> Press <Ctrl>-<right arrow> three times

The cursor moves to the right three words. Continue practicing using all the cursor move-ment commands listed in Table 2-1. When you have finished practicing, press <Home> <Home>-<Up arrow> to return the cursor to the beginning of the document.

3. Now you want to practice deleting text. Move the cursor so that it is on the p in place-ment in the third sentence in the first paragraph. You are going to change this to a capital P.

> Press <Ins>

The word **Typeover** should now appear in the lower-left corner of the screen.

> Type: P

The letter is now an uppercase P. Press <Ins> to return to the insert mode. The word **Type-over** no longer appears in the left corner of the screen. Move the cursor until it is under the s in service, the word following Placement, where the cursor is currently located.

> Press <Del>

> Type: S

Move the cursor to the first f in office, the word following Service.

> Press <Backspace>

> Type: O

You should notice that <Del> deletes the character above the cursor while <Backspace> de-letes the character to the left of the cursor.

4. Next you are going to delete an entire sentence. Move the cursor so that it is on the word I that begins the next sentence, I think this information will help you in your job-search efforts.

> Press <Alt>-<F4>

The words **Block on** start flashing in the lower left-corner of the screen.

> Press . (the period)

Your screen should look like Figure 2-4. The last sentence of the first paragraph should now be highlighted.

> Press <Del>

The prompt **Delete block** appears at the bottom of the screen.

> Enter: Y

The sentence is now deleted from the text.

5. Move the cursor to the first sentence in the second paragraph of the letter. Change the lowercase p and s in placement service to uppercase letters.

6. Move the cursor to the T in These, the first word of the sentence These seminars will be divided up according to majors.

> Press <Alt>-<F4>

> Press . (the period)

> Press <Right arrow> twice to extend the highlighting two more spaces

FIGURE 2-4 Selecting a Box of Text

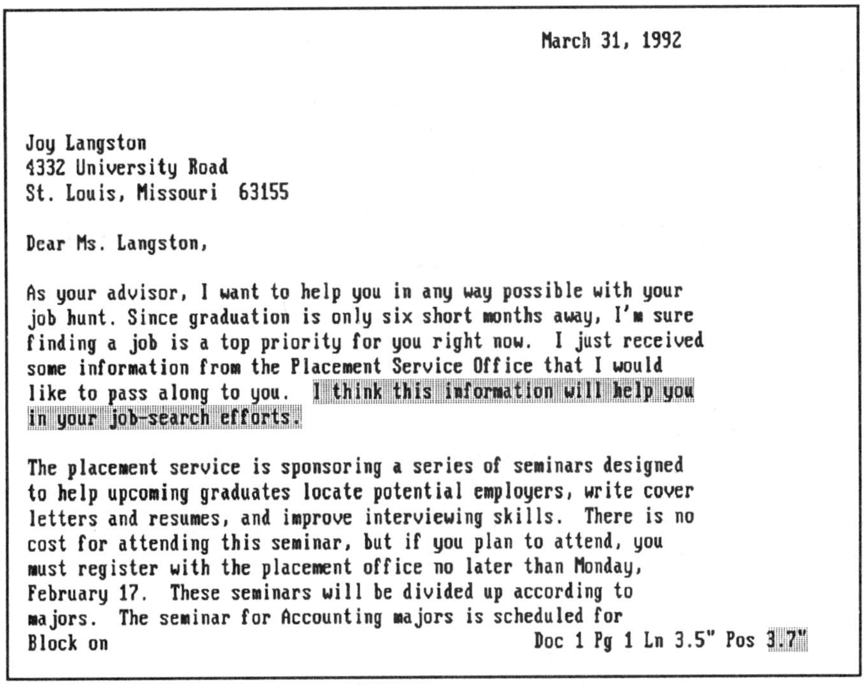

```
                                              March 31, 1992


   Joy Langston
   4332 University Road
   St. Louis, Missouri  63155

   Dear Ms. Langston,

   As your advisor, I want to help you in any way possible with your
   job hunt. Since graduation is only six short months away, I'm sure
   finding a job is a top priority for you right now.  I just received
   some information from the Placement Service Office that I would
   like to pass along to you.  I think this information will help you
   in your job-search efforts.

   The placement service is sponsoring a series of seminars designed
   to help upcoming graduates locate potential employers, write cover
   letters and resumes, and improve interviewing skills.  There is no
   cost for attending this seminar, but if you plan to attend, you
   must register with the placement office no later than Monday,
   February 17.  These seminars will be divided up according to
   majors.  The seminar for Accounting majors is scheduled for
   Block on                              Doc 1 Pg 1 Ln 3.5" Pos 3.7"
```

The entire sentence should be highlighted. The highlighting should stop immediately in front of the T in the word The.

> Press <Del>

The prompt **Delete block** appears.

> Enter: Y

The entire sentence should be deleted.

7. Move the cursor so it is on the letter t in the word it found in the sentence I think it will be well worth your time. This is the last sentence in the third paragraph of the letter.

> Press <Backspace> eight times

The sentence should now read It will be well worth your time.

8. You are now going to save the corrections you just made.

> Press <F7> for EXIT

The prompt **Save document** appears at the bottom of the screen.

> Type: Y

The file name SEMINAR appears next to the **Document to be saved** prompt because the document has already been saved once. If you wanted to keep the original document without the changes you just made, you could enter a new file name. That way, the original document would remain on your disk under the file name SEMINAR and the file with the corrections would be saved under the new file name you entered. In this exercise, you are going to replace the old SEMINAR with the file containing the revisions you just made. Since the file name already appears next to the prompt, you do not have to enter anything.

Press <Enter>

The prompt **Replace** appears at the bottom of the screen. The prompt is asking if you want to replace the original SEMINAR with the document you just created by making corrections.

Enter: Y

The prompt **Exit WP?** appears at the bottom of the screen.

9. You have finished with this Your Turn exercise. You can either exit from the WordPerfect program by pressing Y or you can leave the file on the screen while you read through the following sections by pressing N. The SEMINAR file will be used in the next Your Turn exercise.

Moving Blocks of Text

WordPerfect's block operation feature allows you to define a block of text—either a sentence, paragraph, or page—and then either copy it or move it elsewhere in the document. To be able to move a block of text, it first must be highlighted. Position the cursor under the first letter of the text to be moved. Activate the MOVE function by pressing <Ctrl>-<F4>. A menu appears at the bottom of the screen that offers four options: **1 Sentence; 2 Paragraph; 3 Page; 4 Retrieve**. Select the appropriate number. Depending on the number selected, either a sentence, paragraph, or page is highlighted.

Next the prompt **1 Move; 2 Copy; 3 Delete; 4 Append** appears at the bottom of the screen. If the text is to be moved to another part of the document, enter 1 for **Move.** The prompt **Move cursor; press Enter to retrieve** appears at the bottom of the screen. Move the cursor to the position where the text should be inserted. Press <Enter>. The text is deleted from its original location and is moved to its new location.

The MOVE function can also be used to copy a block of text that is to be repeated a number of times throughout a document. Move the cursor to the beginning of the block of text to be copied. Activate the MOVE function by pressing <Ctrl>-<F4>. Select either **1, 2,** or **3** depending on whether a sentence, paragraph, or page needs to be copied. When the **1 Move; 2 Copy; 3 Delete; 4 Append** prompt appears, enter 2 for **Copy.** The text is copied into a temporary storage location, but also is left in its original position in the document. The block of text can be reproduced as many times as needed. Simply place the cursor at the position where the copied text is to appear and activate the MOVE function <Ctrl>-<F4>. Select 4 for **Retrieve.** The menu **1 Block; 2 Tabular column; 3 Rectangle** appears at the bottom of the screen. Enter 1 for **Block.** This process can be repeated as many times as necessary to place copied text. The text stays in memory until a new block of text is copied or deleted.

YOUR TURN

In this exercise, you are going to practice moving text.

1. Start with the SEMINAR file on your screen. If necessary, start the WordPerfect program and retrieve the SEMINAR file from your data disk.

2. Move the cursor to the A in the word As, the first word in the first sentence of the letter, As your advisor, I want to help you in any way possible with your job hunt. You are going to cut this sentence and move it to a new location.

Press <Ctrl>-<F4> for MOVE

The Move menu appears at the bottom of the screen.

Press 1 for **Sentence**

The entire sentence is highlighted. Your screen should look similar to Figure 2-5. You are going to cut this sentence from its present location and move it to a new location.

Press 1 for **Move**

The sentence is cut from the letter. The prompt **Move cursor; press Enter to retrieve** appears at the bottom of the screen. Move the cursor to the word `I` in the sentence that begins: `I just received some information...`

Press <Enter>

The sentence that was cut is now inserted as the second sentence of the letter.

3. Move the cursor to the first letter of the sentence in the second paragraph that begins: `There is no cost for attending this seminar...` You are going to move this sentence so that it is the last sentence of the paragraph.

Press <Ctrl>-<F4> for MOVE

Enter 1 for **Sentence**

Enter 1 for **Move**

Move the cursor to the space immediately following the period at the end of the last sentence in the paragraph. Press the Space Bar twice so that there are two spaces after the period.

Press <Enter>

The sentence that was cut now appears as the last sentence of the paragraph. Change the `p` and `o` in the words `placement office` in the sentence you just moved to capital letters.

FIGURE 2-5 Using the MOVE Command

```
                                              March 31, 1992


Joy Langston
4332 University Road
St. Louis, Missouri  63155

Dear Ms. Langston,

As your advisor, I want to help you in any way possible with your
job hunt. Since graduation is only six short months away, I'm sure
finding a job is a top priority for you right now.  I just received
some information from the Placement Service Office that I would
like to pass along to you.

The Placement Service is sponsoring a series of seminars designed
to help upcoming graduates locate potential employers, write cover
letters and resumes, and improve interviewing skills.  There is no
cost for attending this seminar, but if you plan to attend, you
must register with the placement office no later than Monday,
February 17.  The seminar for Accounting majors is scheduled for
Saturday, February 22.  I have enclosed a tentative schedule of
events.
1 Move; 2 Copy; 3 Delete; 4 Append: 0
```

4. You want to save the changes you made to the SEMINAR file.

> Press <F7> for EXIT

> Enter Y for Yes

The file name SEMINAR appears next to the **Document to be saved** prompt because the document has already been saved once. In this exercise, you are going to replace the old SEMINAR with the file containing the revisions you just made. Since the file name already appears next to the prompt, you do not have to enter anything.

> Press <Enter>

The **Replace** prompt appears. You do want to replace the old SEMINAR file with the file containing the revisions you just made.

> Enter Y for Yes

5. You have finished with this Your Turn exercise. You can exit from the WordPerfect program by pressing Y to exit, or leave the file on the screen while you read through the following sections by pressing N. The SEMINAR file will be used in the next Your Turn exercise.

Correcting Spelling Mistakes

WordPerfect comes with a very useful function called the Speller. The Speller checks the spelling in a document, and if it finds a misspelled word, it suggests the correct spelling. Although the Speller helps the user find typing and spelling mistakes, it by no means eliminates the need for careful proofreading. For example the Speller would find nothing wrong with the sentence, "The students all plan to enjoy there spring vacation." In this sentence, the word *there* should be *their,* but the word *there* is spelled correctly, therefore it would not be found as a misspelled word needing correction.

To use the Speller, first retrieve the document that is to be checked. Activate the SPELL function by pressing <Ctrl>-<F2>. The Speller can check a word at a time, a page at a time, or it can check the spelling of the entire document. To check the spelling of one word or page, the cursor must be placed anywhere within the word or page before activating the SPELL function. When the Check menu appears, enter 1 for **Word** to check a single word, or enter 2 for **Page** to check the entire page. To check the spelling of an entire document enter 3 for **Document.**

The message **Please wait** appears at the bottom of the screen while the Speller program checks the spelling. If the Speller comes across a word that is not in its dictionary, that word is highlighted in the document and the message **Not found! Select word or menu option** appears at the bottom of the screen along with a replacement list. The replacement list includes words that are similar to the misspelled word, and its purpose is to help you find the correct spelling of the highlighted word. If the highlighted word can be replaced by one of the words in the replacement list, simply press the letter corresponding to the correct word. The Speller replaces the highlighted word with the word selected from the replacement list, and continues checking the spelling.

The Not Found menu contains six options. If a highlighted word in this particular instance is acceptable, enter 1 for **Skip once.** The Speller will continue to check the spelling. If that word is found again, it will be highlighted again. If the highlighted word is acceptable in all cases of its use, enter 2 for **Skip** and the Speller will continue to check the spelling. If that word is found again, the Speller will skip over it. If the word should be added to a supplemental dictionary because it is used often and you want the Speller to recognize it, enter 3 for **Add.**

If the highlighted word needs to be corrected but cannot be corrected by using one of the words from the replacement list, enter 4 for **Edit.** The cursor moves to the first letter of the misspelled word. Make the necessary correction and press <F7> for EXIT.

If you need to look up a word you do not know how to spell, enter 5 for **Look up.** The prompt **Word or word pattern** appears. Enter the word, spelled as closely as possible using "wild-card" characters for those letters you are not sure about. Enter ? if you are unsure of a single letter and * if you are unsure of more than one letter. For example, say you do not know how to spell *boutonniere* but know it begins with a *bo* and has a *t* in it somewhere and ends with an *e*. At the **Word or word pattern** prompt, enter bo*t*e and press <Enter>. A list of words appears on the screen, one of which is *boutonniere*.

The last option on the Not Found menu is 6 for **Ignore numbers**. This option tells the program to ignore all occurrences of words containing numbers.

When the Speller can find no more misspelled words, the message **Word count: nnn Press any key to continue** appears on the screen. The word count provides the total number of words in the document. Press any key to exit from the Speller. Save the revised document.

Difference Box: Using WordPerfect 5.0's Speller on a Computer with Two Floppy Disk Drives
To use the Speller on a computer with two floppy disk drives, you need a WordPerfect Speller disk. First, retrieve the document that is to be checked. Remove the data disk that is in drive B and replace it with the Speller disk. Activate the SPELL function by pressing <Ctrl>-<F2>. Depending on which version of WordPerfect you are using, a message may appear at this point indicating that the program cannot locate the Speller in drive A. If this happens, enter b: and press <Enter> to tell WordPerfect to look for the Speller in drive B. The Check menu appears at the bottom of the screen. Do not remove the WordPerfect Program Disk from drive A or the Speller disk from drive B while checking the document. Once you have finished checking the spelling of your document, remove the Speller disk from drive B. Insert your data disk in drive B. Save the revised document. Make sure you switch the Speller disk with your data disk *before* you save the revised document, or it will be saved on the Speller disk.

YOUR TURN

In this exercise, you are going to practice using the Speller on the SEMINAR file.

1. Start with the SEMINAR file on your screen. If necessary, start the WordPerfect program and retrieve the SEMINAR file from your data disk.

2. You are ready to check the spelling of the document.

        Press <Ctrl>-<F2> for SPELL

The Check menu appears at the bottom of the screen. Your screen should look similar to Figure 2-6. You want to check the spelling of the entire document.

        Enter 3 **for Document**

**FIGURE 2-6 WordPerfect's
Check Menu**

```
                                                    March 31, 1992




Joy Langston
4332 University Road
St. Louis, Missouri  63155

Dear Ms. Langston,

Since graduation is only six short months away, I'm sure finding a
job is a top priority for you right now.  As your advisor, I want
to help you in any way possible with your job hunt. I just received
some information from the Placement Service Office that I would
like to pass along to you.

The Placement Service is sponsoring a series of seminars designed
to help upcoming graduates locate potential employers, write cover
letters and resumes, and improve interviewing skills.  The seminar
for Accounting majors is scheduled for Saturday, February 22.  I
have enclosed a tenative schedule of events.  There is no cost for
attending this seminar, but if you plan to attend, you must
register with the Placement Office no later than Monday, February
17.
Check: 1 Word; 2 Page; 3 Document; 4 New Sup. Dictionary; 5 Look Up; 6 Count: 0
```

Your screen should look similar to Figure 2-7. The Speller finds the word *Langston* and high-
lights it. The Not Found menu appears at the bottom of the screen. The word *Langston*, however, does not need to be changed in this letter.

> Enter 2 for **Skip**

Since you entered 2 for **Skip**, the Speller does not stop at the next occurrence of *Langston.*
If the Speller locates any typing errors or misspelled words that you mistakenly typed when
entering the document, correct them as you continue through this exercise.

**FIGURE 2-7 WordPerfect's
Not Found Menu**

```
                                                    March 31, 1992




Joy Langston
4332 University Road
St. Louis, Missouri  63155

Dear Ms. Langston,

Since graduation is only six short months away, I'm sure finding a
                                      Doc 1 Pg 1 Ln 1.67" Pos 1.4"
{    ▲    ▲    ▲    ▲    ▲    ▲    ▲    ▲    ▲    ▲    ▲    }   ▲    ▲






Not Found: 1 Skip Once; 2 Skip; 3 Add; 4 Edit; 5 Look Up; 6 Ignore Numbers: 0
```

3. The Speller will eventually stop at the word *tenative.* This word is misspelled. When the Speller locates *tenative,* it lists the correct spelling, which is *tentative.* The letter **A** appears in front of *tentative.*

> Press a

The correct spelling of the word replaces the misspelled word in the document.

4. Eventually the Speller also stops on the name *Moser* and offers a list of replacement terms. Since *Moser* is spelled correctly, you can ignore it.

> Press 2 for **Skip**

5. When the Speller completes checking the spelling of the entire document, the word count appears at the bottom of the screen along with the prompt **Press any key to continue**.

> Press any key

6. You now want to save the changes you made.

> Press <F7> for EXIT
>
> Enter Y for Yes
>
> Press <Enter>
>
> Enter Y for Yes

You have finished with this Your Turn exercise. You can either exit from the WordPerfect program by entering Y for Yes, or you can leave the file on the screen while you read the following sections. The SEMINAR file will be used in the next Your Turn exercise.

Viewing a Document

Once a document has been entered and edited, it is a good idea to use WordPerfect's VIEW option to see how the document will look on the page once it is printed. To view a document, press <Shift>-<F7> for PRINT. The print screen appears (see Figure 2-8). To view a document, enter 6 for **View document**. A representation of how the document will appear when printed is displayed on the screen.

After selecting 6, the page on which the cursor was located appears. The following menu appears at the bottom of the screen:

1 100%; 2 200%; 3 Full page; 4 Facing page

The default setting is 3 for **Full page**. This displays the entire page; however, the text on the page cannot be read. To be able to read the text, select 1 or 2 to display the text at 100 percent or 200 percent. If the document contains more than one page, selecting 4 for **Facing page** displays two pages at one time. The pages displayed are the page where the cursor is located and the facing page.

To exit from the print view screen and return to the document, press the Space Bar twice. The document returns to the screen.

Printing a Document

Before printing a document, make sure the computer you are using is hooked up to a printer, that the printer is turned on and is online. In addition, make sure the printer is loaded with paper and that the paper is properly aligned in the printer.

FIGURE 2-8 WordPerfect 5.1's Print Screen

```
Print

        1 - Full Document
        2 - Page
        3 - Document on Disk
        4 - Control Printer
        5 - Multiple Pages
        6 - View Document
        7 - Initialize Printer


Options

        S - Select Printer              HP LaserJet Series II
        B - Binding Offset              0"
        N - Number of Copies            1
        U - Multiple Copies Generated by   Printer
        G - Graphics Quality            High
        T - Text Quality                High




Selection: 0
```

There are several ways to print with WordPerfect. One way is to retrieve the document to be printed. With the document displayed, press <Shift>-<F7> for PRINT. The print screen appears (refer to Figure 2-8). Press 1 to print the entire text or press 2 to print just the page of the text where the cursor is located. To print more than one copy of the document, enter N for **Number of copies**, enter the number of copies to be printed, and press either 1 for **Full document** or 2 for **Page**.

A document can also be printed without retrieving it. Press <F5> for LIST FILES. When the list of all the files in the default directory appears, there is a menu at the bottom of the screen. Move the highlighting to the file you want to print. Press 4 for **Print.** The prompt **Page(s): All** appears next. Press <Enter> to print the entire document. If desired, only certain pages from a document can be printed. Table 2-2 lists examples of entries that can be made at the **Page(s)** prompt to print only specific pages.

TABLE 2-2 Printing Specific Pages from a Document

Enter at Pages Prompt	Pages That Will Print
<Enter>	Entire document
8	Only page 8 will print
8-	Pages 8 to the end of the document will print
8-10	Pages 8 through 10 will print
-8	The first page of the document through page 8 will print
8,10	Page 8 and page 10 will print
8-10,15	Pages 8 through 10 and page 15 will print

YOUR TURN

In this exercise, you are going to print the SEMINAR file. Before starting the exercise, make sure the computer you are using is hooked up to a printer, that the printer is online, and that the paper is properly positioned in the printer.

1. Start with the SEMINAR file on your screen. If necessary, start the WordPerfect program and retrieve the SEMINAR file from your data disk.

2. Before you print the document, you want to preview it on the screen.

> Press <Shift>-<F7> for PRINT
>
> Press 6 for **View document**

The full page should be displayed on the screen. If it is not, press 3 for **Full page**. To be able to read the text, enlarge the display.

> Press 1 for 100%
>
> Press 2 for 200%

While the display is enlarged, you can move through it using the cursor movement keys. Once you have finished viewing the document, press 3 to return the display to **Full page** and press the Space Bar twice to return the document to the screen.

3. Print the SEMINAR file by doing the following:

> Press <Shift>-<F7> for PRINT
>
> Press 1 to print the entire document

The SEMINAR file is printed. Your finished document should look like Figure 2-9.

4. You are now ready to save the final document and exit from the WordPerfect program.

> Press <F7> for EXIT
>
> Press Y for Yes at the **Save document** prompt
>
> Press <Enter> at the **Document to be saved** prompt
>
> Press Y for Yes at the **Replace**
>
> Press Y for Yes at the **Exit WP** prompt

When the system prompt appears, remove your disks and turn off the computer and monitor. Be sure to store the disks safely.

❏ SUMMARY POINTS

■ One main function of a word processor is text editing, which involves entering and manipulating text.

■ Common writing and editing features of word processors include cursor positioning, word wrap, scrolling, insertion, replacement, deletion, spelling correction, block operation, searching, undo, and save.

```
                                                     January 9, 1992


        Joy Langston
        4332 University Road
        St. Louis, Missouri 63155

        Dear Ms. Langston,

        Since graduation is only six short months away, I'm sure finding a
        job is a top priority for you right now.  As your advisor, I want
        to help you in any way possible with your job hunt.   I just
        received some information from the Placement Service Office that I
        would like to pass along to you.

        The Placement Service is sponsoring a series of seminars designed
        to help upcoming graduates locate potential employers, write cover
        letters and resumes, and improve interviewing skills.  The seminar
        for Accounting majors is scheduled for Saturday, February 22.   I
        have enclosed a tentative schedule of events.  There is no cost for
        attending this seminar, but if you plan to attend, you must
        register with the Placement Office no later than Monday, February
        17.

        I hope you plan to attend this seminar.  It will be well worth your
        time.

        Sincerely,



        Professor Herbert Moser

        Enclosure
```

FIGURE 2-9 The SEMINAR Document

■ Word wrap is a feature which automatically moves a word to the beginning of the next line if it crosses the right margin.

■ A block operation feature allows a user to define a block of text (a word, sentence, paragraph, or page) and delete, copy or move it.

Chapter 2: Introduction to WordPerfect 5.1

Command	Keystroke	Function
BLOCK	\<Alt\>-\<F4\>	Highlights a block of text for further action.
CANCEL	\<F1\>	Cancels some commands; returns to document from menus with no action taken. Also allows you to restore the last two blocks of text that were deleted.
DATE/OUTLINE	\<Shift\>-\<F5\>	Automatically inserts the date as either text or code at the cursor's location.
EXIT	\<F7\>	Exits from the current document, giving the user the opportunity to save the document currently on the screen. Also gives the user the opportunity to exit from WordPerfect.
FLUSH RIGHT	\<F6\>	Aligns text following the cursor flush with the right margin.
HELP	\<F3\>	Displays help information, either alphabetically or by key combination.
LIST FILES	\<F5\>	Allows the user to view the files in the default directory, to change directories, to retrieve files, and to perform other file-maintenance tasks.
MOVE	\<Ctrl\>-\<F4\>	Allows you to move, copy, delete, or append blocks of text.
PRINT	\<Shift\>-\<F7\>	Provides full control over printing WordPerfect documents.
RETRIEVE	\<Shift\>-\<F10\>	Allows a file to be retrieved to the text window from disk.
SAVE	\<F10\>	Saves the document currently on screen without exiting the document or the program.
SPELL	\<Ctrl\>-\<F2\>	Allows the user to check the spelling of a word, page, document, or block of text.

❏ WORDPERFECT EXERCISES

1. Assume that the computer is shut off. List all the necessary steps needed to start the WordPerfect program. If you need help remembering how to start WordPerfect, refer to "Getting Started with WordPerfect" earlier in this chapter.

2. Start the WordPerfect program. Enter your name in the upper-left corner of the text window and press \<Enter\>. Using the automatic date feature, enter the date. If you need help with the automatic date feature, refer to the first Your Turn exercise in this chapter. Press \<Enter\> twice. Enter the following document:

```
A soap opera deals with the plights and problems brought about in
the lives of its permanent principal characters by the advent and
interference of one group of individuals after another. Thus, a
soap opera is an endless sequence of narratives whose only cohesive
```

element is the eternal presence of bedeviled and beleaguered
principal characters. A narrative, or story sequence, may run from
eight weeks to several months. The end of one plot is always hooked
up with the beginning of the next, but the connection is
unimportant and soon forgotten. Almost all the villains in the
small town daytime serials are emigres from the cities-gangsters,
white-collar criminals, designing women, unnatural mothers, cold
wives, and selfish, ruthless, and just plain cursed rich men. They
always come up against a shrewdness that outwits them or destroys
them, or a kindness that wins them over to the good way of life.
E. B. White, "Soapland"

3. Make the following editing changes to the paragraph you just entered. If you need to review how to make these changes, refer to "Selecting Blocks of Text," "Deleting Text," and "Moving Blocks of Text" earlier in this chapter.

■ Make the following changes to the first sentence of the paragraph:
   a. Delete the first word, A.
   b. Change the lowercase s in soap, which is now the first word of the paragraph to a capital S.
   c. Add an s to the end of opera to make it plural.
   d. Delete the s at the end of the word deals.
   e. Delete the word its and insert the word their in its place.

■ Delete the following sentence using the block operation function and the <Del> key:
   A narrative, or story sequence, may run from eight weeks to several
   months.

■ Move the cursor to the beginning of the paragraph. Copy the first sentence. Place the copy of this sentence at the end of the text. The sentence should appear both at the beginning and the end of the paragraph when you have finished.

■ Move the cursor to the very end of the document and press <Enter> three times.

■ Type: Version 1

4. Use the Speller to check the spelling of the paragraph. If you need to review how to use the Speller, refer to "Correcting Spelling Mistakes" earlier in this chapter. After you have corrected any spelling errors, proofread the paragraph carefully for any errors the Speller may not have caught. When satisfied that the paragraph is entered correctly, save it.

5. Preview and print the document. If you need help remembering how to preview and print a document, refer to "Viewing a Document" and "Printing a Document" earlier in this chapter.

6. Save the document. Exit from WordPerfect. If you need to review how to save a document and exit from WordPerfect, refer to "Saving a Document" and "Exiting from WordPerfect" earlier in this chapter.

7. Assume that the WordPerfect program has been loaded and that the text window is blank. List all the necessary steps needed to retrieve a document that has been stored on a disk. If you need help remembering how to retrieve a document, refer to "Retrieving a Document" earlier in this chapter.

8. You decide to reenter the sentence previously deleted and to delete the last sentence of the paragraph. Start the computer and load the WordPerfect program. Retype the sentence

    A narrative, or story sequence, may run from eight weeks to several
    months.

in its original location. Delete the last sentence of the paragraph using the block operation function and <Del>. Change the last line of the document, Version 1 to Version 2. Save the revised file using a new file name.

9. Preview the paragraph and then print it.

❏ WORDPERFECT PROBLEMS

To complete the following exercises, you need to use files on the Student File Disk. In order to complete these exercises, you will need to be able to start WordPerfect, exit from WordPerfect, save a document, back up a file on a disk, retrieve a document, select blocks of text, delete text, move blocks of text, correct spelling mistakes, view a document, and print a document.

1. On the Student File Disk there is a WordPerfect file called SPELL. Start the WordPerfect program and retrieve this file. Save this file and rename it SPELL-2. If you need to review how to back up a file on a disk, refer to "Backing Up a File on a Disk" earlier in this chapter. You want to maintain the original SPELL file on your disk.

2. There are many spelling errors in the SPELL-2 file. Use WordPerfect's Speller to check the spelling of the paragraphs. You can assume that proper names and the titles of books and computer names are correct. Correct the spelling of the words that the Speller finds that should be corrected.

3. Proofread the paragraphs carefully to make sure the Speller found all the errors. If there are errors in the document that the Speller did not find, correct them.

4. Move the cursor to the very end of the document. Press <Enter> three times. Enter your name.

5. When you are satisfied that the document is correct, save the SPELL-2 file. Preview the file and print it. Exit from the WordPerfect program.

6. On the Student File Disk there is a WordPerfect file called SUBSCRP. Start the WordPerfect program and retrieve this file. Save this file and rename it SUBSCRP2. You want to maintain the original SUBSCRP file on your disk. If you need to review how to back up a file on a disk, refer to "Backing Up a File on a Disk" earlier in this chapter.

7. The SUBSCRP document is an order to a publishing firm. Enter the current year in the date at the top of the document. Using the block operation function and <Del>, delete the supplier address and replace it with the following new address:

```
Midwest Publishing
112 Lasalle Street
Chicago, IL   60610
```

8. Change the name of the magazine to `News Weekly`.

9. Add the following to the beginning of the first sentence:

`Starting next month,·`

Change the `P` in `Please` from upper case to lowercase.

10. Add the following name to the list of persons receiving the subscription:

```
Mr. Eric Ricard
Engineering Department
```

11. Using the block operation function and <Del>, delete the following sentence:

```
I am accepting your special offer—$15 for the first subscription,
$8 for each additional subscription.
```

12. Delete the name `Helen Turoff`. Enter your name in its place.

13. Use the Speller to check the spelling in your letter. Make any necessary corrections.

14. Save the letter. Preview the letter to make sure it looks all right on the page. Print the letter.

15. Exit from the WordPerfect program. Turn off the computer and monitor. Carefully store the disks.

❏ WORDPERFECT CHALLENGE

Assume you are contemplating relocating to a different city in order to seek employment in your field.

1. Using WordPerfect, write a letter to the Chamber of Commerce of a city where you would like to live. Ask for information about that city, including what the job opportunities in your field are, housing availability and prices, local recreational, social, and cultural offerings, and so on.

2. Proofread your letter carefully. Use the WordPerfect Speller to check for spelling errors. When you are satisfied with your letter, save it.

3. Preview and print your letter.

4. Change the city, state, and zip code of your letter so you can send it to a second city. Make any other necessary changes in the text of the letter so that the letter can appropriately be sent to the second city.

5. Proofread the second letter carefully. Use the Speller to check for spelling errors. When you are satisfied with the second letter, save it by giving it a new file name. That is, you want to keep both the original letter sent to the first city and the second letter addressed to a different city on your disk.

6. Preview and print the second letter.

CHAPTER 3

More WordPerfect 5.1 Features

OUTLINE

❏ INTRODUCTION

Many simple documents such as memos, letters, and short papers can be created with the WordPerfect functions learned in the previous chapter. Resumes, term papers, and other types of documents, however, require the use of more advanced features. These features can make the creation of a complicated document a relatively easy task. This chapter explains how to use formatting features to enhance the appearance of a document and how to add footnotes to a document.

❏ FORMATTING A DOCUMENT

The formatting function of a word processor involves a variety of features that communicate with the printer to tell it how to print the text on paper. Some of the more common formatting features include setting margins and tab stops, selecting single- or double-spaced text, and performing character enhancements, such as underlining and boldfacing.

WordPerfect's default settings provide a standard page format. The user does not have to enter any information. These default settings can be changed, however. The exercises in this chapter will guide you through the process of formatting a document so that it can be custom-designed.

❏ LINE FORMAT

The LINE FORMAT function, which enables the user to set left and right margins, tabs, spacing, justification, and hyphenation, is activated by pressing <Shift>-<F8> for FORMAT and then pressing either 1 or L for **Line**. The Line Format menu for WordPerfect 5.1 has nine options (see Figure 3-1). Table 3-1 explains the purpose of each option. To return to the document from the Line Format menu, press <Esc> twice.

FIGURE 3-1 WordPerfect's Line Format Menu

```
Format: Line

     1 - Hyphenation                    No

     2 - Hyphenation Zone - Left        10%
                           Right        4%

     3 - Justification                  Full

     4 - Line Height                    Auto

     5 - Line Numbering                 No

     6 - Line Spacing                   1

     7 - Margins - Left                 1"
                   Right                1"

     8 - Tab Set                        Rel: -1", every 0.5"

     9 - Widow/Orphan Protection        No



Selection: 0
```

TABLE 3-1 Options from the WordPerfect Line Format Menu

Selection	Description
1- Hyphenation	Hyphenation can be set to Yes or No. If set to No, none of the words are hyphenated. If set to Yes, the user can select where words should be hyphenated. The default setting is No.
2- Hypenation Zone	Sets the limits that determine if a word should be hyphenated or moved to the next line.
3-Justification	Justification can be set to Left, Center, Right or Full. If set to Left, the lines of text are justified at the left margin and ragged at the right margin. If set to Center, lines of text are centered between the margins. If set to Right, the lines of text are ragged at the left margin and justified at the right margin. If set to Full, both the left and right margin are justified, that is, the lines of text are even at the left and right margins.
4-Line Height	Sets the amount of space each line takes up. Line height is measured from the bottom of one line to the bottom of the next line.
5- Line Numbering	Line numbering can be set to Yes or No. If set to Yes, lines are numbered when the document is printed. The numbers do not appear on the screen. If set to No, lines are not numbered. The default setting is No.
6-Line Spacing	Sets the line spacing. A setting of 1.5 = one and one-half lines of spacing; 1 = single spacing, 2 = double spacing; 3 = triple spacing; and so on. The default setting is 1 for single spacing.
7-Margins	Sets the left and right margins. The default setting is 1 inch for both left and right margins.
8-Tab Set	Sets tab stops. The default setting is a tab stop every five spaces.
9-Widow/Orphan Protection	Prevents widows and orphans. An orphan is the first line of a paragraph appearing by itself at the bottom of a page. A widow is the last line of a paragraph appearing by itself at the top of a page.

Left and Right Margins

To set the right and left margins, press either 7 or M for **Margins** from the Line Format menu. The cursor moves to the **Left Margin** setting. Enter the desired left margin setting in inches and press <Enter>. For example enter 1.5 for a 1 1/2-inch left margin. After pressing <Enter>, the cursor moves to the **Right Margin** setting. Enter the desired right margin setting in inches and press <Enter>.

Margin settings are operative from the cursor's location forward. To change margin settings, place the cursor where the new margin settings are to go into effect and enter the new margin settings from the Line Format menu.

Justification

Justification is a feature for making the lines of text in a document line up evenly at the margins. To set the justification for a document, press either 3 or J for **Justification** from the Line Format menu. The cursor moves to the current justification setting. The default setting in WordPerfect is **Full,** which means the lines are printed evenly at both the left and right margins. To turn the justification off so that lines will print unevenly at the right margin, press 3 or J for **Justification** and then press 1 or L for **Left** Justification.

The justification setting is operative from the cursor's location forward. To change the justification setting, place the cursor where the new setting is to go into effect. Change the justification setting from the Line Format menu.

Difference Box: Justification in WordPerfect 5.0

After pressing 3 or J for **Justification** from the the Line Format menu, the options for Justification settings are **Yes** and **No**. If Y for **Yes** is selected, the lines of text will be even, or justified at both the left and right margins. If N for **No** is selected, the lines of text will be even at the left margin, but ragged at the right margin.

Line Spacing

To set the line spacing, press either 6 or S for **Line Spacing.** The cursor moves to the current line spacing setting. WordPerfect's default line spacing is 1 for single-spaced. Enter the desired line spacing and press <Enter>. For example, enter 1.5 for a spacing of one and one-half lines, 2 for double spacing, 3 for triple spacing and so on.

The setting for line spacing is operative from the cursor's location forward. To change the line spacing, place the cursor where the new line spacing is to go into effect. Change the setting for **Line Spacing** from the Line Format menu.

Tab Set

To set tabs, press either 8 or T for **Tab Set** from the Line Format menu. The Tab menu appears at the bottom of the screen (see Figure 3-2). The ruler line that appears represents the width of the document. The 0" at the left end of the ruler indicates the location of the left margin. Along the lines are Ls which indicate the current setting for left tab stops. To set new tabs, you can use the arrow keys to move the cursor along the ruler line. When the cursor reaches the location where the tab is to be set, type either L, C, R, or D. L sets a left tab. Text will align to the left of the tab's location. C sets a center tab. Text will be centered around the tab's location. R sets a right tab. Text will be aligned to the right of the tab's

FIGURE 3-2 The Tab Menu

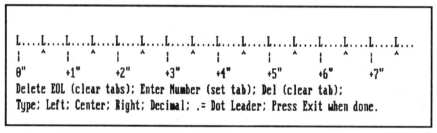

location. D sets a decimal tab. Text will align wherever the period is pressed after pressing <Tab>. Decimal tabs are very useful for entering columns of numbers that include decimals, such as dollar amounts.

Tab settings can also be entered by typing in the location where they are to appear, in inches, and pressing <Enter>. For example, if you wanted a tab at 4 1/4 inches on the page, you would enter 4.25. After pressing <Enter>, an L appears at the location just entered and the cursor moves to that location. To change the new tab setting to another type of tab, simply press C, R, or D.

With WordPerfect you can also set leaders with tab stops. A leader is a character that automatically fills in the space from the cursor's position to the tab stop when the <Tab> key is pressed. The most common leader is a dot or period. This is often used in a table of contents, for example. To set a tab stop with a dot leader, move the cursor to the tab stop that is to be preceded by the dot leaders and type a period. Tab stops that include dot leaders are highlighted on the Tab menu.

To delete all set tabs, position the cursor on or before the first tab setting. Press <Ctrl>-<End>. All the tabs from the cursor forward are deleted. To delete individual tabs, move the cursor to the letter representing the tab stop to be deleted and press <Del>.

When you have finished setting the tabs, press <F7> for EXIT. To return to the text without saving any of the tabs that were set, press <F1> for CANCEL. Tabs can be set as many times as necessary in a document. Only the text entered after tabs have been set will be affected.

❏ INDENTING PARAGRAPHS

In addition to using tab stops, WordPerfect has two INDENT functions that enable the user to easily indent an entire paragraph from either the left margin only or both the left and right margins. The INDENT function that indents a paragraph from both the right and left margins is activated by pressing <Shift>-<F4>. The tab stops also are used for indent stops, so the cursor moves to the next stop when the INDENT function is activated. Every line is then indented an equal distance from the left and right margins. Pressing <Enter> cancels the INDENT function and the lines that follow return to the normal margin.

To indent a paragraph from the left margin only, press <F4>. The paragraph indents one tab stop each time <F4> for INDENT is pressed. Pressing <Enter> cancels the function, and the lines that follow return to the normal margin.

A hanging paragraph, in which the first line begins at the left margin while the remaining lines are indented, can also be created using the INDENT function. To create a hanging indent, press <F4> for INDENT. Then press <Shift>-<Tab> to move the first line of the paragraph one tab stop to the left. Type the paragraph. The first line of the paragraph starts at the left margin while the remaining text is indented. To end a hanging paragraph, press <Enter>.

Difference Box WordPerfect 5.0: The Tab Ruler
In WordPerfect 5.0, the left margin on the tab ruler is not indicated by 0". Instead, it falls where it is set. That is, if the left margin is set for 2 inches, it will fall at 2" on the tab ruler. In WordPerfect 5.0, the 0" indicator on the Tab Ruler always indicates the left edge of the paper rather than the left margin.

YOUR TURN

In this exercise you are going to practice using WordPerfect's various formatting options. Figure 3-3 depicts the final document.

Difference Box WordPerfect 5.0

When instructed to turn off the justification in number 2 of this exercise, you will press N for **No** instead of pressing 1 for **Left.** In addition, when instructed to set the tabs in number 3, use the following directions:

> Type: 1
> Press <Enter>

An L appears at 1 inch. You want to change this to a decimal tab.

> Type: d
> Type: 1.25
> Press <Enter>
> Type: 1.75
> Press <Enter>

There should be a D at 1 inch and an L at 1 1/4 inches and at 1 3/4 inches.

---

1. Start WordPerfect on the computer. If you need to review how to start the program, refer to "Getting Started with WordPerfect" in the previous chapter. There should be a blank text window on the screen. First, you are going to change the left and right margins.

> Press <Shift>-<F8> for FORMAT
>
> Press 1 for **Line**

The Line Format menu should be on your screen.

> Press 7 for **Margins**

The cursor should move to the left margin option. You want to set the margins at 3/4 inch.

> Type: 0.75
>
> Press <Enter>

The cursor moves to the right margin option.

> Type: 0.75
>
> Press <Enter>

2. You want to turn the justification off. Notice that it now says Full next to the **Justification** option. The Line Format menu should still be on your screen.

> Press 3 for **Justification**
>
> Press 1 for **Left**

It should now say **Left** next to the **Justification** prompt.

FIGURE 3-3 Using
Formatting Functions to
Create an Outline

The Placement Service is pleased you are attending one of our job
placement seminars. This is the third year we have sponsored these
seminars and they have proven to be quite successful. The seminar for
Accounting majors is Saturday, February 22, from 8:00 a.m. to 5:00
p.m. The following introduces you to the people leading the seminar
and outlines the day's schedule.

    Dr. Kate Clifford, Head of Placement Service. Dr. Clifford has
been the head of the Placement Service at Washington University
for over fifteen years. Before coming to Washington University,
she worked for the executive recruiting firm, Cyphers and Porter,
Inc.

    Mr. Keith Goldman, Audit Manager, Thales Electronics. As Audit
Manager, Mr. Goldman is responsible for hiring close to twenty
auditors a year. Mr. Goldman's published articles include,
"Marketing Your Accounting Degree" and "The Hiring Trend in
Accounting."

  I. 8:00-8:30 Registration

 II. 8:30-10:00 Locating Employers

    A. Job Opportunities for Accounting Majors and Who is Doing the
        Hiring
    B. Informational Interviews: What They are and How to Get One
    C. Word of Mouth: How Talking to Everyone Can Get You a Job

III. 10:00-12:00 Cover Letters and Resumes

    A. The Contents of a Resume: What Should and Should Not Be
        Included
    B. The Form of a Resume: What a Resume Should and Should Not
        Look Like
    C. How to Write a Cover Letter

 IV. 12:00-1:00 Break for Lunch

  V. 1:00-2:00 Interviewing Skills

    A. First Impressions: How to Make a Positive Impression in the
        First Five Minutes of an Interview
    B. Being Prepared for Any Interview Question
    C. Knowing What Questions You Should Ask

 VI. 2:00-5:00 Utilizing the Placement Service Office

    A. Using the Career Library
    B. Interviews Through the Placement Office

3. Next you want to reset the tab stops. The Line Format menu should still be on your screen.

Press 8 for **Tab Set**

The Tab menu line appears.

Press <Ctrl>-<End> to delete all the tab stops

The left margin is set at 3/4 inch. You are going to set three tabs. You want a decimal tab at 1 inch and left tabs at 1 1/4 inches and 1 3/4 inches. Remember, the 0" marker on the Tab Ruler indicates the left margin.

Type: 0.25

Press <Enter>

An L appears at 1/4 inch. You want to change this to a decimal tab.

Type: d

Type: `0.5`

Press <Enter>

Type: `1`

Press <Enter>

Your screen should look like Figure 3-4. There should be a D at 1/4 inch and an L at 1/2 inches and at 1 inch.

Press <F7>

The Line Format menu returns to the screen. You are ready to start entering the document.

Press <Esc> two times

4. The text window should be on your screen.

Type the following:

```
The Placement Service is pleased you are attending one of our job
placement seminars. This is the third year we have sponsored these
seminars and they have proven to be quite successful. The seminar
for Accounting majors is Saturday, February 22, from 8:00 a.m. to
5:00 p.m. The following introduces you to the people leading the
seminar and outlines the day's schedule.
```

Press <Enter> twice at the end of the paragraph

5. The next two paragraphs are to be indented from the left margin. You want the paragraphs to indent to the second tab stop, so you will have to press <F4> twice.

Press <F4> for INDENT two times

Type the following:

```
Dr. Kate Clifford, Head of Placement Service. Dr. Clifford has been
the head of the Placement Service at Washington University for over
fifteen years. Before coming to Washington University, she worked
for the executive recruiting firm, Cyphers and Porter, Inc.
```

Press <Enter> two times

Press <F4> for INDENT two times

```
Mr. Keith Goldman, Audit Manager, Thales Electronics. As Audit
Manager, Mr. Goldman is responsible for hiring close to twenty
auditors a year. Mr. Goldman's published articles include,
```

FIGURE 3-4 Changing Tab Settings

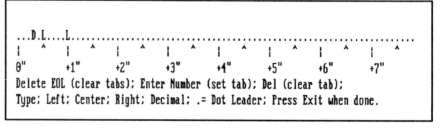

"Marketing Your Accounting Degree" and "The Hiring Trend in Accounting."

> Press <Enter> two times at the end of the second paragraph

6. You are now going to enter the outline.

> Press <Tab>

The words **Align char** appear in the lower-left corner of the screen because the first tab is a decimal tab and it is using a period (.) as the character by which it is going to align the text.

> Type: I.

> Press <Tab>

> Type: 8:00-8:30 Registration

> Press <Enter> two times

> Press <Tab>

> Type: II.

> Press <Tab>

> Type: 8:30-10:00 Locating Employers

> Press <Enter> two times

Notice that the Roman numerals I and II align by the period that follows them. This is because that tab stop is set as a decimal tab. The decimal tab aligns characters at a period.

> Press <Tab> two times

> Type: A.

> Press <F4>

> Type the following:

> Job Opportunities for Accounting Majors and Who is Doing
>   the Hiring

> Press <Enter>

> Press <Tab> two times

> Type: B.

> Press <F4>

> Type the following:

> Informational Interviews: What They are and How to Get One

> Press <Enter>

> Press <Tab> two times

> Type: C.

> Press <F4>

> Type the following:

> Word of Mouth: How Talking to Everyone Can Get You a Job

Press <Enter> two times

Press <Tab>

Type: III.

Press <Tab>

Type: 10:00-12:00 Cover Letters and Resumes

Press <Enter> two times

Press <Tab> two times

Type: A.

Press <F4>

Type the following:

The Contents of a Resume: What Should and Should Not Be
    Included

Press <Enter>

Press <Tab> two times

Type: B.

Press <F4>

Type the following:

The Form of a Resume: What a Resume Should and Should Not
    Look Like

Press <Enter>

Press <Tab> two times

Type: C.

Press <F4>

Type: How to Write a Cover Letter

Press <Enter> two times

You should now be familiar with how the tabs work. Type the rest of the outline as follows:

    IV. 12:00-1:00 Break for Lunch

     V. 1:00-2:00 Interviewing Skills

        A. First Impressions: How to Make a Positive Impression in
           the First Five Minutes of an Interview

        B. Being Prepared for Any Interview Question

        C. Knowing What Questions You Should Ask

    VI. 2:00-5:00 Utilizing the Placement Service Office

        A. Using the Career Library

        B. Interviews Through the Placement Office

7. When you have finished entering the outline, proofread the entire document carefully. Use WordPerfect's Speller to check for spelling errors. If you need to review how to use the Speller, refer to "Correcting Spelling Mistakes" in the previous chapter. Save the letter as PSLETTER, for placement service letter. If you need to review how to save a document, refer to "Saving a Document" in the previous chapter.

8. View the PSLETTER document. If you need to review how to view a document, refer to "Viewing a Document" in the previous chapter. When you view it, make sure all the tabs line up properly. Print the PSLETTER document. If you need to review how to print a document, refer to "Printing a Document" in the previous chapter. Your printed document should look like Figure 3-3. Exit from the WordPerfect program. Turn off the computer and monitor. Carefully store your disks.

❏ CHARACTER ENHANCEMENTS

A character enhancement is any special printing effect. Character enhancements such as underlining and boldfacing are quite useful when creating reports, resumes, and other documents. Whether you can use all the character enhancements included in WordPerfect depends on your printer. Your instructor can tell you which character enhancements your printer is capable of producing.

Boldface

To activate the BOLD function, press <F6>. Any text entered after activating the BOLD function appears in boldface type when printed. To end the BOLD function, press <F6> again.

To make text that has already been entered boldface, use the block operation function to define the text to be made boldface. While the words **Block on** are still flashing in the lower-left corner of the screen, activate the BOLD function by pressing <F6>. The text that was marked with the block operation function will be in boldface when printed. Activating the BOLD function turns the block operation function off. The words **Block on** stop flashing in the lower-left corner of the screen.

Text that is to be printed in boldface appears highlighted on the screen. You may have to adjust the contrast on your monitor in order to see the difference between the regular text and the text to be boldfaced.

Underline

To activate the UNDERLINE function, press <F8>. Any text entered after activating the UNDERLINE function is underlined when printed. To end the UNDERLINE function, press <F8> again.

To underline text that has already been entered, use the block operation function to define the text to be underlined. While the words **Block on** are still flashing in the lower-left corner of the screen, activate the UNDERLINE function by pressing <F8>. The text that was marked with the block operation function will be underlined when printed. Activating the underline function turns the block operation function off. The words **Block on** stop flashing in the lower-left corner of the screen.

Text that is to be underlined appears differently on the screen. If you have a color monitor, text that is to be underlined may appear in a different color. If you have a monochrome monitor, text to be underlined may appear on the screen either underlined or in reverse video, that is, dark letters on a bright background.

Center

Text can be centered by pressing <Shift>-<F6> for the CENTER function. Any text entered after pressing <Shift>-<F6> is automatically centered. Pressing <Enter> cancels the CENTER function and the text that follows returns to the margin settings.

❏ VIEWING COMMAND CODES

WordPerfect is a what-you-see-is-what-you-get word processor. That is, what you see on the screen resembles as closely as possible how the text will look when printed on a piece of paper. However, when most of WordPerfect's functions are activated, command codes are inserted into the text. Because codes are not printed, they do not appear on the screen unless the user wants to view them. Revealing the command codes enables a user to easily delete commands.

Pressing <Alt>-<F3> activates the REVEAL CODES function. When the REVEAL CODES function is activated, the screen is divided in two by the Tab Ruler. The same text is displayed above and below the Tab Ruler, but the text below the Tab Ruler also displays all the codes. The cursor on the bottom window is displayed as a highlighted bar. The cursor can be moved using the arrow keys. Either <Backspace> or <Del> can be used to delete command codes. Pressing <Alt>-<F3> again cancels the REVEAL CODES function and the text window returns to normal.

 YOUR TURN

For this exercise, you are going to create a resume. Figure 3-5 illustrates the final, corrected document. Start with a blank text window on your screen.

Difference Box: WordPerfect 5.0

When instructed to change the justification in number 1 of this exercise, you will press N for **No** instead of pressing 1 for **Left.** When setting the tabs in number 2, set them at 2 and 4.5.

---

1. Before you start typing the resume, some formatting changes need to be made. First, the right margin is not justified.

        Press <Shift>-<F8> for FORMAT

        Press 1 for **Line**

        Press 3 for **Justification**

        Press 1 for **Left**

The word **Left** now appears next to **Justification**.

2. Next, you want to set your tabs.

        Press 8 for **Tab Set**

The Tab menu appears.

FIGURE 3-5 Using Formatting Functions to Create a Resume

```
JOY LANGSTON                              4332 University Road
                                          St. Louis MO 63155
                                          (314) 555-1214

                          Objective

To develop skills in managerial accounting with a major
corporation and to become a controller.

                          Education

B.S. Accounting, Washington University, 1992
Minor: Economics with emphasis in corporate finance.
Significant courses include:

Accounting                       Business
Financial Accounting             Topics in Corporate Management
Cost Accounting                  Industrial Economics
Advanced Accounting              Management Information Systems
Advanced Federal Tax Law         Business Communications

                          Experience

Summers   Intern, Price Waterhouse, Columbus, Ohio 1991
          Worked on various audit assignments, including stock
          inventory at Mills International.

College   Assistant, University Financial Aid Office, 1991
          Reviewed applications for financial aid; verified their
          conformity with tax returns and other supportive
          documents.

          Orientation Leader, University Admissions Office 1990
          Met with prospective students and their parents;
          conducted tours of campus; wrote reports for each
          orientation meeting.

                     Computer Experience

Proficient in running Lotus 1-2-3 and WordPerfect on an IMB PC

                         Activities

Alpha Beta Psi, 1990-1992
Student Senator.  Served on budget committee, 1991-1992

                         References

Credentials and references available upon request.
```

> Press <Ctrl>-<End> to clear all the current tabs
>
> Type: 1
>
> Press <Enter>
>
> Type: 3.5
>
> Press <Enter>

You now have tabs set at 1 inch and 3.5 inches.

> Press <F7> for EXIT
>
> Press <Esc> two times

3. Now you are ready to start typing the resume. The name *Joy Langston* is in all capital letters and boldface.

> Press <F6> for BOLD

Type: JOY LANGSTON

Press <F6> to turn bold off

Press <Enter>

Press <Tab> two times

Type: 4332 University Road

Press <Enter>

Press <Tab> two times

Type: St. Louis, MO 63155

Press <Enter>

Press <Tab> two times

Type: (314) 555-1214

Press <Enter> two times

4. All the titles for the major divisions in the resume are in boldface and centered.

Press <Shift>-<F6> for CENTER

Press <F6> for BOLD

Type: Objective

Press <F6> to turn bold off

Press <Enter> two times

Type the following:

To develop skills in managerial accounting with a major corporation
and to become a controller.

Press <Enter> two times

Press <Shift>-<F6> for CENTER

Press <F6> for BOLD

Type: Education

Press <F6> to turn bold off

Press <Enter> two times

Type the following:

B.S. Accounting, Washington University, 1992

Press <Enter>

Type the following:

Minor: Economics with emphasis in corporate finance.

Press <Enter>

Type the following:

Significant courses include:

Press <Enter> two times

The next subtitles are to be underlined.

        Press <F8> for UNDERLINE

        Type: `Accounting`

        Press <Tab>

        Type: `Business`

        Press <F8> to turn underline off

        Press <Enter>

        Type: `Financial Accounting`

        Press <Tab>

        Type: `Topics in Corporate Management`

        Press <Enter>

        Type: `Cost Accounting`

        Press <Tab>

        Type: `Industrial Economics`

        Press <Enter>

        Type: `Advanced Accounting`

        Press <Tab>

        Type: `Management Information Systems`

        Press <Enter>

        Type: `Advanced Federal Tax Law`

        Press <Tab>

        Type: `Business Communications`

        Press <Enter> two times

        Press <Shift>-<F6> for CENTER

        Press <F6> for BOLD

        Type: `Experience`

        Press <F6> to turn bold off

        Press <Enter> two times

The next two subheadings also are going to be underlined.

        Press <F8> for UNDERLINE

        Type: `Summers`

        Press <F8> to turn underline off

Indent the next paragraph.

        Press <F4> for INDENT

        Type: `Intern, Price Waterhouse, Columbus, Ohio 1991`

        Press <Enter>

> Press <F4> for INDENT
>
> Type the following:

Worked on various audit assignments, including stock inventory at
Mills International.

> Press <Enter> twice
>
> Press <F8> for UNDERLINE
>
> Type: College
>
> Press <F8> to turn underline off
>
> Press <F4> for INDENT
>
> Type: Assistant, University Financial Aid Office, 1991
>
> Press <Enter>
>
> Press <F4> for INDENT
>
> Type the following:

Reviewed applications for financial aid; verified their conformity
with tax returns and other supportive documents.

> Press <Enter> two times
>
> Press <F4> for INDENT
>
> Type the following:

Orientation Leader, University Admissions Office 1990

> Press <Enter>
>
> Press <F4> for INDENT
>
> Type the following:

Met with prospective students and their parents; conducted tours of
campus; wrote reports for each orientation meeting.

> Press <Enter> two times

5. Enter the remainder of the resume using the CENTER and BOLD functions as necessary.

Computer Experience

Proficient in running Lotus 1-2-3 and WordPerfect on an IBM PC

Activities

Alpha Beta Psi, 1990-1992
Student Senator. Served on budget committee, 1991-1992

References

Credentials and references available upon request.

6. Next, save the document.

> Press <F1O> for SAVE
>
> Type: RESUME
>
> Press <Enter>

7. You have decided you want to underline the name at the top. To do this, you have to mark the name as a block of text and activate the UNDERLINE function. Move the cursor under the *J* in *Joy*.

> Press <Alt>-<F4> for BLOCK
>
> Press <End> to highlight to the end of the line
>
> Press <F8> for UNDERLINE

The name will now be underlined when printed.

8. Now you decide to delete the underlining from the subtitles *Summers* and *College*. Move the cursor so that it is under the *S* in *Summers*.

> Press <Alt>-<F3> for REVEAL CODES

The screen is divided in two (see Figure 3-6). Below the Tab Ruler line is the text with all the command codes revealed. Notice the word *Summers* has an [UND] symbol in front of it and an [und] symbol after it. These are the command codes for underlining. Command code symbols that signify the beginning of a code, or where the code is turned on, are always in all uppercase letters. Command code symbols that signify the ending of a code, or where the code is turned off, are always in all lowercase letters. Everything between the two codes, the one that is all uppercase letters and the one that is all lowercase letters, is affected by that code. To delete the underlining, delete one of the underline codes. In the bottom screen, the highlight that is the cursor should be over the *S* in *Summers*.

> Press <Backspace>

Notice both the [UND] and the [und] are deleted. Now you need to delete the underlining from College.

> Press <Down arrow> four times

FIGURE 3-6 Revealing Command Codes

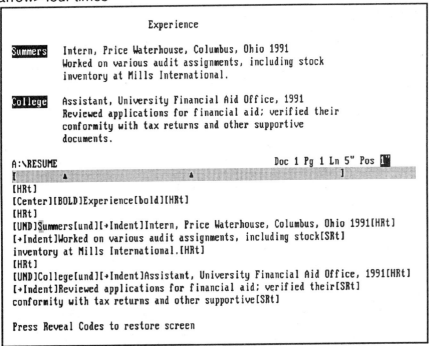

The highlight that is the cursor should be over the *C* in *College* in the lower screen.

> Press <Backspace>

Both the [UND] in front of *College* and the [und] after *College* are deleted.

> Press <Alt>-<F3>

The text window returns to normal.

9. Look over the resume carefully. The formatting should match Figure 3-5. Use the Speller to check for spelling errors. Use the VIEW option to see what the resume will look like when printed. When you are satisfied with the resume, save the document again because changes were made to the resume after it was saved the first time.

10. Print the resume. Your hard copy should look like Figure 3-5. You have finished with this document and can exit from the WordPerfect program.

❏ PAGE FORMAT

The PAGE FORMAT function, which enables the user to set top and bottom margins, headers and footers, and page numbers, is activated by pressing <Shift>-<F8> for FORMAT and then pressing either 2 or P for **Page**. The Page Format menu for WordPerfect 5.1 has eight options (see Figure 3-7). Table 3-2 describes each option. To return to the document from the Page Format menu, press <Esc> two times.

Difference Box WordPerfect 5.0: The Page Format Menu

The Page Format Menu in WordPerfect has nine options. It includes, as option 6, a New Page Number option which allows the user to renumber pages. In WordPerfect 5.1 this option has been incorporated into the submenu for the Page Numbering option.

FIGURE 3-7 The WordPerfect Page Format Menu

```
Format: Page

    1 - Center Page (top to bottom)     No

    2 - Force Odd/Even Page

    3 - Headers

    4 - Footers

    5 - Margins - Top                   1"
                  Bottom                1"

    6 - Page Numbering

    7 - Paper Size                      8.5" x 11"
              Type                      Standard

    8 - Suppress (this page only)




Selection: 0
```

Headers and Footers

Options on the Page Format menu that help users create professional-looking documents include headers or footers. A header is a piece of text that is printed at the top of a page, such as a title that appears on each page. A footer is a piece of text that is printed at the bottom of a page. Oftentimes headers and footers include a page number. Headers and footers can be several lines long. They can be printed on odd-numbered pages only, even-numbered pages only, or on both odd and even pages.

TABLE 3-2 WordPerfect 5.1's Options from the Page Format Menu

Option	Description
1-Center Page (top to bottom)	Centers a page from top to bottom when it is printed.
2-Force Odd/Even Page	Forces the page number on the current page to be an odd or an even page number.
3-Headers	Enables the same text to be printed at the top of each page.
4-Footers	Enables the same text to be printed at the bottom of each page.
5-Margins (top and bottom)	Enables the user to set the top and bottom margins in inches. The default is 1 inch for both the top and bottom margins.
6-Page Numbering	Pages are automatically numbered when printed.
7-Paper Size and Type	Enables the user to specify the size and type of paper on which the document is to be printed.
8-Suppress (this page only)	Enables the user to turn off any combination of page formats for the current page only.

To create a header or footer in a WordPerfect document, press <Shift>-<F8> for FORMAT and either 2 or P for **Page**. To create a header, press 3 for **Headers**. To create a footer, press 4 for **Footers**. Next select either 1 for **Header** (or **Footer**) **A** or 2 for **Header** (or **Footer**) **B**. Headers and footers will print on odd pages only and on even pages only. That is why WordPerfect includes an option for **Header (Footer) A** and **Header (Footer) B**. Header A could, for example, print on even pages only, and Header B could print on odd pages only.

After selecting Header (or Footer) A or B, a menu appears that allows you to designate on which pages this header (or footer) will print. You can specify that it prints on every page, on odd pages, or on even pages. After making this selection, a blank window appears. Enter the header (or footer) and press <F7> for EXIT.

Headers and footers do not appear on the screen. If you want to see what headers and footers will look like when printed, use the VIEW option.

❏ FOOTNOTES AND ENDNOTES

One of the most tedious tasks involved in writing documents such as term papers is typing the footnotes. WordPerfect simplifies this task tremendously.

Footnotes and endnotes provide information about a cited work. The only difference between footnotes and endnotes is that footnotes appear at the bottom of the page and endnotes are compiled at the end of the document. Footnotes and endnotes created with WordPerfect are automatically numbered. All the user has to do is type the text of the note.

To create a footnote or an endnote, the cursor must be placed at the space where the note number is to appear. Activate the FOOTNOTE function by pressing <Ctrl>-<F7>. The Note menu appears. Type 1 for **Footnote** to create a footnote. Type 2 for **Endnote** to create an endnote. Next type 1 for **Create**. A special editing screen appears. The number of the note is in the upper-left corner of the screen. Enter the note and press <F7> for EXIT. The document returns to the text window and the note number is automatically added in the document.

To edit a note that has already been entered, activate the FOOTNOTE function <Ctrl>-<F7>. When the Note menu appears, select **Footnote** or **Endnote**, depending on which type of note is being edited. Next select **2** for **Edit**. The prompt **Footnote (Endnote) Number?** appears. Enter the number of the footnote or endnote that is to be edited and press <Enter>. The note is retrieved and changes can be made to it. Once the changes are made, press <F7> for EXIT. The document returns to the screen.

To delete a footnote or endnote, move the cursor to the note number in the document. Press <Backspace> or <Del> to delete the note number. The prompt **Delete [note]** appears. Press Y for **Yes** and the note is deleted. The numbering of the remaining notes is automatically revised as necessary.

Footnotes do not appear on the screen. If you want to see what footnotes will look like when printed, use the VIEW option.

❑ SEARCH AND REPLACE

If you have ever written a lengthy document and discovered that a key term has been used incorrectly throughout the text, you know how difficult and time -consuming it is to correct the mistake. This problem has been eliminated by incorporating a search and find routine in WordPerfect and most other word processors. The user tells the program the specific character string to search for, and the program finds and positions the cursor at the first occurrence of the string.

WordPerfect can search for text in a forward or reverse direction. The SEARCH function activated by pressing <F2> searches for the specified text forward from the cursor's position. The SEARCH function activated by pressing <Shift>-<F2> searches for the specified text backward from the cursor's position. Once the SEARCH function is activated, the **Srch** prompt appears at the bottom of the screen with an arrow that indicates the direction of the search. Enter the character string to be searched for and press either <F2> or <Shift>-<F2> again. The cursor stops after the first match is found.

In addition to searching for a particular string of text, WordPerfect can search for one string of text and replace it with another string of text. To replace text throughout an entire document, press <Home> <Home> <Up arrow> to move the cursor to the beginning of the document. Next, press <Alt>-<F2> for REPLACE. The prompt **w/Confirm?** appears at the bottom of the screen. If you want to confirm each replacement, press Y for **Yes**. If you want the program automatically to make all the replacements without your having to confirm each one, press N for **No**. When the **Srch** prompt appears at the bottom of the screen, enter the text that is to be replaced. Once the text to be replaced is entered, press <Alt>-<F2> again. The prompt **Replace with** appears. Enter the new text that is to replace the text being removed and press <Alt>-<F2>. If you selected Y at the **w/Confirm** prompt, WordPerfect will stop each time it finds the text that is to be replaced. You can then confirm whether or not the text should be replaced in that particular instance. If you selected N at the prompt, WordPerfect automatically makes all the replacements.

 YOUR TURN

In this exercise, you are going to type a paper that includes a header and footnotes. A blank text window should be on the screen.

1. The first step in creating this document is to enter a header.

> Press <Shift>-<F8> for FORMAT
>
> Press 2 for **Page**
>
> Press 3 for **Headers**
>
> Press 1 for **Header A**

The Header menu appears at the bottom of the screen.

> Press 2 for **Every page**

A special screen appears in which the header is entered.

> Type: `Job Placement Seminar`
>
> Press <Alt>-<F6> for FLUSH RIGHT

The cursor jumps to the right side of the screen.

> Press <Ctrl>-B

The symbol ^B appears on the screen. This is the symbol WordPerfect uses to automatically number pages. When the page is printed, the ^B symbol will be replaced with the appropriate page number.

> Press <Enter>
>
> Press <F7> for EXIT

The Page Format menu returns to the screen. Usually, headers are not printed on the first page of a report. You do not want your header to print on the first page.

> Press 8 for **Suppress (this page only)**

Difference Box WordPerfect 5.0: Press 9 for Suppress (this page only)

> Press 1 for **Suppress All Page Numbering, Headers and Footers**
>
> Press <Esc> twice

The Format menu returns to the screen.

2. Next, you want to turn justification off.

> Press 1 for **Line**

Press 3 for **Justification**

Press 1 for **Left**

Difference Box WordPerfect 5.0: Press N for **No**.

---

3. This term paper uses both double- and single-spacing. The body of the paper is double-spaced and the quotations are single-spaced. As you type the paper, you will switch back and forth between double- and single-spacing. Because the default setting is single-spacing, you need to switch to double-spacing to begin typing the body of the paper. The Line Format menu should still be on the screen.

Press 6 for **Line**

Type: 2 for double-spacing

Press <Enter>

Press <Esc> two times

The editing window returns to the screen.

4. Now you are ready to begin typing the paper. First type the title.

Press <Shift>-<F6> for CENTER

Press <F8> for UNDERLINE

Type: Interviews: Wretched or Rewarding?

Press <F8> to turn underline off

Press <Enter>

Type the following:

For many people, interviews have a peculiar Dr. Jekyll and Mr. Hyde quality to them. While these people are job hunting, they anxiously await the phone call or letter issuing the coveted invitation for an interview. After all their hard work of scouting out the job market, finding openings in their field, writing resumes and cover letters, an interview seems like a well-deserved reward. But, once attained the golden interview turns into a nerve-shattering monster. Sleepless nights are spent worrying over such questions as what will I wear, what will I say, what if they ask a question I can't answer? All of a sudden, the job hunter feels like the hunted as visions of the mighty interviewer, whose sole purpose is to expose all the inadequacies of the interviewee, become inescapable.

Interviews do not have to turn into such horrible monsters. Exposing some of the myths about interviews helps to alleviate the fear we all attach to the interviewing process.

Often, the interviewee has a totally inaccurate image of the interviewer. Many prospective employees assume the interviewer is highly skilled in conducting interviews. This is not necessarily the case as Richard Boles points out in the following quotation:

5. Now you are ready to type the first quotation. The cursor should still be in the space following the colon. Press <Enter> once to create space between the text and the quotation. The quotation should be single-spaced.

Press <Shift>-<F8> for FORMAT

Press 1 for **Line**

Press 6 for **Line spacing**

Type: 1 to change to single-spaced

Press <Enter>

Press <Esc> two times

The quotation needs to be indented from each margin.

Press <Shift>-<F4> for INDENT

Type the quotation as follows:

. . . the interviewer may be as uncomfortable with this process as you are and as ill-equipped to know how to find out what he or she wants to know as the newest college graduate just coming into the job market.

You now need to create the first footnote.

Press <Ctrl>-<F7> for FOOTNOTE

Press 1 for **Footnote**

Press 1 for **Create**

The special screen for entering the footnote text appears. Notice that the 1 for footnote 1 has already been inserted.

Type the footnote as follows, underlining the title of the book:

Boles, Richard, <u>What Color Is Your Parachute?</u>, Berkeley: 10 Speed Press, 1983, P. 181.

Press <F7> for EXIT

The 1 for footnote 1 is automatically placed in the text.

Press <Shift>-<F8> for FORMAT

Press 1 for **Line**

Press 6 for **Line spacing**

Type: 2 for double-spacing

Press <Enter>

Press <Esc> two times

Press <Enter> to create space after the quotation

Type the following:

This is not the impression most people looking for jobs have of
those who have the power to hire or not, hire them.

Boles explains why interviewers may be so uncomfortable with the
process:

6. Now you are ready to type the second quotation. The cursor should still be in the space following the colon. Press <Enter> once to create space between the text and the quotation. The quotation should be single spaced.

> Press <Shift>-<F8> for FORMAT
>
> Press 1 for LINE
>
> Press 6 for **Line spacing**
>
> Type: 1 to change to single-spaced
>
> Press <Enter>

The quotation needs to be indented from each margin.

> Press <Shift>-<F4> for INDENT
>
> Type the quotation as follows:

The odds are very great that the executive who does the
interviewing was hired because of what they could contribute to the
company, and not because they were such a great interviewer. In
fact, their gifts in this arena may be rather miserable.

You now need to enter the second footnote.

> Press <Ctrl>-<F7> for FOOTNOTE
>
> Press 1 for **Footnote**
>
> Press 1 for **Create**

The special screen for entering the footnote text appears.

> Type the footnote as follows:

Ibid.

> Press <F7> for EXIT
>
> Press <Shift>-<F8> for FORMAT
>
> Press 1 for **Line**
>
> Press 6 for **Line spacing**
>
> Type: 2 for double-spacing
>
> Press <Enter>
>
> Press <Esc> two times
>
> Press <Enter> to create space after the quotation.
>
> Type the following:

David Roman agrees with Boles. Roman states

> Press <Enter>

Press <Shift>-<F8> for FORMAT

Press 1 for **Line**

Press 6 for **Line spacing**

Type: 1 to change to single-spaced

Press <Enter>

The quotation needs to be indented from each margin.

Press <Shift>-<F4> for INDENT

Type the quotation as follows:

```
As interviewers, . . . managers . . . may be out of their element.
They're in the business of running a . . . department, not of
interviewing job applicants.
```

You now need to enter the third footnote.

Press <Ctrl>-<F7> for FOOTNOTE

Press 1 for **Footnote**

Press 1 for **Create**

The special screen for entering the footnote text appears.

Type the footnote as follows:

```
Roman, David, "Why MIS/DP Job Interviews Go Wrong," in Computer
Decisions, November 19, 1985, p. 66.
```

Press <F7> for EXIT

Press <Shift>-<F8> for FORMAT

Press 1 for **Line**

Press 6 for **Line spacing**

Type: 2 for double-spacing

Press <Enter>

Press <Esc> twice

Press <Enter> to create space after the quotation

Type the remainder of the text as follows:

```
Since the person running the interview is probably just as
uncomfortable as you are, there are several things you as an
interviewee can do to take advantage of the situation and turn the
interview into a pleasant and rewarding experience.
```

7. You now discover that you misspelled a name throughout the text. The author's name is Bolles, not Boles. You are going to use the REPLACE command to locate and correct all occurrences of Boles.

Press <Alt>-<F2> for REPLACE

The prompt **w/Confirm?** appears. The prompt is asking if you want the program to stop at each correction so that you can confirm it.

> Press Y for Yes

The prompt **Srch** appears in the lower-left corner of the screen.

> Type: Boles
>
> Press <Alt>-<F2> for REPLACE

The prompt **Replace with** appears in the lower-left corner of the screen.

> Type: Bolles
>
> Press <Alt>-<F2> for REPLACE
>
> Press Y

The cursor moves to the next occurrence of Boles.

> Press Y

Continue to replace all occurrences of Boles with Bolles. When finished, the computer beeps. The corrections have now been made in the text, but footnote 1 still contains a misspelling of the author's name, so you need to edit a footnote.

> Press <Ctrl>-<F7> for FOOTNOTE
>
> Press 1 for **Footnote**
>
> Press 2 for **Edit**
>
> Type: 1 for Footnote number 1
>
> Press <Enter>

The first footnote appears on the screen. Change the spelling of *Boles* to *Bolles*. Press <F7> to exit from the note screen after the correction has been made.

8. Next, you decide the word *interviewee* is too informal for this paper. You are going to search through the document and individually replace each occurrence of *interviewee*.

> Press <Home> <Home>-<Up arrow> to move to the beginning of the document
>
> Press <F2> for SEARCH

The prompt **Srch** appears in the lower-left corner of the screen with Boles entered as the search string because that was the last text searched for.

> Type: interviewee
>
> Press <F2> for SEARCH

The cursor stops at the first occurrence of *interviewee*.

> Press <Backspace> to delete *interviewee*
>
> Type: applicant
>
> Press <F2> for SEARCH

The prompt appears with *interviewee* entered as the search string.

> Press <F2>

The cursor stops at the next occurrence of *interviewee*.

Press <Backspace> to delete *interviewee*

Type: `person being interviewed`

Press <F2> two times

The cursor stops at the next occurrence of *interviewee.*

Press <Backspace> to delete *interviewee*

Type: `prospective employee`

Change the word an preceding prospective to `a`.

9. Return the cursor to the beginning of the document. Use WordPerfect's Speller to check the spelling in the entire document. Correct any errors. Use the VIEW function to see your header and footnotes. Save the document as PAPER. Print the paper. Once the paper is printed, you have finished this Your Turn exercise. Exit from the WordPerfect program.

❏ SUMMARY POINTS

■ Word processors, such as WordPerfect, include formatting features that determine how the text is printed on paper.

■ Common formatting features include setting tab and margin stops, single- or double-spacing the text, and performing character enhancements.

■ Common character enhancements include underlining and boldfacing.

■ Headers and footers are pieces of text that are printed on every page in a document. A header is printed at the top of a page, and a footer is printed at the bottom of a page.

■ Search and find routines locate a specific string of characters.

❏ COMMAND SUMMARY

Command	Keystoke	Function
BOLD	<F6>	Turns boldface on and off.
CENTER	<Shift>-<F6>	Center text between left and right margins.
FOOTNOTE	<Ctrl>-<F7>	Inserts a footnote at the cursor location; allows existing footnotes to be edited.
FORMAT	<Shift>-<F8>	Allows the user to change line, page, document, or other formats to customize the appearance of a document.
Line Format	<Shift>-<F8> <1>	Allows the user to access the hyphenation, justification, line height, line numbering, line spacing, left and right margins, tab set, and widow/orphan options.

Page Format	<Shift>-<F8> <2>	Allows the user to access the center page, force odd/even page, headers, footers, top and bottom margins, page numbering, paper size and type, and supress (this page only) options.
INDENT	<F4>	Temporarily changes the left margin of a paragraph to the next tab stop each time <F4> is pressed. To indent both the left and right margins, press <Shift>-<F4>.
REPLACE	<Alt>-<F2>	Allows all instances of particular text and codes to be replaced automatically, either with or without manual confirmation.
REVEAL CODES	<Alt>-<F4>	Splits the screen, displaying text and formatting codes in the lower half.
SEARCH FORWARD	<F2>	Allows the user to search for text or codes from the cursor to the end of the document.
SEARCH BACKWARD	<Shift>-<F2>	Allows the user to search for text or codes from the cursor to the beginning of the document.
UNDERLINE	<F8>	Turns underlining on and off.

❑ WORDPERFECT EXERCISES

1. Changing the Format of a Document

If you need help answering the questions that follow, refer to "Left and Right Margins," "Line Spacing," "Page Format," "Character Enhancements," and "Footnotes and Endnotes" earlier in this chapter.

a. Describe the process for setting margins. Open a new document and set the top margin at 2 inches. Set the left margin to 2 inches.

b. How do you change the spacing in a document? Change to double-spacing for this exercise.

c. Center, underline, and boldface the title of the document, which is `Monitoring Chemical Spills`

d. Type the following:

`Since the chemical spill at the Union Carbide plant in Bhopal, India, that resulted in the deaths of more than 2,000 people, chemical companies have become more interested in computerized tracking and warning systems designed to protect communities around their plants. The old method for predicting the path and level of toxicity of a chemical cloud (still in use at many chemical plants) involves the use of lengthy charts and tables and relies on human calculations.`

`Safer Emergency Systems, Inc., has designed computerized emergency systems for 25 chemical plants. The system combines a computer, a 19-inch color graphics screen, and a printer with`

sensors placed at key locations in the plant to detect leaks early
and sound alarms in the central computer. A tower placed on the
rooftop of a building in a nearby open field has sensors that help
plot the temperature and direction of a chemical cloud.

e. What is the procedure for inserting footnotes in a WordPerfect Document? Insert the following
footnote after the first paragraph.

Johnson, Dale, <u>Safety with the Computer,</u> Chicago: University Press,
1985, p. 74.

f. Use WordPerfect's Speller to check the spelling of your document. Proofread it carefully, correcting
any errors you find. Save and print the document.

2. Setting Tabs

If you need help answering the questions that follow, refer to "Tab Set" earlier in this chapter.

a. How do you set a decimal tab using WordPerfect? Open a new document and set a left tab at 1
inch and a decimal tab at 4 inches.

Difference Box WordPerfect 5.0
Set the left tab at 2 inches and a decimal tab at 5 inches.

---

b. Type the following. The title should be centered and in boldface. The first column should align at
the first tab stop. The decimal points in the second column should align at the second tab stop.

JANUARY EXPENSES

Rent	$250.00
Movies	6.00
Food	75.39
Clothes	38.54
Books	43.95
Car Insurance	158.00
Dry Cleaning	8.50
Gasoline	22.50
Telephone	27.57
Savings	125.00
Stamps	5.00

c. Save and print the document.

d. How do you set tabs that use dot leaders? Start a new document. Set a left tab at 1 inch. Set a right tab with leaders at 5 inches. The title should be centered and boldface. The left column should align at the tab stop at 1 inch. Type the following:

Difference Box WordPerfect 5.0
Set the left tab at 2 inches. Set a right tab with leaders at 5 inches.

<pre>
            THE TRAGEDY OF HAMLET, PRINCE OF DENMARK
      Claudius . . . . Paul Halcomb
      Hamlet . . . . Jeffery Spencer
      Polonius . . . . Nathan Criswell
      Horatio . . . . Keith Janeskowski
      Laertes . . . . Richard Gorman
      Voltimand . . . . David Knoles
      Cornelius . . . . Terry Lynch
      Rosencrantz . . . . Luther Rabaldo
      Guildenstern . . . . Maarty Reily
      Osric . . . . Eugene Rondeau
      Marcellus . . . . Arthur Singletary
      Bernardo . . . . Peter Cook
      Francisco . . . . Charles Bartholomiew
      Reynaldo . . . . Donald Porter
      Gravedigger I . . . . Bruce Wilcox
      Gravedigger 2 . . . . Ralph Tidwell
      Fortinbras . . . . Daniel Vasquez
      Gertrude . . . . Amy Osterholm
      Ophelia . . . . Anne Hamilton
      Ghost of Hamlet's father . . . . . . Art Gammon
</pre>

e. Proofread the document carefully. Correct any errors you find. Save and print the document.

❑ WORDPERFECT PROBLEMS

To complete the following exercises, you need to use files on the Student File Disk. In order to complete these exercises, you will need to be able to set left and right margins, change the page format, and use the search and replace function.

1. On the Student File Disk there is a WordPerfect file called APPLY. Start the WordPerfect program and retrieve this file. Save this file and rename it APPLY-2. If you need to review how to back up a file on a disk, refer to "Backing Up a File on a Disk" in the previous chapter. You want to maintain the original APPLY file on your disk.

2. Read the APPLY-2 file. APPLY-2 is a solicited application letter used to answer an advertisement for an accounting job. Assume that you have just graduated from your college with a major in marketing rather than accounting. You are looking for a job in the marketing field. Delete the sender address. Replace it with your own address.

3. Change the date to the current date.

4. Delete the company address and replace it with the address of a company that you know.

5. Delete the phrase `Daily Mirror` on `April 9` from the first sentence of the letter. Insert the following to take its place: `in the Tribune No. 350`
Make sure that the word *Tribune* is underlined.

6. Using the REPLACE command, replace all occurrences of the word *accounting* with the word *marketing.*

7. In the second paragraph, delete `Washington University`. Enter the name of your college.

8. Delete the following sentence:
`As an intern at Price Waterhouse, I worked on the audit of Mills International.`

9. Insert the following in place of the sentence just deleted:

`As a project assignment, I conducted a market survey on fast food business in Northwest Missouri. This survey was used for the implementation of a new fast food chain in the area.`

10. Move the cursor to the name of the applicant. Replace the name *Joy Langston* with your own name.

11. Proofread the letter carefully. Correct any errors you find. Save the letter. Print the letter.

12. Now that you have seen a hard copy of the letter, you would like to make some changes to the format design. Make the following changes:
    a. Change the top margin to 1 1/2 inches.
    b. Set the right and left margins so that they are both 1 1/2 inches.
    c. Set the right margin so that it will not be justified when it is printed.

13. Save the letter. Print it again.

❑ WORDPERFECT CHALLENGE

Assume you have written a report on computers for a class you are taking. You are going to enter your report into WordPerfect.

1. Start a new document. Change the left and right margins to 1 1/2 inches. Change the line spacing to double-spaced. You want a header that includes automatic page numbers. Create the following header:
`Computer Report`

2. Enter the report as follows. When you come to the quotation, change to single-spacing. Enter the footnote information provided at the end of the document. After entering the quotation, change back to double-spacing for the remainder of the report.

Computers and Communications

The term Information Revolution has been coined to describe a major aspect of our contemporary society. Today, information is considered to be an important commodity, much like manufactured products during the Industrial Revolution. In order for businesses or individuals to succeed in today's society, there has to be easy access to the enormous amount of information that exists. The free flow of information, be it information between two individuals in the same room or information between two corporations on opposite sides of the world, involves communication. Computers have greatly enhanced communications on an international level as well as an individual level.

This report covers the following three areas of computers and communications.

1. Satellites
2. Desktop Publishing
3. Information Networks

Satellites allow people to telephone international points, transmit high-speed computerized data to destinations thousands of miles away, and view events at a video conference as they occur in distant places. Video-teleconferencing employs a two-way full motion video plus a two-way audio system and provides the most effective simulation of face-to-face communication. Videoconferencing is best suited for planning groups, project teams, training seminars, and other groups that want a sense of full participation

Publication provides one of the most widely used sources of communication. Desktop publishing has simplified the publishing process, resulting in a tremendous increase of publications and thus an increase in the exchange of ideas and information. Because it is affordable and in the long run can save a company money, more companies are using desktop publishing.

> A typical microcomputer-based desktop publishing system with a laser printer and hard disk drive would cost between $5,000 and $12,000. This can be a very insignificant cost to a business that would spend considerably more to have documents professionally typeset and printed.[1]

Typically, a company's Corporate Communications Department utilizes desktop publishing to create publications such as company reports, newsletters, and presentation graphics.

Not only have computers enhanced the communications within and among corporations, they have also improved the communications or flow of ideas and information on the individual level. Information networks provide online services that enable subscribers to shop and bank from home, book airline tickets, look up facts in an encyclopedia, and send and receive electronic mail. Students in high school and college are learning how to use online services because they contribute to successful education.

Whether communications are occurring around the world, in the classroom, or in the home, computers are playing an important role.

Enter the following information for the footnote:

Steven Mandell, <u>Computers and Information Processing</u> (St. Paul: West Publishing, 1989), p. 352.

3. Use WordPerfect's Speller to check the spelling of the report. Proofread the report carefully. Correct any errors you find. Save the report. Print the report.

CHAPTER 4

Introduction to Lotus 1-2-3, Release 2.2

OUTLINE

❏ INTRODUCTION

A manual spreadsheet is used to record business transactions and to perform calculations. A spreadsheet program uses a computer's memory capability to solve mathematically oriented problems. With a spreadsheet program, columns of numbers can be set up to keep track of money or objects. This chapter looks at some of the features that make spreadsheet programs so popular. It also provides instructions on how to get started using Lotus 1-2-3, Release 2.2.

❏ GUIDE TO LOTUS 1-2-3

This chapter introduces Lotus 1-2-3, Release 2.2, a software package that combines a spreadsheet with file management and graphics functions. This chapter focuses on 1-2-3's spreadsheet.

Identifying Parts of the Worksheet

When a new 1-2-3 worksheet is loaded into the computer, a screen like the one shown in Figure 4-1 appears. Numbers listed down the left side of the grid represent the rows. The letters listed across the top of the grid represent the columns.

Each cell in the spreadsheet has a cell address or coordinate. The coordinate of a cell consists of a letter for its column and a number for its row. For example, the coordinate or cell address C4 represents the cell where column C and row 4 intersect. The cell pointer is a highlighted bar that indicates which cell or cells are active or can accept information. The cell indicated by the cell pointer is called the active cell. In Figure 4-1, the cell pointer is in cell A1, so A1 is the active cell.

The top three lines of the screen constitute the control panel. The first line of the control panel is the status line, which provides information such as the cell address, the cell contents, and whether the cell contains a label, value, or formula.

FIGURE 4-1 A Blank Lotus 1-2-3 Worksheet

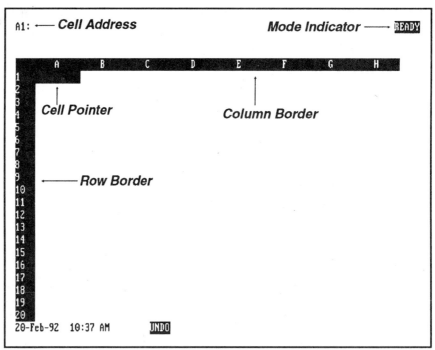

The second line of the control panel, the entry line, is a work line that displays data as it is typed in at the keyboard. The entry line is called a work line because the data appearing there can be edited and changed before <Enter> is pressed. Once <Enter> is pressed, however, the data moves from the entry line to the status line and enters the worksheet. The entry line may also contain a menu of Lotus 1-2-3 options.

The third line of the control panel, the prompt line, contains either a submenu or an explanation of a specific command.

The mode indicator, in the upper-right corner of the worksheet, displays 1-2-3's current mode of operation. Lotus 1-2-3 is always in the READY mode when first started. This is the mode that enables you to move the cell pointer around the worksheet. Typing any other valid character or command activates one of the other modes. Table 4-1 describes some of 1-2-3's mode indicators.

In the bottom-left corner of the worksheet is the error message area. If a mistake is made, error messages provide a brief description of what has gone wrong.

In the bottom-right corner of the screen are the status indicators. Status indicators appear when certain 1-2-3 keys are used or when particular program conditions exist. Table 4-2 describes some of 1-2-3's status indicators.

Getting Started With Lotus 1-2-3

Some of the procedures for using Lotus 1-2-3 depend on whether you are using a system with two floppy disk drives or one with a hard disk drive. The directions in this chapter are for a hard disk drive. Differences for systems with two floppy disk drives are written in Difference Boxes.

Each of the following sections introduces one or more features of Lotus 1-2-3. At the end of each section, there is a hands-on activity marked **Your Turn**. Be sure to read the preceding section carefully before trying the hands-on activity.

The key on the IBM-PC keyboard marked ⏎ is the <Enter> key, also called the <Return> key. Whenever you are instructed to press <Enter>, press the key marked ⏎ .

TABLE 4-1 Lotus 1-2-3 Mode Indicators

Indicator	Description
EDIT	An entry is being edited.
ERROR	An error was made; 1-2-3 is waiting for <Enter> or <Esc> to be pressed in response to the error.
HELP	1-2-3's Help facility is being used.
LABEL	A label is being entered.
MENU	A menu is displayed and a menu option is being selected.
POINT	1-2-3 is pointing to a cell or a range of cells.
READY	1-2-3 is waiting for a command or cell entry.
VALUE	A number or formula is being entered.
WAIT	1-2-3 is calculating; commands cannot be processed.

TABLE 4-2 Lotus 1-2-3 Status Indicators

Status Indicator	Description
CALC	Formulas in the worksheet need to be recalculated; Pressing <F9> for CALC recalculates the formulas.
CAPS	The <Caps Lock> key is on; pressing <Caps Lock> again turns it off.
DIRC	A formula that refers to itself is included in the worksheet.
END	The <End> key is on; pressing <End> again turns it off.
NUM	The <Num Lock> key is on; pressing <Num Lock> again turns it off.
OVR	The <Ins> key is on; as you type, characters at the cursor's location are replaced by new characters entered (called overstriking); pressing <Ins> again turns overstriking off so that new characters are inserted and characters at the cursor's location move to the right to make room for them.
SCROLL	The <Scroll lock> key is on; pressing <Scroll Lock> again turns it off.
UNDO	The keys <Alt>-<F4>, for UNDO, can be pressed to cancel the last procedure performed.

The following symbols and type faces appear throughout the chapter. This is what they mean:

Select WORKSHEET	Italicized text indicates that a specific option from a menu should be selected.
Press <Enter>	The angle brackets (< >) are used to signify a specific key on the keyboard. Press the key whose name is enclosed by the angle brackets.
Press <Alt-<F4>	If a hyphen appears between two keys to be pressed, it means the keys have to be pressed together. Hold down the first key while tapping the second key once. In this example, the user would hold down the <Alt> key while pressing the <F4> key once.
Enter range of labels	The information in boldface indicates phrases or menu selections that appear on the computer screen.
WORKSHEET command	All capital letters indicate the name of a command.
Type: `Budget`	Typewriter font indicates text that is to be entered into a worksheet.

To use Lotus 1-2-3 on a hard disk drive, the program will first have to be installed on the hard drive. Follow these steps to access Lotus 1-2-3 from a hard drive on which it has been installed.

1. Turn on the computer and monitor.

2. A prompt may appear asking you to enter the date. If it does, type the current date using numbers and hyphens, for example, `11-15-92`. Press <Enter>.

3. A prompt may appear asking you to enter the time. If it does, you can either press <Enter> to bypass this prompt, or you can enter the time using a 24-hour format. For example, enter `16:30:00` if it is 4:30 p.m. Press <Enter> after entering the time.

4. When the system prompt C> appears on the screen, type `cd\` and the name of the directory in which Lotus 1-2-3 is stored on the hard drive. For example, if the program is stored in a directory named 123, type `cd\123` and press <Enter>. Insert the data disk, the disk onto which the Lotus files you create are stored, into drive A.

5. The system prompt C> appears. Type either `Lotus` or `123` and press <Enter>. If you type `Lotus`, the Lotus Access System appears (see Figure 4-3). The menu pointer is on 1-2-3. You can either press <Enter> or type `1` to select 1-2-3. You can bypass the Access System by typing `123`. This takes you directly to a blank worksheet.

Notice in Figure 4-2 there are five options included in the menu at the top of the screen. The first option, 1-2-3, activates Lotus and places a blank worksheet on the screen. PRINTGRAPH enters the Lotus graphics printing program so that a graph that has been created can be printed. The PRINTGRAPH option

FIGURE 4-2 The Lotus 1-2-3 Access System

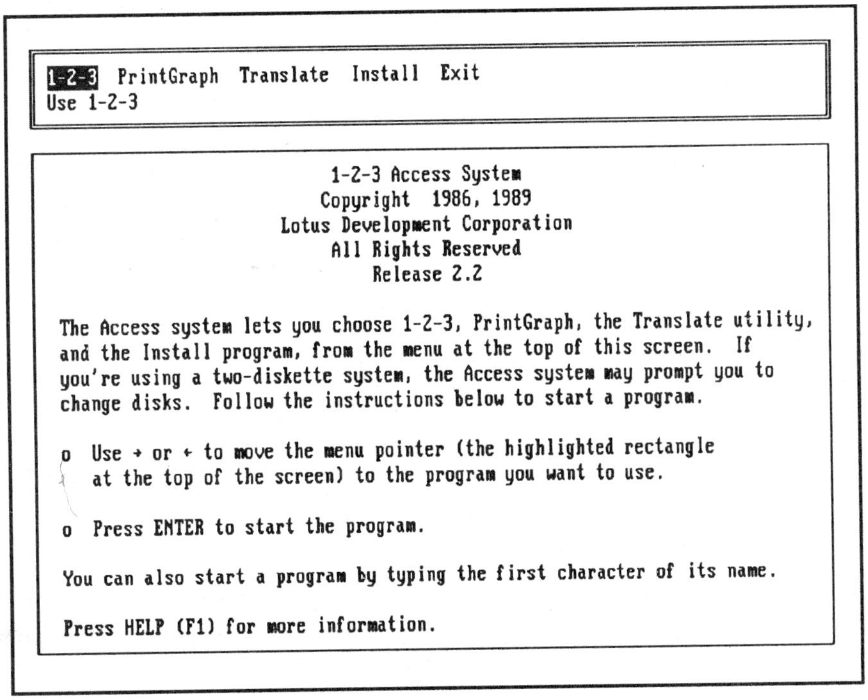

```
1-2-3  PrintGraph  Translate  Install  Exit
Use 1-2-3

                    1-2-3 Access System
                    Copyright  1986, 1989
                 Lotus Development Corporation
                     All Rights Reserved
                        Release 2.2

   The Access system lets you choose 1-2-3, PrintGraph, the Translate utility,
   and the Install program, from the menu at the top of this screen.  If
   you're using a two-diskette system, the Access system may prompt you to
   change disks.  Follow the instructions below to start a program.

   o  Use + or + to move the menu pointer (the highlighted rectangle
      at the top of the screen) to the program you want to use.

   o  Press ENTER to start the program.

   You can also start a program by typing the first character of its name.

   Press HELP (F1) for more information.
```

will be covered in Chapter 5. TRANSLATE allows a user to read files from certain other programs. INSTALL begins the procedure to install Lotus 1-2-3. Finally, EXIT exits the Lotus program to the system prompt.

Moving around the Worksheet

The Lotus 1-2-3 worksheet contains 256 columns, which are labeled A-IV, and 8,192 rows, which are numbered 1-8192. The part of the worksheet that appears on the screen at one time is the window. For example, in Figure 4-1, cells A1 through H20 appear in the window.

There are several ways to move around the 1-2-3 worksheet and to see parts of the worksheet outside the window. The first is by using the pointer-movement keys (also called cursor control keys) located on the numeric keypad at the right of the keyboard. Table 4-3 lists the pointer-movement keys and describes where the cell pointer moves when each key is pressed. In addition, if the keyboard includes arrow keys separate from the numeric keypad, these keys will move the cell pointer in the direction the arrow is pointing.

The other way to move the cell pointer around the worksheet is by using the GOTO key. The GOTO key is the <F5> key, one of the ten function keys at the left of the keyboard. Pressing <F5> moves the cell pointer to any cell on the worksheet. For example, if the cell pointer is in cell A1 and you want to go to cell R30, simply press <F5>, type R30, and press <Enter>. The cell pointer immediately moves to cell R30. The GOTO key quickly moves the cell pointer large distances in the spreadsheet.

Using the Function Keys

Lotus 1-2-3 uses the function keys <F1> through <F1O> to perform special operations. These function keys are located either at the left side or along the top of the keyboard. A function can be performed either by pressing the function key alone or in conjunction with the <Alt> key. Table 4-4 lists some of the operations that can be performed using the function keys. When the instructions in this chapter say to press, for example, <F5>, this means to press the function key labelled **F5.**

TABLE 4-3 Pointer-Movement Keys

Key	Description
<Home>	Pressing <Home> returns the cell pointer to cell A1.
<PgUp>	Pressing <PgUp> moves the cell pointer up twenty cells.
<PgDn>	Pressing <PgDn> moves the cell pointer down twenty cells.
<Up arrow>	Pressing <Up arrow> moves the cell pointer one cell up.
<Right arrow>	Pressing <Right arrow> moves the cellpointer one cell to the right.
<Down arrow>	Pressing <Down arrow> moves the cell pointer one cell down.
<Left arrow>	Pressing <Left arrow> moves the cell pointer one cell to the left.
<Ctrl>-<Left arrow>	Pressing these keys together moves the cursor eight columns to the left.
<Ctrl>-<Right arrow>	Pressing these keys together moves the cursor eight columns to the right.

TABLE 4-4 The Function Keys

Key	Description
\<F1\>	HELP; displays a Help screen related to the current task being performed.
\<F2\>	EDIT; puts 1-2-3 in the EDIT mode so that the contents of the selected cell can be edited.
\<F5\>	GOTO; moves the cell pointer to a designated cell.
\<F9\>	CALC; recalculates all the formulas in a worksheet.
\<F10\>	GRAPH; displays the current graph.
\<Alt\>-\<F4\>	UNDO; cancels any changes made to the worksheet since 1-2-3 was last in the READY mode. Pressing \<Alt\>-\<F4\> again restores the changes.

Difference Box: Selecting the Directory on a Computer with Two Floppy Disk Drives

If you are using a computer with two floppy disk drives, you want drive B to be the current directory, since the disk onto which you want to save your Lotus files is in drive B. To find where the current directory is located, type the slash character < / > to view the Main menu. Type F for FILE and then D for DIRECTORY. The entry line reads **Enter current directory:** followed by either **A:** or **B:** If it says B:\, the location of the current directory does not need to be changed. It is already in drive B, where your data disk is. If it says A:\, the current directory has to be changed to drive B.

To change the drive, activate the Main menu. Type W for WORKSHEET, G for GLOBAL, D for DEFAULT, and D again for DIRECTORY. The entry line reads **Enter default directory.** Press \<Esc\> to erase the current directory designation. Type **B:** and press \<Enter\> to change the current directory designation to drive B. The previous submenu returns. Type U for UPDATE to save the change from drive A to drive B. After a few seconds, the same submenu returns. Type Q for QUIT to return to the READY mode.

YOUR TURN

In this exercise you are going to start Lotus 1-2-3 and practice moving the cell pointer around the worksheet. This exercise assumes the Lotus program is stored in a directory named 123. If Lotus 1-2-3 is stored in a different directory in the computer you are using, ask your instructor for directions.

1. Turn on the computer and monitor. Place your disk in drive A.

2. If a prompt appears asking you to enter the date, enter today's date using numbers and hyphens. For example, if the date is September 28, 1993, you would do the following:

> Enter: 09-28-93
>
> Press \<Enter\>

If a prompt appears asking you to enter the time, press \<Enter\> or enter the time in a 24-hour format and press \<Enter\>.

3. The system prompt C> should be on the screen.

        Type: `cd\123`

        Type: `123`

        Press <Enter>

A blank worksheet should be on your screen.

4. You are ready to practice moving the cell pointer.

        Press <Down arrow> three times

The cell address in the status line should say A4.

        Press <Right arrow> ten times

The cell address should be K4.

        Press <PgDn>

Watch the row border. The cell pointer remains in the same place and the row numbers change. The cell address should be K24.

        Press <Ctrl>-<Right arrow>

The cell address should be L24.

        Press <Home>

The cell pointer moves back to A1. Pressing <Home> always brings the cell pointer back to A1.

        Press <F5>, the GOTO key

The prompt **Enter address to go to** appears in the entry line.

        Type: `L24`

        Press <Enter>

The cell pointer immediately moves to cell L24. Check the cell address to make sure that is the location of the cell pointer.

        Press <PgUp>

The cell address should be L4.

        Press <Home>

        Press <F5>

        Type: `Z1988`

        Press <Enter>

Continue to practice moving the cell pointer with the pointer-movement keys and with <F5>, the GOTO key. When you have finished, press <Home> to return to cell A1.

5. You have finished with this Your Turn exercise. Leave the worksheet on your screen while you read the following sections.

                                                                          Chapter 4: Introduction to Lotus 1-2-3

Menus and Menu Options

For the Main menu to be activated, Lotus must be in the READY mode. Typing the slash key < / > or the less-than key (<) activates the READY mode, and the Main menu appears in the entry line of the control panel (see Figure 4-3). The Main menu lists eleven options. When the Main menu is first selected, the menu pointer, the highlight indicating which option is currently selected, is on the WORKSHEET option.

There are two ways to select an option. The first is by highlighting the option with the menu pointer. To highlight an option, move the menu pointer to the option using the <Left arrow> and <Right arrow> keys. When the option is highlighted, press <Enter>. The second way to select an option is by pressing the first letter of the option name. Selecting an option using this second method is faster, as it eliminates having to move the menu pointer and press the <Enter> key.

In addition to the Main menu, Lotus 1-2-3 has several submenus. That is, when you select one option on the Main menu, a submenu with additional options moves to the entry line. For example, if you select the WORKSHEET option from the Main menu, a submenu with ten additional options moves from the prompt line to the entry line.

If a menu is activated by mistake, or if you begin to use an option and decide you do not want that option, pressing <Esc> lets you back out of any selection one menu at a time until you return to the READY mode. Each time <Esc> is pressed, the current menu is replaced with the one previous to it.

Getting Help With Lotus 1-2-3

Lotus 1-2-3 includes a Help facility that provides information about how to use the program. To call up the Help facility, press <F1>, the HELP key. As soon as <F1> is pressed, the worksheet disappears and a detailed explanation of the current activity on the worksheet appears. After you have read the information provided by the Help facility, press <Esc>. The worksheet returns to the screen.

FIGURE 4-3 The Lotus 1-2-3 Main Menu

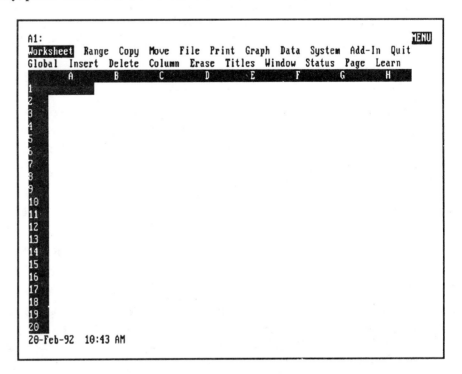

If an error is made in a worksheet, ERROR appears in the mode indicator and you cannot continue working until the error is corrected. If this happens, press <F1>. Information regarding the error message appears. Use this information to help you correct the error.

Difference Box: Using 1-2-3's Help Facility on a Computer System with Two Floppy Disk Drives

If you want to use the Help facility on a computer with two floppy disk drives, take the 1-2-3 system disk out of drive A. Place the Help Disk into drive A. Press <F1>, the HELP key. As soon as <F1> is pressed, the worksheet disappears and a detailed explanation of the current activity on the worksheet appears. When you have finished using the Help facility, take the Help Disk out of drive A and place the 1-2-3 system disk into drive A. Press <Esc>.

Saving and Retrieving Files

Worksheets are permanently saved in files on your data disk. Once saved, a file can be retrieved at any time to be used and changed as necessary. Lotus saves files to a directory located on a disk. When instructed to save a file, Lotus checks the location of the current directory. On a computer with a hard drive, the current directory can be for drive A or drive C. The default setting is for drive C. Your data disk, however, is in drive A, so you want the current directory to be drive A.

To find where the current directory is located, type the slash character < / > to view the Main menu. Type F for FILE and then D for DIRECTORY. The entry line reads **Enter current directory:** followed by either **C:** or **A:**. If it says **A:**, the location of the current directory does not need to be changed. If it says **C:**, the current directory has to be changed to drive A.

To change the drive, activate the Main menu. Type W for WORKSHEET, G for GLOBAL, D for DEFAULT, and D again for DIRECTORY. The entry line reads **Enter default directory**. Press <Esc> to erase the current directory designation. Type A:\ and press <Enter> to change the current directory designation to drive A. The previous submenu returns. Type U for UPDATE to save the change from drive C to drive A. After a few seconds, the same submenu returns. Type Q for QUIT to return to the READY mode.

Difference Box: Selecting the Directory on a Computer with Two Floppy Disk Drives

If you are using a computer with two floppy disk drives, you want drive B to be the current directory, since the disk onto which you want to save your Lotus files is in drive B. To find where the current directory is located, type the slash character </> to view the Main menu. Type F for FILE and then D for DIRECTORY. The entry line reads **Enter current directory:** followed by either **A:** or **B:**. If it says **B:**, the location of the current directory does not need to be changed. If it says **A:**, the current directory has to be changed to drive B.

To change the drive, activate the Main menu. Type W for WORKSHEET, G for GLOBAL, D for DEFAULT, and D for DIRECTORY. The entry line reads **Enter default directory**. Press <Esc> to erase the current directory designation. Type B:\ and press <Enter> to change the current directory designation. The previous submenu returns. Type U for UPDATE to save the change to drive B. After a few seconds, the same submenu returns. Type Q for QUIT to return to the READY mode.

Once the current directory designation is drive A on a computer with a hard drive or drive B on a computer with two floppy disk drives, a worksheet can be saved. To save a worksheet in a file, type a slash < / > to view the Main menu. Next, select the FILE command and the SAVE command.

You are then prompted to specify a file name. A file name can be up to eight characters long, and it can be a combination of letters and numbers. Try to give the file a name that indicates the information contained on that worksheet. Type the name of the file and press <Enter>. The mode indicator switches to WAIT for a few seconds and then changes to READY. When 1-2-3 returns to the READY mode, the worksheet has been saved.

When 1-2-3 saves the worksheet, an extension is automatically added to the name given the worksheet. The extension is separated from the file name by a period. The extension given to the file name depends on whether the original Lotus 1-2-3 or Lotus 1-2-3 Release 2 or 2.2 is being used. The first release of 1-2-3 adds the extension WKS to the file name, and releases 2 and 2.2 add the extension WK1.

To retrieve an existing file, type the slash < / > when the worksheet is in the READY mode, Type F for FILE and R for RETRIEVE. 1-2-3 then prompts you to enter the name of the file to be retrieved. The files stored on the disk are listed on the prompt line. To select a file to retrieve, highlight its name using the arrow keys, if necessary, and press <Enter>.

The entry line can display up to five file names. If there is more than one file on the disk, the file names are listed alphabetically from left to right. If there are more than five files saved on the disk, press <Down arrow> to see the next five files. Once the line containing the name of the file to be retrieved is reached, use <Left arrow> and <Right arrow> to highlight it and press <Enter>. Pressing <Home> returns the menu pointer to the first file name in the list.

Saving an Amended File

Once a worksheet has been created, it can be retrieved and changes can be made to it. Data can be added or deleted, values and labels can be changed, and so on. When a previously saved file has been retrieved and amended, there are two methods by which to save it.

The first method is to save the amended file as a new file, in which case the original file remains in 1-2-3's memory and can be retrieved again if necessary. The second method is to replace the original file with the amended file, so that only the amended file is saved and the original file is erased from memory.

To save an amended file, first select the FILE option from the Main menu. Next select SAVE. The prompt **Enter name of file to save** appears. The response to this prompt determines whether the amended file replaces the original file or is saved as a new file.

To save the amended file as a new file, type in a different file name and press <Enter>. To replace the original file, press <Enter>, indicating that the file name of the original file is to be used as the file name of the amended file. After pressing <Enter>, you can either select CANCEL, REPLACE, or BACKUP. Selecting CANCEL cancels the command leaving the file intact. Selecting REPLACE replaces the original file with the current file. If you select BACKUP, two things happen. First, 1-2-3 copies the last version of the worksheet that was saved to a backup file with the same file name but with the extension BAK. It then saves the changes that were made to the current worksheet with the existing file name and the WK1 extension.

Quitting a File and Quitting the Access System

When you no longer want to work on a particular worksheet, you need to leave 1-2-3. Be sure to save the file before leaving 1-2-3. Once the file is saved, type a slash < / > to view the Main menu. Next type Q for QUIT. The prompt **No Yes** appears on the entry line of the control panel, and NO is highlighted. Pressing the <Enter> key at this point cancels the QUIT command and returns the worksheet to the READY mode.

If you do not wish to cancel the QUIT command, move the menu pointer to YES and press <Enter>. If 1-2-3 was started directly, by typing 123 at the C> system prompt, then the operating system prompt appears immediately. If 1-2-3 was started through the Access System by typing Lotus, the Access System screen appears. If the Access System menu appears, move the menu pointer to EXIT and press <Enter>. The operating system prompt appears.

If you do not want to exit from the Lotus program, but you do want to leave one worksheet to start working on a new one, type a slash < / > to activate the Main menu. Type W to select WORKSHEET and E to select ERASE. The prompt **No Yes** appears on the entry line of the control panel, and NO is highlighted. Pressing <Enter> at this point cancels the ERASE command and returns the worksheet to the READY mode. To start a new worksheet, highlight YES and press <Enter>. A blank worksheet appears. Make sure the current worksheet has been saved before using the WORKSHEET, ERASE command. As long as the worksheet was saved to the disk, using the ERASE command simply wipes it off the screen, it does not erase it from the disk.

 YOUR TURN

A blank worksheet should still be on your screen from the last Your Turn exercise. The cell pointer should be in cell A1. If you are using a computer with a hard disk drive, make sure your data disk is in drive A. If you are using a computer with two floppy disk drives, make sure your data disk is in drive B.

1. First, you are going to practice making menu selections.

Press / (the slash key)

Note that the mode indicator says MENU, the current cell address is A1, and the WORK-SHEET option on the Main menu is highlighted. Read the prompt line. This is a submenu for the WORKSHEET command.

Press <Right arrow>

The cell pointer is now on RANGE and a submenu for the RANGE command is in the prompt line.

Press <Right arrow>

Now the cell pointer is on the COPY option. A description of the COPY command appears in the prompt line.

2. Move through the Main menu one command at a time by pressing <Right arrow>. When the cell pointer is on QUIT press <Right arrow> once. The cell pointer moves back to the WORKSHEET option. The cell pointer should now be on WORKSHEET.

> Press <Enter>

The WORKSHEET submenu now appears on the entry line. The cell pointer is on GLOBAL, the first option in the submenu. The prompt line describes the GLOBAL command.

> Press <Right arrow>

The cell pointer moves to the second command.

> Press <Left arrow>

The cell pointer moves back to the GLOBAL option.

> Press <Esc>

Pressing <Esc> moves Lotus 1-2-3 back one command level. The Main menu is now back in the entry line.

> Press <Esc>

The entry and prompt lines are empty, and the mode indicator has changed from the MENU mode to the READY mode.

3. Next, practice making menu selections by typing the first letter of the command.

> Press / (the slash key)

The Main menu appears.

> Press P for PRINT

The PRINTER command is immediately activated.

> Press <Esc>
>
> Press R for RANGE

The RANGE command is immediately activated.

> Press N for NAME

The NAME command is activated.

> Press D for DELETE

The DELETE command is activated.

> Press <Esc> three times

Pressing <Esc> moves you backward through all the menus and returns you to the READY mode. You should now be familiar with the two methods for selecting a command: highlighting it and pressing <Enter> or pressing the first letter of the command name. When instructed to *Select* a command, use whichever method you prefer for selecting the command.

4. Next you want to find out where the current directory is located.

> Press /
>
> *Select WORKSHEET*
>
> *Select GLOBAL*

> *Select DEFAULT*
>
> *Select DIRECTORY*

If the entry line reads **Enter default directory: A:**, press <Enter>. Then press <Esc> four times to return to the READY mode and skip to number 5 in this exercise. If the entry line reads **Enter default directory C:**, change the location of the default directory by doing the following:

> Press <Esc>
>
> Type: A:\
>
> Press <Enter>

Difference Box: If using a computer system with two floppy disk drives, change the default directory to B:\

Notice that in the upper-right corner of the Default Settings screen it now says **Directory: A:**. This shows you that the default directory is now set for A:.

> *Select UPDATE*
>
> Press <Esc> four times to return to the READY mode

5.   A blank worksheet should be on your screen, and you should be in the READY mode. The cell pointer should be in A1. You are going to practice saving and retrieving a file.

> Type: Lotus 1-2-3
>
> Press <Enter>

Something is now entered into the worksheet. You are ready to save this worksheet.

> Press /
>
> *Select FILE*
>
> *Select SAVE*

The prompt **Enter name of file to save** appears.

> Type: PRACTICE
>
> Press <Enter>

The worksheet is now saved as a file on your disk. Next you want to erase the worksheet from the screen. Remember, this removes it from the screen only.

> Press /
>
> *Select WORKSHEET*
>
> *Select ERASE*
>
> *Select YES*

You should have a blank worksheet on your screen. Now you are going to retrieve the PRAC-TICE file.

> Press /
>
> *Select FILE*

Select RETRIEVE

Your screen should look like Figure 4-4. The filename PRACTICE.WK1 appears in the prompt line and it is already highlighted.

Press <Enter>

The worksheet with "Lotus 1-2-3" entered into cell **A1** appears on the screen.

6. Next you want to make a change to the file.

Press <Down arrow>

The cell pointer should be in A2.

Type: `Practice File`

Press <Enter>

The PRACTICE file has now been amended, because new data has been entered into A2. You are going to save the amended file.

Press */*

Select FILE

Select SAVE

The prompt **Enter name of file to save** appears. To save the amended file as a separate file from the original PRACTICE file, enter a new file name. To replace the original PRACTICE file with the amended PRACTICE FILE, which now has data in A2, do the following instead:

Press <Enter>

Select REPLACE

The mode indicator returns to READY, and the new practice worksheet remains on the screen.

FIGURE 4-4 Retrieving a File

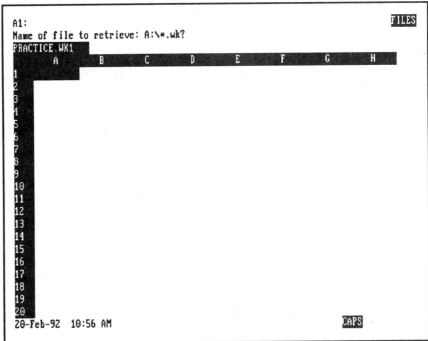

7. Now you want to practice using the Help feature.

>Press <F5>

The prompt **Enter address to go to** appears in the prompt line.

>Type: G8200

>Press <Enter>

ERROR appears in the mode indicator.

>Press <F1>

Your screen should look like Figure 4-5. Read the information on the screen. The last line of the screen **Invalid cell or range address** identifies your error. You specified a row that does not exist, row 8200. The final row on the worksheet is 8192. Notice at the bottom of the screen the option ERROR MESSAGE INDEX is highlighted.

>Press <Right arrow>

The option HELP INDEX is now highlighted.

>Press <Enter>

The Help Index appears on the screen. The Help Index lists and accesses all the Help screens available on 1-2-3. The highlighting is now on ABOUT 1-2-3 HELP.

>Press <Enter>

Read the information that appears on the screen. After reading about 1-2-3 Help, press <Right arrow> to move the highlighting to HELP INDEX, and press <Enter>. Select other Help screens and read about them. After becoming familiar with using the Help screens, press <Esc> to return to the worksheet. ERROR is still in the mode indicator. Press <Esc> again to erase the invalid cell address.

FIGURE 4-5 Using the Help Feature

```
A2: 'Practice File                                              HELP
Enter address to go to: G8200

_____

Invalid cell or range address -- The following conditions could have caused
  this error:
  o A cell or range specified in a command used a nonexistent address or
    range name.
  o A cell or range specified in a command does not contain enough rows and/or
    columns for 1-2-3 to complete the command.  This error will occur, for
    example, if you use /Graph Name Table and specify a range that contains less
    rows than 1-2-3 needs to list all the graph names in the worksheet.
  o A cell specified as the location argument for a {DISPATCH} advanced
    macro command contained an entry that did not evaluate to a location.
  o The cell or range specified in a Macro Library Manager Name-List command
    caused the Macro Library Manager to try to enter a range name in a cell
    that is beyond the last row in the worksheet.


Invalid number input -- You specified an invalid number for the command you were
  using.  Enter a number within the range indicated in the command prompt.

_____

Error Message Index                                        Help Index
Invalid cell or range address
```

8. You are now ready to exit from the program. It is a good practice to always save your worksheet one last time before quitting.

> Press *I*
>
> *Select FILE*
>
> *Select SAVE*
>
> Press <Enter>
>
> *Select REPLACE*

Now you are ready to quit.

> Press *I*
>
> *Select QUIT*
>
> *Select YES*

If the Access System menu appears, select EXIT. Turn off the computer and monitor. Store your disks carefully.

❏ CREATING A WORKSHEET

In previous sections, you learned how to move around the worksheet and how to use menus and submenus. You used two commands, SAVE and RETRIEVE, and you entered data into the worksheet (when you typed "Lotus 1-2-3" into cell A1). This section introduces more commands and basic worksheet moves by having you create a monthly budget.

Entering Labels

As explained at the beginning of the chapter, one of three categories of data can be entered in a cell: a label, a value, or a formula. Labels usually are letters or words, used as titles or captions to help identify the items in a column or a row.

Labels can be entered only when the worksheet is in the READY mode. If an attempt is made to enter a label while in any other mode, 1-2-3 beeps and nothing happens. Before you enter a label, check to make sure the worksheet is in the READY mode.

Entering a label in a cell involves three steps:

1. First, the cell pointer has to be moved to the cell where the label is to be entered. Either the GOTO key <F5> or the pointer-movement keys can be used to move the cell pointer.

2. Next, the label is typed. As soon as you start typing the label, the mode indicator changes to LABEL and the label appears in the entry line.

3. The final step is to store the label in the cell. There are two ways to store the label. The first is by pressing <Enter>. The second is by pressing the up, down, left, or right pointer-movement keys. As soon as one of these keys is pressed, the label is stored in the cell.

Three things happen once the label is stored: The label moves to the status line, it appears in the appropriate cell on the worksheet, and the mode indicator returns to READY.

Using the pointer-movement keys, rather than <Enter>, to store a label can be a timesaver because the pointer-movement keys perform two functions with one keystroke. If <Enter> is pressed to store the label, the label is stored, but the cell pointer remains in the same cell. Before you can make the next entry, the cell pointer has to be moved to a new cell. If <Up arrow>, <Down arrow>, <Left arrow>, or <Right arrow> is used to store a label, the cell pointer also moves automatically one cell in the direction the arrow is pointing. For example, if labels must be entered in cells A1, A2, A3, and A4, time is saved by pressing <Down arrow> after each label is typed, because the cell pointer moves to the next cell where the label is to be entered.

A typing error can be corrected before <Enter> or one of the cell pointer keys is pressed by using <Backspace>, which is located to the left of the <Num Lock> key. <Backspace> should not be confused with the left pointer-movement key, which also has a left arrow on it. Each time <Backspace> is pressed, one character is erased. After erasing the mistake, retype and store the label.

There are two ways to edit data already stored in a cell. One way is to go to the cell where the label is located, retype the entire label, and store it. The new label replaces the old one. Once a label has been replaced, it is erased from memory and cannot be retrieved. The second way is to use the EDIT key, <F2>, which allows the information in the entry line to be edited. To use the EDIT key, go to the cell to be edited, press <F2>, and make the correction.

The default setting for the width of a cell in Lotus 1-2-3 is nine characters. That is, unless otherwise specified, a cell can hold only nine characters. When entering labels, however, Lotus 1-2-3 uses an automatic spill-over feature: If a label longer than nine characters is entered, it spills over automatically into the next cell.

YOUR TURN

Start the Lotus 1-2-3 program. If you need to review how to load the program, refer to "Getting Started with Lotus 1-2-3" earlier in this chapter. A blank worksheet should be on your screen. You are going to enter labels into the worksheet.

1. Make sure the worksheet is in the READY mode and that the current cell address is A1.

Type: MONTHLY BUDGET

Press <Enter>

Notice that the title MONTHLY BUDGET spills over into cell B1 because it is longer than nine characters. Also, notice that the cell pointer remains in cell A1.

2. Go to cell A3. Use either the GOTO key <F5> or the pointer-movement key <Down arrow>. When you are instructed to go to a specific cell, always check the cell address to make sure the cell pointer is in the correct cell.

In cell A3, type Income

Press <Down arrow>

Notice that the cell pointer automatically moves one cell down, to cell A4.

Press the Space Bar twice and type Take-home Pay

Press <Down arrow> three times

The cell address now should read A7.

        Type: `Expenses`

        Press <Enter>

3. By now you should be familiar with the three steps involved in entering a label: going to a specific cell location, typing the label, and pressing either <Enter>, <Up arrow>, <Down arrow>, <Left arrow>, or <Right arrow>. For the remainder of this chapter, when instructed to "Enter `A Label` in A1", for example, this means go to cell A1, type "A Label," and press either <Enter>, <Up arrow>, <Down arrow>, <Left arrow>, or <Right arrow>

        Enter `Rent` in A9

        Enter `Phone` in A10

        Enter `Food` in A11

        Enter `Personal` in A12

        Enter `Clothing` in A13

        Enter `Transportation` in A14

        Enter `Student Loan` in A15

        Enter `Car Loan` in A16

        Enter `Insurance` in A17

        Enter `Savings` in A18

        Enter `TOTAL` in A20

        Enter `Budgeted` in C7

        Enter `Actual` in D7

        Enter `Difference` in E7

        Enter `Per of Income` in G7

        Move the cell pointer to D1 and enter your name.

4. Now practice using <F2>, the EDIT key.

        Go to G7

        Press <F2>

The mode indicator reads EDIT and the label moves from the status line to the entry line.

        Press <Left arrow> ten times

The cursor is one space to the right of the *r in Per.*

        Press <Backspace> three times to erase Per

        Type: `%`

        Press <Enter>

When all the labels are entered, your screen should look like Figure 4-6. Save the worksheet under the file name BUDGET1. If you need to review how to save a worksheet, refer to "Saving and Retrieving Files" earlier in this chapter. You are finished with this Your Turn exercise.

FIGURE 4-6 Entering Labels in the BUDGET1 Worksheet

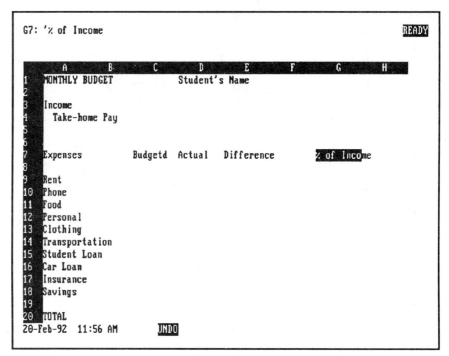

You can either exit from the program, or you can leave the worksheet on your screen while you read the following section.

Entering Values

Values are either numbers or formulas. Like all spreadsheet programs, Lotus 1-2-3 processes labels and values differently. A value, unlike a label, can be used in an arithmetic calculation. A label can spill over into several cells, but a value must be confined to one cell. Because 1-2-3 distinguishes labels from values, care must be taken in making entries.

The first character of an entry distinguishes it as either a label or a value. Because most labels are words, 1-2-3 assumes that an entry is a label if its first character is a letter. If the first character is a number, 1-2-3 assumes the entry is a value. For the most part, the following rules apply:

- The entry is interpreted as a value if the first character is one of the following: 0 1 2 3 4 5 6 7 8 9 + - (. @ _ # $.
- If the first character is any character other than those listed above, the entry is interpreted as a label.

Values are entered into a cell in the same way as labels. The worksheet must be in the READY mode. The cell pointer is moved to the appropriate cell, the number is typed into the cell, and the number is stored in the cell by pressing <Enter>, <Up arrow>, <Down arrow>, <Left arrow>, or <Right arrow>.

Values also are edited the same way as labels. A value can be edited with <Backspace> before it has been stored in the cell. After a value has been stored, it can be changed either by typing a new entry or by using the <F2> key.

YOUR TURN

Start the Lotus 1-2-3 program if necessary. Retrieve the BUDGET1 worksheet if necessary. If you need to review how to retrieve a worksheet, refer to "Saving and Retrieving Files" earlier in this chapter. The BUDGET1 worksheet should be on your screen. You are going to enter values into the worksheet.

1.   Move the cell pointer to C4

Enter: 1100

Notice that the mode indicator changes to VALUE as soon as a number is entered.

2.   Enter the remaining values as follows:

Enter 240 in C9
Enter 20 in C10
Enter 200 in C11
Enter 100 in C12
Enter 70 in C13
Enter 120 in C14
Enter 40 in C15
Enter 150 in C16
Enter 50 in C17
Enter 110 in C18
Enter 240 in D9
Enter 35 in D10
Enter 178 in D11
Enter 95 in D12
Enter 114 in D13
Enter 108 in D14
Enter 40 in D15
Enter 150 in D16
Enter 50 in D17
Enter 90 in D18

3.   When all the values have been entered, your worksheet should look like Figure 4-7. Save the amended worksheet under the file name BUDGET1. Replace the original BUDGET1. If you need to review how to save an amended file, refer to "Saving an Amended File" earlier in this chapter. You are finished with this Your Turn exercise. You can either exit

FIGURE 4-7 Entering Values in the BUDGET1 Worksheet

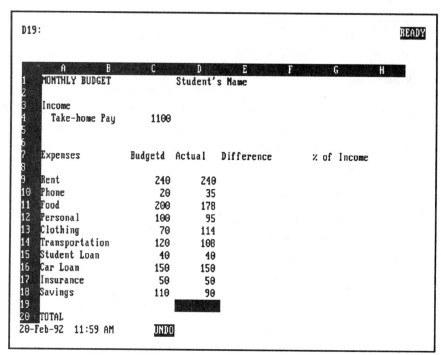

```
D19:                                                              READY

        A       B       C       D       E       F       G       H
1   MONTHLY BUDGET              Student's Name
2
3   Income
4      Take-home Pay        1100
5
6
7   Expenses            Budgetd  Actual  Difference      % of Income
8
9   Rent                   240     240
10  Phone                   20      35
11  Food                   200     178
12  Personal               100      95
13  Clothing                70     114
14  Transportation         120     108
15  Student Loan            40      40
16  Car Loan               150     150
17  Insurance               50      50
18  Savings                110      90
19
20  TOTAL
    20-Feb-92  11:59 AM       UNDO
```

from the program, or you can leave the worksheet on your screen while you read the following section.

Ranges

A range is a rectangular block of one or more cells in the worksheet that 1-2-3 treats as one unit. A range can be composed of a single cell, one row, one column, or a block of rows and columns that form a rectangle (see Figure 4-8). Ranges are among the valuable assets of electronic spreadsheets. Instead of performing a particular function on one cell at a time, the user can define a range of cells and have a function performed on the entire range. For example, ranges can be used to copy, move, or erase entire sections of a worksheet.

FIGURE 4-8 Ranges

THESE ARE RANGES	THESE ARE NOT RANGES

YOUR TURN

Start the Lotus 1-2-3 program if necessary. Retrieve the BUDGET1 worksheet if necessary. The BUDGET1 worksheet should be on your screen.

1. In this exercise you are going to practice working with ranges.

> Go to cell A5
>
> Type: \= (the backslash key followed by the equal sign)
>
> Press <Enter>

Notice that, even though the equal sign was typed only once, the double lines fill the entire cell. That is because the backslash was typed before the equal sign. In Lotus 1-2-3, the backslash functions as a repeating label prefix. Whatever is typed after the backslash repeats itself until it fills the entire cell.

> Type: /
>
> *Select COPY*

The message **Enter range to copy FROM: A5..A5** appears in the entry line, and the mode indicator says POINT. A5 is the current location of the cell pointer, and it is also a one-cell range. You are now going to copy this one-cell range. Because A5 is the only cell to be copied, press the <Enter> key. The entry line now reads **Enter range to copy TO: A5**. You now need to indicate the range of cells where you want the double lines copied to. There are two ways to indicate a range. The first way is to type the cell addresses that comprise the range, separated by a period:

> Type: B5.H5
>
> Press <Enter>

2. The second way to indicate a range is to extend the highlighting to include all the cell addresses that constitute the range:

> Go to A8
>
> Type: \- (the backslash key followed by a hyphen)
>
> Press <Enter>
>
> Type: /
>
> *Select COPY*

The prompt **Enter range to copy FROM: A8..A8** appears in the entry line. Again, this one-cell range is what you want to copy, so press <Enter>. The prompt **Enter range to copy TO: A8** now appears in the entry line. This time you are going to indicate the range by expanding the highlighting. The range must first be "anchored" before the highlighting can be expanded. Typing a period after the cell address where the highlighting is to begin anchors the highlighting—that is, it indicates the address of the first cell in the range.

Type: . (period) to anchor the first cell of the range in cell A8

Notice that the entry line of the control panel now reads **Enter range to copy TO: A8..A8**. Once the period was pressed, 1-2-3 automatically added ..A8. You can tell if a range is anchored by looking at this notation by the prompt. If there is only one cell address, such as A8, the range is not anchored. If there is a notation of a range, such as A8..A8, the range is anchored.

Press <Right arrow> seven times

Notice that the highlighting now extends through the range of cells A8-H8, and that the notation by the prompt in the entry line now reads A8..H8.

Press <Enter>

Pressing <Enter> confirms the range indicated by the highlighting. The single line is copied into that range of cells.

3. Save the amended worksheet under the file name BUDGET1. Replace the original BUDGET1. If you need help reviewing how to save an amended file, refer to "Saving an Amended File" earlier in this chapter. You are finished with this Your Turn exercise. You can either exit from the program, or you can leave the worksheet on your screen while you read the following section.

Entering Formulas

Formulas are mathematical expressions. When writing formulas with 1-2-3, you can use addition, subtraction, multiplication, division, and exponentiation, as well as advanced financial and statistical analysis. Formulas can contain references to particular cells (using their cell addresses) and can indicate mathematical operations to be performed on the values within those cells.

Formulas are entered on a worksheet in the same way that labels and numbers are entered-by typing them into cells. A formula typically is created by entering either a value or a cell address, then a mathematical operator, and then another value or cell address, and so on. The mathematical operators most frequently used in formulas are:

+   add
-   subtract
*   multiply
/   divide

Formulas often contain cell addresses. For example, a formula might be A5 + A6 + A7. Because formulas are values, and Lotus assumes an entry beginning with a letter is a label, formulas often begin with a plus sign (+) to indicate that what follows is a formula, not a label. If the previous example were entered into a worksheet, it would be entered as + A5 + A6 + A7.

There are two ways to enter formulas into cells: (1) by typing the formula, and (2) by pointing to the cells included in the formula. The following exercise uses both methods.

YOUR TURN

Start the Lotus 1-2-3 program if necessary. Retrieve the BUDGET1 worksheet if necessary. The BUDGET1 worksheet should be on your screen. You are going to enter formulas into the worksheet.

1.   First, you are going to enter formulas by typing them.

> Go to C20
>
> Type: `240+20+200+100+70+120+40+150+50+110`

Notice that the mode indicator changes to VALUE and that the formula you typed appears in the entry line.

> Press <Enter>

The mode indicator changes to READY, the formula moves to the status line, and the sum (1,100) appears in cell C20. The next formula is entered using cell addresses rather than numbers:

> Go to D20
>
> Type: `+D9+D1O+D11+D12+D13+D14+D15+D16+D17+D18`

Remember that the plus sign (+) must be the first character typed, to indicate to Lotus that this is a value, not a label.

> Press <Enter>

Again, the sum appears in the cell where the formula was entered, even though you used cell addresses rather than numbers in the formula.

2.   When the formula is long, like this one, typing in all the numbers or cell addresses is time-consuming, and making a typing error is easy. A more efficient way to enter formulas is by pointing to the cells included in the formula. Reenter the two formulas just entered using this method:

> Go to C20
>
> Type: `+`
>
> Using <Up arrow>, move to C18

Notice that the mode indicator says POINT and that +C18 is in the entry line. You had to use <Up arrow> key rather than the <F5> to move to C18 because the GOTO key, <F5>, does not function while you are pointing to cells in a formula.

> Type: `+`

The cell pointer moves back to C20.

> Using <Up arrow>, move to C17
>
> Type: `+`

Again, the cell pointer moves back to C20.

        Move to C16

        Type: +

        Move to C15

        Type: +

        Move to C14

        Type: +

        Move to C13

        Type: +

        Move to C12

        Type: +

        Move to C11

        Type: +

        Move to C10

        Type: +

        Move to C9

        Press <Enter>

The formula, using cell addresses, is in the status line. The sum is in cell C20. Using the same pointing method, reenter the formula for cell D20.

3. The column titled Difference shows the difference between what was budgeted for the month and what was actually spent. Enter formulas in cells E9 through E18 to show this difference:

        Go to E9

        Type: +

        Move to C9

        Type: −

        Move to D9

        Press <Enter>

The formula appears in the status line, the mode indicator says READY, and the difference appears in cell E9.

        Go to E10

        Type: +

        Move to C10

        Type: −

        Move to D10

        Press <Enter>

Because $15 more than what was budgeted was actually spent, the number appears as a negative.

> Go to E11
>
> Type: +
>
> Move to C11
>
> Type: −
>
> Move to D11
>
> Press <Enter>

Continue to enter formulas into cells E12 through E18 that calculate the difference between what was budgeted and what was actually spent.

4. Save the amended worksheet under the file name BUDGET1. Replace the original BUDGET1. If you need to review how to save an amended file, refer to "Saving an Amended File" earlier in this chapter. You are finished with this Your Turn exercise. You can either exit from the program, or you can leave the worksheet on your screen while you read the following section.

Formatting Cells

Values in a Lotus 1-2-3 worksheet can be formatted. That is, they can be made to appear with dollar signs, with commas, or rounded off to a certain number of decimal places. Either one cell or a range of cells can be formatted.

To format a cell, first select the RANGE option from the Main menu. Then select FORMAT. The options for the FORMAT command appear in the entry line. Table 4-5 lists these options and the functions they perform.

If Fixed, Scientific, Currency, Comma (,), or Percent is selected as a format, 1-2-3 prompts you to enter the number of decimal places you would like displayed. Up to fifteen decimal places can be displayed. No matter how many decimal places are actually displayed, however, 1-2-3 remembers the number to maximum precision. That is, formatting a value only changes the way it is displayed; the value itself does not change. For example, suppose the value in cell B 12 is 13.9812. If cell B12 is formatted using the Fixed option to be rounded to two decimal places, the number 13.98 appears in cell B12 on the worksheet. If B12 is used in a formula, however, 1-2-3 uses 13.9812 in its calculations; it does not use 13.98.

 YOUR TURN

Start the Lotus 1-2-3 program if necessary. Retrieve the BUDGET1 worksheet if necessary. The BUDGET1 worksheet should be on your screen You are going to practice using the FORMAT command.

1. You are going to format a range of cells as Currency.

> Go to C9

TABLE 4-5 FORMAT Command Options

Option	Description
Fixed	Values are rounded to a fixed number of places; for example, 8.67.
Scientific	Exponential notation; for example, 2.56E+05.
Currency	Dollars and cents; for example, $30.45.
,	Commas are added to long numbers; for example, 32,450. Negative numbers are placed in parentheses; for example, (5,469).
General	No fixed number of decimal places is set; for example, 8.671.
+/-	Horizontal bar graph; displays a bar of plus signs for the value of a positive integer or minus signs for the value of a negative integer; for example, 3.3 would be displayed as +++.
Percent	Value is multiplied by 100 and a percent sign is added; for example, 58%.
Date	Date format; for example, DD-MMM-YY (28-Sep-93).
Text	Displays the formula in the cell.
Hidden	Hides the cell entries.
Reset	Returns cell or cells to the global default format which, if not changed, is General.

> Type: /
>
> *Select RANGE*
>
> *Select FORMAT*
>
> *Select CURRENCY*

Lotus 1-2-3 prompts you to enter the number of decimal places. The default setting is 2. Select the default setting by pressing <Enter>. The entry line reads **Enter range to format: C9..C9**.

> Press <Down arrow> nine times, or until the range reaches C18
>
> Press <Right arrow> two times

The range from C9 to E18 is now selected, as indicated in the entry line.

> Press <Enter>

All the values in cells C9 to E18 now appear in the currency format. Notice that the negative numbers now appear within parentheses rather than having a minus sign in front of them. The status line reads **C9: (C2) 240**. The C2 within parentheses indicates how the cell has been formatted. It stands for Currency rounded to 2 decimal places.

2. The column titled % of Income is used for figuring out what percentage of the monthly take-home pay was actually spent on each of the budgeted expenses. The formula used to figure this percentage is the amount spent divided by the monthly take-home pay. For example, the formula to be entered into G9 is 240/1100 or D9/C4. Enter the appropriate formulas into cells G9 through G18. Remember, if you use cell addresses in your formulas, you must use the + prefix.

3. Next, format cells G9-G18 using the Percent format option:

Go to G9

Type: /

Select RANGE

Select FORMAT

Select PERCENT

The entry line reads **Enter number of decimal places (0..15): 2**.

Type: 0

Press <Enter>

Press <Down arrow> nine times, or until the cell range G9 through G18 is selected

Press <Enter>

The percentages appear in column G. In the first line of the control panel, (PO) stands for the Percentage format carried out to 0 decimal places.

4. Save the amended worksheet under the file name BUDGET1. Replace the original BUDGET1. You are finished with this Your Turn exercise. You can either exit from the program, or you can leave the worksheet on your screen while you read the following section.

Erasing A Cell

Erasing a cell or a range of cells on a 1-2-3 worksheet is easy. First select RANGE from the Main menu; then select ERASE. The prompt ENTER RANGE TO ERASE appears. Using the <Left arrow>, <Right arrow>, <Up arrow> and <Down arrow>, select the range to be erased and press <Enter>.

If a value that has been used in a formula is erased, the formula using that value automatically recalculates without the value.

    YOUR TURN

Start the Lotus 1-2-3 program if necessary. Retrieve the BUDGET1 worksheet if necessary. The BUDGET1 worksheet should be on your screen.

1. You are going to practice erasing a cell.

Go to A12

Type: /

Select RANGE

Select ERASE

The prompt **Enter range to erase: A12..A12** appears in the entry line. Only one cell, A12, is to be erased, so press <Enter>.

Enter Spending $ in A12

2. Save the amended worksheet under the file name BUDGET1. Replace the original BUDGET1. You are finished with this Your Turn exercise. You can either exit from the program, or you can leave the worksheet on your screen while you read the following sections.

❏ CHANGING THE APPEARANCE OF A WORKSHEET

Having a worksheet that is easy to read is important. Lotus 1-2-3 includes such options as being able to align labels, adjust column widths, and insert and delete rows and columns, in order to help create a neat and easily understandable worksheet. These options are discussed in the following sections.

Aligning Labels

A label prefix determines the alignment of a label—that is, whether it aligns on the left side of the cell, is centered within the cell, or is aligned on the right side of the cell. A label prefix is the first character typed when entering a label. Table 4-6 lists the label prefixes and explains their functions. Lotus 1-2-3's default prefix is the apostrophe. That is, if no prefix is indicated, Lotus aligns the labels on the left side of the cell.

Label prefixes also enable a heading that begins with a number to be used as a label. For example, if you wanted to use 1996, 1997, and 1998 as labels, Lotus would read them as values unless you used a label prefix. Just as the plus sign is typed in as the first character of a formula beginning with a cell address, so a label prefix must be the first character of a label beginning with a number. In this example, you could type the following into the cells: ^1996, ^1997, ^1998. (The label prefix character does not appear in the cell as part of the label.)

There are two methods for setting up label prefixes. The first is to type in the prefix as part of the title. The second, which is explained in the following exercise, is to align a range of labels.

YOUR TURN

Start the Lotus 1-2-3 program if necessary. Retrieve the BUDGET1 worksheet if necessary. The BUDGET1 worksheet should be on your screen.

1. You are going to practice aligning labels.

Go to A7

Type: /

TABLE 4-6 Label Prefixes

Label Prefix	Purpose
' (apostrophe)	To align labels on the left side of the cell
^ (caret)	To center labels within the cell
" (double quotation mark)	To align labels on the right side of the cell
\ (backslash)	To repeat a single character or a set of characters for the length of the cell

Select RANGE

Select LABEL

Left, **Right**, and **Center** appear in the entry. Currently the labels are aligned at the left side of the cell. Move the menu pointer to **Right** and press <Enter>. The prompt, **Enter range of labels A7..A7** appears in the entry line.

Press <Right arrow> seven times

The range of cells from A7 through H7 is selected.

Press <Enter>

Move the cell pointer through row 7. Notice that each label is preceded by the label prefix ".

2. Now center the labels.

Go to A7

Type: /

Select RANGE

Select LABEL

Select CENTER

Enter the range of labels A7 through H7

Press <Enter>

Move the cell pointer through row 7. Now the ^ label prefix is in front of each label.

3. Save the amended worksheet under the file name BUDGET1. Replace the original BUDGET1. You are finished with this Your Turn exercise. You can either exit from the program, or you can leave the worksheet on your screen while you read the following section.

Adjusting Column Widths

The default column width in Lotus 1-2-3 is nine characters. The column width can be adjusted, however, from one to seventy-two characters. The width of individual columns can be set, or the width of all the columns in the worksheet can be set.

 YOUR TURN

Start the Lotus 1-2-3 program if necessary. Retrieve the BUDGET1 worksheet if necessary. The BUDGET1 worksheet should be on your screen.

1. In this exercise you are going to practice changing the column widths.

Go to C4

In the previous hands-on exercise, when cells were changed to the Currency format, cells C4, C20, and D20 were not formatted. Now you are going to format these cells.

Type: /

> *Select RANGE*
>
> *Select FORMAT*
>
> *Select CURRENCY*
>
> Press <Enter> to accept the default setting at two decimal places
>
> Press <Enter> again to accept a range of one cell, C4

Notice that asterisks now fill C4. Changing the format to Currency added enough characters to 1,100 that it is now too long to fit in the column at its present width. Look at the control panel. Even though asterisks appear on the worksheet, Lotus still has the value of 1,100 stored in C4.

2. Keep the cell pointer at C4. You are going to change the width of the column so that the actual value, rather than asterisks, appears on the worksheet in cell C4.

> Type: /
>
> *Select WORKSHEET*
>
> *Select COLUMN*
>
> *Select SET-WIDTH*

Enter column width (1..240): 9 now appears in the entry line, because 9 is the current width of the column.

> Press <Right arrow> once

Notice that the 9 in the entry line changed to a 10. The current column width is now 10. $1,100.00 now appears on the worksheet in C4. A column width of 10 is enough space for this value.

> Press <Enter>

The control panel now reads **C4: (C2) [W10] 1100**. This indicates that cell C4 is formatted as currency carried out to two decimal places, the width of C4 is 10, and the value in C4 is 1,100.

3. Now you are going to format cell C20 as Currency.

> Go to C20
>
> Type: /
>
> *Select RANGE*
>
> *Select FORMAT*
>
> *Select CURRENCY*
>
> Press <Enter> to accept the default setting at two decimal places
>
> Press <Enter> again to accept a range of one cell, C20

Because the width of the column is 10, the value appears in C20. When you are changing the width of a column, the cell pointer can be on any cell in the column. Move the cell pointer to any cell in column D and change the width of column D to 10. Then format D20 as Currency, carried out to two decimal places.

4. Column F is too wide. Move the cell pointer to column F

Type: /

Select WORKSHEET

Select COLUMN

Select SET-WIDTH

The prompt **Enter column width (1..240)** appears in the entry line.

Type: 3

Press <Enter>

The column width of column F is now 3.

5. Save the amended worksheet under the file name BUDGET1. Replace the original BUDGET1. You are finished with this Your Turn exercise. You can either exit from the program, or you can leave the worksheet on your screen while you read the following section.

Inserting and Deleting Rows and Columns

Sometimes the appearance of a worksheet can be enhanced by adding a row or column. Perhaps a row or column has to be added to accommodate additional data, or data that is no longer relevant has to be deleted from a worksheet. Adding or deleting rows and columns on a Lotus worksheet is a simple task that involves pointing to the location where the row or column is to be added or deleted.

To add a row or column, first position the cell pointer. The cell pointer must be positioned to the right of where a column is to appear and under where a row is to appear. Select the WORKSHEET option from the Main menu. Next select INSERT. The option of selecting either COLUMN or ROW appears next. After you select ROW or COLUMN, the prompt **Enter column (row) insert range** appears in the entry line. If only one column or row is to be inserted, simply press <Enter>. If more than one column or row is to be inserted, the range of the insertion can be indicated either by using the pointer movement keys or by typing in the range. Once <Enter> is pressed, the row or column is added, and the worksheet returns to the READY mode.

Deleting a row or column is similar to adding a row or column. Select WORKSHEET from the Main menu, and select DELETE. Next you choose to delete either a row or a column, and indicate the range of columns or rows to be deleted. Pressing <Enter> deletes the designated rows or columns and the worksheet returns to the READY mode.

Be very careful when deleting rows and columns. Once a row or column is deleted, it is erased from memory and cannot be retrieved. Accidentally deleting a row when you intended to delete a column could be disastrous.

 YOUR TURN

Start the Lotus 1-2-3 program if necessary. Retrieve the BUDGET1 worksheet if necessary. The BUDGET1 worksheet should be on your screen.

1. In this exercise you are going to delete row 6 from the worksheet.

Go to A6

Type: /

Select WORKSHEET

Select DELETE

Select ROW

Press <Enter>, because you want to delete row 6 only

2. Now you are going to add a row between Take-Home Pay and the double lines.

Go to A5

Type: /

Select WORKSHEET

Select INSERT

Select ROW

Press <Enter>, because you want to add one row only.

Your worksheet should look like Figure 4-9 when completed.

3. Save the amended worksheet under the file name BUDGET1. Replace the original BUDGET1. You are finished with this Your Turn exercise. You can either exit from the program, or you can leave the worksheet on your screen while you read the following section.

❏ PRINTING A WORKSHEET

There are times when it is useful to have a hard copy of a worksheet. Printing a Lotus worksheet is described in this section.

FIGURE 4-9 Changing the Appearance of the BUDGET1 Worksheet

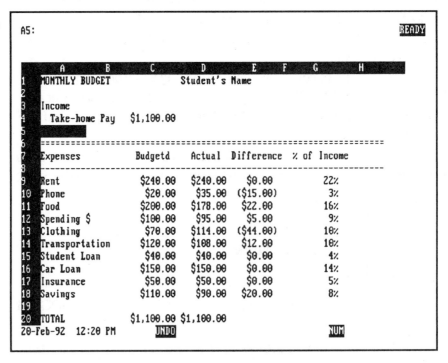

Chapter 4: Introduction to Lotus 1-2-3

TABLE 4-7 Print Options

Option	Description
RANGE	Specifies the range of the worksheet to be printed. The range must be specified even if all the data on the worksheet is being printed.
LINE	Advances the paper one line.
PAGE	Advances the paper one page.
OPTIONS	Allows a number of choices to be made regarding the appearance of the worksheet. These choices include specifying a header or footer to be printed on each page, setting margins, specifying border columns and rows, and specifying the number of lines per page.
CLEAR	Resets some or all of the print settings.
ALIGN	Resets the alignment of the paper to the top of the page.
GO	Starts the printing process.
QUIT	Returns 1-2-3 to the READY mode.

Before printing a worksheet, make sure to save the file so that the hard copy will include the latest changes or additions. Select the PRINT option from the Main menu. The options PRINTER and FILE appear next. A Lotus worksheet can be sent directly to a printer, or it can be stored in a print file for later processing. Select PRINTER. Eight PRINTER options appear in the entry line. These options offer choices regarding the appearance and format of the printout. Table 4-7 lists the PRINTER options and describes their functions.

The only PRINTER option that must be selected is RANGE. After you select range, the prompt **Enter print range** appears in the entry line. To specify the range to be printed, move the cell pointer to the first cell to be printed. The address of that cell appears after the prompt in the entry line. Type a period (.) to anchor the range, and then move the cell pointer to the last cell to be printed. Press <Enter>. The PRINTER options return to the entry line.

Make sure the printer is connected to your computer and is online. First, select ALIGN and then select GO from the PRINTER options, and the worksheet is printed. The PRINTER options remain in the entry line after the worksheet has been printed. When you no longer want to print, select QUIT and the worksheet returns to the READY mode.

YOUR TURN

Start the Lotus 1-2-3 program if necessary. Retrieve the BUDGET1 worksheet if necessary. The BUDGET1 worksheet should be on your screen.

1. In this exercise you are going to print the BUDGET1 worksheet. Make sure the computer you are using is hooked up to a printer, that the printer is turned on, has plenty of paper, and is online.

Type: /

Select PRINT

Select PRINTER

Your screen should look like Figure 4-10. The PRINTER options are in the entry line and the current Print Settings are displayed in the remainder of the screen.

2. You need to select the range of cells you want to print.

>   *Select RANGE*
>
>   Move the cell pointer to A1

Remember, <F5> cannot be used to go to a specific cell when the mode indicator says POINT.

>   Type a period (.) to anchor the range
>
>   Press <Right arrow> 7 times to select the columns A through H
>
>   Press <Down arrow> 19 times to select the rows 1 through 20

The entire worksheet should now be highlighted.

>   Press <Enter>

3. The worksheet is no longer highlighted, and the PRINTER options return to the entry line.

>   *Select ALIGN*
>
>   *Select GO*

The BUDGET1 worksheet is printed. It should look like Figure 4-11.

4. Save the amended worksheet under the file name BUDGET1. Replace the original BUDGET1. You are finished working with the BUDGET1 worksheet. Exit from the Lotus program. If you need to review how to exit from the program, refer to "Quitting a File and Quitting the Access System" earlier in this chapter.

FIGURE 4-10 The Print Settings Screen

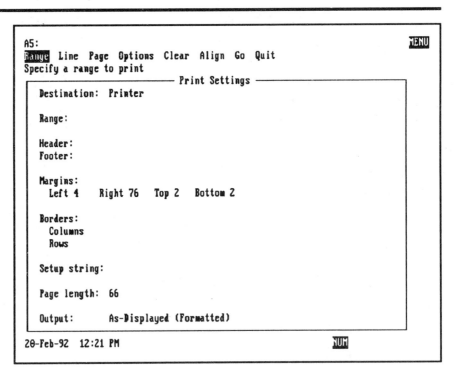

```
A5:                                                              MENU
Range  Line  Page  Options  Clear  Align  Go  Quit
Specify a range to print
                            ── Print Settings ──
   Destination:  Printer

   Range:

   Header:
   Footer:

   Margins:
     Left 4      Right 76    Top 2    Bottom 2

   Borders:
     Columns
     Rows

   Setup string:

   Page length:  66

   Output:       As-Displayed (Formatted)

   20-Feb-92  12:21 PM                             NUM
```

Chapter 4: Introduction to Lotus 1-2-3

```
MONTHLY BUDGET              Student's Name

Income
  Take-home Pay    $1,100.00

===================================================================
Expenses            Budgetd    Actual  Difference  % of Income
-------------------------------------------------------------------
Rent                $240.00   $240.00     $0.00        22%
Phone                $20.00    $35.00   ($15.00)        3%
Food                $200.00   $178.00    $22.00        16%
Spending $          $100.00    $95.00     $5.00         9%
Clothing             $70.00   $114.00   ($44.00)       10%
Transportation      $120.00   $108.00    $12.00        10%
Student Loan         $40.00    $40.00     $0.00         4%
Car Loan            $150.00   $150.00     $0.00        14%
Insurance            $50.00    $50.00     $0.00         5%
Savings             $110.00    $90.00    $20.00         8%

TOTAL             $1,100.00 $1,100.00
```

FIGURE 4-11 The BUDGET1 Worksheet

❏ SUMMARY POINTS

- A spreadsheet program simulates the operations of a calculator and stores the results in the computer's memory.
- An electronic spreadsheet is displayed as a table of columns and rows.
- The three categories of items which can be entered into an electronic spreadsheet are labels, values, and formulas.
- Labels are used to identify the contents of a spreadsheet. A value is a single piece of numeric information used in the calculations of a spreadsheet.
- A formula is a mathematical expression that is assigned to a cell in the spreadsheet.
- The two major areas of a worksheet are the control panel and the window. The control panel displays important information about the worksheet. The window is the portion of the worksheet which is currently displayed.

❏ COMMAND SUMMARY

Command	Keystroke	Function
EDIT	\<F2\>	Puts 1-2-3 in EDIT mode.
GOTO	\<F5\>	Moves to a specific cell.
HELP	\<F1\>	Displays a 1-2-3 Help screen.
PERIOD		Anchors the pointer.

Command	Function
/Copy	Copies data from one part of a worksheet to another.
/File Retrieve	Retrieves a file from disk.
/File Save	Saves the current file, either with the same or a different name.
/Print Printer Go	Starts printing.
/Print Printer Options	Allows the user to set print options before printing.
/Print Printer Range	Specifies a range of data to print.
/Quit	Exits the worksheet.
/Range Erase	Erases specified data.
/Range Format	Changes the appearance of specified numbers.
/Range Label	Changes the alignment of specified labels.
/Worksheet Delete Column	Removes columns (and any data in them).
/Worksheet Delete Row	Removes rows (and any data in them).
/Worksheet Insert Column	Inserts blank columns.
/Worksheet Insert Row	Inserts blank rows.

❑ LOTUS 1-2-3 EXERCISES

1. Assume that the computer is shut off. List all the necessary steps to start the Lotus program. If you need help remembering how to start Lotus, refer to "Getting Started with Lotus 1-2-3" earlier in this chapter. Make sure your data disk is in the proper drive.

2. A blank worksheet should be displayed on the screen. List all the necessary steps for checking to see where the current directory is located. If you need help remembering how to check the location of the current directory, refer to "Saving and Retrieving Files" earlier in this chapter. If necessary, change the current directory to drive A for a computer system with a hard drive or drive B for a computer system with two floppy drives.

3. Now you are going to enter a new worksheet. Enter your name in cell Al. Assume that you want to prepare the following report on the total quantity of items ordered by customers during the past week. Enter the worksheet as follows:

	A	B	C	D	E	F	G	H	I
1	YOUR NAME								
2									
3	Summary of Products Ordered During Week 30								
4									
5	PRODUCT NAME		CODE	MON	TUE	WED	THR	FRI	TOTAL
6									
7	Skirts		1	80	90	50	70	110	
8	Shorts		2	120	130	110	140	150	
9	Blouses		3	30	30	20	60	70	
10	Shirts		4	180	170	150	180	180	
11	Socks		5	110	105	120	140	150	
12	Jeans		6	165	170	140	150	170	
13									
14	TOTAL								

4. After you enter Summary of Products Ordered During Week 30 in cell A3, in which cell(s) is the text displayed? What do you call this?

5. List the steps necessary for changing the width of a column. If you need to review how to adjust the column width, refer to "Adjusting Column Widths" earlier in this chapter. Change the width of columns B, C, D, E, F, G, and H to 6.

6. List the steps necessary for aligning labels. If you need to review how to align labels, refer to "Aligning Labels" earlier in this chapter. Align the labels in cells C5 through 15 so that they are centered in the cell.

7. You are now ready to compute the totals and complete the report.
   a. Start with the totals per day. Move the cell pointer to D14. This should be the cell for the total of Monday's orders. Total orders for Monday are +D7 + D8 + D9 + D10 + D11 + D12. Enter this formula in D14 using the pointing method.
   b. Enter the appropriate formulas in cells E14, F14, G14 and H14 using the pointing method.
   c. Move the cell pointer to I7. This should contain the total for skirts ordered during week 30, that is the sum of cells D7 through H7. Enter the appropriate formula in cell 17.
   d. Enter the appropriate formulas in cells I8, I9, I10, I11, I12, and I14. What is the grand total of products ordered during the week?

8. Next you want to improve on the appearance of the report. You want to draw a horizontal line between the last line of data and the totals. Move the cell pointer to cell A13.

   Type: \-

What appears in cell A13? Repeat this entry in cells B13 through I13.

9. The report is now ready. Save the worksheet under the name SALE30. If you need to review how to save a worksheet, refer to "Saving and Retrieving Files" earlier in this chapter.

10. Print the report. If you need to review how to print a report, refer to "Printing a Worksheet" earlier in this chapter.

❏ LOTUS 1-2-3 PROBLEMS

To complete the following exercises, you need to use files on the Student File Disk. In order to complete these exercises, you will need to be able to start Lotus 1-2-3, save and retrieve files, save an amended file, quit a file and quit the Access System, specify ranges, enter formulas, format cells, align labels, adjust column widths, insert and delete rows and columns, and print a worksheet.

1. On the Student File Disk is a Lotus 1-2-3 file called PAY.WK1. Start the Lotus program and retrieve this file. Save the file and rename it PAY-2 in order to maintain the original PAY.WK1 on the disk.

2. Enter your name in cell Al. Look the worksheet over carefully. This worksheet is used to compute the net pay for six employees working at Hi-Tech Manufacturing. Not all of the worksheet is displayed in the window. Move the cell pointer around the worksheet to make sure you have viewed the entire worksheet.

3. Right now the labels in cells C6 through J6 are awkward because they are left-justified. Format the labels in row 6 so that they are right-justified.

4. Change the column width of columns, C, D, E, F, and G to 5.

5. Insert a row between the labels in row 6 and the data that starts in row 7.

6. Enter a formula in cell H8 that totals the hours David Lawhon worked during the week. Enter the other formulas as needed in cells H9, H10, H11, H12, and H13.

7. Column I lists each employee's hourly wage. Format these numbers as Currency with two decimal places.

8. Column J computes the gross pay. The gross pay is the total hours worked times the rate. The symbol Lotus uses for multiplication is the asterisk (*). Using cell addresses, enter a formula in cell J8 that multiplies the total hours worked by David Lawhon by his rate. (Hint: Remember to precede the first cell address with a plus sign so that Lotus does not think this is a label.) Enter the other formulas as needed in cells J9, J10, J11, J12, and J13.

9. Add a row of hyphens using the repeating label prefix in the row of space between the labels in row 6 and the remaining data in the worksheet.

10. Format the values in the GROSS PAY column as Currency with two decimal places.

11. Save and print the payroll report.

It is the end of the month and once again you are low on funds. You want to create a worksheet to help you keep track of where your money goes during the month.

1. Using Lotus 1-2-3, start a new worksheet. You need places in your worksheet to keep track of your income and your disbursements. The following sample ledger sheet might provide you with some ideas as to how to set up your worksheet:

Date	Income					Disbursements			
	Work		Other		TOTAL INCOME	Expenditures		Savings	TOTAL DISBURSEMENTS
	Job	Amount	Description	Amount		Description	Amount	Amount	

2. Create a worksheet to keep track of your income and expenses for a month. Enter appropriate data regarding your financial status. Make sure to include your name somewhere on your worksheet.

3. Format all the cells that have dollar amounts entered as Currency with two decimal places. Make sure all your columns have appropriate column widths.

4. At the bottom of your worksheet enter formulas that compute your total income for the month as well as your total disbursements for the month. Enter a formula that subtracts your total disbursements from your total income. Enter appropriate labels that identify your formulas.

5. Format the worksheet as necessary to make it neat and easy to read. Align labels as necessary, add lines of hyphens or equal signs to separate labels from data, insert rows if necessary, and so on.

6. When you are satisfied with your worksheet save it and print it.

CHAPTER 5

More Lotus 1-2-3 Features

OUTLINE

❏ INTRODUCTION

In the previous chapter, the fundamentals for creating basic Lotus 1-2-3 worksheets were covered. Lotus 1-2-3 also has many advanced features that simplify the task of creating more complex worksheets. These features, such as the COPY and MOVE commands, sorting, and the @functions ("at functions"), are covered in this chapter.

Also covered in this chapter is the concept of spreadsheet analysis. Spreadsheet analysis (or what-if analysis) is the mental process of evaluating information contained within an electronic spreadsheet. Often it involves comparing various results generated by the spreadsheet. A model, in terms of a spreadsheet, is a numeric representation of a real-world situation. For example, a home budget is a numeric representation of the expenses involved in maintaining a household and therefore can be considered a model. The chapter concludes with a section on how to create graphs using Lotus 1-2-3.

❏ EDITING A WORKSHEET

Just as word processing programs do, spreadsheet programs include commands that make editing a worksheet quick and easy. Two of these commands are COPY and MOVE.

The COPY Command

Some of the data entered into complex worksheets is repetitive. For example, the same labels or formulas may be repeated. Lotus 1-2-3 has a COPY command that copies any cell or cells in the worksheet and inserts them in another part of the worksheet.

The COPY command is one of the options from 1-2-3's Main menu. After the user selects COPY, the prompt **Enter range to copy FROM** appears in the entry line. The range to be copied is then selected, either by using the pointer-movement keys or by typing the range of cells. After this range has been selected, the prompt **Enter range to copy TO** appears in the entry line. Move the pointer to the first cell of the range where the data is to be copied, and press <Enter>. All the data is copied to the new range. You do not need to specify a range equal in size to the range that was copied. You should, however, make sure there is no data in the range where the data will be written. If there is data in that range, the COPY command will write over it, and that data will be irretrievably lost.

The MOVE Command

Lotus 1-2-3 also includes a MOVE command. The difference between COPY and MOVE is that when data is copied it remains in the original location as well as appearing in the location where it is copied. When data is moved, it appears in the new location only; it is removed from the original location.

To move data, select MOVE from the Main menu. After selecting MOVE, the prompt **Enter range to move FROM** appears in the entry line. The range to be moved is then selected, either by using the pointer-movement keys or by typing the range of cells. After this range has been selected, the prompt **Enter range to move TO** appears in the entry line. Move the pointer to the first cell of the range where the data is to be moved, and press <Enter>. All the data is moved to the new range. It no longer appears in the original range. Before moving a range, make sure there is no data in the range where the data will be written. If there is data in that range, the MOVE command will write over it, and that data will be irretrievably lost.

YOUR TURN

Because you are now familiar with Lotus commands, the hands-on exercises in this chapter use an abbreviated method to indicate what commands are to be selected. For example, the following instructions indicate that you should type a slash to activate the Main menu, select WORKSHEET from the Main menu options, and select ERASE from the worksheet options:

> / WORKSHEET ERASE

1. Load the Lotus 1-2-3 program. A blank worksheet should be on your screen. Enter the following labels in the cells indicated:

Cell	Label
Al	REGION ONE SALES
A2	First Quarter
A4	NAME
C4	JAN
D4	FEB
E4	MAR
F4	TOTAL

2. You realize you forgot to leave a space to enter your name. You want to move everything you just entered down two rows. To do this, you are going to use the MOVE command.

> Go to A1
>
> / MOVE

Your screen should look like Figure 5-1. The prompt is asking you to enter the range of cells you want to move.

> Press <Down arrow> three times
>
> Press <Right arrow> five times

The entry line should now say **Enter range to move FROM: A1..F4**

> Press <Enter>

The entry line should now say **Enter range to move TO: A1.** You want to move everything down two rows.

> Press <Down arrow> twice

The cell pointer should now be in cell A3.

> Press <Enter>

All the data should now be moved down two lines. Enter your name in cell A1.

3. You also want to keep track of Region Two sales. Instead of entering all the labels a second time, you are going to copy them.

FIGURE 5-1 Using the Move Command

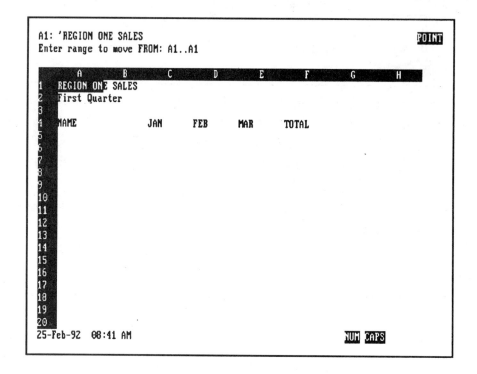

```
A1: 'REGION ONE SALES                                          POINT
Enter range to move FROM: A1..A1

        A       B       C       D       E       F       G       H
1  REGION ONE SALES
2  First Quarter
3
4  NAME            JAN     FEB     MAR     TOTAL
5
6
7
8
9
10
11
12
13
14
15
16
17
18
19
20
25-Feb-92  08:41 AM                                     NUM CAPS
```

Go to A3

/ COPY

The entry line should now say **Enter range to copy FROM: A3..A3**.

Press <Down arrow> three times

Press <Right arrow> five times

The range of cells highlighted should be A3 through F6.

Press <Enter>

Go to A18

Press <Enter>

The range of cells is now copied to the new location.

Go to A18

Press <F2>

The contents of cell A18 moves to the entry line.

Press <Left arrow> nine times

The cursor should be under the *O* in *ONE*

Press <Del> three times

Type: TWO

Press <Enter>

4.   Enter the following labels into the worksheet:

Cell	Label	Cell	Label
A8	Gray, Betsy	A23	Frye, Jo
A9	Mian, Ted	A24	Abbot, Steve
A10	Flores, Donna	A25	Flynn, Lane
A11	Schultz, Ed	A26	Flynn, Laura
A12	Maines, Sandra	A27	Zak, Tom
A13	West, John	A28	Coe, Amy

5.   Make sure your data disk is in the appropriate drive and that the default directory is set to that drive. Save the worksheet under the file name FIRSTQTR. You have finished with this Your Turn exercise. You can either leave the worksheet on your screen while you read the following section, or you can exit from the Lotus program.

The Difference between GLOBAL and RANGE Commands

Many Lotus 1-2-3 commands can be applied either to a specific range of cells or to the entire worksheet. For example, if every value in a particular worksheet is currency, the entire worksheet can be formatted one time and all the values in that worksheet will appear as currency.

To use the GLOBAL command, first select WORKSHEET from the Main menu. Next, select GLOBAL and a menu of all the GLOBAL options appears. Table 5-1 lists these options and describes their functions.

TABLE 5-1 GLOBAL Options

Option	Description
Format	Sets a global format (For example, the entire worksheet could be formatted as currency.)
Label-Prefix	Sets a global label alignment prefix (For example, centering all the labels in the worksheet.)
Column-Width	Sets a global column width. (For example, every column could be 12 characters wide.)
Recalculation	Determines when, in what order, and how many times formulas in the worksheet are recalculated
Protection	Prevents changes from being made to cells
Default	Enables the user to select default settings for such things as the type of printer being used and its connection; the directory 1-2-3 automatically uses when searching for files; international display formats; the method of using the Help facility; and the type of clock display on the screen.
Zero	Determines whether values of zero are displayed on the screen

YOUR TURN

In this exercise you are going to globally format the FIRSTQTR worksheet. Start the Lotus program if necessary and retrieve the FIRSTQTR file.

1.   Enter the following values in the cells indicated:

Cell	Value	Cell	Value
C8	4280	C23	6890
C9	6080	C24	8970
C10	5880	C25	8760
C11	6260	C26	6600
C12	6700	C27	9300
C13	6500	C28	4880
D8	6300	D23	8200
D9	6600	D24	7420
D10	5000	D25	6980
D11	6550	D26	7280
D12	3800	D27	6390
D13	4670	D28	8000
E8	5400	E23	5730
E9	2990	E24	6290
E10	7800	E25	5020
E11	6980	E26	7330
E12	5890	E27	5980
E13	4370	E28	8310

2.   All the values entered are currency, so you are going to format the entire worksheet as currency.

/ WORKSHEET GLOBAL FORMAT CURRENCY

The prompt **Enter number of decimal places** appears.

Press <Enter> to accept the default setting of 2

Asterisks appear in the cells because the columns are not wide enough to display the values. You are going to change the column width of the entire worksheet.

/ WORKSHEET GLOBAL COLUMN-WIDTH

The prompt ENTER GLOBAL COLUMN WIDTH appears.

Type: 12

Press <Enter>

Your screen should look like Figure 5-2. The worksheet is now globally formatted for currency and for a column width of 12. A value entered in any cell on the worksheet appears on the screen as currency, and every column on the worksheet has a width of 12 characters.

3.   Save the amended FIRSTQTR file. You have finished with this Your Turn exercise. You can either leave the worksheet on your screen while you read the following section, or you can exit from the Lotus program.

FIGURE 5-2 Using the GLOBAL Command

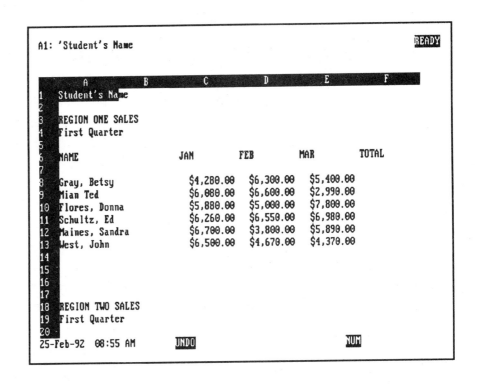

```
A1: 'Student's Name                                              READY

        A           B          C          D          E          F
1   Student's Name
2
3   REGION ONE SALES
4   First Quarter
5
6   NAME                      JAN        FEB        MAR        TOTAL
7
8   Gray, Betsy            $4,280.00  $6,300.00  $5,400.00
9   Mian Ted               $6,080.00  $6,600.00  $2,990.00
10  Flores, Donna          $5,880.00  $5,000.00  $7,800.00
11  Schultz, Ed            $6,260.00  $6,550.00  $6,980.00
12  Maines, Sandra         $6,700.00  $3,800.00  $5,890.00
13  West, John             $6,500.00  $4,670.00  $4,370.00
14
15
16
17
18  REGION TWO SALES
19  First Quarter
20
25-Feb-92  08:55 AM       UNDO                   NUM
```

❏ FUNCTIONS

In the previous chapter, you learned how to enter formulas either by typing them or by using the pointing method. Using 1-2-3's @functions is a quicker and more accurate way to enter certain formulas. Functions reduce the number of keystrokes needed to enter a formula as well as reduce the likelihood of an error occurring. The @functions are built-in formulas that perform specialized calculations.

In Lotus, these functions are called "at functions" because each one begins with the "at" character (@). An @function is composed of three parts: the at symbol (@), the name of the function, and an argument or arguments enclosed by parentheses. The argument, which indicates what the function applies to, can be a single value or a range of cells.

Lotus includes both simple @functions, such as one that adds a range of cells, and more complex @functions, such as those that calculate loans, annuities, and cash flows over a period of time. Lotus includes eight categories of functions:

Mathematical @functions

Logical @functions

Special @functions

String @functions

Date and Time @functions

Financial @functions

Statistical @functions

Database @functions

Table 5-2 lists some of the more commonly used @functions.

TABLE 5-2 @Functions

Function	Description
@AVG	Calculates the average of a list of values
@MAX	Determines the maximum value in a list
@MIN	Determines the minimum value in a list
@SUM	Determines the sum of a list of values
@RAND	Determines a random number between 0 and 1
@ROUND	Rounds a value to a specified number of places
@SQRT	Determines the positive square root of a value

Order of Precedence

When more complex formulas are used on a worksheet, Lotus performs calculations in a specific order of precedence. The order of precedence, or order of operations, is the order in which calculations are performed in a formula that contains several operators. Table 5-3 shows operators that can be used in formulas, together with the order in which the operations are performed. If a formula contains operations that have the same precedence, they are performed sequentially from left to right.

There is a way to override the order of precedence listed in Table 5-3. Operations contained within parentheses are calculated before operations outside the parentheses. The operations within the parentheses are performed according to the order of precedence.

Take, for example the formula C12 + B12 * C12. If the contents of cell C12 is 2 and the contents of cell B12 is 5, the result of this formula is 12. Since multiplication is the second order of operations and addition is the third order of operations, Lotus would perform the multiplication first (5 * 2 = 10) and then the addition (2 + 10 = 12). If, however, the formula was entered as (C12 + B12) * C12, the result would be 14. In this case, Lotus would first perform the addition within parentheses (2 + 5 = 7) and then perform the multiplication (7 * 2 = 14).

TABLE 5-3 Order of Precedence

Order	Operator	Operation
First	^	Exponentiation
Second	*, /	Multiplication, Division
Third	+, -	Addition, Subtraction

YOUR TURN

In this exercise you are going to add some @functions to the FIRSTQTR worksheet. Start the Lotus program if necessary and retrieve the FIRSTQTR file.

1.   Column F keeps track of each sales representative's total sales for January, February, and March. You are going to enter a function that computes this total.

FIGURE 5-3 Using @ Functions

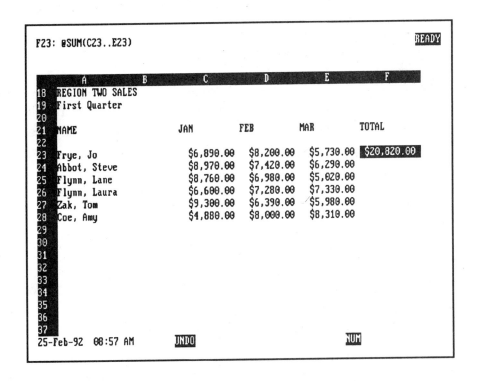

```
F23: @SUM(C23..E23)                                          READY

         A          B          C          D          E          F
18  REGION TWO SALES
19  First Quarter
20
21  NAME                   JAN        FEB        MAR        TOTAL
22
23  Frye, Jo            $6,890.00  $8,200.00  $5,730.00  $20,820.00
24  Abbot, Steve        $8,970.00  $7,420.00  $6,290.00
25  Flynn, Lane         $8,760.00  $6,980.00  $5,020.00
26  Flynn, Laura        $6,600.00  $7,280.00  $7,330.00
27  Zak, Tom            $9,300.00  $6,390.00  $5,980.00
28  Coe, Amy            $4,880.00  $8,000.00  $8,310.00
29
30
31
32
33
34
35
36
37
25-Feb-92  08:57 AM         UNDO                        NUM
```

Go to F8

Type: @SUM(C8..E8)

Press <Enter>

The total of cells C8, D8, and E8 appears immediately in cell F8.

Go to F23

Type: @SUM(C23..E23)

Press <Enter>

Your worksheet should look like Figure 5-3. Notice that the formula using the @SUM function is in the status line.

2. Save the amended FIRSTQTR file. You have finished with this Your Turn exercise. You can either leave the worksheet on your screen while you read the following section, or you can exit from the Lotus program.

Copying Functions

Previously you learned how to use the COPY command to copy labels. The COPY command also can be used to copy functions, but it works differently in this case, as explained in this section.

When a cell containing a function is copied, Lotus does not copy the value displayed in the cell on the worksheet. Rather, Lotus copies the function displayed in the status line. When the function is copied, Lotus automatically inserts the appropriate argument or arguments. For example, suppose a worksheet contains a list of values in columns B, C, and D, and a sum for each column needs to be calculated. First, the @SUM function is used to calculate the total for column B. Then, that function is copied into columns C and D to calculate the totals for those columns. Lotus automatically inserts the appropriate range of cells in the arguments for each function.

YOUR TURN

In this exercise you are going to copy the @SUM functions in the FIRSTQTR worksheet. Start the Lotus program if necessary and retrieve the FIRSTQTR file.

1. First, you are going to copy the @SUM function in F8 to cells F9 through F13.

>   Go to F8

>   / COPY

The prompt **Enter range to copy FROM** appears. You want to copy the @function in F8.

>   Press <Enter>

The prompt **Enter range to copy TO: F8** appears in the entry line. The mode indicator says POINT. The cell pointer is not anchored because there is only one cell address in the prompt.

>   Press <Down arrow> to move to F9

>   Press . (period) to anchor the cell pointer in F9

Notice the prompt now says **Enter range to copy TO: F9..F9**. You know the cell pointer is now anchored because two cell addresses appear in the prompt.

>   Press <Down arrow> four times

Your screen should look like Figure 5-4. The prompt says **Enter range to copy TO F9..F13**.

>   Press <Enter>

The totals for F9 through F13 appear. Go to F9. The @function in the status line should be @SUM(C9..E9). Lotus automatically changed the argument from (C8..E8) to (C9..E9).

FIGURE 5-4 Copying
@Functions

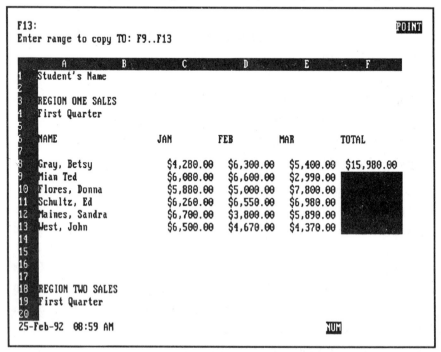

2. Now you want to copy the @function in F23 into cells F24 through F28.

> Go to F23
>
> / COPY
>
> Press <Enter> to copy F23
>
> Press <Down arrow> to move the cell pointer to F24
>
> Press . (period) to anchor the cell pointer in F24
>
> Press <Down arrow> four times to move the cell pointer to F28
>
> Press <Enter>

The totals appear in cells F24 through F28.

3. Save the amended FIRSTQTR file. You have finished with this Your Turn exercise. You can either leave the worksheet on your screen while you read the following section, or you can exit from the Lotus program.

❏ SORTING

Data that has been entered into a worksheet can be sorted in many different ways. It can be sorted alphabetically or numerically in ascending or descending order.

To sort data in a worksheet, select DATA from the Main menu. Next, select SORT. The Sort Settings window appears on the screen (see Figure 5-5). The first step in sorting data in a worksheet is to specify the range that is to be sorted. You have to be very careful in specifying the data range to be sorted. Lotus only moves those cells that are specified in the data range. Therefore, to keep the data intact, all the cells related to the data that is to be sorted must be included in the data range. Lotus will not move any cells

FIGURE 5-5 The Sort Settings Window

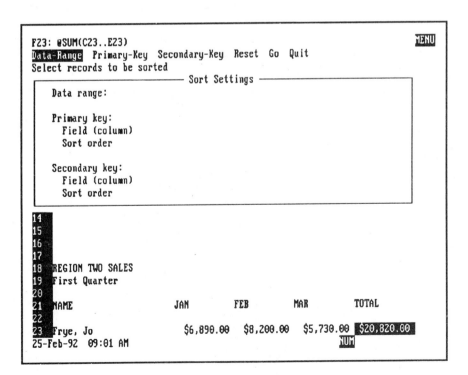

that are not included in the sort data range. You could end up with scrambled data , where some cells were moved and some cells were not. It is a good idea to make a copy of your worksheet before sorting it just in case a mistake is made. That way you can go back to the original worksheet and start over if necessary.

After the data range to be sorted has been selected, the primary key has to be selected. The primary key tells Lotus specifically which data to sort on. After selecting the primary key, you indicate whether the sort should be in ascending or descending order. You can also indicate a secondary key, which is the second data item Lotus would use to sort on. For example, look at Figures 5-6a and 5-6b. The first screen shows an unsorted worksheet. The store names and order amounts are entered in random order. The second screen shows the worksheet sorted using the store name as the primary key and the order amount as the

FIGURE 5-6a An Unsorted Worksheet

A1: 'OCTOBER ORDERS READY

	A	B	C	D	E	F	G
1	OCTOBER ORDERS						
2							
3	STORE				ORDER AMOUNT		
4	==						
5	Lige Green Flower & Gifts				$2,500.45		
6	Lexa's Greenhouse				$1,800.17		
7	Johnson's Baskets				$1,250.25		
8	Jones Decorating Center				$1,967.98		
9	Diamond Hill Flower Shop				$3,850.67		
10	Where the West Begins				$3,356.75		
11	Zachary's Gifts and Such				$4,298.50		
12	Daisy Patch Flowers				$980.58		
13	Jana's House				$2,500.45		
14	Lige Green Flower & Gifts				$383.45		
15	Diamond Hill Flower Shop				$876.53		
16	Autumn Place				$1,250.25		
17	Lexa's Greenhouse				$256.90		
18	Diamond Hill Flower Shop				$32.56		
19	Jan's Flowers & Wedding Catering				$2,845.25		
20							

25-Feb-92 09:26 AM UNDO NUM

FIGURE 5-6b Sorted Worksheet

A1: 'OCTOBER ORDERS READY

	A	B	C	D	E	F	G
1	OCTOBER ORDERS						
2							
3	STORE				ORDER AMOUNT		
4	==						
5	Autumn Place				$1,250.25		
6	Daisy Patch Flowers				$980.58		
7	Diamond Hill Flower Shop				$32.56		
8	Diamond Hill Flower Shop				$876.53		
9	Diamond Hill Flower Shop				$3,850.67		
10	Jana's House				$2,500.45		
11	Jan's Flowers & Wedding Catering				$2,845.25		
12	Johnson's Baskets				$1,250.25		
13	Jones Decorating Center				$1,967.98		
14	Lexa's Greenhouse				$256.90		
15	Lexa's Greenhouse				$1,800.17		
16	Lige Green Flower & Gifts				$383.45		
17	Lige Green Flower & Gifts				$2,500.45		
18	Where the West Begins				$3,356.75		
19	Zachary's Gifts and Such				$4,298.50		
20							

25-Feb-92 09:30 AM UNDO NUM

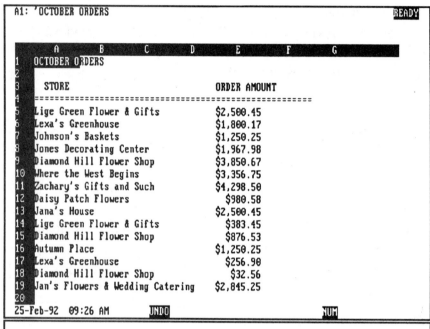

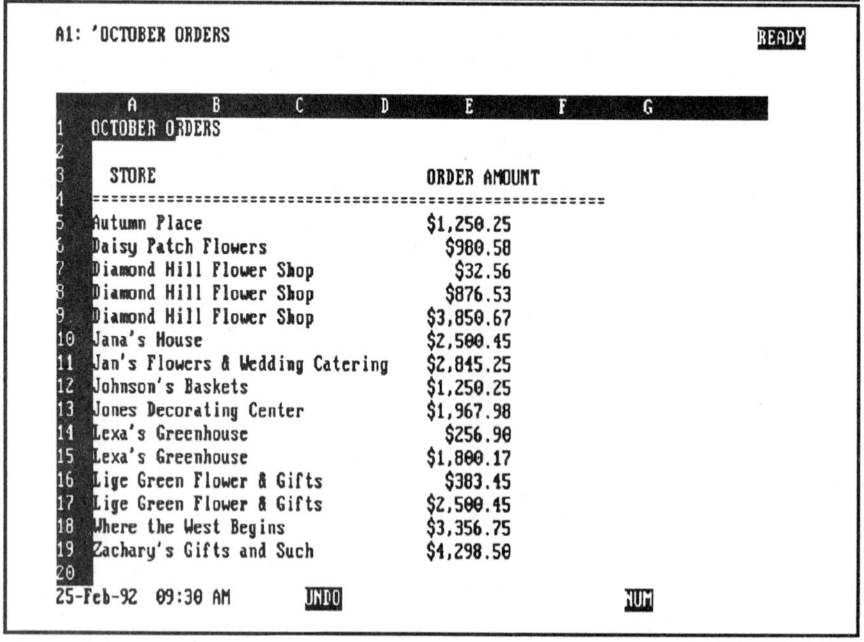

secondary key. Notice the stores are all grouped together and their order amounts listed in ascending order.

Once the data range, primary key, and, if desired, secondary key have been indicated, select GO and the worksheet is immediately sorted. The sorted worksheet can then be saved as a separate file.

YOUR TURN

In this exercise you are going to sort the FIRSTQTR worksheet. Start the Lotus program if necessary and retrieve the FIRSTQTR file.

1. Before you start the FIRSTQTR worksheet, you are going to make a copy of it, just in case you make a mistake and need to start over.

> / FILE SAVE
>
> Type: FIRSTSRT
>
> Press <Enter>

You will keep the FIRSTQTR file on your disk as a backup copy just in case you need it.

2. The first step in sorting the file is to select the data range. First you are going to sort the Region One sales representatives in order by the total amount each one sold.

> Go to A8
>
> / DATA SORT

The Sort Settings window should appear on your screen. First you are going to select the data range on which you want to sort.

> Select *DATA-RANGE*

The prompt in the entry line should say **Enter data range: A8**

> Press . (period)
>
> Press <Right arrow> five times
>
> Press <Down arrow> five times

Your screen should look like Figure 5-7. Even though you are only going to sort by each sales representative's total amount, all the data related to that data has to be included in the data range. If you selected column F only, the cells in column F would be the only ones to move during the sort. When you were finished, the data would all be scrambled and the total amounts would no longer coincide with the appropriate sales representative. Look at the Sort Settings window. The range A8..F13 should now appear as the data range.

3. Next you need to select the primary key. You are going to sort on the total amount sold, so data in column F is the primary key.

> Press <Enter>
>
> Select *PRIMARY-KEY*

To specify the primary key, you indicate any cell in the column you want 1-2-3 to use to sort the data. To sort on the TOTAL column, you need to move the cursor to any cell in column F.

FIGURE 5-7 Selecting the Data-Range on which to Sort

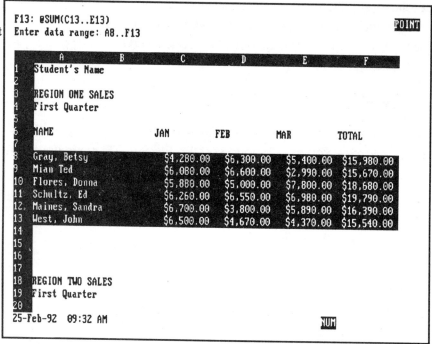

```
F13: @SUM(C13..E13)                                              POINT
Enter data range: A8..F13

            A          B         C          D          E          F
1    Student's Name
2
3    REGION ONE SALES
4    First Quarter
5
6    NAME                     JAN        FEB        MAR       TOTAL
7
8    Gray, Betsy           $4,280.00  $6,300.00  $5,400.00  $15,980.00
9    Mian Ted              $6,080.00  $6,600.00  $2,990.00  $15,670.00
10   Flores, Donna         $5,880.00  $5,000.00  $7,800.00  $18,680.00
11   Schultz, Ed           $6,260.00  $6,550.00  $6,980.00  $19,790.00
12   Maines, Sandra        $6,700.00  $3,800.00  $5,890.00  $16,390.00
13   West, John            $6,500.00  $4,670.00  $4,370.00  $15,540.00
14
15
16
17
18   REGION TWO SALES
19   First Quarter
20
25-Feb-92  09:32 AM                                             NUM
```

Go to F8

Press <Enter>

The prompt **Sort order (A or D)** appears in the entry line. The prompt is asking if you want the sort to be in ascending or descending order. You want the totals sorted in ascending order.

Type: A

Press <Enter>

You are now ready to sort the data.

Select GO

In a moment the worksheet returns to the screen. Look at the TOTAL column for Region One sales. It should be listed in ascending order.

4. Next, sort Region One sales in alphabetical order by sales representative.

/ DATA SORT

The Sort Settings window appears. The range of cells A8 through F13 should still be selected as the data range, so you do not have to select the data range again. You do, however, have to change the primary key.

Select PRIMARY-KEY

Go to A8

Press <Enter>

Press <Enter> to accept ascending as the sort order

Select GO

The Region One sales data should now be sorted alphabetically by sales representative.

5. Now you want to sort the data for Region Two alphabetically by sales representative.

> / DATA SORT

The Sort Settings window appears. You need to change the data range.

> *Select DATA-RANGE*
>
> Press <Esc> to cancel the current data-range settings
>
> Go to A23
>
> Press . (period) to anchor the cell pointer
>
> Press <Right arrow> five times
>
> Press <Down arrow> five times

The data range A23..F28 should be selected

> Press <Enter>

Since column A is still selected as the primary key, you do not need to reset it.

> *Select GO*

The Region Two sales data is now sorted alphabetically by sales representative.

6. Save the amended FIRSTSRT file. You have finished with this Your Turn exercise. You can either leave the worksheet on your screen while you read the following section, or you can exit from the Lotus program.

❏ ABSOLUTE AND RELATIVE CELL ADDRESSING

Earlier in this chapter, you learned how to copy functions. When Lotus copies functions or formulas, it uses what is called relative cell addressing. That is, the address of a cell is relative to its position on the worksheet. The column letter and row number change according to the position of the cell where the formula or function is copied.

Let's look at an example to help clarify this concept. Say you entered the function @SUM(C8..E8) in cell F8. If this function is copied to cells F9 through F13, the following appears in these cells:

F9	@SUM(C9..E9)
F1O	@SUM(C1O..E1O)
F11	@SUM(C11..E11)
F12	@SUM(C12..E12)
F13	@SUM(C13..E13)

Lotus automatically changed the row number to reflect the row number of the row into which the function was copied. If a formula or function is copied across columns rather than down rows, the column letters are automatically changed to reflect the column letter of the column into which the function or formula is copied.

Some formulas, however, need to use absolute cell addresses rather than relative cell addresses. What this means is that a column letter or row number (or both) of a cell address has to remain absolute, that is, unchanged, no matter where that formula is copied.

To indicate to Lotus that a column or row should be absolute, a dollar sign is entered before the column letter or row number. For example, if the formula $A12*5 is copied, the row number is relative, so it may change. The column letter A, however, is absolute because it has the dollar sign in front of it. Therefore, it will never change no matter where this formula is copied. If the formula A$12*5 is copied, the column letter is relative, so it may change when copied. The row number 12 is absolute because the dollar sign is in front of it, so it will never change when copied. Finally, if the formula A12*5 is copied, the entire cell address, A12, will never change no matter where in the worksheet that formula is copied because both the column and row are absolute.

YOUR TURN

In this exercise you are going to use absolute cell addressing in a formula for the FIRSTSRT worksheet. Start the Lotus program if necessary and retrieve the FIRSTSRT file.

1. The sales representatives earn a commission on their total sales each quarter. You are going to enter a formula that calculates their commission earnings.

> Go to C3
>
> Type: Commission Rate
>
> Press <Enter>
>
> Go to E3
>
> Type: .10
>
> Press <Enter>

The figure is the percentage rate the sales representatives earn in commission. It is appearing as currency, because you previously globally formatted the worksheet as currency. You need to format this cell as percentage.

> / RANGE FORMAT PERCENT
>
> Press <Enter> to accept default of two decimal places
>
> Press <Enter> to format cell E3

2. Next you need to enter the formula that calculates the commissions.

> Go to G6
>
> Type: COMMISSION
>
> Press <Enter>
>
> Go to G8
>
> Type: +F8*E3
>
> Press <Enter>

Since the commission percentage rate appears in cell E3 only, that specific cell can never change no matter where this formula is copied. Now copy the formula in G8 to cells G9 through G13. The cell pointer should still be in G8.

/ COPY

Press <Enter> to copy cell G8 only

Press <Down arrow> to move the cell pointer to G9

Press . (period) to anchor the cell pointer in G9

Press <Down arrow> four times

The range of cells G9 through G13 should be highlighted.

Press <Enter>

Move the cursor down through column G to look at the formulas. Notice that the first cell address in the formula changes because it is relative, but the address E3 never changes because both the column and row are absolute.

3. Now figure the commission rate for the Region Two sales representatives.

Go to G21

Type: COMMISSION

Press <Enter>

Go to G23

Type: +F23*E3

Press <Enter>

/ COPY

Press <Enter> to copy cell G23

Press <Down arrow> to move cell pointer to G24

Press . (period) to anchor the cell pointer in G24

Press <Down arrow> four times

The range of cells G24 through G28 should be highlighted.

Press <Enter>

The commissions for Region Two are calculated.

4. Save the amended FIRSTSRT file. You have finished with this Your Turn exercise. You can either leave the worksheet on your screen while you read the following section, or you can exit from the Lotus program.

❏ FREEZING TITLES

Up to this point, all the worksheets you have used fit within the window. More complex and larger worksheets, however, may not fit within the window. As the user moves around a large worksheet, columns and rows of information scroll off the computer screen. Usually this is not a problem, unless titles identifying the rows and columns also scroll off the screen. A screen full of numbers with no identifying labels can be confusing. Lotus solves that problem by including a feature that "freezes" titles. If a row or column of titles is frozen, those titles do not scroll off the computer screen as the user moves around a large worksheet.

TABLE 5-4 Titles Options

Option	Description
Both	The rows above the cell pointer and the columns to the left of the cell pointer will not scroll off the screen.
Horizontal	The rows above the cell pointer will not scroll off the screen.
Vertical	The columns of the screen to the left of the cell pointer will not scroll off the screen.
Clear	All the existing titles are unfrozen.

To freeze titles, the user must position the cell pointer one row below the rows to be frozen and one column to the right of the columns to be frozen. After positioning the cell pointer, select the WORKSHEET option from the Main menu, then select TITLES. There are four TITLES options from which to select. Table 5-4 lists these options and describes their functions.

The cell pointer keys cannot be used to move into a row or column that has been frozen. To go to a cell within a row that is frozen, use the GOTO key, <F5>.

A second copy of the title rows and/or title columns is displayed on the screen. There are two ways to remove this second copy. If the CLEAR option is selected from the TITLES menu, all the existing titles are unfrozen and the second copy is removed. Another way to remove the second copy is to press <PgDn> and then <PgUp> for rows, or <Tab> and <Shift>-<Tab> for columns.

YOUR TURN

In this exercise you are going to practice freezing titles. Start the Lotus program if necessary and retrieve the FIRSTSRT file.

1.　All of the FIRSTSRT file does not fit in the window at one time. If you move the cell pointer over to display the COMMISSION column, the names of the sales representatives scroll off the screen. You want to freeze columns A and B on the screen, so that the names will not scroll off.

　　　　　Press <Home>

The cell pointer moves to A1. You have to move the cell pointer one column to the right of the columns you want to freeze.

　　　　　Go to C1

　　　　　/ WORKSHEET TITLES VERTICAL

　　　　　Columns A and B are now frozen.

　　　　　Press <F5> for GOTO

　　　　　Type:　G1

　　　　　Press <Enter>

Your screen should look like Figure 5-8. Columns A and B remain on the screen so you can identify the commission figures.

FIGURE 5-8 Freezing Titles

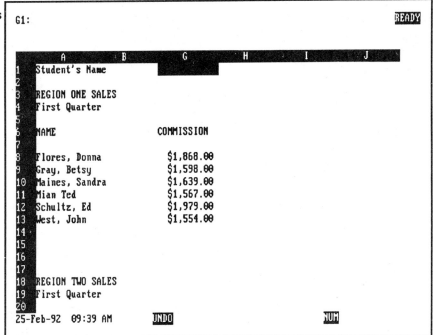

Press <Down arrow> to view the Region Two sales

Press <Left arrow> twice

The other months scroll back onto the screen so you can view them.

2. You are now ready to clear the titles.

/ WORKSHEET TITLES CLEAR

Columns A and B are no longer frozen on your screen.

3. Save the FIRSTSRT file. You have finished with this Your Turn exercise. You can either leave the worksheet on your screen while you read the following section, or you can exit from the Lotus program.

❏ SPREADSHEET ANALYSIS

Once a worksheet has been created, it is easy to experiment with various options. After changes are made, Lotus automatically recalculates the worksheet to reflect those changes. Numerous alternatives to a single plan can be projected and evaluated, so the spreadsheet is an invaluable tool in decision making.

YOUR TURN

In this exercise you are going to experiment with what-if analysis by making changes to the commission percentage rate. Start the Lotus program if necessary and retrieve the FIRST-SRT file.

1. Right now the commission rate is 10 percent. The regional sales manager wants to know how the commissions would be affected if commissions went down to 8 percent. First you want to freeze column A so the names will always appear on the screen.

> Press <Home>
>
> Go to C1
>
> / WORKSHEET TITLES VERTICAL

Now the sales representatives' names will always appear on the screen.

> Go to G8

Jot down on a piece of paper all the sale representatives' commissions.

> Go to E3
>
> Type: .08
>
> Press <Enter>

Now look at the commission rates. Lotus automatically recalculated them to reflect an 8 percent commission rate. Change the commission rate to 12 percent and look at the change.

2. You can continue to experiment with what-if analysis by changing the percentage rate. When you have finished experimenting, change the percentage rate back to 10 percent.

3. Save the FIRSTSRT file. You have finished with this Your Turn exercise. You can either leave the worksheet on your screen while you read the following sections, or you can exit from the Lotus program.

❏ GRAPHICS

The purpose of business graphics is to develop charts and analytical graphs for financial analysis. Numeric data can be transformed into multicolored charts and graphs for analyzing markets, forecasting sales, comparing stock trends, and planning business and home finances. Frequently used in presentations and reports, business graphics often can present information more effectively than a column of numbers. Two of the more commonly used types of graphs are bar graphs and pie charts.

Bar Graphs and Pie Charts

A bar graph can be used to make a quantitative comparison of several subjects' performances. Numeric values are represented as vertical bars, each of which depicts the value of a single cell in the worksheet. The X axis, a horizontal line, has labels identifying what each bar represents. The Y axis, a vertical line, has scaled numeric divisions corresponding to the worksheet values being represented.

Two types of bar graphs often are used in analytical graphs. A simple bar graph depicts the changes in one set of values, whereas a multiple bar graph depicts the relationships among changes in several sets of values. For example, a simple bar graph might chart how many blue jeans a clothing store sold in the spring, summer, fall, and winter (see Figure 5-9). A multiple bar graph might compare the numbers of blue jeans sold to the numbers of corduroy slacks and chino pants sold in the spring, summer, fall, and winter. Each season would have three bars above it; one bar for blue jeans, one for corduroy slacks, and one for chino pants (see Figure 5-10).

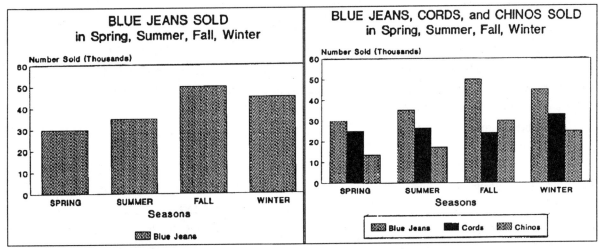

FIGURE 5-9 A Simple Bar Graph   **FIGURE 5-10 A Multiple Bar Graph**

In Figures 5-9 and 5-10, the vertical line or Y axis contains the numeric data ranges from 0 to 60. Notice the word *Thousands* in parentheses at the top of the graph. This means each of the numeric values along the vertical line should be multiplied by 1,000. The first bar in the graph in Figure 5-9 reaches the 30 mark on the Y axis. This means 30,000 blue jeans were sold in the spring.

A pie chart represents a whole subject divided into parts. It looks like a circle divided into wedges, like slices of a pie, and shows the relationships among the sizes of the wedges and the whole pie. The pie stands for the total, and each wedge stands for one data item. In Figure 5-11, the entire pie represents the total number of pants sold in winter. Each wedge represents one style of pants. This pie chart indicates that in winter, 44 percent of all the pants sold were blue jeans, 32 percent were corduroy, and 24 percent were chinos.

With Lotus 1-2-3, data contained in a worksheet can be transformed easily into a graph. In addition, if a number is changed on the worksheet, that change is immediately reflected in the graph. Five different types of graphs can be drawn with 1-2-3: line graphs, bar graphs, stacked-bar graphs, pie charts, and XY graphs. Bar graphs, line graphs, and pie charts are covered in this chapter.

FIGURE 5-11 A Pie Chart

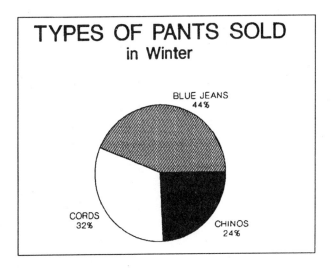

Creating a Bar Graph and a Line Graph

In order to use 1-2-3's graphics feature, your computer must be equipped with certain hardware. It must have either a color graphics board and a color (or monochrome) monitor, or a board that enables you to display graphics on a monochrome monitor. Without this hardware, the computer will beep when you try to display a graph. The graph can, however, be saved in a file and then printed through the PrintGraph feature of the Lotus Access System.

Commands from the 1-2-3 GRAPH menu are used to create a graph. The first step is to retrieve the file containing the data to be used for the graph. Next, the graph type has to be selected. To select the type of graph, choose the GRAPH option from the Main menu. The GRAPH options appear in the entry line and the Graph Settings window appears (see Figure 5-12). Table 5-5 describes the function of each option.

After you have selected TYPE from the GRAPH menu, the options LINE, BAR, XY, STACKED-BAR, and PIE appear in the entry line. Select the type of graph to be drawn. Once the type of graph has been selected, the GRAPH menu appears in the entry line. The next step in creating a graph is to specify which data ranges are to be used for the graph and what labels are to be used to describe that data. The options used to accomplish this step are the range commands (X, A, B, C, D, E, F) from the GRAPH menu.

The X option is used to select the range of labels. On a bar graph, each label on the X axis corresponds to a bar or multiple bars. On a line graph, each label corresponds to a data point in the line. The A-F options are used to specify ranges of data. Up to six ranges can be specified for a bar or line graph. After the data ranges and labels have been chosen, the graph can be viewed using the VIEW option in the GRAPH menu.

FIGURE 5-12 The Graph Settings Window

```
A1: 'Student's Name                                                        MENU
Type  X  A  B  C  D  E  F  Reset  View  Save  Options  Name  Group  Quit
Line  Bar  XY  Stack-Bar  Pie
      ┌────────────────────── Graph Settings ──────────────────────┐
      │ Type: Line              Titles: First                       │
      │                                 Second                      │
      │   X:                            X axis                      │
      │   A:                            Y axis                      │
      │   B:                                                        │
      │   C:                                    Y scale:   X scale: │
      │   D:                            Scaling Automatic  Automatic│
      │   E:                            Lower                       │
      │   F:                            Upper                       │
      │                                 Format   (G)        (G)     │
      │   Grid: None       Color: No    Indicator Yes       Yes     │
      │                                                             │
      │     Legend:             Format:  Data labels:      Skip: 1  │
      │   A                     Both                                │
      │   B                     Both                                │
      │   C                     Both                                │
      │   D                     Both                                │
      │   E                     Both                                │
      │   F                     Both                                │
      └─────────────────────────────────────────────────────────────┘
   25-Feb-92  10:00 AM                                        NUM
```

TABLE 5-5 Graph Options

Option	Description
Type	Enables the user to select which of the five types of graphs is to be drawn
X, A-F (Ranges)	Enables the user to select which of the five types of graphs is to be drawn
Reset	Enables the user to select the ranges of the worksheet from which the graph is to be drawn and labeled
View	Enables the user to view the current graph
Save	Saves the current graph as a file for later printing
Options	Enables the user to add legends or titles to the graph or to alter its appearance
Name	Enables the user to save the current graph settings under a graph name
Group	Enables the user to set all the graph data ranges at once
Quit	Returns the worksheet to the READY mode

Adding Options to a Graph

After a basic graph has been created, it can be enhanced using the options found in the OPTIONS menu. The OPTIONS menu enables the user to add legends that identify shading patterns used in bar graphs or pie charts and symbols used as the data points in line graphs, add titles to the graph, include horizontal and vertical grid lines and so on. Table 5-6 lists the options found in the OPTIONS menu and describes their functions.

Saving and Naming a Graphics File

After a graph has been created in Lotus 1-2-3 it must be *both* saved and named. There is an important difference between these two commands found in the GRAPH menu.

TABLE 5-6 Options from the OPTIONS Menu

Option	Description
Legend	Creates legends for the data ranges in a graph
Format	In line and XY graphs, sets whether data points are connected with lines, whether symbols are used to mark the points, whether both symbols and lines are used, or neither symbols nor lines are used
Titles	Adds graph titles and axis titles to a graph
Grid	Adds or removes grid lines from a graph
Scale	Determines the axis scaling and sets the format of the numbers that appear along the axis
Color	Displays graphs in color on a color monitor
B&W	Displays graphics in black and white
Data-labels	Identifies a range of cells as labels for the data points in a line graph or the bars in a bar graph
Quit	Returns to the GRAPH menu

If you want to print a graph, it has to be saved using the SAVE option. After selecting SAVE from the GRAPH menu, the prompt **Enter graph file name:** appears in the entry line. The name of the graph can be up to eight characters long. Lotus automatically adds the extension PIC to the name of the graph. If you exit from a worksheet without saving a graph, that graph cannot be printed. A graph must be saved as a PIC, that is with the PIC extension that Lotus automatically provides, before it can be printed.

Graphs are linked to the worksheet from which they were created. If you create a graph and want to be able to retrieve that graph at a later date, it must be named using the NAME option from the GRAPH menu. If you exit from a worksheet without naming the graph you created, it is impossible to retrieve that graph. Your only option at that point is to recreate the graph from scratch. To name a graph, select NAME from the GRAPH menu. Next select CREATE. The prompt **Enter graph name** appears in the entry line. You can use the same graph name when saving and naming a graph. Once a graph has been named, it can be retrieved by selecting NAME from the GRAPH menu and then selecting USE. A list of all the graphs that have been created using the current worksheet appears in the prompt line. Highlight the name of the graph you want to retrieve and press <Enter>.

Remember, if you want to be able to print a graph, you must save it using the SAVE option from the GRAPH menu. If you want to be able to retrieve a graph you created at a later date, you must name the graph using the NAME option from the GRAPH menu. Finally, after creating one or more graphs from a worksheet, the worksheet file must be saved before exiting from that particular worksheet.

YOUR TURN

You are going to create a simple bar graph, a multiple bar graph, and a line graph using the FIRSTSRT.WK1 file. Start the Lotus program if necessary and retrieve the FIRSTSRT file.

1. First you are going to create a simple bar graph that shows the sales figures for Donna Flores in January, February, and March.

> / GRAPH

The Graph Settings window appears. Notice that the type of graph is set for line. You want to change it to bar.

> *Select TYPE*

> *Select BAR*

The type of graph is now listed as a bar graph in the Graph Settings window.

2. Next you have to select the data ranges. Range X selects the labels. In this graph the labels are the months.

> *Select X*

The worksheet returns to the screen. The prompt **Enter x-axis range** appears.

> Go to C6

> Press . (period) to anchor the cell pointer in C6

> Press <Right arrow> two times

The range of cells C6 through E6 should now be highlighted.

> Press <Enter>

The Graph Settings window returns to the screen. Notice the range C6..E6 is now entered in the Graph Settings window next to the X range.

> *Select A*

The worksheet returns to the screen. The A range is Donna's sales in January, February, and March.

> Go to C8
>
> Press . (period) to anchor the cell pointer in C8
>
> Press <Right arrow> two times
>
> Press <Enter>

You can now view the graph.

> *Select VIEW*

Your screen should look like Figure 5-13. When you have finished viewing the bar graph, press the Space Bar.

3. Next, you want to create a multiple bar graph. You want to show entire Region One sales for the first quarter. To do this, you need to select the rest of the sales representatives as the B, C, D, E, and F data ranges.

> *Select B*
>
> Go to C9
>
> Press . (period) to anchor the cell pointer in C9
>
> Press <Right arrow> two times

**FIGURE 5-13 Creating a
Simple Bar Graph**

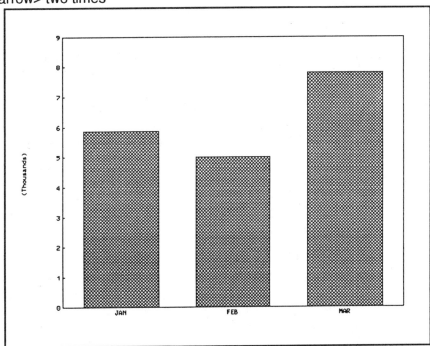

Press <Enter>

Select C

Go to C10

Press . (period) to anchor the cell pointer in C10

Press <Right arrow> two times

Press <Enter>

Select D

Go to C11

Press . (period) to anchor the cell pointer in C11

Press <Right arrow> two times

Press <Enter>

Select E

Go to C12

Press . (period) to anchor the cell pointer in C12

Press <Right arrow> two times

Press <Enter>

Select F

Go to C13

Press . (period) to anchor the cell pointer in C13

Press <Right arrow> two times

Press <Enter>

Select VIEW

Your screen should look like Figure 5-14. You now have six bars, one for each sales representative over each month. You cannot tell by looking at the graph, however, what these
bars represent.

4. To help clarify the graph, you are going to enhance it using options from the OPTIONS
menu.

Press the Space Bar to clear the graph from the screen.

Select OPTIONS

Select LEGEND

Select A

Type: Flores

Press <Enter>

Select LEGEND

Select B

Type: Gray

FIGURE 5-14 Creating a Multiple Bar Graph

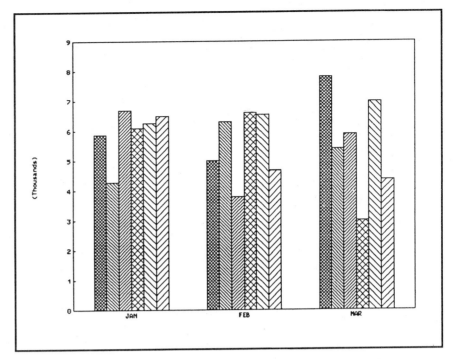

Press <Enter>

Select LEGEND

Select C

Type: Maines

Press <Enter>

Select LEGEND

Select D

Type: Mian

Press <Enter>

Select LEGEND

Select E

Type: Schultz

Press <Enter>

Select LEGEND

Select F

Type: West

Press <Enter>

The sales representatives' names are now all entered in the legend portion of the Graph Settings window. Next you want to add some titles.

Select TITLES

Select FIRST

Type: REGION ONE SALES

Press <Enter>

Select TITLES

Select SECOND

Type: First Quarter

Press <Enter>

Select TITLES

Select X-AXIS

Type: Month

Press <Enter>

Select TITLES

Select Y-AXIS

Type: Sales

Press <Enter>

View the graph again.

Select QUIT

Select VIEW

Your screen should look like Figure 5-15. Now the graph is much easier to understand.

5.   Before you create a line graph, you must save and name this bar graph.

Press the Space Bar to clear the graph from the screen

Select SAVE

FIGURE 5-15 Adding Options to a Graph

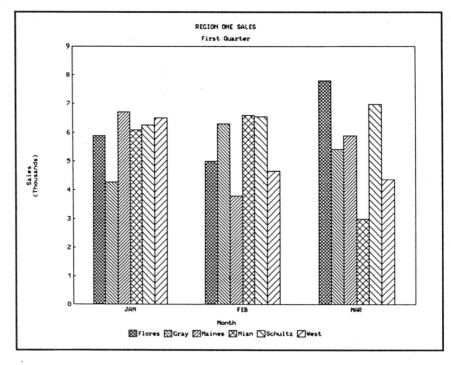

Application Software Manual

The prompt **Enter graph file name** appears in the entry line.

> Type: `R1-BAR`
>
> Press <Enter>
>
> *Select NAME*
>
> *Select CREATE*
>
> Type: `R1-BAR`
>
> Press <Enter>

Now you can create a line graph using the same data selected for the bar graph.

> *Select TYPE*
>
> *Select LINE*

You want to include the grid option on the line graph.

> *Select OPTIONS*
>
> *Select GRID*
>
> *Select HORIZONTAL*
>
> *Select QUIT*
>
> *Select VIEW*

Your screen should look like Figure 5-16. You now need to save and name the line graph.

> Press the Space Bar to clear the graph from the screen
>
> *Select SAVE*
>
> Type: `R1-LINE`
>
> Press <Enter>

FIGURE 5-16 Creating a Line Graph

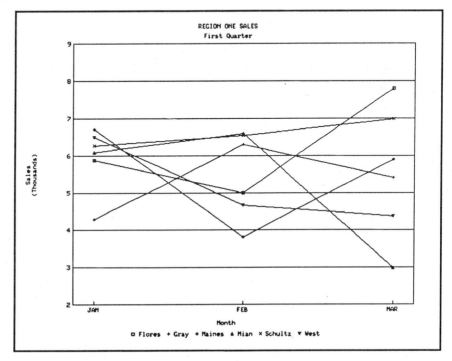

Select NAME

Select CREATE

Type: `R1-LINE`

Press <Enter>

6. You have finished creating graphs for now. You must be sure to save the entire worksheet now so that all the graph settings will be saved.

Press <Esc>

Select FILE

Select SAVE

Press <Enter>

Select REPLACE

You have finished with this Your Turn exercise. You can either leave the worksheet on your screen while you read the following section, or you can exit from the Lotus program.

Creating a Pie Chart

Creating a pie chart is slightly different from creating bar graphs or line graphs. Up to six data ranges can be graphed in a line or bar graph. In a pie chart only one data range can be graphed. That is because a pie chart represents a picture of one subject divided into parts. The entire pie chart represents the total of one category while each wedge in the pie represents one data item within that category. A pie chart cannot represent two categories at the same time.

When creating a pie chart, Lotus allows you to create what are called exploded wedges. An exploded wedge is a wedge, or slice, that has been separated from the rest of the pie for emphasis (see Figure 5-17). Often the largest or smallest wedge of the pie is exploded to draw attention to that wedge. In Figure 5-17, the smallest wedge has been exploded.

To explode a wedge in a Lotus pie chart, you first have to enter code numbers on the worksheet that correspond to each wedge in the pie. These code numbers also designate the shading pattern used for that wedge. Lotus includes seven shading patterns numbered 1 through 7. To designate shading patterns for

FIGURE 5-17 Pie Chart with One Wedge Exploded

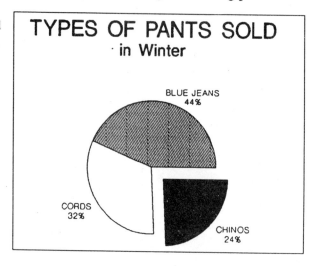

the wedges in the pie chart, enter a different number from 1 to 7 for each wedge in the pie chart. Then, select that range of code numbers as the B range for the pie chart. To explode a wedge, add 100 to the code number for that wedge.

 YOUR TURN

You are going to create a pie chart using the FIRSTSRT.WK1 file. Start the Lotus program if necessary and retrieve the FIRSTSRT file.

1. The settings for the last graph you created will still be current, so the first step is to clear all the graph settings.

> / GRAPH RESET

You can clear all the graph settings, or you can clear individual parts of the graph. You want to clear all the graph settings.

> *Select GRAPH*

The Graph Settings window is now all clear.

2. For this pie chart, you want to show the total sales figures for Region Two. Remember, a pie chart can only show one data range.

> *Select TYPE*
>
> *Select PIE*
>
> *Select X*
>
> Go to A23
>
> Press . (period) to anchor the cell pointer in cell A23
>
> Press <Down arrow> five times
>
> Press <Enter>
>
> *Select A*
>
> Go to F23
>
> Press . (period) to anchor the cell pointer in cell F23
>
> Press <Down arrow> five times
>
> Press <Enter>
>
> *Select VIEW*

Your screen should look like Figure 5-18. Notice that Lotus automatically computed the percentage of each wedge to the total.

3. Next you want to add some options to the pie chart as well as some shading patterns.

> Press the Space Bar to clear the graph from the screen
>
> *Select OPTIONS*
>
> *Select TITLES*

FIGURE 5-18 Creating a Pie Chart

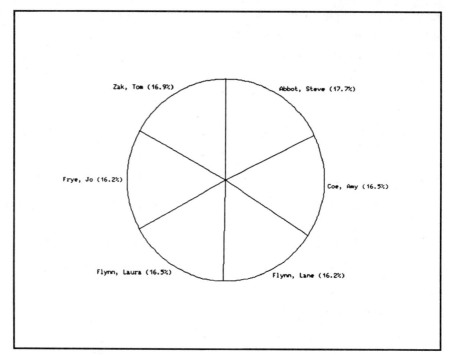

Select *FIRST*

Type: REGION ONE TOTAL SALES

Press <Enter>

Select *TITLES*

Select *SECOND*

Type: First Quarter

Press <Enter>

Now you want to add codes for shading patterns.

Press <Esc> three times

The worksheet should be in the ready mode. Enter the following codes in the cells indicated:

Cell	Code Number	Cell	Code Number
H23	1	H26	4
H24	2	H27	5
H25	3	H28	6

Format the code numbers as GENERAL.

Go to H23

/ RANGE FORMAT GENERAL

Press <Down arrow> five times

Press <Enter>

Now you want to select these code numbers as the B data range.

/ GRAPH B

164   **Application Software Manual**

Go to H23

Press . (period) to anchor the cell pointer in H23

Press <Down arrow> five times

Press <Enter>

Select VIEW

Now each wedge has a different shading pattern.

4. Next you want to explode the wedge that represents the largest total sales, which is the wedge for Steve Abbot at 17.7 percent.

Press the Space Bar to erase the graph from the screen

Press <Esc> two times to return the worksheet to the READY mode

The code number that corresponds to Steve Abbot's wedge is in cell H23. You need to add 100 to this code number to explode his wedge.

Go to H23

Type: 101

Press <Enter>

/ GRAPH VIEW

Your screen should look like Figure 5-19.

5. Next, you want to both save and name the pie chart.

Press the Space Bar to clear the graph from the screen.

Select SAVE

Type: R2-PIE

**FIGURE 5- 19 Exploding a
Wedge of a Pie Chart**

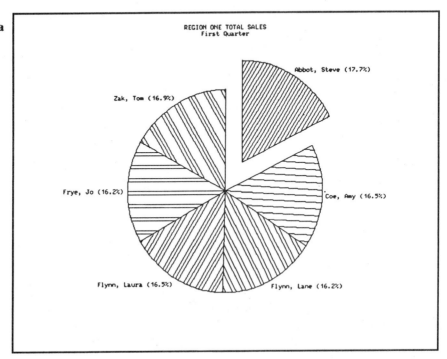

Press <Enter>

Select NAME

Select CREATE

Type: `R2-PIE`

Press <Enter>

6. You have finished creating graphs for now. You must be sure to save the entire worksheet now so that all the graph settings will be saved.

Press <Esc>

Select FILE

Select SAVE

Press <Enter>

Select REPLACE

You have finished with this Your Turn exercise. You can either leave the worksheet on your screen while you read the following section, or you can exit from the Lotus program.

❏ PRINTING A GRAPH

Before trying to print a graph, you need to perform three steps. First, make sure the printer is capable of printing graphics. Next, check to make sure the 1-2-3 Install program for the printer has been run. The printer you will be using to print the graphs has to be installed properly before the graphs can be printed. Finally, make sure the printer is properly hooked up to the computer, is turned on, and has plenty of paper.

The PrintGraph program is started from the Access System menu, so you need to exit from 1-2-3 before you can print a graph. Before exiting, make sure the final version of the worksheet and graph file or files have been saved. If you accessed 1-2-3 by typing `Lotus` at the system prompt, the Access System menu appears after exiting. If you started by typing `123,` the operating system prompt appears. At the system prompt, type `Lotus` and the Access System menu appears on the screen.

When the Access System menu appears, select PRINTGRAPH. The PrintGraph screen appears (see Figure 5-20). The PrintGraph menu has six options, which are described in Table 5-7.

Difference Box: Printing Graphs on a Computer with Two Floppy Disk Drives

To print a graph using a computer with two floppy disk drives, you need the Lotus System Disk, the PrintGraph Disk, and the data disk containing the graph files you want to print. Boot the computer with the DOS disk. When the A> system prompt appears on the screen, take the DOS disk out of drive A. Place the Lotus System Disk into drive A. Place your data disk into drive B. Type: `Lotus` and press <Enter>. The 1-2-3 Access System menu appears. Take the Lotus System Disk out of Drive A and place the PrintGraph Disk into drive A. Select PRINTGRAPH from the Access System menu. The PrintGraph menu appears on the screen.

Application Software Manual

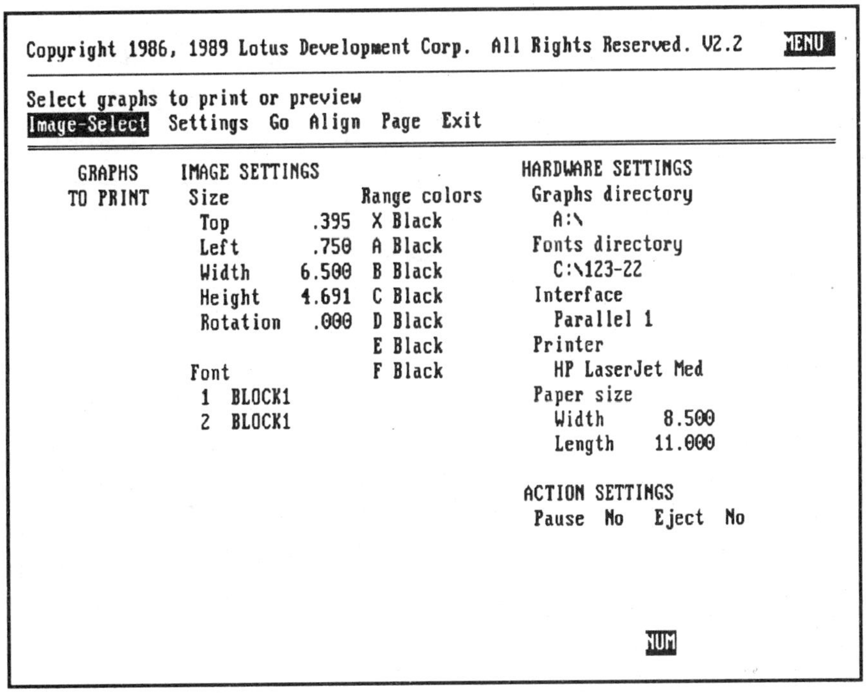

FIGURE 5-20 The PrintGraph Screen

```
Copyright 1986, 1989 Lotus Development Corp.  All Rights Reserved.  V2.2   [MENU]

Select graphs to print or preview
[Image-Select]  Settings  Go  Align  Page  Exit

        GRAPHS     IMAGE SETTINGS                    HARDWARE SETTINGS
        TO PRINT     Size                              Graphs directory
                       Top      .395   Range colors      A:\
                       Left     .750   X Black          Fonts directory
                       Width   6.500   A Black            C:\123-22
                       Height  4.691   B Black          Interface
                       Rotation .000   C Black            Parallel 1
                                       D Black          Printer
                                       E Black            HP LaserJet Med
                     Font              F Black          Paper size
                     1  BLOCK1                            Width    8.500
                     2  BLOCK1                            Length  11.000

                                                        ACTION SETTINGS
                                                        Pause  No    Eject  No




                                                               [NUM]
```

Selecting Hardware Settings

Before printing a graph, the hardware settings must be set properly. The Graphs Directory must be set to the drive where the file containing the graphs you want to print is located. The PrintGraph program uses fonts to print labels and titles for graph files. The PrintGraph fonts are located in the same directory as the PrintGraph program. The Fonts Directory has to be set for the location of the PrintGraph program files.

The current Graphs Directory setting is listed under HARDWARE SETTINGS on the screen. If you are using a computer with a hard disk drive, and your graph files are in drive A, the Graphs Directory should be set for A:. If you are using a computer with two floppy disk drives and your graph files are in drive B, the Graphs Directory should be set for B:. If it is necessary to set the Graphs Directory, select SETTINGS from the PrintGraph menu. The SETTINGS menu appears. Select HARDWARE from the SETTINGS menu and the HARDWARE menu appears. Select GRAPHS-DIRECTORY from the HARDWARE menu. The prompt, **Enter directory containing graph files** appears. Type the drive letter followed by a colon and press <Enter>. The HARDWARE menu returns to the screen.

The current Fonts Directory setting is listed under HARDWARE SETTINGS on the screen. If you are using a computer with a hard disk drive, and your PrintGraph files are in the 123 directory in drive C, the Fonts Directory should be set for C:\123. If you are using a computer with two floppy disk drives and your PrintGraph files are in drive A, the Fonts Directory should be set for A:.

If it is necessary to set the Fonts Directory, select SETTINGS from the PrintGraph menu. The SETTINGS menu appears. Select HARDWARE from the SETTINGS menu and the HARDWARE menu appears. Select FONTS-DIRECTORY from the HARDWARE menu. The prompt, **Enter directory containing font (.FNT) files** appears. Type the drive letter where the PrintGraph program is located followed by a colon and press <Enter>. The HARDWARE menu returns to the screen.

Another setting needs to be made from the HARDWARE menu. Graphs can be printed at high density or low density. If you are using a dot-matrix printer, high density graphs look much better, but they take longer to print. Low-density graphs are of draft quality, but they print much faster. The difference between the high-density and low-density setting is how many dots per inch the printer prints. The high-density setting prints more dots per inch, which produces a high-quality graph and, consequently, slows down the printing time. The low-density setting prints fewer dots per inch, which speeds up the printing time but produces a graph of poorer quality. To set the resolution of the printer, select PRINTER from the HARDWARE menu. A menu with the printers that have been installed appears. There should be a low-density and a high-density option for your printer. Move the highlight to the option you wish to select and press the Space Bar. The number symbol (#) appears next to the setting you selected. To turn a selection off, move the highlight to it and press the Space Bar again. After the printer has been selected, press <Enter>. The HARDWARE menu returns to the screen. To return to the PrintGraph menu, press <Esc>.

Difference Box: Setting the Directories on a Computer with Two Floppy Disk Drives

Look at the settings for the Graph Directory and the Fonts Directory listed under HARDWARE SETTINGS. For a computer with two floppy disk drives, the setting for the Graph Directory should be B:\, and the setting for the Fonts Directory should be A:\. If these settings are not correct, use the following steps to change them.

> *Select SETTINGS*
> *Select HARDWARE*
> *Select GRAPHS-DIRECTORY*
> Type: B:\
> Press <Enter>
> *Select FONTS-DIRECTORY*
> Type: A:\
> Press <Enter>
> Press <Esc> twice to return to the PrintGraph menu

Selecting the Size of the Graph

Graphs can be printed on a full sheet of 8 1/2- by 11-inch paper, printed half size so that two graphs will fit on one page, or you can use your own settings to tailor the graph to whatever size you choose. The option that allows you to do this is the IMAGE option on the SETTINGS menu. Select SIZE from the IMAGE menu. From the SIZE menu you can select FULL to print the graph on a full sheet of paper, HALF to print the graph on a half sheet of paper, or set your own dimensions by selecting MANUAL.

Selecting an Image to Print

The IMAGE-SELECT option from the PrintGraph menu allows you to designate which graphs you want to print. Select IMAGE-SELECT from the PrintGraph menu. A list of the graph files, that is files with the PIC extension, found in the Graph Directory appears. Select the graph or graphs you wish to print by moving the highlight to the graph name and pressing the Space Bar. If you want to view a graph before selecting it, highlight the graph name and press <F1O>. When you have finished viewing the graph, press the Space Bar to erase the graph from the screen.

YOUR TURN

In this exercise you are going to print the graphs you created. The Access System menu has to be on the screen. If a worksheet is on the screen, save it and select QUIT from the Main menu. If the system prompt appears, enter `Lotus` to retrieve the Access System menu. If you are starting the Lotus program, type `Lotus` at the system prompt.

1. The Access System menu should be on your screen.

   Select PRINTGRAPH

The PrintGraph menu appears. Look at the settings for the Graph Directory and the Fonts Directory listed under HARDWARE SETTINGS. For a computer with a hard disk drive, the setting for the Graph Directory should be A:\ and the setting for the Fonts directory should be C:\123. If these settings are not correct, use the following steps to change them.

   Select SETTINGS

   Select HARDWARE

   Select GRAPHS-DIRECTORY

   Type: `A:\`

   Press <Enter>

   Select FONTS-DIRECTORY

   Type: `C:\123`

   Press <Enter>

   Press <Esc> twice to return to the PrintGraph menu

2. Next, set the printer resolution.

   Select SETTINGS

   Select HARDWARE

   Select PRINTER

Move the highlight to the low-density setting for your printer.

   Press the Space Bar

   Press <Enter>

   Select QUIT

Now you want to select to print on a half-page of paper.

   Select IMAGE

   Select SIZE

   Select HALF

   Select QUIT to exit from the SIZE menu

   Select QUIT to exit from the IMAGE menu

FIGURE 5-21 Selecting the Graphs to Print

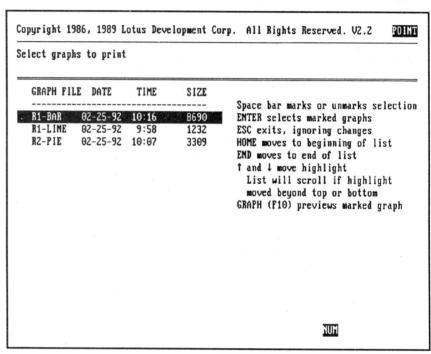

```
Copyright 1986, 1989 Lotus Development Corp.  All Rights Reserved. V2.2   POINT

Select graphs to print


   GRAPH FILE  DATE      TIME    SIZE
   -----------------------------------       Space bar marks or unmarks selection
   R1-BAR     02-25-92  10:16   8690          ENTER selects marked graphs
   R1-LINE    02-25-92   9:58   1232          ESC exits, ignoring changes
   R2-PIE     02-25-92  10:07   3309          HOME moves to beginning of list
                                              END moves to end of list
                                              ↑ and ↓ move highlight
                                                 List will scroll if highlight
                                                 moved beyond top or bottom
                                              GRAPH (F10) previews marked graph




                                                                      NUM
```

Select QUIT to exit from the SETTINGS menu

3. Now you want to select your graphs to print.

> *Select IMAGE-SELECT*

Your screen should look like Figure 5-21. The three graph files are listed, Move the highlight to each one and press the Space Bar. There should be a number symbol (#) next to each graph name. When there is a number symbol next to each graph name, press <Enter>.

4. You are ready to print the graphs.

> *Select ALIGN*

> *Select GO*

After a few moments, the graphs should begin to print.

5. You have finished with this Your Turn exercise. To exit from the PrintGraph program, select EXIT and select YES. The Access System menu appears. Select EXIT. Turn off the monitor and computer. Carefully store your disks.

❑ SUMMARY POINTS

- ■ Spreadsheet analysis is the mental process of evaluating information contained within a spreadsheet. It often involves comparing various results generated by a spreadsheet.
- ■ A model is a numeric representation of a real-world situation.
- ■ Functions, built-in formulas included in a spreadsheet program, save time by reducing the number of keystrokes needed to enter a formula as well as reduce the likelihood of error.
- ■ Formulas involving several operators are calculated according to the order of precedence. Parentheses can be used to override the order of precedence.
- ■ Analytical graphs are used in business for financial analysis.

- Bar graphs can be used to provide a quantitative comparison of several subjects' performances. Pie charts depict one subject divided into parts, showing the relationships between the parts and the whole.

❏ COMMAND SUMMARY

Command	Function
/ Copy	Copies data from one part of a worksheet to another.
/ Move	Moves data from one place to another within a worksheet.
/ Worksheet Global Column-width	Changes the default column width for an entire worksheet.
/ Worksheet Global Format	Changes the default appearance of all numbers in a worksheet.
/ Worksheet Global Label-Prefix	Changes the default alignment of all labels in a worksheet.
/ Worksheet Titles	Freezes the rows above the cell pointer (Horizontal), the columns to the left of the cell pointer (Vertical) or both.

Lotus 1-2-3 Graphics

A-F	Sets the A-F data ranges, which contain the numbers to be graphed.
Name	Creates, displays, deletes, and lists named graphs.
Options	Adds enhancements to graphs; sets the scaling for the graph axes.
Quit	Returns to 1-2-3 READY mode.
Reset	Resets some or all of the current graph settings to the default settings.
Save	Saves the current graph in a graph (.PIC) file so it can be printed with PrintGraph, Allways, or another program.
Type	Sets the graph type (bar, line, pie, stack-bar, or XY).
View	Displays the current graph.
X	Sets the X data range, which contains the X-axis labels, X-axis values, or pie slice labels.

Lotus 1-2-3 PrintGraph

Go	Prints the selected graphs.
Image-select	Designates which graphs should be printed.
Settings Hardware Fonts-directory	Sets the directory to the current location of the PrintGraph program, where the PrintGraph fonts are located.
Settings Hardware Graphs-directory	Sets the directory to the current location of the files containing the graphs to be printed.
Settings Hardware Printer	Sets the high density or low density option for the printer.
Settings Image Size	Sets the size of the graph to be printed.

In this exercise you are going to design a model to help you follow your performance and determine your final grade in the courses you are taking. If you need help completing this exercise, refer to the COPY command, Copying Functions, and Sorting sections earlier in this chapter.

1. Assume you are a business major taking the following courses during the Fall Semester:

Course	Credit Hours
ACCT 221	3
MIS 200	3
POLS 360	3
ECON 310	3
STATS 210	3

Load the Lotus program. A new worksheet should be on the screen.

2. Enter your name in cell Al. Enter the remaining data for the worksheet as follows:

	A	B	C	D	E	F	G	H	I	J
1	Your Name									
2				ASSIGNMENTS						
3	Fall Semester									
4									TOTAL	
5	COURSE	CR. HRS.	1	2	3	4	5	TOTAL	POSSIBLE	PERC.
6										
7	ACCT 221	3	180	80	95	178			600	
8	MIS 200	3	180	190	170	190	188		1000	
9	POLS 360	3	45	47	80				200	
10	ECON 310	3	75	180	140	184			650	
11	STATS 210	3	150	180	170'				600	

3. Enter an @SUM function in H7 that totals your scores in ACCT 221. Copy this function to cells H8 through H11.

4. In cell J7 enter a formula using cell addresses that computes your percentage for each course. (Hint: The percentage would be + TOTAL/TOTAL POSSIBLE.) Copy the formula to cells J8 through J11.

5. Format cells J7 through J11 as percent with two decimal places. What is your standing in Accounting 221 ? In Economics 31O?

6. Reduce the size of columns B, C, D, E, F, G, and H to 7 characters.

7. You realize that in MIS 200, your professor gave a last assignment that does not show in your records. The assignment was worth 50 points and you received a grade of 47. Insert a column before the TOTAL column to include this new assignment. Type the assignment number (6) and your grade in the appropriate

cells. Reduce the column width of this column to 7 characters. Change the total possible points for the course and correct the formula in order to include this new grade in your total. What is your standing in MIS 200?

8. Sort your worksheet so the courses are listed from the highest grade percentage to the lowest grade percentage.

9. Save the worksheet. Name the file GRADE.

10. Print the GRADE file.

❏ LOTUS 1-2-3 PROBLEMS   1–8

To complete the following exercises, you need to use files of the Student File Disk. If you need help completing this exercise, refer to the COPY command, Order of Precedence, Copying Functions, Absolute and Relative Cell Addressing, and Freezing Titles sections earlier in this chapter.

1. On the Student File Disk is a file called BILLS. Save the file and rename it BILLS-2. This spreadsheet file contains information on bills that a family is paying off over time. Enter your name in cell D1. Carefully read the information in the worksheet. Column A lists all the bills that are being paid off over time. Column C lists the yearly interest rate on each bill. Column D lists the total amount due on each bill as of January 1. Columns E, G, and I list the monthly payment made on each bill in January, February, and March. Since the entire worksheet cannot be seen on the screen at one time, freeze the labels in column A.

2. Format the values in column C so they appear as percent with one decimal place (for example, 21.3%). Format the block of cells D8 through J17 to currency with two decimal places.

3. Change the column width of columns D through J to 14 characters.

4. Move the cell pointer to cell D17. Enter a formula that finds the total of cells D8 through D15. Copy the formula in cell D17 to cells E17 through J17. Zeros will appear in the cells.

5. In column E, enter the following as the monthly payment for each bill:

MasterCard	100.00
JC Penney	30.00
Discover	50.00
Lord & Taylor	75.00
Car Loan	233.56
Student Loan	103.00

Copy the monthly payment amount just entered into the corresponding cells in columns G and I.

6. The purpose of the Total Due (Month) columns F, H, and J is to project what the total amount left on each bill will be the following month. To make this calculation, the monthly payment has to be subtracted from the total amount due. This provides the new total amount due on the bill. Interest will accrue on that amount over the month, however. To calculate the interest charge for the month, the new total amount due has to be multiplied by the yearly interest rate and then divided by twelve. The interest charge accrued for the month then has to be added to the total amount due on the bill for that month.

Move the cell pointer to cell F8. The purpose of this cell is to calculate the total amount of February's MasterCard bill. Enter a formula that makes this calculation. To help you out, the general form the formula should take is:

(((Total amount due-monthly payment)*interest rate)/12)+(Total amount due-monthly payment)

Use cell addresses rather than figures when entering the formula, and make sure that the reference to column C is absolute (that is $C8, to make column C absolute). Be sure to include all the parentheses in their proper locations in order to get the order of operations correct. What is the formula that belongs in cell F8? $(((D8-E8)*\$C8)/12)+(D8-E8)$

7. Copy the formula you entered in F8 to cells F9 through F11 and cells F14 through H15. Then repeat the same steps for columns H and J. $H8-I8$
   $F8/G8$

8. Unfreeze the titles. Save the worksheet. You are ready to print the worksheet. Since it is so long, you have to print it in two parts. First, use the / PRINT PRINTER OPTIONS MARGINS menu to set the left and right margins to 0. Print the block of cells A1 through F17. Next, print the block of cells G1 through J17.

❑ LOTUS 1-2-3 CHALLENGE

You have a part-time job at the A-Mart department store. The store manager finds out you know how to create graphs using Lotus 1-2-3 and has asked for your help.

1. The A-Mart department store has three local branches. The store manager has asked you to create a graph summarizing the monthly sales of these three stores. Following is the data you have been given for the graph:

	Jan	Feb	March	April	May	June
Branch 1	$84,000	$75,000	$69,000	$78,000	$82,000	$ 40,000
Branch 2	$81,000	$91,000	$93,000	$97,000	$104,000	$114,000
Branch 3	$83,000	$62,000	$78,000	$85,000	$ 84,000	$ 90,000

2. Create and print a bar graph that will best illustrate A-Mart's sales figures. Be sure to supply all the appropriate titles for the graph. Include a legend for the graph. Remember to both save and name the graph file and to save the worksheet file before printing your graph. Print the graph using the high-density option.

Application Software Manual

CHAPTER 6

Introduction to dBASE III PLUS

OUTLINE

❑ INTRODUCTION

Schools, hospitals, restaurants, and all types of businesses store data. The ability to retrieve, sort, and analyze data quickly and efficiently can make the difference between a company's success and failure. The types of data collected include employee records, bills, supply lists, budgets, and insurance information. Before microcomputers became standard business equipment, the most common way to organize data was to store the records in folders in file cabinets. File cabinets use a lot of space, however, and sometimes several departments may keep the same data. This duplication of data is a waste of time, effort, and space, and can lead to confusion or errors if one copy is changed. Database management software is a program that computerizes record-keeping tasks. The purpose of this chapter is to explain dBASE III PLUS, a sophisticated and powerful data management tool.

❑ GUIDE TO dBASE III PLUS

A data manager software package, like dBASE III PLUS is used to organize files and to store the type of data that is kept in folders in a manual filing system. Each data item that is stored, such as a first name, a last name, an address, an invoice amount, is called a field. A group of related fields forms a record. A business may keep a personnel record on each employee. This record would contain fields such as the employee's name, address, salary, and so on. A file is a group of related records. All the personnel records could make up one file. The business might have other files for customers, vendors or inventory, for example. Fields, records and files can all be easily created using dBASE III PLUS.

Some of the directions for using dBASE III PLUS vary depending on whether the computer has two floppy disk drives or a hard disk drive. The directions in this chapter are written for computers with a hard disk drive. Differences for computers with two floppy disk drives are written in Difference Boxes.

Each of the following sections introduces one or more features of dBASE III PLUS. At the end of each section there is a hands-on activity marked with the symbol **Your Turn**. Do not try the hands-on activity until after you have carefully read the section preceding it.

dBASE III PLUS refers to the key marked ⏎ as the <Enter> key. Throughout this chapter, when you are instructed to press the <Enter> key, press the key marked ⏎ .

The following symbols and typefaces are used throughout the chapter. This is what they mean:

Press <Ctrl>-A	<Ctrl> is always used together with another key. In this example
Add new record? **File is already open**	Boldface indicates words or phrases that appear on the computer screen. The text could be a prompt or a message.
Type: Number	Typewriter font indicates text that is to be entered into a file.
Select *LIST*	Italics indicates selecting a command from an available menu.
The ADDRESS file The TOOLS option	Capital letters indicate the name of a file or the name of a menu option or command.

There are two ways to enter commands in dBASE III PLUS. One is by using the Assistant Menu. The second way is by typing commands at the dot prompt. For beginning users of dBASE III PLUS, entering commands using the Assistant Menu is easier. Therefore, this chapter approaches learning the dBASE III PLUS program by using the Assistant Menu. Typing commands at the dot prompt is not covered.

Getting Started with dBASE III PLUS

To use dBASE III PLUS on a hard disk drive, the program will first have to be installed on the hard drive. Follow these steps to access dBASE III PLUS from a hard drive on which it has been installed.

1.   Turn on the computer and monitor.

2.   A prompt may appear asking you to enter the date. If it does, type the current date using numbers and hyphens, for example 1-15-93. Press <Enter>.

3.   A prompt may appear asking you to enter the time. If it does, you can either press <Enter> to bypass this prompt, or you can enter the time using a 24-hour format. For example, enter 16:30:00 if it is 4:30 p.m. Press <Enter> after entering the time.

4.   When the system prompt C> appears on the screen, enter cd\ and the name of the directory in which dBASE III PLUS is stored on the hard drive. For example, if the program is stored in a directory named DBPLUS, enter cd\dbplus and press <Enter>.

5.   The system prompt C> appears again. Enter dbase and press <Enter>. When dBASE III PLUS has been started properly, the Assistant Menu appears on the screen.

Difference Box: Starting dBASE III PLUS on a Computer with Two Floppy Disk Drives

To boot the computer and start dBASE III PLUS, you need a DOS disk, dBASE III PLUS System Disk #1, dBASE III PLUS System Disk #2, and a formatted data disk. All the files you create are saved on your data disk. Follow these steps to boot the computer and start dBASE III PLUS.

1.   Insert the DOS disk into Drive A. Close the disk drive door. Turn on the computer and monitor.

2.   A prompt appears asking you to enter the date. Enter the current date using numbers and hyphens, for example 1-15-93 and press <Enter>.

3.   A prompt appears asking you to enter the time. You can either press <Enter> to bypass this prompt, or you can enter the time using a 24-hour format. For example, enter 16:30:00 if it is 4:30 p.m. Press <Enter> after entering the time.

4.   When the system prompt A appears, take the DOS disk out of Drive A. Place the dBASE III PLUS System Disk #1 into Drive A. Close the disk drive door. Enter dbase and press <Enter>.

5.   After a few moments the message **Insert system disk 2 and press enter, or press ctrl-C to abort** appears at the bottom of the screen. Take System Disk #1 out of Drive A. Place System Disk #2 into Drive A, shut the disk drive door, and press <Enter>.

When dBASE III PLUS has been started properly, the Assistant Menu appears on the screen.

   YOUR TURN

In this exercise, you are going to start dBASE III PLUS on the computer. This exercise assumes that the dBASE III PLUS program is stored in a directory named dbplus. If dBASE III

PLUS is stored in a different directory in the computer you are using, ask your instructor for directions.

1.　Turn on the computer. If a prompt appears asking you to enter the date, type today's date using numbers and hyphens. For example, if the date is September 28, 1993, you would do the following:

> Type: 09-28-93
>
> Press <Enter>

If a prompt appears asking you to enter the time, either press <Enter> or enter the time in a 24-hour format and press <Enter>.

2.　The system prompt C> should appear on the screen.

> Type: cd\dbplus
>
> Press <Enter>

The system prompt C> should appear on the screen again.

> Type: dbase
>
> Press <Enter>

The Assistant Menu appears on the screen. Your screen should look like Figure 6-1. Leave the Assistant Menu on the screen while you read the following section.

❏ USING THE ASSISTANT MENU

A menu is a list of choices or options shown on the display screen from which the user selects a command or option. The Assistant Menu acts as a home base for the dBASE III PLUS program. All the commands

FIGURE 6-1 The Assistant Menu

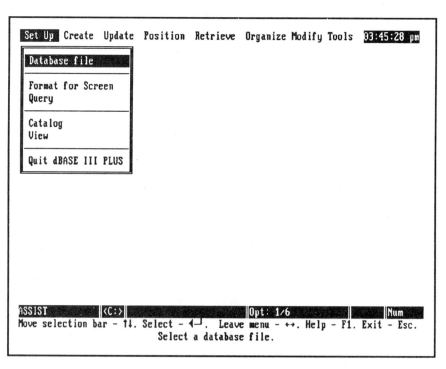

needed to create and maintain a database file are in the Assistant Menu. Before creating database files, you must understand the components of the Assistant Menu (refer to Figure 6-1).

At the top of the Assistant Menu is a Menu Bar that lists eight options: SET UP, CREATE, UPDATE, POSITION, RETRIEVE, ORGANIZE, MODIFY, and TOOLS. To the right of the Menu Bar is a space that keeps track of the current time. If you did not enter the correct time when the dBASE III PLUS program was first loaded, the time that appears on the screen will be incorrect.

When the Assistant Menu first appears after loading the dBASE III PLUS program, the Set Up Menu is open. The options from the Set Up Menu are listed in a pull-down menu. Each of the options on the Menu Bar has a corresponding pull-down menu.

There are four lines at the bottom of the screen. The first is called the Action Line; it is located immediately above the highlighted bar. In Figure 6-1 the Action Line is empty, but in the next hands-on exercise you will see an entry in it. The highlighted bar is called the Status Bar. It keeps track of what you are doing. For example, in Figure 6-1 the first box in the Status Bar shows that you are using the Assistant Menu, and the second box indicates which disk drive the computer is currently accessing. The remaining boxes in the Status Bar will be explained in the following hands-on exercise.

Underneath the Status Bar is the navigation line. The navigation line explains how to move between the menus and menu options. Finally, the message line at the bottom of the screen describes the option currently selected. In Figure 6-1, the message **Select a database file** describes the option currently highlighted, which is the DATABASE FILE option from the Set Up Menu.

As you use the Assistant Menu, get in the habit of reading the Status Bar and the action, navigation, and message lines. They provide useful information that will help you to work with database files.

There are two ways to open a menu on the Menu Bar. The first method is to use the right and left arrow keys located on the numeric keypad at the right of the keyboard. Pressing the right arrow key moves the highlighting on the Menu Bar to the right. Pressing the left arrow key moves the highlighting to the left. As a new menu is opened, its pull-down menu appears. If the highlighting is on the Set Up Menu, which is the first menu on the Menu Bar, pressing the left arrow key moves the highlighting to the Tools Menu, the last one on the bar. Conversely, if the highlighting is on the Tools Menu, pressing the right arrow key moves the highlighting to the first menu, the Set Up Menu.

The second way to open a menu is to press the letter corresponding to the first letter of the name of the menu. For example, if you want to open the Retrieve Menu, press R. If you want to open the Update Menu, press U, and so on.

Pressing the up arrow and down arrow keys moves the highlighting up and down through a pull-down menu. When the option you want is highlighted, press <Enter> to select the option. Typically, another menu appears after you press <Enter>. The method for moving through that menu and all subsequent menus is the same: Press the up or down arrow key until the desired option is highlighted, and press <Enter>. You cannot select an option from within a pull-down menu by entering the first letter of the option's name. That method works only if you are selecting an option from the Menu Bar. To make a selection from a pull-down menu, highlight the option and press <Enter>.

If you choose an option from a menu and then decide you do not want it, press <Esc> to cancel the selection. Each time <Esc> is pressed, you are taken back one step. Continue to press <Esc> until you are back to the desired menu. If <Esc> is pressed from one of the menus on the Menu Bar, the entire screen goes blank except for the Status Bar and a dot at the bottom of the screen. It is called a dot prompt. If you were entering commands by typing them at the dot prompt rather than selecting them from the Assistant Menu, you would want this dot prompt on your screen. However, in this section you will only be entering commands using the Assistant Menu. If the dot prompt appears on the screen, type `assist` and press <Enter>. The Assistant Menu will reappear.

❏ GETTING HELP WITH dBASE III PLUS

dBASE III PLUS has a very useful Help feature. When using dBASE III PLUS you can obtain information about the menu option currently selected by pressing <F1>. If you get lost or stuck while trying to perform an operation, try to solve the problem by pressing <F1> and reading the Help screen that appears. The Help feature provides information only on the menu option that is highlighted.

❏ QUITTING dBASE III PLUS

The command to exit from dBASE III PLUS is found in the Set Up Menu. The last option on the Set Up Menu, QUIT dBASE III PLUS, allows the user to exit from dBASE III PLUS and return the DOS system prompt to the screen. The only way you can exit from dBASE III PLUS is by selecting this option. If you exit using any other method, you risk losing information stored in your data files. When the system prompt appears and the red light on the disk drive is off, you can remove your disk from the disk drive and turn off the computer and monitor.

 YOUR TURN

In this exercise, you are going to practice moving around the Assistant Menu, selecting menu options, using the Help feature, and quitting from dBASE III PLUS. Before you begin, place the Student File Disk that came with this book in Drive A.

> **Difference Box:**
> If you are using a computer with two floppy disk drives, place the Student File disk that came with this book into Drive B.

1. The Assistant Menu should be on your screen from the previous exercise. First, practice moving along the Menu Bar. Currently the Set Up Menu is open.

    Press <Right arrow>
Notice that the Create Menu is now open.

    Press <Right arrow>
Now the Update Menu is open.

    Press <Right arrow> five times
The Tools Menu is now open.

    Press <Right arrow>

Notice that the highlighting moved back to the beginning of the Menu Bar and the Set Up Menu is open.

        Press <Left arrow>

The Tools Menu is now open.

        Press <Left arrow> two times

Now the Organize Menu is open.

        Press <Right arrow> four times

The highlighting wrapped around to the beginning of the Menu Bar and the Create Menu is now open. Try making selections from the Menu Bar by pressing the first letter of the option.

        Type: O

The Organize Menu is open.

        Type: T

The Tools Menu is open.

        Type: P

The Position Menu is open.

        Type: C

The Create Menu is open.

        Press <Down arrow> two times

The highlighting moved down to the VIEW option on the Create Menu.

        Press <Down arrow> four times

Notice that the highlighting moved from the LABEL option, the last on the list, to the DATA-BASE FILE option, the first on the list.

        Press <Up arrow>

The highlighting moved back to LABEL, the last option on the list.

        Press <Right arrow>

The Update Menu is open.

        Press <Down arrow>

Notice that nothing happened. None of the options on the Update Menu are available to you now. That is because you have not yet accessed any files that could be updated.

2.   Practice making menu selections.

        Press <Left arrow> two times

The Set Up Menu should be open with the DATABASE FILE highlighted. Select the DATA-BASE FILE option.

        Press <Enter>

A submenu listing all of the possible disk drives that can be used appears.

        If necessary, highlight A:

Press <Enter>

A list of all the dBASE III PLUS files stored on the Student File disk in drive A is displayed.

Highlight the file name CUSTOMER.DBF

Press <Enter>

The prompt **Is the file indexed? [Y/N]** appears. Indexed files are covered in Chapter 7.

Type: N

The Set Up Menu remains open. Look at the Status Bar; some of its entries have changed. The first box still has ASSIST in it because you are using the Assistant Menu. The second box has <A:> in it because you are accessing disk drive A. The third box always displays the name of the file that currently is being used. CUSTOMER now appears in this box. It was accessed when the CUSTOMER.DBF file was highlighted from the list of files on the disk in Drive A and <Enter> was pressed.

Rec: 1/12 appears in the fourth box. This box provides information on the status of the records in the current file. The first number tells you which record the program is currently accessing and the second number reports the total number of records in the current database file. Therefore, Rec: 1/12 means that the computer is currently accessing record 1, and there are a total of twelve records in the CUSTOMER file. The next box, which is currently empty, indicates the status of <Ins> and <Del>. <Ins> and <Del>, the insert and delete keys, are used when editing a database file. The last box in the Status Bar indicates the status of <Caps Lock>. If the capitals lock key is on, CAPS appears in this box.

Press <Caps Lock>

Caps should now appear in the box. Anything you type while **Caps** appears in the Status Bar will be in all capital letters.

Press <Caps Lock>

The last box in the Status Bar should be empty again. <Caps Lock> is a toggle switch, which means that if you press it once it is on, if you press it a second time it is off, and pressing it a third time turns it on again.

3.   Next, practice pressing <Esc> to cancel a selection.

Type: R

Press <Down arrow>

DISPLAY is highlighted.

Press <Enter>

A new menu appears and the entry **Command: DISPLAY** is in the Action Line. The Action Line always displays the command that was selected from the Assistant Menu.

Press <Down arrow>

Specify scope is highlighted.

Press <Enter>

A third menu appears. Next, escape from all of the menus.

Press <Esc>

The third menu disappears.

Press <Esc>

The second menu disappears. You have moved back to the options on the Menu Bar.

Press <Esc>

The Assistant Menu disappears from the screen and the dot prompt appears at the bottom of the screen. Notice that ASSIST no longer appears in the Status Bar. This is because the Assistant Menu was canceled the last time <Esc> was pressed. It is easy, however, to retrieve the Assistant Menu.

Type: assist

Press <Enter>

The Assistant Menu returns to the screen.

4. Next, look at the CUSTOMER file.

Type: U

Press <Down arrow>

EDIT is highlighted.

Press <Enter>

Record 1 from the CUSTOMER file appears on the screen, which should look like Figure 6-2. The CUSTOMER file keeps track of customers' names, addresses, and business-related numbers. At the top of the screen is an editing and cursor-movement menu. The purpose of this menu is to remind you what keys to press for editing and moving the cursor through the record. Underneath the menu is a record from the CUSTOMER file. You can tell from the entry **Rec: 1/12** on the Status Bar that this file contains twelve records and the current record is 1. Each record contains seven fields: First Name, Last Name, Address, City, State, ZIP, and Cnumber.

5. Look at the menu at the top of the screen. The first box indicates how to move the cursor from character to character and word to word. The second box indicates how to move the

FIGURE 6-2 Record 1 from the CUSTOMER File

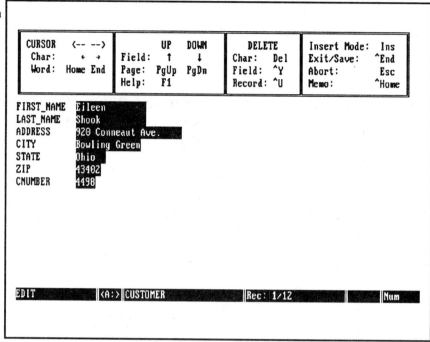

```
┌──────────────────────────────────────────────────────────────────────────┐
│ CURSOR    <-- -->            UP   DOWN    DELETE        Insert Mode:  Ins  │
│ Char:      ←  →      Field:   ↑    ↓      Char:   Del   Exit/Save:   ^End  │
│ Word:   Home End     Page:  PgUp PgDn     Field:  ^Y    Abort:       Esc   │
│                      Help:    F1          Record: ^U    Memo:      ^Home   │
└──────────────────────────────────────────────────────────────────────────┘

   FIRST_NAME   Eileen
   LAST_NAME    Shook
   ADDRESS      920 Conneaut Ave.
   CITY         Bowling Green
   STATE        Ohio
   ZIP          43402
   CNUMBER      4498
```
```
EDIT          │<A:>│CUSTOMER          │Rec: 1/12         │Num
```

cursor from field to field and record to record. The last two boxes have information on editing a record. Practice moving around a record and moving from record to record.

Press <Right arrow>

The cursor moves to the next character, the *i* in *Eileen*.

Press <Down arrow>

The cursor moves down to the next field, the LAST_NAME field.

Press <Down arrow> again

The cursor moves down to the ADDRESS field.

Press <End>

The cursor moves to the second word in the ADDRESS field.

Press <End> again

The cursor moves to the next word in the ADDRESS field.

Press <Home>

The cursor moves to the left one word.

Press <Home> again

The cursor moves one word to the left.

Press <PgDn>

Record 2 appears. The entry in the Status Bar now reads **Rec 2/12**.

Press <PgDn> again

Record 3 appears.

Press <Down arrow> seven times

The cursor moved through record 3 and now record 4 appears.

> Press <PgUp>

Record 3 appears again. Pressing <PgUp> brought the previous record to the screen. Notice that the cursor is in the first field in record 3.

> Press <Up arrow>

Record 2 appears on the screen. There are two ways to move from record to record. First, pressing <PgUp> brings the previous record to the screen, and pressing <PgDn> brings the next record to the screen. The second way is to move the cursor to the first or last field in the record and press <Up arrow> or <Down arrow>. Pressing <Up arrow> when the cursor is in the first field in the record brings the previous record to the screen. Pressing <Down arrow> when the cursor is in the last field in the record brings the next record to the screen.

> Press <Ctrl>-<End>

The Assistant Menu returns to the screen.

6. Next you are going to practice accessing the Help feature.

> Type: C
>
> Press <F1>

A Help screen appears that describes the CREATE option, which is used with the dot prompt. Notice the prompt at the bottom of the screen in the navigation line: **Press any key to continue work in ASSIST.**

> Press any key

7. The Assistant Menu returns to the screen.

> Type: R
>
> Press <Down arrow> four times
>
> Press <F1>

A Help screen describing the SUM command appears. Read the screen.

> Press any key to return to the Assistant Menu

8. Now you are going to exit from dBASE III PLUS.

> Type: S
>
> Press <Up arrow>

9. The option QUIT dBASE III PLUS should be highlighted.

> Press <Enter>

The message **END RUN dBASE III PLUS** and the system prompt return to the screen. Take your disk out of Drive A and turn off the computer and monitor.

❏ DEFINING THE STRUCTURE OF A DATABASE FILE

The first step in creating a database file is to define its structure. That is, you have to decide what fields will be included in each record, the names of the fields, maximum number of characters each field is likely to contain, and whether the data to be stored in a field is alphanumeric, numeric, or logical. Although the structure of a database file can be edited and changed after it has been created, prior planning can be a time-saver. Before entering the structure on the computer, take some time to think about and organize the data to be stored in the database file you are creating.

Naming a Database File

Before the structure of a database file can be defined, the file has to be named. To name a database file, the CREATE option, the second choice on the Menu Bar in the Assistant Menu, must be selected. To choose it, either move the highlighting using the arrow keys to CREATE and press <Enter>, or type the letter C. When CREATE has been selected, the Create Submenu appears.

The first option in the Create Submenu is DATABASE FILE, and it is highlighted. Select this option by pressing the <Enter> key. The Drive Selection Submenu appears. Select Drive A. The prompt **Enter the name of the file** appears in the middle of the screen. You can now enter a name for the database file.

File names can be up to eight characters long. The first character must be a letter, but the name can contain numbers and underscore characters. The file name cannot contain any blank spaces. The file name MY DATA would not be acceptable because of the space. The file name would be acceptable if an underscore instead of a space were used: MY_DATA.

If you make a mistake while typing in the file name, use <Backspace> to delete the error and retype the entry. Once <Enter> has been pressed, the only way to change the file name is to cancel the operation by pressing <Esc>. If <Esc> is pressed, the prompt **Are you sure you want to abandon operation? (Y/N)** appears. Pressing Y for Yes cancels the operation for naming a file, and you can start the file-naming procedure again. Pressing N for No enables you to continue creating the database file and keep the file name that was entered.

dBASE III PLUS automatically adds a file extension to file names. A file extension is a period and three letters that follow the file name. File extensions help identify different types of files. When creating a database file, dBASE III PLUS automatically adds the file extension dbf (for database file) after the file name. An example of another type of file that can be created with dBASE III PLUS is a label form file, which is used for creating mailing labels. dBASE III PLUS adds the file extension lbl (for label) after a label form file. By looking at the file extensions, a user can easily tell the difference between a database file and a file that contains a form for mailing labels.

Defining Fields

Defining a field consists of establishing the field's name, type, and width. A field name identifies its contents. Common field names are LASTNAME, FIRSTNAME, CITY, STATE. Notice there are no spaces in LASTNAME or FIRSTNAME. Like file names, field names cannot contain any spaces. Underscores, in addition to letters and numbers, are permitted. Therefore, LAST_NAME or FIRST_NAME would be acceptable field names. A field name may include up to ten characters; the first character must be a letter.

The field type identifies the kind of data stored in the field. A field can be defined as one of the following types: character, date, logical, memo, and numeric. Character fields are used to store data composed of any of the letters, numbers, or special characters found on the keyboard. Date fields are used to store dates.

Chapter 6: Introduction to dBASE III PLUS

Unless instructed to do otherwise, dBASE III PLUS stores and displays dates in the mm/dd/yy format (m stands for month, d stands for day, and y for year).

Logical fields are used to store data based on the response to a true/false question. An example of a logical field might be PAID. If a customer had paid for an item, either a T, for true, or Y, for yes, would be the data entered into the PAID field. If the customer had not paid, F, for false, or N, for no, would be entered into the field.

Memo fields are used to store large blocks of text. They hold the same kind of data as that of character fields (letters, numbers, and special characters). However, memo fields can store 5,000 characters or more, while character fields can store only up to 254 characters. Memo fields, for example, might contain notes on the individual records.

Numeric fields are used to store numbers that are used in mathematical formulas. A numeric field can be either integer or decimal. An integer number is one that would never have a decimal place. The number of books checked out of a library is an example of an integer number.

Not all fields that store numbers are numeric. A field is defined as numeric only if the numbers stored in it are used in a computation. Fields that store ZIP codes, Social Security, telephone, or employee numbers would be character rather than numeric fields because those numbers would not be used in a formula. Fields that store the quantity of an item ordered or the cost of an item would be numeric because those numbers could be used in a formula. Multiplying the number stored in the QUANTITY field by the number stored in the COST field would result in the total amount owed, for example.

The field width is the maximum number of characters required to store information in the field. For example, in a STATE field the width would be two because the maximum number of characters the field would have to hold is two (for example, OH for Ohio, MA for Massachusetts, CA for California). Because the field width that is defined for each field takes up memory space, it is a good idea to know as closely as possible how many storage characters are necessary for all fields. That is, if a database file contains a LASTNAME field, it is a waste of memory to define the field width as thirty if most of the last names stored in the file are going to be twenty characters or less.

Each type of field has a limit regarding how many characters it can store. Character fields have a maximum field width of 254. Date fields always have a field width of eight. The only possible width for a logical field is one, because the entry will always be one letter (T, F, Y, or N). dBASE III PLUS automatically inserts a field width of eight whenever a date field is defined and a field width of one whenever a logical field is defined, since these are the only possible widths for these two fields. When defining the width of a numeric field, decimal points and negative signs must be considered because they count as digits. The maximum width of a numeric field is nineteen.

 YOUR TURN

In this exercise you are going to boot your computer, load the dBASE III PLUS program, name a database file, and define the fields for that file.

1.   Turn on the computer and monitor.

2.   A prompt may appear asking you to enter the date. If it does, type the current date using numbers and hyphens. For example if the date is September 28, you would do the following:

> Type: `09-28-93`
>
> Press <Enter>

If a prompt appears asking you to enter the time, either press <Enter> or enter the time in a 24-hour format and press <Enter>.

3.   The system prompt C> should appear on the screen.

> Type: `cd\dbplus`
>
> Press <Enter>

4.   The system prompt C> appears again.

> Type: `dbase`
>
> Press <Enter>

The Assistant Menu appears on the screen. Place the formatted disk that is your data disk in Drive A.

5.   You are ready to create the database file.

> Type `c` for CREATE

The Create Submenu appears. The DATABASE FILE option is already highlighted.

> Press <Enter>

The Drive Selection Submenu appears.

> Highlight A:
>
> Press <Enter>

Difference Box:

If you are using a computer with two floppy disk drives, highlight B: and press <Enter> when the Drive Selection Submenu appears.

Your screen should look like Figure 6-3. The prompt **Enter the name of the file** appears.

> Type: `Library`
>
> Press <Enter>

Your screen should look like Figure 6-4. This is the dBASE III PLUS field definition form.

6.   The purpose of the file you are creating is to keep track of books in a personal library. For each book, you are going to keep a record of the following information:

1.	Number	Allocated sequentially to each new book
2.	Title	Title of the book
3.	Author	Author's last and first name
4.	Date of purchase	Month and year when the book was purchased

FIGURE 6-3 Creating a Database File

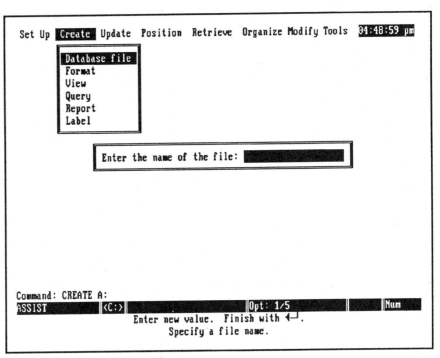

```
Set Up  Create  Update  Position  Retrieve  Organize Modify Tools  04:48:59 pm
          ┌────────────────┐
          │ Database file  │
          │ Format         │
          │ View           │
          │ Query          │
          │ Report         │
          │ Label          │
          └────────────────┘

              ┌──────────────────────────────────────────────┐
              │ Enter the name of the file: ▓▓▓▓▓▓▓▓▓▓▓▓▓▓▓▓  │
              └──────────────────────────────────────────────┘




Command: CREATE A:
ASSIST          |<C:>|                      |Opt: 1/5        |        |Num
                    Enter new value.  Finish with ◄┘.
                         Specify a file name.
```

5. Cost   Amount paid for the book

6. Usage   School or personal usage

7. Start defining the six fields in the field definition form. The blinking cursor should be under the heading FIELD NAME.

        Type: NUMBER

        Press <Enter>

FIGURE 6-4 The Field Definition Form

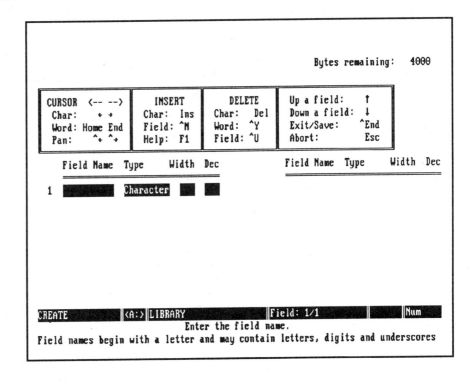

```
                                                Bytes remaining:    4000

   ┌──────────────┬──────────────┬──────────────┬─────────────────────┐
   │ CURSOR <-- --│   INSERT     │   DELETE     │ Up a field:      ↑   │
   │ Char:   ← →  │ Char:  Ins   │ Char:  Del   │ Down a field:    ↓   │
   │ Word: Home End│ Field: ^N   │ Word:  ^Y    │ Exit/Save:    ^End   │
   │ Pan:   ^← ^→  │ Help:  F1   │ Field: ^U    │ Abort:         Esc   │
   └──────────────┴──────────────┴──────────────┴─────────────────────┘

        Field Name  Type    Width  Dec        Field Name  Type     Width  Dec
        ─────────────────────────────         ────────────────────────────
     1  ▓▓▓▓▓▓▓▓   Character  ▓▓   ▓▓




   CREATE        |<A:>|LIBRARY          |Field: 1/1      |        |Num
                         Enter the field name.
   Field names begin with a letter and may contain letters, digits and underscores
```

The cursor moves to the FIELD TYPE column. You want this field to be a character/text field, so press the <Enter> key to accept the character/text default setting. The cursor moves to the field width column. Choose 3 as the width for the NUMBER field, because it is doubtful that you will own more than 999 books:

> Type: 3
>
> Press <Enter>

Because the field type is not numeric, the cursor automatically skips the decimal column and jumps down so that you can enter the information on the second field.

8. Enter the information on the remaining fields as follows. If you notice a typing mistake before you have pressed <Enter>, use <Backspace> to delete the characters and retype the entry. If you notice a typing mistake in a field that has already been entered, use the <Up arrow>, <Down arrow>, <Left arrow>, and <Right arrow> keys to move the cursor to the entry where the mistake occurred. Then use the <Del> key to delete characters and the <Ins> key to insert characters to help you correct the error.

> Type: TITLE
>
> Press <Enter>
>
> Press <Enter> again
>
> Type: 25
>
> Press <Enter>
>
> Type: LAST_NAME
>
> Press <Enter>
>
> Press <Enter> again
>
> Type: 15
>
> Press <Enter>
>
> Type: FIRST_NAME

At this point, the computer beeps and the cursor automatically moves to the FIELD TYPE column. This happens because the field name FIRST_NAME is ten characters wide, which is the maximum width that a field name can be. dBASE does not accept more than ten characters for a field name, so it automatically moves the cursor to the next column. The beep alerts you to the fact that the cursor has moved to the next column so you do not have to press the <Enter> key. Again, accept the default setting for FIELD TYPE and enter the field width:'

> Press <Enter>
>
> Type: 15
>
> Press <Enter>
>
> Type: PUR_MONTH
>
> Press <Enter>
>
> Press <Enter> again
>
> Type: 2

Press <Enter>

Type: PUR_YEAR

Press <Enter>

Press <Enter> again

Type: 2

Press <Enter>

Type: COST

Press <Enter>

The COST field is not a character/text field. It is a numeric field with two decimal places. Notice what the prompt line at the bottom of the screen says: **Press SPACE to change the field type.**

Press the Space Bar once

The word **Numeric** now appears in the FIELD TYPE column for the COST field.

Press <Enter>

Type: 8

Press <Enter>

This time the cursor moves to the decimal column, because the field type is numeric. Two decimal places are required.

Type: 2

Press <Enter>

Type: USAGE

Press <Enter>

You want the USAGE field to be a logical field. This time, instead of pressing the Space Bar to select the field type, use L for LOGICAL.

Type: L

dBASE III PLUS immediately selects logical for the field type, 1 for the field width, and moves the cursor to the next line. (You could also select LOGICAL by pressing the Space Bar several times or select NUMERIC by entering N.)

9. All the fields for this data file are now defined. Your screen should look like Figure 6-5. Look over all your entries to make sure there are no mistakes. If there are mistakes use the <Up arrow>, <Down arrow>, <Left arrow>, <Right arrow> and <Ins> keys to correct them.

Now end the field definition process.

Press <Ctrl>-<End>

The message **Press ENTER to confirm. Any other key to resume.** appears at the bottom of the screen. If you want to enter more data fields or edit fields already entered, press any key. To end the field definition process press <Enter> one more time.

Press <Enter>

FIGURE 6-5 Defining the Fields for the LIBRARY File

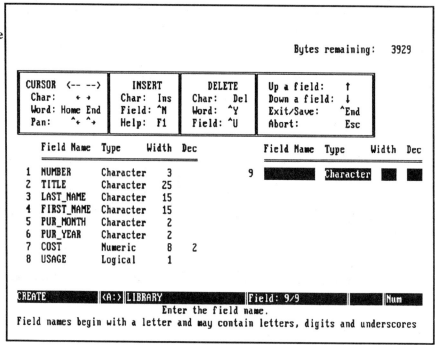

```
                                                          Bytes remaining:    3929

 ┌─────────────────┬──────────────┬──────────────┬────────────────────────┐
 │ CURSOR  <-- -->  │   INSERT     │   DELETE     │ Up a field:      ↑      │
 │  Char:    ← →    │ Char:  Ins   │ Char:  Del   │ Down a field:    ↓      │
 │  Word: Home End  │ Field: ^N    │ Word:  ^Y    │ Exit/Save:      ^End    │
 │  Pan:    ^← ^→   │ Help:  F1    │ Field: ^U    │ Abort:           Esc    │
 └─────────────────┴──────────────┴──────────────┴────────────────────────┘

      Field Name  Type     Width  Dec          Field Name  Type     Width  Dec

   1  NUMBER      Character   3            9  ▓▓▓▓▓▓▓▓  Character  ▓▓   ▓▓
   2  TITLE       Character  25
   3  LAST_NAME   Character  15
   4  FIRST_NAME  Character  15
   5  PUR_MONTH   Character   2
   6  PUR_YEAR    Character   2
   7  COST        Numeric     8    2
   8  USAGE       Logical     1


 �as CREATE        <A:> LIBRARY              Field: 9/9              Num
                         Enter the field name.
      Field names begin with a letter and may contain letters, digits and underscores
```

After a few seconds the field definition form disappears and the message **Input data records now? (Y/N)** appears on the screen. The data structure has now been saved.

> Type: N

The Assistant Menu returns to the screen. Leave the Assistant Menu on the screen while you read the following section.

Displaying the Structure of a Database File

After the structure for a database file has been defined, the user can view the structure. By displaying the structure on the screen, a user can find out what fields are included in the file, its field names, widths, and field types.

Before the structure of a database file can be displayed, however, the file has to be active. The file whose name appears in the Status Bar is the active file. If you want to display the structure of a file other than the one whose name is in the Status Bar, or if there is no file name listed in the Status Bar, you must first access the database file. To access the database file, select the SETUP option from the Menu Bar in the Assistant Menu. Next, select the DATABASE FILE option from the Set Up Submenu, the disk drive where the files are stored, and the name of the file whose structure you want to display. The prompt **Is the file indexed? [Y/N]** appears on the screen. Indexed files are covered in Chapter 7. For now you will enter N in response to this prompt. After responding to the prompt, the file name appears in the Status Bar.

To display the structure of a database file whose name is in the Status Bar, select the TOOLS option from the Menu Bar in the Assistant Menu. Next, select the LIST STRUCTURE option from the Tools Submenu. The prompt **Direct the output to the printer? [Y/N]** appears on the screen. If you wish to have a hard copy of the structure for future reference, type Y. If you do not need a hard copy of the structure, type N. The structure of the database file then appears on the screen. To exit from the display, press any key. The Assistant Menu returns to the screen.

YOUR TURN

In this exercise you are going to display the structure of the LIBRARY database file. Look at the Status Bar. Notice that the file name LIBRARY appears. Because the LIBRARY file is currently active, you do not have to access it.

1.   The Assistant Menu should be on your screen.

Type T for TOOLS

Move the highlight to LIST STRUCTURE from the Tools Submenu

Press <Enter>

2.   The prompt **Direct the output to the printer? [Y/N]** appears on the screen. You do not need a hard copy of the structure.

Type: N

3.   The structure for the LIBRARY database file appears. Your screen should look like Figure 6-6. Notice that the first line displays the disk drive where the file is stored and its file name. The second line lists the number of records that are stored in the database file. Because no records have been added to the LIBRARY database file, a zero appears in this line. The next thing listed is the date of the last change made to the file. Finally, the field numbers, names, types, widths, and the decimal places for each field in the database file are listed.

FIGURE 6-6 The Structure of the LIBRARY File

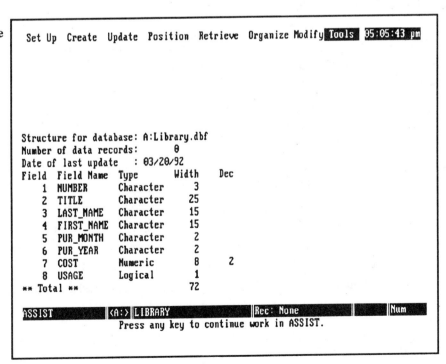

4. Look the structure over carefully.

   Press any key

The Assistant Menu returns to the screen. You can either exit from dBASE III PLUS or leave the Assistant Menu on the screen while you read the following section.

Editing the Structure of a Database File

It is easy to make changes to the structure of a database file. Fields can be added, deleted, or redefined; field names, widths, or types can be changed.

The database file to be edited must be active. That is, its name has to appear in the Status Bar. If you want to edit the structure of a file other than the one whose name is in the Status Bar, or if there is no file name listed in the Status Bar, access the database file by selecting the SETUP option from the Menu Bar in the Assistant Menu. Select the DATABASE FILE option from the Set Up Submenu, select the disk drive where the files are stored and the name of the file whose structure you want to display. The prompt **Is the file indexed? [Y/N]** appears on the screen. Until you learn about indexed files, you will enter N in response to this prompt. After responding to the prompt, the file name appears in the Status Bar.

Once the database file to be edited is active, select the MODIFY option from the Menu Bar in the Assistant Menu. Next, select DATABASE FILE from the Modify Submenu. The structure for the database file, along with a menu, appears on the screen. The words MODIFY STRUCTURE appear in the Status Bar.

To edit the structure of the database file, move the cursor to the field that is to be changed. Pressing the up arrow key moves the cursor up a field; pressing the down arrow key moves the cursor down a field. Pressing the left and right arrow keys moves the cursor one character to the left or right, respectively. Pressing <End> moves the cursor through the structure category by category. That is, the cursor jumps from the field name, to the type, width, decimal (if there is an entry in that column), and then down to the field name of the following field, and so on.

To insert a character, position the cursor where the character is to be inserted, press <Ins> and enter the character or characters. To delete a character, position the cursor under the character to be deleted and press <Del>.

To insert a new field, position the cursor where the field is to be inserted and press <Ctrl>-N. A new field is inserted and all the fields following the new field move down one position. The field's name, type, width, and, if necessary, decimal places must then be entered. To delete a field, position the cursor on the field to be deleted and press <Ctrl>-U. The field is deleted and all the fields following the deleted field move up one position. If only a word, rather than an entire field, is to be deleted, place the cursor on that word and press <Ctrl>-Y. The word is deleted and a new entry can be made.

After all of the changes have been made, pressing <Ctrl>-<End> saves the changes and exits the MODIFY STRUCTURE command. The prompt **Press ENTER to confirm. Any other key to resume** appears on the screen. If all the editing changes have been made, press <Enter>. The changes are saved and the Assistant Menu returns to the screen. If you want to cancel the option to save the database structure, press any key other than <Enter>. You can then continue to make changes to the database structure.

YOUR TURN

In this exercise, you are going to make changes to the LIBRARY database.

1. The Assistant Menu should be on your screen and the LIBRARY file should be active. If necessary, start the dBASE III PLUS program. Check the Status Bar to make sure that the LIBRARY file is active. If it is not, use the SET UP option to access the LIBRARY database file. The word LIBRARY should appear in the Status Bar.

>   Type M for MODIFY

>   Press <Enter> to select DATABASE FILE from the Modify Submenu

2. Your screen should look like Figure 6-7. At the top of the screen is a menu that lists the keys used to move the cursor, insert, and delete. Underneath the menu is the structure for the LIBRARY database file. You want to add a new field to the file. Some of the books have more than one author, but only one author's name is stored in each database record. The field you are going to add is a logical field named CODE. If a book has more than one author, you will enter Y for Yes. If it has only one author, you enter N for No.

3. The cursor should be in field 1, the NUMBER field.

>   Press <Down arrow> four times

The cursor is now in field 5. You want to insert a new field 5 so that the CODE field comes right after the author's first name.

>   Press <Ctrl>-N

FIGURE 6-7 Modifying the Structure of a Database File

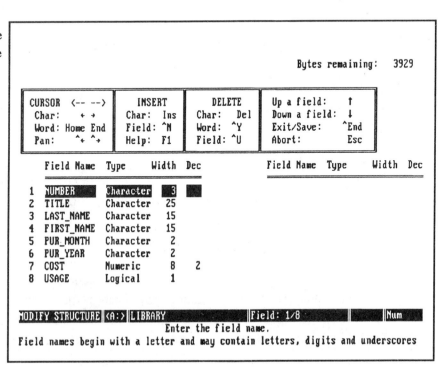

A new field 5 is added. You can now enter the new field name.

    Type: CODE

    Press <Enter>

    Type: L

4. You now want to switch the order in which the fields appear. You want the COST field to come right after the CODE field. To do this, delete the COST field from where it now appears and reinsert it in its new location. First you have to move the cursor to the COST field.

    Press <Down arrow> two times

The cursor should be in the COST field.

    Press <Ctrl>-U

The COST field is deleted and all the fields that came after it moved up one spot.

    Press <Up arrow> two times

The cursor should now be in field 6, the PUR_MONTH field.

    Press <Ctrl>-N

There is now room to add a new field 6.

    Type: COST

    Press <Enter>

    Press N to enter the NUMERIC field type

    Type: 8

    Press <Enter>

    Type: 2

    Press <Enter>

The COST field is now inserted in its new location. You are now ready to save the edited LIBRARY database file.

    Press <Ctrl>-<End>

The prompt **Press ENTER to confirm. Any other key to resume** appears at the bottom of the screen.

    Press <Enter>

The Assistant Menu returns to the screen. You can either exit from dBASE III PLUS or you can leave the Assistant Menu on the screen while you read the following section.

❏ ENTERING DATA INTO A DATABASE FILE

Once the structure for the database file has been completed, records can be entered into the file. Records can be added immediately following the creation of the database file structure. When creating the database file structure for the first time, the prompt **Input data now? [Y/N]** appears as soon as you press <Ctrl>-<End> to save the database file structure. Pressing Y, for Yes, enables you to begin entering records.

Records do not have to be entered as soon as the database file structure is completed. If you choose to enter records at a later point, make sure the database file to which the records are to be added is the active file. The active file is the file whose file name appears in the Status Bar. If the file to receive the records is not the active file, access that file by selecting SET UP from the Menu Bar on the Assistant Menu, and selecting DATABASE FILE from the Set Up Submenu. Next, select the disk drive where the file is stored and, finally, select the appropriate file name.

Once the file is active, access the data-entry form by selecting UPDATE from the Menu Bar in the Assistant Menu, and then selecting APPEND from the Update Submenu. The data-entry form appears on the screen along with a menu. The data is entered on the data-entry form in the space provided for each field. After typing the data for one field, press <Enter> and the cursor moves to the next field. If the data fills the field completely, you do not have to press <Enter>; the cursor automatically moves to the next field. After data for the last field in the record has been added, a blank data-entry form for the next record appears. dBASE III PLUS saves the data that is entered record by record. That is, once the blank entry-form for the next record appears, the previous record is saved.

If you make a typing mistake while entering data into a field and have not pressed <Enter>, use <Backspace> to delete your mistake and type the entry again. If you notice a mistake that has already been entered into a field, use the up or down arrow keys to move the cursor to that field. Use either <Backspace> or <Del> to delete the error and enter the correction.

If you want to move back to check the entries in a previous record, press <PgUp>. Pressing <PgUp> moves to the previous record. To move to the next record in the file, press <PgDn>.

As you enter each record into the database file, dBASE III PLUS assigns it a record number. The record number for the current record is displayed in the Status Bar. dBASE III PLUS displays two record numbers separated by a slash. The first is the number of the current record; that is, the record that appears on the screen. The second is the total number of records in the database file.

Remember, when creating the structure for a database file, capitalization does not matter because dBASE III PLUS automatically capitalizes all the field names. Capitalization does, however, make a difference when entering records into the database file. dBASE III PLUS stores the data in the records exactly as you enter them, including whatever capitalization is used.

When all the records have been entered, end the data-entry process by using one of two methods. The first is by pressing <Enter> when the blank data-entry form for the next record appears. For example, say there are twenty records in a database file and you have just entered all the data for record 20. A blank data-entry form for record 21 appears on the screen. Pressing <Enter> when the blank form for record 21 appears terminates the data-entry process. Only twenty records will be saved (records 1 through 20); the empty record 21 will not be saved.

Another way to end the data-entry process is by pressing <Ctrl>-<End>. It does not matter what record appears on the screen if you press <Ctrl>-<End> to end. For example, say there are twenty records in a database file and you have entered all of them. Before ending the entry process you want to return to record 10 to check and make sure you entered the data in that record correctly. You would press <PgUp> to return to record 10. Once you had checked that record, you could leave it on the screen and press <Ctrl>-<End>. All the records in the file would be saved without having to return to record 20.

If a blank data-entry form is on the screen when you press <Ctrl>-<End>, that record will be saved in the database file. For example, say you entered the twenty records and pressed <Enter> after data for the last field in record 20 was entered. A blank data-entry form for record 21 appears on the screen. If <Ctrl>-<End> is pressed while this blank form is on the screen, dBASE III PLUS saves all twenty-one records; record 21 is saved although it contains no data. If this happens, the blank record can be removed. Later in this chapter you will learn how to delete an unwanted database record.

YOUR TURN

In this exercise you are going to enter fifteen records into the LIBRARY file. Check to make sure the LIBRARY file is the active file. If the file name LIBRARY does not appear on the Status Bar, access the file by selecting SET UP from the Menu Bar on the Assistant Menu, DATABASE FILE from the Set Up Submenu, the disk drive where the LIBRARY file is stored, and finally the LIBRARY file.

1. When the LIBRARY file is the active file, you are ready to access the data-entry form.

     Type U for UPDATE

     Press <Enter> to select APPEND from the Update Submenu

A blank data-entry form appears. Your screen should look like Figure 6-8.

2. The cursor is in the space next to NUMBER.

     Type: 1

     Press <Enter>

     Type: A Short Course in PL/C

     Press <Enter>

FIGURE 6-8 A Data-Entry Form

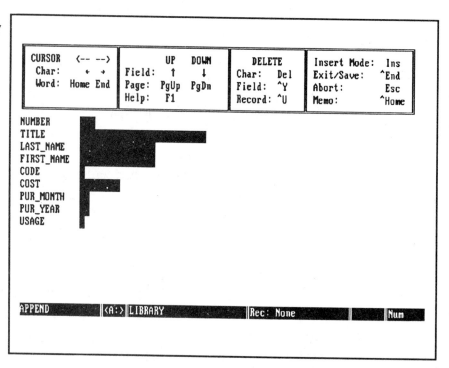

Type: Clark

Press <Enter>

Type: Ann

Press <Enter>

Type: N

The computer beeps and the cursor automatically moves to the next field although you did not press <Enter>. This happens because the field width is one and you typed one character. The beep alerts you to the fact that the cursor is already in the next field. This also occurs with the rest of the entries in this record.

Type: 25.00

Type: 07

Type: 93

Type: N

After you enter the last field, dBASE III PLUS automatically advances to the next record.

3. You are now going to add fourteen more records to the LIBRARY file.

Enter the following information:

No.	Title	Last Name	First Name	Code	Cost	Mo	Year	Use
2	Accounting Today	Asman	Mark	Y	50.50	01	93	Y
3	Advanced Structured COBOL	Welburn	Tyler	N	35.00	10	91	N
4	Business Policies	Christensen	Roland	Y	45.00	01	90	Y
5	COBOL for the 90's	Spence	John	N	28.00	11	91	N
6	Computers are Fun	Rice	Jean	Y	34.00	02	90	N
7	Consumer Behavior	Williams	Terrel	N	40.00	01	91	N
8	Economics	McConnel	Campbell	N	65.00	12	90	N
9	International Marketing	Kramer	Roland	N	52.00	09	91	Y
10	Introduction to BASIC	Mandell	Steven	N	54.00	01	90	N
11	Using 1-2-3	Leblond	Geoffrey	Y	21.50	04	92	N
12	Discovering PC DOS	Worcester	Clark	N	18.50	07	92	N
13	Harbrace College Handbook	Hodges	John	N	16.75	10	90	Y
14	Facts from Figures	Morney	M	N	16.00	11	91	N
15	Financial Accounting	Eskew	Robert	Y	38.80	09	92	Y

4. When all the records are entered, number 16 appears on the screen. Since record 16 is empty and you do not want to save it, you are going to exit by pressing <Enter> rather than pressing <Ctrl>-<End>.

Press <Enter>

The fifteen records are saved and the Assistant Menu returns to the screen. Notice that the Status Bar now says **Rec:15/15**, which means there are fifteen records in the file and dBASE III PLUS is currently pointing to record 15.

5. You have finished with this Your Turn exercise. You can either leave your work on the screen while you read the following sections, or you can exit from dBASE III PLUS.

❏ UPDATING A DATABASE FILE

Very rarely is a database file ever finalized. Typically, changes such as adding or deleting records and updating the data stored in the records are continually made to a database file. Editing a database file is a very easy operation using the Assistant Menu.

Editing a Record

To edit records in an active database file, first select the UPDATE option from the Menu Bar in the Assistant Menu. Next select EDIT from the Update Submenu. The current record, whose number is displayed in the Status Bar, appears on the screen. The word EDIT appears in the Status Bar.

If the record that is displayed is not the record needing to be edited, press <PgUp> or <PgDn> to browse through the records until the one you want to edit is displayed. Pressing the up and down arrow keys moves you through the records as long as you do not go past the first or last field. For example, if the cursor is in the first field of the record and you press <Up arrow>, the previous record appears on the screen. If the cursor is in the last field of the record and you press <Down arrow> the next record appears on the screen.

Once the appropriate record is displayed, use the up and down arrow keys to move to the field to be edited. Use the left and right arrow keys to move through the characters in a particular field. Use <Backspace> or <Del> to delete characters. If you want to insert characters, press <Ins>. If you try to enter characters without pressing <Ins> first, the characters you enter will type over the characters that were already there. Typing over characters is, of course, another method for editing data.

After making editing changes to one record, you can edit other records by pressing <PgUp> or <PgDn>. As many data records can be edited as necessary.

When the editing process is complete, there are two ways to exit from the editing process. If you want to save all the changes that were made, press <Ctrl>-<End>. If you want to leave the editing process but you do not want to save the changes made to the current record, press <Esc>.

YOUR TURN

In this exercise you are going to edit several of the records in the LIBRARY database file.

1. The Assistant Menu should be on your screen and the LIBRARY file should be active. If necessary, start the dBASE III PLUS program. Check the Status Bar to make sure that the LIBRARY file is active. If it is not, use the SET UP option to access the LIBRARY database file. The word LIBRARY should appear in the Status Bar. When the LIBRARY file is active, start the process of editing the records.

Chapter 6: Introduction to dBASE III PLUS

Type U for UPDATE

Move the highlight to EDIT from the Update Submenu

Press <Enter>

Record 15 appears on the screen. Notice the words **EDIT** and **Rec: 15/15** in the Status Bar. This means that record 15 is currently displayed, and there are a total of fifteen records in the LIBRARY database file.

2. The LIBRARY file needs to be edited because you are now using three more of your books at school.

Press <PgUp> until record 1 is on the screen

Press <Down arrow> until the cursor is in the USAGE field

Type: Y

The computer beeps and record 2 appears. The other two books you are now using at school are record 3, Advanced Structured COBOL, and record 12, Discovering PC DOS.

Edit those two records so that Y is entered into the USAGE field rather than N

3. The records have now all been edited. You are ready to exit from the editing procedure.

Press <Ctrl>-<End>

4. You have finished with this Your Turn exercise. You can either leave your work on the screen while you read the following section, or you can exit from dBASE III PLUS.

Browsing Through Records

Records can also be listed for editing by using the BROWSE option from the Update Submenu. To list records using the BROWSE option, select UPDATE and BROWSE; records from the current database file are displayed. Instead of displaying one record at a time, however, the BROWSE option displays a set of records. Up to seventeen records can be displayed vertically down the screen, and up to eighty characters can be displayed horizontally across the page. If a data record contains more than eighty characters, only the first eighty are displayed.

 YOUR TURN

In this exercise you are going to use the BROWSE option to display records from the LIBRARY file.

1. The Assistant Menu should be on your screen and the LIBRARY file should be active. If necessary, start the dBASE III PLUS program. Check the Status Bar to make sure that the LIBRARY file is active. If it is not, use the SET UP option to access the LIBRARY database file. The word LIBRARY should appear in the Status Bar. When the LIBRARY file is active, you can browse through records.

Type U for UPDATE

Move the highlight to BROWSE from the Update Submenu

Press <Enter>

Records 13 through 15 should be displayed on your screen.

2. Notice that only six of the nine fields in the LIBRARY file are displayed. Whenever you use the BROWSE option, only those fields that will fit across the screen horizontally are displayed. To see all the fields in a database file, use the EDIT option. Also notice the Editing Menu at the top of the screen. Records can be edited from the BROWSE option.

Press <Right arrow>

The cursor moves to the 3 in 13.

Press <Right arrow> twice

The cursor moves to the next field. You can move through a record using <Left arrow> and <Right arrow>.

Press <Up arrow>

Record 12 appears.

Press <Up arrow> until record 1 appears

Notice that only records 1-14 are displayed; the rest scrolled off the screen.

Press <Down arrow> until record 15 is highlighted

Press <Down arrow> one more time

The message **Add new records? (Y/N)** appears. New records can be added using the BROWSE option.

Type: N

Press <Ctrl>-<End>

3. You have finished with this Your Turn exercise. You can either leave your work on the screen while you read the following section, or you can exit from dBASE III PLUS.

Adding a Record

To add a record to an active database file, select the UPDATE option from the Menu Bar in the Assistant Menu. Next, select APPEND from the Update Submenu. A blank data-entry form appears on the screen. The word APPEND is in the Status Bar. The letters EOF are in the area of the Status Bar that indicates what record is currently active. EOF stands for End Of File. When records are added to an existing database file using the APPEND command, they appear at the end of the existing file.

The data-entry form is filled out using the same method as that for entering data into the database file for the first time. As many records as necessary can be added. Pressing <PgDn> or <Enter> after entering data into the last field in the file accesses another blank data-entry form. When all the records have been added, press <Ctrl>-<End> or <Enter> when the next blank data-entry form appears; either ends the process of adding records to the file.

YOUR TURN

In this exercise, add five new records to the LIBRARY file.

1. The Assistant Menu should be on your screen and the LIBRARY file should be active. If necessary, start the dBASE III PLUS program. Check the Status Bar to make sure that the LIBRARY file is active. If it is not, use the SET UP option to access the LIBRARY database file. The word LIBRARY should appear in the Status Bar. When the LIBRARY file is active, you can add records to the database file.

> Type ʊ for UPDATE
>
> If necessary, highlight the APPEND option
>
> Press <Enter> to select APPEND from the Update Submenu

A blank data-entry form appears on the screen. In the Status Bar, the indicator **Rec: EOF/15** appears. This means that you are at the end of the file and there are a total of fifteen records in the LIBRARY database file.

2. You are now ready to add the five new records. The cursor should be in the NUMBER field. Enter the following:

No.	Title	Last Name	First Name	Code	Cost	Month	Year	Usage
16	Getting Things Done	Bliss	Edwin	N	23.60	02	91	N
17	Intermediate Algebra	Mangan	Frances	N	22.30	09	90	Y
18	Management	Glueck	William	N	28.45	07	02	N
19	Learning to Program in C	Plum	Thomas	N	48.90	07	92	N
20	Information Systems	Burch	John	Y	52.60	01	92	Y

When all the data is entered, save the records and end the process of adding records to a database file. A blank form for record 21 is on the screen. You do not want to save the blank form, so exit by pressing <Enter> rather than pressing <Ctrl>-<End>.

> Press <Enter>

The Assistant Menu returns to the screen.

3. You have finished with this Your Turn exercise. You can either leave your work on the screen while you read the following section, or you can exit from dBASE III PLUS.

Deleting a Record

Deleting records using dBASE III PLUS is a two-step process. First, mark the records for deletion and then remove the marked records from the database file. By marking the records first, you have the option of retrieving the material before it is permanently removed from the database file. Once records are removed from the database file they are irretrievable, so be careful when deleting them. You do not want to lose data that you may need at a later point.

To mark records for deletion, select UPDATE from the Menu Bar on the Assistant Menu. Next, select EDIT from the UPDATE Submenu. Access the record that is to be deleted so that it appears on the screen. Pressing <Ctrl>-U marks the record for deletion. The word DEL appears in the right corner of the Status Bar indicating that the record has been marked for deletion.

<Ctrl>-U is a toggle. That is, if pressed once it is active and the record is marked; if pressed again it is no longer active, and the record is not marked. Pressing <Ctrl>-U a third time marks the record again.

When all the records to be deleted are marked, press <Ctrl>-<End> to exit from the EDIT function. At this point, the records are only marked; they have not been removed from the database file. If you decide to retain the records, remove the deletion marks by selecting UPDATE from the Menu Bar and RECALL from the Update Submenu. Then select the marked records to be recalled.

To delete marked records from the database file, select UPDATE from the Menu Bar on the Assistant Menu. Next, select PACK from the Update Submenu. When PACK has been selected, the records are permanently removed from the database file.

YOUR TURN

In this exercise you are going to delete a record from the LIBRARY database file.

1. The Assistant Menu should be on your screen, and the LIBRARY file should be active. If necessary, start the dBASE III PLUS program. Check the Status Bar to make sure that the LIBRARY file is active. If it is not, use the SET UP option to access the LIBRARY database file. The word LIBRARY should appear in the Status Bar. When the LIBRARY file is active, you can delete records.

      Type U for UPDATE

      Move the highlight to EDIT from the Update Submenu

      Press <Enter>

One of the records from the LIBRARY database file appears on your screen.

      Press <PgUp> until record 17 appears on your screen

      Press <Ctrl>-U

Your screen should look like Figure 6-9. Notice that the word **Del** appears in the Status Bar.

      Press <Ctrl>-U again

Because <Ctrl>-U is a toggle, the word **Del** is no longer in the Status Bar and record 17 is no longer marked for deletion.

      Press <Ctrl>-U a third time

Again, record 17 is marked for deletion. Leave it marked. Look at the Status Bar. It should say **Rec: 17/20**, which means there are 20 records in the database file.

      Press <Ctrl>-<End>

FIGURE 6-9 Deleting a Record

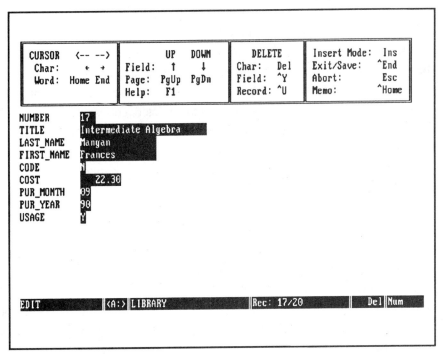

```
┌──────────────────────────────────────────────────────────────────────────────┐
│ ┌───────────────┬──────────────────┬──────────────────┬─────────────────────┐ │
│ │ CURSOR  <-- -->│        UP   DOWN │     DELETE       │ Insert Mode:  Ins   │ │
│ │ Char:     ← →  │ Field:  ↑    ↓   │ Char:    Del     │ Exit/Save:    ^End  │ │
│ │ Word:  Home End│ Page:  PgUp PgDn │ Field:   ^Y      │ Abort:        Esc   │ │
│ │                │ Help:   F1       │ Record:  ^U      │ Memo:         ^Home │ │
│ └───────────────┴──────────────────┴──────────────────┴─────────────────────┘ │
│                                                                                │
│   NUMBER      17                                                               │
│   TITLE       Intermediate Algebra                                             │
│   LAST_NAME   Mangan                                                           │
│   FIRST_NAME  Frances                                                          │
│   CODE        N                                                                │
│   COST             22.30                                                       │
│   PUR_MONTH   09                                                               │
│   PUR_YEAR    90                                                               │
│   USAGE       Y                                                                │
│                                                                                │
│ EDIT          │<A:>│LIBRARY              │Rec: 17/20        │    Del │Num       │
└──────────────────────────────────────────────────────────────────────────────┘
```

2. You are now ready to permanently remove record 17 from the LIBRARY database file. The Update Submenu should appear on your screen. Notice that, according to the Status Bar, there are now a total of twenty records in the LIBRARY database file.

> Move the highlight to PACK from the Update Submenu
>
> Press <Enter>

The message **19 records copied** appears at the bottom of the screen.

> Press any key to return to the Assistant Menu

Now look at the Status Bar. Notice that there are now a total of nineteen records in the LIBRARY database file. Check to make sure the record was deleted.

> Type ʊ for UPDATE
>
> Move the highlight to EDIT from the Update Submenu
>
> Press <Enter>

Record 1 should be on the screen.

> Press <PgDn> until record 17 appears on the screen

Record 17 is now the record for the book *Management* rather than *Intermediate Algebra.*

> Press <Ctrl>-<End> to return to the Assistant Menu

3. You have finished with this Your Turn exercise. You can either leave your work on the screen while you read the following section, or you can exit from dBASE III PLUS.

Displaying and Printing a Database File

To display records, the database file whose records you wish to display must be the active file. Select the RETRIEVE option from the Menu Bar on the Assistant Menu. Next, select the LIST option from the

Retrieve Submenu. A submenu for the LIST option appears. The option EXECUTE THE COMMAND is highlighted. Selecting this option causes all the fields from all records to be listed on the computer screen. Usually all the fields in a record will not fit on one line across the screen. dBASE III PLUS displays the fields that do not fit on the following line. Listing the records in this fashion, however, is confusing and difficult to read. Usually you will want to select specific fields from the records that you want to list.

To select specific fields from a record to be listed, choose the CONSTRUCT A FIELD LIST option from the List Submenu. When this option is selected, a list of all the fields in the database structure is displayed on the screen. The first field name in the list is highlighted. You can move the highlighting by pressing the up or down arrow keys. The field name, type, width, and decimal points, if there are any, of the highlighted field appear in another box on the screen. To select a field to be included in the list, press <Enter> when the field is highlighted. The name of the field just selected appears in the Action Line. You can then highlight another field and press <Enter>. The name of the second field appears in the Action Line. The order in which the fields are selected determines the order in which they will appear in the list. You can select as many fields as you want.

Once all the fields have been selected, press <Right arrow> to exit from the selection process. Next, select EXECUTE THE COMMAND from the List Submenu. The prompt **Direct the output to the printer? [Y/N]** appears on the screen. If the list is to be printed, the computer must be connected to a printer and the printer must be online. Press Y for Yes to print the list. If the list is to be displayed only on the screen, press N for No. The data stored in all the records for the fields that were selected is then listed on the screen and, if Y was pressed, printed. If a database file contains more records than will fit on the screen, the first records in the file scroll off the top of the screen. Press any key and the Assistant Menu returns to the screen.

If you press Y to print the list, you may notice that the last line of the list does not print. Some printers have a buffer area that stores individual characters in a line before printing that line. This print buffer is like a holding zone. Because of the particular way the dBASE III PLUS program works, a printer with a print buffer will not print the very last line. To print the last line, you must enter the dot prompt mode. Do not move the paper in the printer once the first part of the list is printed. When the first part of the list has finished printing, press any key to return to the Assistant Menu. Then press <Esc>. The Assistant Menu disappears and the dot prompt appears at the bottom of the screen. Enter the word Eject and press <Enter>. This dot prompt command ejects the last line from the print buffer and prints it at the end of the list where it belongs. To return to the Assistant Menu, enter Assist and press <Enter>.

 YOUR TURN

In this exercise you are going to display and print the records in the LIBRARY database file.

1. The Assistant Menu should be on your screen and the LIBRARY file should be active. If necessary, start the dBASE III PLUS program. Check the Status Bar to make sure that the LIBRARY file is active. If it is not, use the SET UP option to access the LIBRARY database file. The word LIBRARY should appear in the Status Bar.

In order to print the files, your computer must be hooked up to a printer, and the printer must be loaded with paper and online. If your computer is not hooked up to a printer, you can display the records as instructed in this exercise.

>Type R for RETRIEVE
>
>Move the highlight to LIST from the Retrieve Submenu
>
>Press <Enter>
>
>Move the highlight to EXECUTE THE COMMAND from the List Submenu
>
>Press <Enter>

The prompt **Direct the output to the printer? [Y/N]** appears on the screen.

>Type: N

Your screen should look like Figure 6-10. Look at your screen closely. Note that records 1 through 9 scrolled off the top of the screen. Second, notice that all the fields from all the records are listed. Because the fields did not all fit on one line, the data for each record is listed on two lines. For each record, the COST, PUR_MONTH, PUR_YEAR, and USAGE fields appear on the second line. Finally, notice that the entries in the CODE and USAGE fields are all either T or F even though you entered a Y or N. dBASE III PLUS automatically changes a Y entry into a logical field to a T for True and it changes an N entry into a logical field to an F for False.

2. As they appear now, the records are very confusing to read. To make the records easier to read, display only a few fields at a time from each record.

>Press any key to end the display process

The Retrieve Submenu appears. The LIST option is already highlighted.

FIGURE 6-10 Listing Records

```
 Set Up  Create  Update  Position  Retrieve  Organize Modify Tools  06:30:57 pm
     10  10      Introduction to BASIC      Mandell      Steven         .F.
 54.00 01          90      .F.
     11  11      Using 1-2-3                Leblond      Geoffrey       .T.
 21.50 04          92      .F.
     12  12      Discovering PC DOS         Worcester    Clark          .F.
 18.50 07          92      .T.
     13  13      Harbrace College Handbook Hodges        John           .F.
 16.75 10          90      .T.
     14  14      Facts from Figures         Morney       M              .F.
 16.00 11          91      .F.
     15  15      Financial Accounting       Eskew        Robert         .T.
 38.80 09          92      .T.
     16  16      Getting Things Done        Bliss        Edwin          .F.
 23.60 02          91      .F.
     17  18      Management                 Glueck       William        .F.
 28.45 07          02      .F.
     18  19      Learning to Program in C  Plum          Thomas         .F.
 48.90 07          92      .F.
     19  20      Information Systems        Burch        John           .T.
 52.60 01          92      .T.

 ASSIST          <A:> LIBRARY                    Rec: 17/19            Num
               Press any key to continue work in ASSIST.
```

Press <Enter>

Move the highlight to CONSTRUCT A FIELD LIST from the List Submenu

Press <Enter>

A list of all the fields in the LIBRARY database file appears in the upper-left corner of the screen. A box containing a description of the structure for the first field, NUMBER, appears in the center of the screen (see Figure 6-11).

3. You can move through the list of field names by pressing the <Up arrow> or <Down arrow>.

Press <Down arrow> two times

The highlighting is now on the LAST_NAME field. Notice that the structure for the LAST_NAME field is also displayed in the box in the center of the screen.

Press <Down arrow> four times

The highlighting is on the PUR_MONTH field and its structure is displayed in the center box.

Press <Up arrow> two times

The highlighting is on the CODE field and its structure is displayed in the center box.

4. Now you are ready to select the specific fields to be displayed in the list. First, display the LAST_NAME, TITLE, and USAGE fields.

Press <Up arrow> until the field name LAST_NAME is highlighted

Press <Enter>

Look at the Action Line. Notice that it says **Command: LIST LAST_NAME**. The name of the field just selected appears in the Action Line.

Press <Up arrow> to highlight the TITLE field

FIGURE 6-11 Constructing a Field List

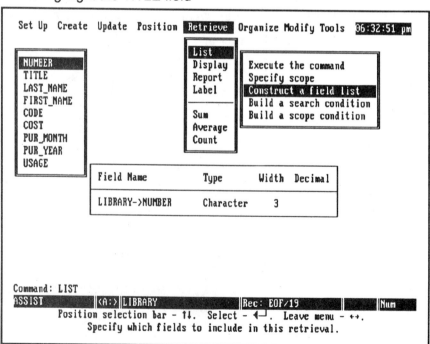

Chapter 6: Introduction to dBASE III PLUS

Press <Enter>

Press <Down arrow> until the USAGE field is highlighted

Press <Enter>

You have finished selecting the fields to be displayed. Your screen should look like Figure 6-12. Notice that all the field names selected appear in the Action Line at the bottom of the screen.

5. You are ready to leave the selection process.

Press <Right arrow>

The list of fields from the LIBRARY database file leaves the screen. The List Submenu is still on the screen.

Move the highlight to EXECUTE THE COMMAND

Press <Enter>

The prompt **Direct the output to the printer? [Y/N]** appears on the screen.

Type: Y

The database file prints and your screen should look like Figure 6-13. Before moving the paper in the printer, take a close look at what was printed. If the last record printed is record 18, your printer is holding record 19 in the print buffer. The following steps enable you to print record 19.

Press any key

Press <Esc>

The Assistant Menu disappears and the dot prompt appears at the bottom of the screen.

Type: Eject

FIGURE 6-12 Selecting Fields from a Database File

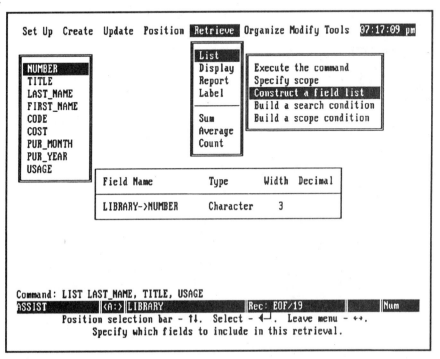

FIGURE 6-13 Listing Selected Files

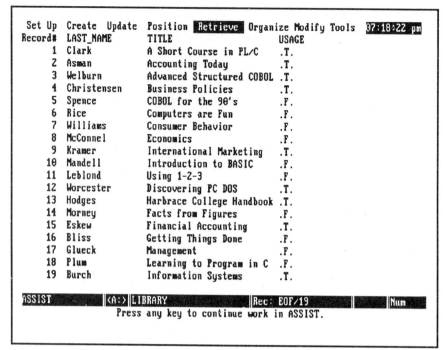

```
Set Up  Create  Update  Position  Retrieve  Organize Modify Tools  07:18:22 pm
Record#  LAST_NAME        TITLE                      USAGE
     1   Clark            A Short Course in PL/C      .T.
     2   Asman            Accounting Today           .T.
     3   Welburn          Advanced Structured COBOL  .T.
     4   Christensen      Business Policies          .T.
     5   Spence           COBOL for the 90's         .F.
     6   Rice             Computers are Fun          .F.
     7   Williams         Consumer Behavior          .F.
     8   McConnel         Economics                  .F.
     9   Kramer           International Marketing     .T.
    10   Mandell          Introduction to BASIC      .F.
    11   Leblond          Using 1-2-3                .F.
    12   Worcester        Discovering PC DOS         .T.
    13   Hodges           Harbrace College Handbook  .T.
    14   Morney           Facts from Figures         .F.
    15   Eskew            Financial Accounting       .T.
    16   Bliss            Getting Things Done        .F.
    17   Glueck           Management                 .F.
    18   Plum             Learning to Program in C   .F.
    19   Burch            Information Systems        .T.

ASSIST          <A:>LIBRARY              Rec: EOF/19         Num
           Press any key to continue work in ASSIST.
```

Press <Enter>

The last line of the list is printed. A second dot prompt appears at the bottom of the screen.

Type: `Assist`

Press <Enter>

The Assistant Menu returns to the screen. Look at the hard-copy of the list. The LAST_NAME, TITLE, and USAGE fields for all the records are printed. This time, reading the list is very easy. Notice that the fields are printed in the order they were selected (LAST_NAME precedes TITLE) rather than in the order in which they appear in the data-entry form (TITLE precedes LAST_NAME).

Press any key to exit from the display

6. The Retrieve Submenu appears on the screen.

Move the highlight to LIST from the Retrieve Submenu

Press <Enter>

Move the cursor to CONSTRUCT A FIELD LIST

Press <Enter>

This time display the COST, PUR_YEAR, and TITLE fields, in that order.

Press <Down arrow> until COST is highlighted

Press <Enter>

Press <Down arrow> until PUR_YEAR is highlighted

Press <Enter>

Press <Up arrow> until TITLE is highlighted

Press <Enter>

Look at the Action Line. It should say **Command: LIST COST, PUR_YEAR, TITLE**.

> Press <Right arrow>
>
> Move the highlight to EXECUTE THE COMMAND from the List Submenu
>
> Press <Enter>
>
> Type: Y

Again, the database file is printed. Your hard copy should look like Figure 6-14.

> Press any key to exit from the display

7. You have finished with this Your Turn exercise. You can either leave your work on the screen while you read the following section, or you can exit from dBASE III PLUS.

❏ MANAGING FILES WITH THE TOOLS OPTION

After working with dBASE III PLUS, you will begin to accumulate a lot of files on your data disk. Appropriate management of the files is extremely important. The TOOLS option on the Menu Bar in the Assistant Menu includes several commands that enable users to maintain files that have been created and stored. The following sections explain these options from the Tools Submenu.

Setting the Disk Drive

The first option on the Tools Submenu is SET DRIVE. If the disk drive the computer is currently accessing needs to be changed, select this option from the Tools Submenu. Another submenu appears with the letters of the disk drives available for selection. For example, if you are using a computer with two floppy disk drives, the letters A: and B: appear. Highlight the drive to be accessed and press <Enter>.

FIGURE 6-14
Printing Records in a File

Record#	COST	PUR_YEAR	TITLE
1	25.00	93	A Short Course in PL/C
2	50.50	93	Accounting Today
3	35.00	91	Advanced Structured COBOL
4	45.00	90	Business Policies
5	28.00	91	COBOL for the 90's
6	34.00	90	Computers are Fun
7	40.00	91	Consumer Behavior
8	65.00	90	Economics
9	52.00	91	International Marketing
10	54.00	90	Introduction to BASIC
11	21.50	92	Using 1-2-3
12	18.50	92	Discovering PC DOS
13	16.75	90	Harbrace College Handbook
14	16.00	91	Facts from Figures
15	38.80	92	Financial Accounting
16	23.60	91	Getting Things Done
17	28.45	02	Management
18	48.90	92	Learning to Program in C
19	52.60	92	Information Systems

Copying a File

There are two methods for copying files. One is used to copy a file that is open (a file whose name is displayed in the Status Bar). The other method is used to copy files that are not open. Making at least one copy, called a backup, of any file you create is extremely important. If anything should happen to your original file (for example, if it is accidentally erased) and you do not have a backup copy, all of your valuable work is lost forever.

The command to copy a file that is already open is found in the Organize Submenu. First, make sure the file whose name appears in the Status Bar is the file you want to copy, and then select the ORGANIZE option from the Menu Bar in the Assistant Menu. Next, select COPY. A menu with disk drive options appears. Select the disk drive where the new file is to be stored. The prompt **Enter the name of the file** appears. You must enter a file name that is different from the original file name. The new file name can be up to eight characters long. Ending the file name with the letters *BK* is a convenient way to easily identify the files on your disk that are backup copies. Enter the file name and press <Enter>. Another submenu appears. Select EXECUTE THE COMMAND. When the number of records that were copied appears in the Action Line at the bottom of the screen, you can press any key to return to the Assistant Menu.

To copy a file that is not open, select the TOOLS option from the Menu Bar in the Assistant Menu. Next, select COPY FILE. A menu with disk drive options appears. Select the disk drive where the file to be copied is stored. Another menu appears that lists all the files that are stored on the disk drive just selected. Select the file to be copied. Again, a menu with disk drive options appears. This time, select the disk drive where the new file is to be stored. The remainder of the procedure for copying an unopened file is similar to that for copying an opened file. The prompt **Enter the name of the file** appears. The file name can be up to eight characters long; ending it with the letters *BK* (for backup) will easily identify the file as a backup copy. Press <Enter> after the file name has been entered. When the number of records that were copied appears in the Action Line at the bottom of the screen, press any key to return to the Assistant Menu.

If you try to copy a file that is open using the COPY FILE command from the Tools Submenu, the message **File is already open** appears. If you get this error message, press <Enter> to get back to the Assistant Menu, and copy the file using the COPY command from the Organize Submenu.

YOUR TURN

In this hands-on exercise, you are going to make a copy of the LIBRARY file.

1. The Assistant Menu should be on your screen and the LIBRARY file should be active. The word LIBRARY should appear in the Status Bar. Because the LIBRARY file is open, use the COPY command from the ORGANIZE option on the Menu Bar of the Assistant Menu.

> Type o for ORGANIZE
>
> Move the highlight to COPY from the Organize Submenu
>
> Press <Enter>

Move the highlight to A:

Press <Enter>

Difference Box: If you are using a computer with two floppy disk drives, move the highlight to B: after selecting COPY from the Organize Submenu.

---

2.   The prompt **Enter the name of the file** appears.

Type: LIBRYBK

Press <Enter>

Move the highlight to EXECUTE THE COMMAND

Press <Enter>

When the file is copied, the message **19 Records copied** should appear in the Action Line at the bottom of your screen.

Press any key to return to the Assistant Menu

3.   You have finished with this Your Turn exercise. You can either leave your work on the screen while you read the following section, or you can exit from dBASE III PLUS.

Renaming a File

If it is necessary to change the name of a file, it can be easily accomplished with the RENAME option on the Menu Bar of the Assistant Menu. After selecting RENAME, a submenu with a list of the disk drives appears. Select the disk drive where the file to be renamed is stored. A list of all the files stored on that disk appears. Select the file to be renamed. The prompt **Enter the name of the file** appears. Enter the new file name, including the extension. When renaming files, you *must include the extension* in the new file name. That is, you must enter DBF at the end of the new file name. After typing the new file name with the DBF extension, press <Enter>. The message **Press any key to continue work in ASSIST** appears once the file has been renamed.

YOUR TURN

In this exercise you are going to rename the LIBRYBK file.

1.   The Assistant Menu should be on your screen and the LIBRARY file should be active. The word LIBRARY should appear in the Status Bar.

Type T for TOOLS

Move the highlight to RENAME from the Tools Submenu

Press <Enter>

Move the highlight to A:

Press <Enter>

2. A list of all the files stored on your disk in Drive A (Drive B on computers with two floppy disk drives) appears.

> Move the highlight to LIBRYBK.DBF
>
> Press <Enter>

The prompt **Enter the name of the file** appears.

> Type: `LIBRYBK2.DBF`
>
> Press <Enter>

When the message **Press any key to continue work in ASSIST** appears, the file has been renamed.

3. You have finished with this Your Turn exercise. You can either leave your work on the screen while you read the following section, or you can exit from dBASE III PLUS.

Listing the File Directory

It is often very useful to be able to list the names of the files that are stored on a disk. After creating several files you might forget some of their names or need to know how much storage space you have on your disk. You can access this information by listing the file directory.

The DIRECTORY command is found on the Tools Submenu. To list the file directory, select DIRECTORY and then choose the disk drive on which the files are stored. Another submenu appears that lists extensions used in dBASE III PLUS. You can list all the files that are stored or only those with a particular extension. For example, if you want the names of all database files, you can list only those that have a DBF extension rather than all the files that are stored. After selecting which files you want to list in the directory, the names of the designated files appear on the screen. When all the files are listed, press any key to return to the Assistant Menu.

 YOUR TURN

In this exercise, you are going to practice listing the file directory.

1. The Assistant Menu should be on your screen and the LIBRARY file should be active. The word LIBRARY should appear in the Status Bar. The Tools Submenu should be open. If necessary, type T for TOOLS.

> Move the highlight to DIRECTORY
>
> Press <Enter>
>
> Move the highlight to A:
>
> Press <Enter>

2. The submenu listing dBASE III PLUS extensions appears. Your screen should look like Figure 6-15. The only file extension you have been instructed to use is DBF for database file.

> Move the highlight to DBF DATABASE FILES

The two database files LIBRARY.DBF and LIBRYBK2.DBF should be listed on your screen. Also, the bytes of memory used by the two files and bytes of memory remaining on your disk are listed. Bytes are used for measuring computer memory. A byte is what the computer treats as one unit of information. Periodically checking the available memory is useful to see how much room you have left on your disk. If you think you may be running out of disk space, find out by listing the directory of the disk.

> Press any key to return to the Assistant Menu

3. You have finished with this Your Turn exercise. You can either leave your work on the screen while you read the following section, or you can exit from dBASE III PLUS.

Erasing a File

The command to erase a file is also found on the Tools Submenu. To erase a file, select the TOOLS option from the Menu Bar in the Assistant Menu. Next, select ERASE from the Tools Submenu. A list of disk drives appears; select the drive where the file to be erased is stored. A list of all the database files stored on the disk in the drive you selected appears next. Select the file you want to erase. Be absolutely certain this is the file to be erased before pressing <Enter>. When the <Enter> key is pressed, the file is deleted

FIGURE 6-15 Listing the File Directory

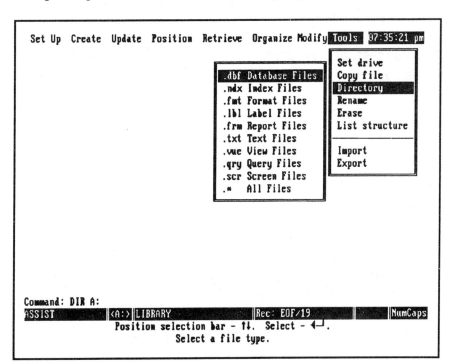

from the disk. If a file is mistakenly selected for deletion and the <Enter> key is pressed, the file is lost unless there is a backup copy.

After pressing <Enter> the message **File has been deleted** appears in the Action Line. To return to the Assistant Menu, press any key.

 YOUR TURN

In this hands-on exercise, you are going to make another copy of the LIBRARY.DBF file and then erase the copy.

1. The Assistant Menu should be on your screen and the LIBRARY file should be active. The word LIBRARY should appear in the Status Bar.

> Type o for ORGANIZE
>
> Move the highlight to COPY from the Organize Submenu
>
> Press <Enter>
>
> Move the highlight to A:
>
> Press <Enter>
>
> Type: LIBRYBK.DBF
>
> Press <Enter>
>
> Move the highlight to EXECUTE THE COMMAND
>
> Press <Enter>

> **Difference Box:**   If you are using a computer with two floppy disk drives, move the highlight to B: after selecting COPY from the Organize Submenu.

2. The message **19 records copied** that appears in the Action Line indicates that there is now a second copy of LIBRARY.DBF. Next, delete the copy made earlier.

> Press any key to return to the Assistant Menu
>
> Type T for TOOLS
>
> Move the highlight to ERASE from the Tools Submenu
>
> Press <Enter>
>
> Move the highlight to A:
>
> Press <Enter>
>
> Move the highlight to LIBRYBK2.DBF

> **Difference Box:** If you are using a computer with two floppy disk drives, move the highlight to B: after selecting ERASE from the Tools Submenu.

Before pressing <Enter>, be certain that you have the right file name highlighted.

Press <Enter>

The message **File has been deleted** appears in the Action Line.

Press any key to return to the Assistant Menu

3. You have finished with this Your Turn exercise. You can either leave your work on the screen while you read the following section, or you can exit from dBASE III PLUS.

❑ RELATIONAL AND LOGICAL OPERATORS

At times it is useful to be able to display specific records. For example, you might want to display only those records that meet certain conditions. Using the LIBRARY file as an example, suppose you want to know which books cost more than $40. Relational operators enable the user to display only those records that meet certain conditions, such as "cost more than $40." Table 6-1 defines the relational operators available in dBASE III PLUS.

TABLE 6-1 Relational Operators

Relational Operator	Relation
=	Equal to
<	Less than
>	Greater than
<=	Less than or equal to
>=	Greater than or equal to
<> or #	Not equal to

To display only those records that meet certain requirements, first select the RETRIEVE option from the Main Menu Bar. Next, select DISPLAY. From the Display Submenu, select BUILD A SEARCH CONDITION. A list of all the fields from the current file appears. Select the search field, that is, the field on which the search is to be based. For example, if you want to find all the books in the LIBRARY file that cost more than $40, the COST field is the search field on which the search is based.

Once a search field has been selected, a menu listing all the relational operators appears. Select a relational operator. If the search field is character/text, the prompt **Enter a character string** appears. If the search field is numeric, the prompt **Enter a numeric value** appears. After either a character string or numeric value has been entered, a logical operator can be selected.

Logical operators allow more than one condition to be set up for displaying records. For example, say you want to display only the records of books from the LIBRARY file that cost more than $40 and were purchased in 1990. To conduct this kind of search, it is necessary to select a logical operator. Table 6-2 lists and explains the logical operators.

If a logical operator is selected, a list of the fields from the current file appears again and another search condition can be set up. When all the desired conditions have been set up, select NO MORE CONDITIONS. Next select EXECUTE THE COMMAND. All the records that meet the designated conditions will be displayed.

TABLE 6-2 Logical Operators

Logical Operator	Comparison
.AND.	Both expressions must be true.
.OR.	Either one expression or the other must be true (or both).

YOUR TURN

In this hands-on exercise, you are going to practice using relational and logical operators.

1. The Assistant Menu should be on your screen and the LIBRARY file should be active. The word LIBRARY should appear in the Status Bar. First, display all the books that cost more than $40.

> Type R for RETRIEVE
>
> Move the highlight to DISPLAY from the Retrieve Submenu
>
> Press <Enter>
>
> Move the cursor to BUILD A SEARCH CONDITION from the Display Submenu
>
> Press <Enter>

A list of the fields in the LIBRARY file appears at the left of the screen. A description of the highlighted field appears in the center of the field. Because you are interested in locating records of all books that cost more than $40, select the COST field.

> Move the highlight to COST
>
> Press <Enter>

A menu of the relational operators appears. Your screen should look like Figure 6-16.

> Move the highlight to > GREATER THAN
>
> Press <Enter>

The prompt **Enter a numeric value** appears.

> Type: 40.00
>
> Press <Enter>

Another menu appears that enables you to add more conditions. For this situation, however, you do not want to add more conditions.

> Move the highlight to NO MORE CONDITIONS
>
> Press <Enter>
>
> Move the highlight to EXECUTE THE COMMAND
>
> Press <Enter>

A list of the seven books costing more than $40 appears. Look over the list carefully.

> Press any key

FIGURE 6-16 Relational Operators

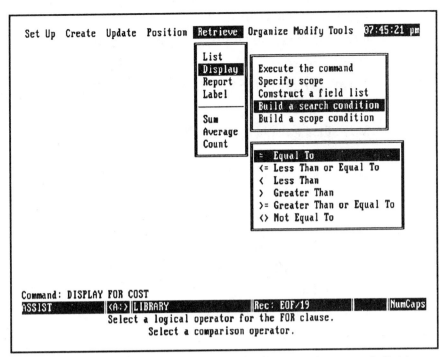

2. Now display all books that were purchased after 1990. PUR_YEAR is the search field.

> Type R for RETRIEVE
>
> Move the highlight to DISPLAY from the Retrieve Submenu
>
> Press <Enter>
>
> Move the cursor to BUILD A SEARCH CONDITION
>
> Press <Enter>

A list of the fields in the LIBRARY file appears at the left of the screen.

> Move the highlight to PUR_YEAR
>
> Press <Enter>
>
> Move the highlight to > GREATER THAN
>
> Press <Enter>
>
> The prompt **Enter a character string (without quotes)** appears.
>
> Type: 90
>
> Move the highlight to NO MORE CONDITIONS
>
> Press <Enter>
>
> Move the cursor to EXECUTE THE COMMAND

Look at the PUR_YEAR field and note that all the years listed are after 1990. All the records cannot fit on the screen. Press any key to see the remaining records.

> Press any key
>
> Press any key to return to the Assistant Menu

3. Now you want to know how many books you have by the author Steven Mandell.

Type R for RETRIEVE

Move the cursor to DISPLAY from the Retrieve Submenu

Press <Enter>

Move the highlight to BUILD A SEARCH CONDITION from the Display Submenu

Press <Enter>

Move the highlight to LAST_NAME

Press <Enter>

Move the highlight to = EQUAL TO

Press <Enter>

Type: Mandell

The character string must be entered exactly as it appears in the record. For example, if you type *mandell* instead of *Mandell,* dBASE III PLUS cannot find the record.

Press <Enter>

Move the highlight to NO MORE CONDITIONS

Press <Enter>

Move the highlight to EXECUTE THE COMMAND

Press <Enter>

The one book by Mandell in your personal library is displayed on the screen.

Press any key

4. Now suppose you want to combine the first two commands to display the titles of all the books purchased after 1990 that cost more than $40. The logical operator .AND. must be selected.

Type R for RETRIEVE

Move the highlight to DISPLAY from the Retrieve Submenu

Press <Enter>

Move the cursor to BUILD A SEARCH CONDITION from the Display Submenu

Press <Enter>

Move the highlight to COST

Press <Enter>

Move the highlight to > GREATER THAN

Press <Enter>

Type: 40.00

Press <Enter>

Next, select a logical operator.

Move the highlight to COMBINE WITH .AND.

Press <Enter>

Now you are ready to build the second search condition, which is all books purchased after 1990.

> Move the highlight to PUR_YEAR
>
> Press <Enter>
>
> Move the highlight to > GREATER THAN
>
> Press <Enter>
>
> Type: 9 0
>
> Move the highlight to NO MORE CONDITIONS
>
> Press <Enter>
>
> Move the highlight to EXECUTE THE COMMAND
>
> Press <Enter>

dBASE III PLUS displays the books that cost more than $40 and were purchased after 1990.

> Press any key

5. You have finished with this Your Turn exercise. You can either leave your work on the screen while you read the following section, or you can exit from dBASE III PLUS.

❏ GOING TO A SPECIFIC RECORD

A specific data record can be displayed by using the GOTO RECORD option from the Position Menu. The options from the Goto Record Submenu are TOP, BOTTOM, and RECORD. If TOP is selected, record 1 becomes the active record. If BOTTOM is selected, the last record in the file becomes the active record. If RECORD is selected, the prompt **Enter a numeric value** appears. Enter the number of the record that you want placed in active status and press <Enter>.

  YOUR TURN

In this hands-on exercise, you are going to practice going to specific records.

1. The Assistant Menu should be on your screen and the LIBRARY file should be active. The word LIBRARY should appear in the Status Bar. Practice using the GOTO RECORD option.

> Type P for POSITION
>
> Move the highlight to GOTO RECORD from the Position Submenu
>
> Press <Enter>
>
> Move the cursor to TOP from the Goto Record Submenu
>
> Press <Enter>

Notice that the Status Bar now says **Rec: 1/19**. The first record in the file is now the active record.

> Type R for RETRIEVE

Move the highlight to DISPLAY from the Retrieve Submenu

Press <Enter>

Move the highlight to EXECUTE THE COMMAND from the Display Submenu

Press <Enter>

Record 1 is displayed.

Press any key

2. Now you want to display the last record in the file.

Type P for POSITION

Move the highlight to GOTO RECORD

Press <Enter>

Move the highlight to BOTTOM

Press <Enter>

Notice that the Status Bar now says **Rec: 19/19**. The last record in the file is now the active record.

Type R for RETRIEVE

Move the highlight to DISPLAY from the Retrieve Submenu

Press <Enter>

Move the highlight to EXECUTE THE COMMAND

Press <Enter>

Record 19 is now displayed.

Press any key

3. Now you want to go to a specific record.

Type P for POSITION

Move the highlight to GOTO RECORD from the Position Submenu

Press <Enter>

Move the highlight to RECORD from the Goto Record Submenu

Press <Enter>

Type: 15

Press <Enter>

Notice that the Status Bar now says **Rec: 15/19**. The fifteenth record in the file is now the active record.

Type R for RETRIEVE

Move the highlight to DISPLAY from the Retrieve Submenu

Press <Enter>

Move the highlight to EXECUTE THE COMMAND from the Display Submenu

Press <Enter>

Record 15 is displayed.

Press any key

4. You have finished with this Your Turn exercise. You can either leave your work on the screen while you read the following section, or you can exit from dBASE III PLUS.

❏ dBASE III PLUS SUMMARY COMMANDS

Thus far this section has introduced dBASE III PLUS commands that enable users to create, edit, and display data files. When a file has been created, it can provide valuable information about a variety of subjects through the use of summary commands. In fact, the summarizing of data is one of dBASE's most significant functions. The SUMMARY commands SUM, AVERAGE, and COUNT are found in the Retrieve Menu.

Count

The COUNT option can be used in several ways to tally the records in a file. An unconditional COUNT command counts all the data records in a file. To use the unconditional COUNT command, select COUNT from the Retrieve Menu, then EXECUTE THE COMMAND. A message such as **28 records** appears on the screen; this indicates the total number of records currently stored in the file.

A conditional COUNT command counts only records that meet a specified condition. To build a condition for the COUNT command, first select COUNT from the Retrieve Menu, and then BUILD A SEARCH CONDITION. Building a condition on which to base the COUNT command is exactly the same as building a condition on which to display only records that meet a specific condition.

More than one condition can be specified in the COUNT command by selecting the option COMBINE WITH .AND., or the option COMBINE WITH .OR. These logical operators perform the same functions when used with the COUNT option that they do when used with the DISPLAY option.

 YOUR TURN

In this hands-on exercise, you are going to practice using the COUNT option.

1. The Assistant Menu should be on your screen and the LIBRARY file should be active. The word LIBRARY should appear in the Status Bar. Because you want to count the records in the file, it is necessary to make sure the first record in the file is the active record.

Type P for POSITION

Move the highlight to GOTO RECORD from the Position Submenu

Press <Enter>

Move the cursor to TOP from the Goto Record Submenu

Press <Enter>

The Status Bar should read **Rec: 1/19**

Type R for RETRIEVE

Move the highlight to COUNT from the Retrieve Submenu

Press <Enter>

Move the highlight to EXECUTE THE COMMAND

Press <Enter>

The message **19 records** appears at the bottom of the screen because the LIBRARY file currently has nineteen data records stored in it.

Press any key

2. Now you want to find out how many books you purchased in 1992.

Type R for RETRIEVE

Move the highlight to COUNT from the Retrieve Submenu

Press <Enter>

Move the highlight to BUILD A SEARCH CONDITION

Press <Enter>

A list of the fields in the LIBRARY file appears.

Move the highlight to PUR_YEAR

Press <Enter>

Move the highlight to = EQUAL TO

Press <Enter>

Type: 92

Move the highlight to NO MORE CONDITIONS

Press <Enter>

Move the highlight to EXECUTE THE COMMAND

Press <Enter>

A message displaying how many books were purchased in 1992 appears at the bottom of the screen.

Press any key

3. Now you want to know how many books you purchased in 1992 that cost $25 or more.

Type R for RETRIEVE

Move the highlight to COUNT from the Retrieve Submenu

Press <Enter>

Move the highlight to BUILD A SEARCH CONDITION

Press <Enter>

Move the highlight to PUR_YEAR

Press <Enter>

Move the highlight to = EQUAL TO

Press <Enter>

Type: 92

Move the highlight to COMBINE WITH .AND.

Press <Enter>

Move the highlight to COST

Press <Enter>

Move the highlight to > = GREATER THAN OR EQUAL TO

Press <Enter>

Type: 25.00

Press <Enter>

Move the highlight to NO MORE CONDITIONS

Press <Enter>

Move the highlight to EXECUTE THE COMMAND

Press <Enter>

A message displaying how many books were purchased in 1992 that cost $25 or more appears at the bottom of the screen.

Press any key

4. You have finished with this Your Turn exercise. You can either leave your work on the screen while you read the following section, or you can exit from dBASE III PLUS.

Sum

The contents of numeric fields can be added using the SUM option from the Retrieve Menu. The unconditional SUM command calculates the sum of all the values in the specified data field. To use the unconditional SUM command, select SUM from the Retrieve Menu. Next, select EXECUTE THE COMMAND. If there is only one numeric field in the file, dBASE III PLUS automatically totals all the entries made in that field. If there is more than one numeric field, you must designate the field for which you want to calculate a total. The SUM command also can include relational and logical operators.

 YOUR TURN

In this hands-on exercise, you are going to practice using the SUM option.

1. The Assistant Menu should be on your screen and the LIBRARY file should be active. The word LIBRARY should appear in the Status Bar. Find the total cost of the books in your library by using the SUM command.

Type R for RETRIEVE

Move the highlight to SUM from the Retrieve Submenu

Press <Enter>

Move the highlight to EXECUTE THE COMMAND

A message appears displaying the total cost of the nineteen records.

Press any key

2. Now you are going to find out how much money you spent on books in 1992.

Type R for RETRIEVE

Move the highlight to SUM from the Retrieve Submenu

Press <Enter>

Move the highlight to BUILD A SEARCH CONDITION

Press <Enter>

Move the highlight to PUR_YEAR

Press <Enter>

Move the highlight to = EQUAL TO

Press <Enter>

Type: 92

Move the highlight to NO MORE CONDITIONS

Press <Enter>

Move the highlight to EXECUTE THE COMMAND

Press <Enter>

A message appears displaying the total cost of the books purchased in 1992.

Press any key

3. You want to know how much money you spent in 1992 for books that cost $25 or more.

Type R for RETRIEVE

Move the highlight to SUM from the Retrieve Submenu

Press <Enter>

Move the highlight to BUILD A SEARCH CONDITION

Press <Enter>

Move the highlight to PUR_YEAR

Press <Enter>

Move the highlight to = EQUAL TO

Press <Enter>

Type: 92

Move the highlight to COMBINE WITH .AND.

Press <Enter>

Move the highlight to COST

Press <Enter>

Move the highlight to > = GREATER THAN OR EQUAL TO

Press <Enter>

Type: 25.00

Press <Enter>

Move the highlight to NO MORE CONDITIONS

Press <Enter>

Move the highlight to EXECUTE THE COMMAND

Press <Enter>

A message appears displaying the total amount spent on books costing $25 or more in 1992.

Press any key

4. You have finished with this Your Turn exercise. You can either leave your work on the screen while you read the following section, or you can exit from dBASE III PLUS.

Average

The AVERAGE option from the Retrieve Menu calculates an average value for the contents of a numeric field. The unconditional AVERAGE command computes the average using the specified field from all the records. The conditional AVERAGE command computes the average using the numeric fields that meet the specified conditions. The AVERAGE command also can include logical operators.

YOUR TURN

In this hands-on exercise, you are going to practice using the AVERAGE option.

1. The Assistant Menu should be on your screen and the LIBRARY file should be active. The word LIBRARY should appear in the Status Bar. Find the average cost of all your books.

Type R for RETRIEVE

Move the highlight to AVERAGE from the Retrieve Submenu

Press <Enter>

Move the highlight to EXECUTE THE COMMAND

Press <Enter>

A message appears displaying the average cost of all your books.

Press any key

2. You are now finished working with the LIBRARY file. Exit from dBASE III PLUS.

Type S for SET UP

Move the highlight to QUIT dBASE III PLUS from the Set Up Submenu

Press <Enter>

Take your disks out of the computer. Turn the computer and monitor off.

❑ SUMMARY POINTS

■ A data manager (data management package) can be used for the same purposes as a manual filing system: to record and file information.

■ Each data item stored, such as a first name, a last name, and address, or an invoice amount, is called a field.

■ A group of related fields forms a record.

■ A group of related records is a file.

■ Defining the structure of a database file involves deciding what fields will be included in each record, the names of the fields, the width of the field and whether the data stored in a field is alphanumeric, numeric or logical.

■ Once data has been entered into a database file, the file can be updated, which includes editing records, adding records and deleting records.

❑ COMMAND SUMMARY

Command	Description
<Ctrl>-<End>	Exits from a file or saves a record.
<Ctrl>-N	Inserts a new line or field definition.
<Ctrl>-<PgDn>	Zooms in; enters editing line for text or expressions.
<Ctrl>-<PgUp>	Zooms out; exits editing line for text or expressions.
<Ctrl>-T	Erases one word to the right of the cursor position.
<Ctrl>-U	Marks a record for deletion in Browse or Edit mode; deletes a field definition.
<Ctrl>-Y	Erases to the end of the line in Append or Edit.

Main Menu	Secondary Menu	Description
Create	Database file	Creates a new database file.
Modify	Database file	Allows you to change the structure of the database once it has been created.
Organize	Copy	Copies a file that is already open.
Position	Goto Record	Allows you to go to a specific record or to the beginning or end of a database.
Retrieve	Average	Calculates an average value for the contents of a numeric field.
Retrieve	Count	Counts the records in a file that meet a specified condition.
Retrieve	Display	Allows you to display only those records that meet certain requirements.
Retrieve	List	Allows you to display or print specified fields from the records.
Retrieve	Sum	Calculates the sum of numeric fields.
Setup	Database file	Retrieves a database file for use.
Setup	Quit dBASE III PLUS	Exits the program.
Tools	Copy file	Allows you to copy a database file without leaving dBASE.

Main Menu	Secondary Menu	Description
Tools	Directory	Lists the names of files stored on a disk.
Tools	Erase	Erases a file from the disk.
Tools	List structure	Displays the structure of the active database file.
Tools	Rename	Allows you to rename a database file without leaving dBASE.
Tools	Set Drive	Allows you to specify the drive and/or directory that data files are stored in.
Update	Append	Allows you to add records to a database.
Update	Browse	Allows you to view or edit multiple records on screen at a single time in a column format.
Update	Edit	Allows you to view or edit a database record by record.
Update	Pack	Permanently removes records that have been marked for deletion from a database file.
Update	Recall	Allows you to recall records that have been marked for deletion.

❏ dBASE III PLUS EXERCISES

1. Assume that the computer is shut off. List all the necessary steps needed to start the dBASE III PLUS program. If you need help remembering how to start dBASE III PLUS, refer to "Getting Started with dBASE III PLUS earlier in this chapter.

2. Start the dBASE III PLUS program. Assume you have been hired by Kenneth Fretwell, D.D.S., to establish a database management system for his office. Use dBASE III PLUS to create a database file named PATIENTS. If you need to review how to name a database file, refer to "Naming a Database File" earlier in this chapter.

3. Your PATIENTS file has eight fields. For each field, enter the following into the field description form. If you need to review how to define fields, refer to "Defining Fields" earlier in this chapter.

Field Name	Type	Width	Dec
First_Name	Character	10	
Last_Name	Character	10	
Address	Character	15	
City	Character	10	
St	Character	2	
ZIP	Character	5	
Age	Character	2	
Balance	Numeric	6	2

4. Enter the following data in the PATIENTS file. If you need to review how to enter data into a file, refer to "Entering Data into a Database File" earlier in this chapter.

First_Name	Last_Name	Address	City	St	ZIP	Age	Balance
David	Busch	552 Wallace	Columbus	OH	43216	27	58.60
Patricia	Busch	552 Wallace	Columbus	OH	43216	28	0
Tom	Allen	67 Curtis	Columbus	OH	43216	78	8.90
Eileen	Spires	890 Pine	Columbus	OH	43216	56	120.00
Dave	Jenkins	10 W. Wooster	Columbus	OH	43216	13	93.50
Pamela	Weaver	16 Clough	Columbus	OH	43216	10	0
Bradley	Busch	552 Wallace	Columbus	OH	43216	7	25.00
William	Bentley	77 Palmer	Dayton	OH	45401	45	0

After the eighth record has been added, press <Enter> to end the process of adding data records.

5. Proofread all the records you entered. Make any corrections necessary and save the changes. If you need to review how to edit files, refer to "Editing a Database File" earlier in this chapter.

6. Add the following records to the PATIENTS file. If you need to review how to add records, refer to "Adding a Record" earlier in this chapter.

First_Name	Last_Name	Address	City	St	ZIP	Age	Balance
Wilma	Lukes	909 Clough	Columbus	OH	43216	89	280.09
Douglas	Swartz	9 Main	Dayton	OH	45401	32	46.90
Linda	Plazer	12 Vine	Columbus	OH	43216	25	176.00
Ann	Bressler	25 Baldwin	Columbus	OH	43216	25	0

7. Tom Allen and William Bentley changed dentists. Delete their records from the file. If you need to review how to delete records, refer to "Deleting a Record" earlier in this chapter.

8. The Busch family moved. Their new address is 41 Normandie in Columbus. Update their records and assume their ZIP code is the same.

9. Dr. Fretwell is going to start a No Cavities Club for children under the age of 16. List all of Dr. Fretwell's patients who are eligible for membership in the club. Refer to "Relational and Logical Operators" earlier in this chapter.

10. What is the total balance due from all of the patients? Which patients owe more than $35? Which patients have a zero balance? For help, refer to "Relational and Logical Operators" and "Sum" earlier in this chapter.

11. Print a hard copy of the PATIENTS file. If you need to review how to print a dBASE III PLUS file, refer to "Displaying and Printing a Database File" earlier in this chapter.

❏ dBASE III PLUS PROBLEMS 1-13

To complete the following exercises, you need to use files on the Student File disk. In order to complete these exercises, you will need to be able to start dBASE III PLUS, quit dBASE III PLUS, define the structure of a database file, name a database file, define fields, display the structure of a database file, edit the structure of a database file, enter data into a database file, add a record, copy a file, use relational and logical operators, go to a specific record, and calculate an average.

1. On the Student File disk there is a dBASE III PLUS file called PAYROLL. Start the dBASE III PLUS program and retrieve this file. Make a copy of this file and call the copy PAYROLL1. That way, if you make a mistake, you will always have the original file.

2. Assume that you are working in the payroll department of a company. The company uses dBASE III PLUS to keep information regarding employees' names, addresses, job names, and hourly salaries. Access the PAYROLL1 database file. How do you display a file's structure? Display the structure of the PAYROLL1 file. How many fields are there in the file? How many numeric fields? What is the width of the field JOBNAME? The field STATUS defines the personnel status (F for full-time and P for part-time). What is its type? How many data records are in the file?

3. Now you want to see the records of the employees. Display all the records. What option do you select to ensure that all the records will be displayed? What is the name of the employee corresponding to record 5? What is his job title? What is the name of the last employee?

4. Now you want to list only the last name, first name, and job title of all employees. Describe the steps necessary to obtain this information.

5. Now list the same information for full-time employees only. How many full-time employees are employed by the company?

6. List the last name, first name, employee number, and job title for all part-time employees who are writers.

7. What is the average hourly wage of all the employees? Which employees earn more than $9 an hour?

8. The payroll department manager wants you to create a new database file that will store information about the employees who worked during March. The file should contain the following information:

Field Name	Field Type	Width	Dec
EMPLNUM	N	3	
MONTH	N	2	
ENDPER	C	6	
NORMHRS	N	5	2

The EMPLNUM field keeps track of the employee number; the MONTH field keeps track of the month of work; the ENDPER field keeps track of the ending period; and the NORMHRS field keeps track of the total hours of work. Create the new database file and name it MONTH3.

9. Enter the structure of the new file using the information in step 8. What prompt does dBASE III PLUS display when all of the fields have been entered? Answer N and use the LIST STRUCTURE option from the Tools Menu to review the file structure. ⎨ PRESS ENTER to confirm. Any other Key to resume

INPUT Data records now? (Y/N)

10. The payroll department manager wants you to add a new field to the MONTH3 database file. This field is to keep track of the number of overtime hours an employee puts in. Add the field as follows:

Field Name	Field Type	Width	Dec
OVERTIME	N	6	2

11. You need to edit the structure of the MONTH3 database file. Change the field width of the NORMHRS field to 6.

12. When you are satisfied with the structure of the MONTH3 database file, use the appropriate command to save your modifications.

13. What is the command to add records to a file? Using this command, enter the following data into the file: Update - Append   89202

EMPLNUM	MONTH	ENDPERIOD	NORMHRS	OVERTIME
0	3	033193	160.00	30.00
2	3	033193	160.00	40.00
3	3	033193	160.00	0.00
4	3	033193	140.00	0.00
6	3	033193	160.00	0.00
7	3	033193	160.00	20.00
8	3	033193	160.00	20.00
9	3	033193	160.00	0.00
10	3	033193	160.00	0.00
11	3	033193	100.00	0.00
13	3	033193	160.00	0.00
14	3	033193	80.00	0.00
15	3	033193	90.00	0.00

Save the data. Exit from dBASE III PLUS.

Assume a video rental store has asked you for help in setting up a dBASE III PLUS file that will help them keep track of the rental of video cassettes. The video store would like you to create a file for them that includes the following data for each video tape:

Item number:	This is a number the store assigns each tape. It is a five digit number preceded by a V. For example, V-78902.
Title:	This would be the name of the movie. For example, *Out of Africa.*
Price:	This would be what the video store charges to rent the movie overnight.
Status:	This would keep track of whether the movie is currently in the store or is rented out. For example, a *Y* for Yes might indicate the movie is in the store available for rental and a *N* for No might indicate the movie is currently loaned out.

1.   Create a new database file named VIDEO.DBF that can keep track of the information required by the video store.

2.   Make up information on twelve movies and enter the data for those twelve movies into the VIDEO.DBF file. Select six of the movies as being rented out and the other six as being in the store available for rent. Vary the rental price of the movies. The video store charges more to rent new releases than it does to rent older movies.

3.   Now you want to demonstrate to the video store how the VIDEO file can be used. Print a list of all the movies that are currently out on loan.

4.   The video store wants to know on an average how much they charge to rent movies. Find the average rental cost of all the movies.

5.   Someone comes into the video store and wants to know if one of the movies in your database file is out on loan. Find and print the record of that one movie to see whether or not it is available.

 **CHAPTER 7**

More dBASE III PLUS Features

OUTLINE

❏ INTRODUCTION

The previous chapter presented all the commands needed to create a database file with dBASE III PLUS. Once a file has been created, it can be manipulated in many useful ways. The purpose of this chapter is to introduce the more advanced dBASE III PLUS commands that make it possible to efficiently arrange data stored in a database file so that it can be used to create a report.

The directions in this chapter are written for computers with a hard drive. Differences for computers with two floppy drives are written in Difference Boxes.

❏ SORTING A DATABASE FILE

As discussed in the previous chapter, a database file is made up of records that a user enters into the data-entry form. As each record is entered, dBASE III PLUS automatically assigns a chronological record number to it. The data records are stored in the file in the order in which they are entered, but this may not be the order that provides the most useful information. For example, records in a payroll file are not entered in alphabetical order. They are added when employees are hired and deleted when workers leave a company. To be useful, a database program must be able to arrange a payroll file in alphabetical order. In dBASE III PLUS, the SORT option found in the Organize Menu enables users to rearrange data records according to the contents of a specified field, which is called the key field. In the example of a payroll file being sorted alphabetically by last name, the field containing the last names would be the key field.

Sorting physically rearranges the records in the active database file. To maintain the original database file, dBASE III PLUS copies the sorted database file into what is called the target file. The user must designate a new file name for the target file. When the sorting procedure is complete, the data records in the target file are arranged by the key field as specified.

YOUR TURN

The Your Turn exercises in this chapter use a slightly different format than the Your Turn exercises in the previous chapter. By now, you should be familiar with how to select a menu option using dBASE III PLUS. That is, you move the highlight bar to the option you wish to select and press <Enter>. Instead of including both steps in the instructions, the exercises in this chapter simply tell you to *Select* a particular option. For example, instead of telling you,

> Move the highlight to DISPLAY
>
> Press <Enter>

The instructions tell you to

> *Select DISPLAY*

Whenever you see the instruction *Select*, it means both to move the highlight to that option and to press <Enter>.

You are going to sort a database file using the SORT option from the Organize Menu. You will create a file called STUDENT that contains the names, classifications, grade-point averages, birth dates, Social Security numbers, account balances, and addresses of students at a college. Numbers are used to designate a student's classification: 4 = senior, 3 = junior, 2 sophomore, and 1 = freshman.

1. Start dBASE III PLUS. Using the CREATE option, create a database file named STUDENT. Enter the following information in the field definition form:

Field	Field Name	Type	Width	Dec
1	NAME	Character	20	
2	YEAR	Character	1	
3	GPA	Numeric	4	2
4	BIRTHDATE	Date	8	
5	SSNUMBER	Character	11	
6	ACCOUNT	Numeric	8	2
7	ADDRESS	Character	15	
8	CITY	Character	10	
9	STATE	Character	2	
10	ZIP	Character	5	

Press <Ctrl>-<End>

If the entries are correct, press <Enter>. If they are not correct, make the necessary corrections and press <Ctrl>-<End> and <Enter>.

2. When the field information has been entered you may input data into the records. The prompt **Input data records now? (Y/N)** should be on the screen.

Type: Y

Enter the information contained in Table 7-1.

TABLE 7-1 Records for the STUDENT File

Name	Yr	GPA	BDate	SSNumber	Account	Address	City	St	ZIP
Faulks, Tim	4	3.20	03/01/71	343-61-1101	286.59	78 Main St.	Miami	FL	32109
Bulas, Irene	3	3.00	07/19/72	289-89-4672	1203.87	908 W. Summit	Oak Hill	TX	78746
Klein, Tom	4	2.55	10/20/71	278-45-7891	96.95	12 Yong St.	Hampton	NC	27710
Wilcox, Bill	1	2.00	06/08/74	524-68-4099	0.00	6 Williams Rd.	Anadale	TX	78756
Ornelas, Tina	2	3.12	03/05/73	468-71-9002	2005.32	123 First St.	Amarillo	TX	79107
Lord, Pamela	4	3.78	03/03/71	208-46-4096	576.94	98 Pike St.	El Paso	TX	79910
Busch, Brad	3	3.70	04/04/67	782-28-1598	803.52	32 Badner	Dallas	TX	75221
Weaver, Chris	2	2.15	10/10/73	411-69-4664	68.07	909 Clough	Lubbock	TX	79408
Engel, Chuck	4	2.34	10/10/66	778-61-8723	12.18	14 Indian Rd.	Houston	TX	77002
Wilks, Cleo	1	3.81	11/02/74	428-18-9972	1096.20	76 Gorrel	Laredo	TX	78040
Bressler, Ann	1	2.08	07/16/69	789-22-6615	0.00	45 S. Luke St.	Pasadena	TX	77501
Hocks, Arthur	3	2.89	03/12/72	558-79-5151	446.29	90 Kellog Rd.	Lubbock	TX	79408
DeSalvo, Liz	4	2.22	06/14/71	879-43-6291	0.00	9. W. Second	Dallas	TX	75221
Freidman, Mark	2	3.98	09/02/74	217-64-4049	33.68	3426 Little St	Pasadena	TX	77501
Crope, Trish	1	3.21	03/11/71	491-10-9984	175.50	67 Baldwin	Oak Hill	TX	78746

3. When the records have been entered, use the SORT option from the Organize Menu to sort all the records alphabetically by name.

Select ORGANIZE

Select SORT

Select NAME

Next, name the target file on which the sorted database will be stored. To do this you must press the right arrow key.

Press <Right arrow>

A list of disk drive options appears. Select the drive where the floppy disk, onto which the sorted database file is to be stored, is located.

Select A:

Difference Box: If you are using a computer with two floppy disk drives, select B: as the drive where the floppy disk is located.

The prompt **Enter the name of the file** appears. Enter a name for the target file.

Type: Alphaname

Press <Enter>

ALPHANAME is the name of the file that now stores the records listed in alphabetical order by name. After pressing <Enter>, the message **100% Sorted 15 Records sorted** appears.

Press any key

4. To see the new sorted file, select the DATABASE FILE option from the Set Up Menu to change the active file to ALPHANAME. Currently, STUDENT is the active file.

Select SET UP

Select DATABASE FILE

Select A:

Difference Box: On computers with two floppy disk drives, select B:.

Select ALPHANAM.DBF

Type: N

To check if the records have been sorted alphabetically by name, use the DISPLAY option from the Retrieve Menu.

Select RETRIEVE

Select DISPLAY

Select SPECIFY SCOPE

Select ALL

Select CONSTRUCT A FIELD LIST

> *Select NAME*
>
> Press <Right arrow>
>
> *Select EXECUTE THE COMMAND*

The names should appear on the screen listed in alphabetical order.

> Press any key

5. Now you are going to sort all the records by GPA in ascending order. The sorted file will be called GPA.

> *Select SET UP*
>
> *Select DATABASE FILE*
>
> *Select A:*

Difference Box: If you are using a computer with two floppy disk drives, select B:.

> *Select STUDENT.DBF*
>
> Type: N
>
> *Select ORGANIZE*
>
> *Select SORT*
>
> *Select GPA*
>
> Press <Right arrow>
>
> *Select A:*

Difference Box: If you are using a computer with two floppy disk drives, select B:.

> Type: GPA
>
> Press <Enter>

The records are now sorted by grade-point average.

> Press any key

6. Look at the records sorted by grade-point average.

> *Select SET UP*
>
> *Select DATABASE FILE*
>
> *Select A:*

Difference Box: If you are using a computer with two floppy disk drives, select B:

> *Select GPA.DBF*
>
> Type: N
>
> *Select RETRIEVE*
>
> *Select DISPLAY*

> *Select SPECIFY SCOPE*
>
> *Select ALL*
>
> *Select CONSTRUCT A FIELD LIST*
>
> *Select NAME*
>
> *Select GPA*
>
> Press <Right arrow>
>
> *Select EXECUTE THE COMMAND*

The names and GPAs should appear on the screen listed in order by GPA.

> Press any key

7. You have finished with this Your Turn exercise. You can either leave your work on the screen while you read the following section, or you can exit from dBASE III PLUS.

Conditional Sorts

A condition can be added to the dBASE III PLUS SORT option dictating that only those records that satisfy the condition are included in the sort. dBASE III PLUS tests each record for the condition and includes the record in the sort only if the condition is met.

To sort only a selected set of records, you must first create a query file that specifies the conditions for selecting records. To create a query file, select QUERY from the Create Menu. Next, select the drive where the new query file is to be stored, and then enter a file name for the file. A query table, by which you can designate the conditions for the sort, appears.

  YOUR TURN

Use the STUDENT file to perform a conditional sort. You want to know which students have a GPA of 3.5 or more. If necessary, start the dBASE III PLUS program.

1. First, make the STUDENT file the active file.

> *Select SET UP*
>
> *Select DATABASE FILE*
>
> *Select A:*

Difference Box: If you are using a computer with two floppy disk drives, select B:.

> *Select STUDENT.DBF*
>
> Type: N

Now that the STUDENT file is the active file, you are ready to create the query file.

> *Select CREATE*
>
> *Select QUERY*

Select A:

Difference Box: If you are using a computer with two floppy disk drives, select B:.

The prompt, **Enter the name of the file** appears.

> Type: `Deanlist`
>
> Press <Enter>

Your screen should look like Figure 7-1, which is the query table.

2. You are now ready to designate the condition for the sort. Remember, you want only grade-point averages that are equal to or greater than 3.5.

> *Select FIELD NAME*
>
> *Select GPA*
>
> *Select OPERATOR*
>
> *Select >= MORE THAN OR EQUAL*
>
> *Select CONSTANT/EXPRESSION*
>
> Type: `3.5`
>
> Press <Enter>

Your screen should look like Figure 7-2. You have created the condition and are ready to exit from the query table.

> *Select EXIT*
>
> *Select SAVE*

FIGURE 7-1 A Query Table

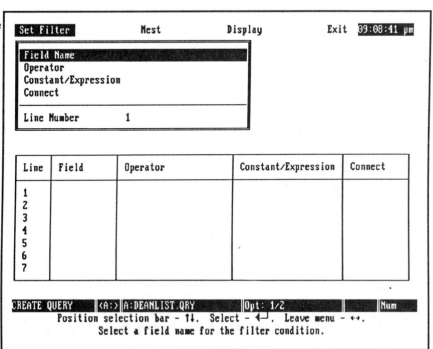

FIGURE 7-2 Creating a Sort Condition

```
┌─────────────────────────────────────────────────────────────────────┐
│ ▐Set Filter▌          Nest          Display          Exit ▐09:13:41 pm▌│
│  ┌───────────────────────────────────────────┐                        │
│  │ Field Name        GPA                      │                        │
│  │ Operator          More than or equal       │                        │
│  │ Constant/Expression 3.5                    │                        │
│  │▐Connect                                   ▌│                        │
│  │                                            │                        │
│  │ Line Number       1                        │                        │
│  └───────────────────────────────────────────┘                        │
│                                  ·                                      │
│  ┌──────┬───────┬──────────────────┬─────────────────────┬──────────┐ │
│  │ Line │ Field │ Operator         │ Constant/Expression │ Connect  │ │
│  ├──────┼───────┼──────────────────┼─────────────────────┼──────────┤ │
│  │ 1    │ GPA   │ More than or equal│ 3.5                 │          │ │
│  │ 2    │       │                  │                     │          │ │
│  │ 3    │       │                  │                     │          │ │
│  │ 4    │       │                  │                     │          │ │
│  │ 5    │       │                  │                     │          │ │
│  │ 6    │       │                  │                     │          │ │
│  │ 7    │       │                  │                     │          │ │
│  └──────┴───────┴──────────────────┴─────────────────────┴──────────┘ │
│                                                                        │
│ ▐CREATE QUERY    ▌▐<A:>▌▐A:DEANLIST.QRY    ▌ ▐Opt: 4/5    ▌  ▐Num▌    │
│         Position selection bar - ↑↓.  Select - ←┘.  Leave menu - ↔.   │
│             Select a logical connector for the filter condition.       │
└─────────────────────────────────────────────────────────────────────┘
```

3. Next, sort the STUDENT file by the conditions established in the query file. First, set up the DEANLIST query file.

> *Select SET UP*
>
> *Select QUERY*
>
> *Select A:*

Difference Box: If you are using a computer with two floppy disk drives, select B:.

> *Select DEANLIST.QRY*

Now that you have set up the DEANLIST query file, only those records that meet the query conditions will be sorted.

> *Select ORGANIZE*
>
> *Select SORT*
>
> *Select GPA*
>
> Press <Right arrow>
>
> *Select A:*

Difference Box: If you are using a computer with two floppy disk drives, select B:.

> Enter: Dean
>
> Press <Enter>

The message **100% Sorted 4 Records sorted** appears at the bottom of the screen.

> Press any key

4. To see the names and corresponding grade-point averages on the dean's list, make DEAN the active file.

> *Select SET UP*
>
> *Select DATABASE FILE*
>
> Select A:

Difference Box: If you are using a computer with two floppy disk drives, select B:.

> *Select DEAN.DBF*
>
> Type: N
>
> *Select RETRIEVE*
>
> *Select DISPLAY*
>
> *Select SPECIFY SCOPE*
>
> *Select ALL*
>
> *Select CONSTRUCT A FIELD LIST*
>
> *Select NAME*
>
> *Select GPA*
>
> Press <Right arrow>
>
> *Select EXECUTE THE COMMAND*

Four records are displayed, each one showing the student's name and GPA. The GPA values range from 3.98 to 3.70.

> Press any key

5. You have finished with this Your Turn exercise. You can either leave your work on the screen while you read the following section, or you can exit from dBASE III PLUS.

❏ INDEXING A FILE

In some respects the INDEX option is similar to the SORT option. Both can arrange records in ascending order, alphabetically, chronologically or numerically, and place the newly sorted file into a separate target file. There are, however, some significant differences between the two options.

Indexed files, unlike sorted files, automatically update changes made to the database. For example, if a record is added or deleted, or if the information stored in a record is edited, the changes are made automatically in all open INDEX files. Thus, as the database grows larger or is modified, the records do not have to be reordered constantly.

With the INDEX option, as with the SORT option, the field being indexed must be a numeric, character, or date field. When a file is indexed, it must be the active file before it can be viewed.

YOUR TURN

Use the INDEX option to create three indexed files for fields SSNUMBER, ZIP, and YEAR. The students' Social Security numbers are used as their identification numbers. The index on the SSNUMBER field will list the students according to these identification numbers. The index on the ZIP field will list the students according to ZIP code. The list could be used for a mass mailing. The index on the YEAR field will list the students according to their class; senior, junior, sophomore, or freshman. If necessary, start the dBASE III PLUS program.

1. First, make STUDENT the active file.

> *Select SET UP*
>
> *Select DATABASE FILE*
>
> *Select A:*

Difference Box: If you are using a computer with two floppy disk drives, select B:.

> *Select STUDENT.DBF*
>
> Type: N

2. Now that STUDENT is the active file, set up the INDEX files.

> *Select ORGANIZE*
>
> *Select INDEX*
>
> Type: SSNUMBER
>
> Press <Enter>
>
> *Select A:*

Difference Box: If you are using a computer with two floppy disk drives, select B:.

> Type: ID_NUMBER
>
> Press <Enter>

The message **100% indexed 15 Records indexed** appears.

> Press any key

Next, index on the ZIP field to a file name MAILING. That is, you are going to create a file called MAILING in which the records are arranged in ascending order by ZIP code. Producing a mass mailing would be much easier with the records arranged by ZIP code.

> *Select ORGANIZE*
>
> *Select INDEX*
>
> Type: ZIP
>
> Press <Enter>

Select A:

Difference Box: If you are using a computer with two floppy disk drives, select B:.

Type: MAILING

Press <Enter>

The message **100% indexed 15 Records indexed** appears.

Press any key

Now you want to index on the YEAR field to a file name CLASS. That is, you are going to create a file called CLASS in which the records are arranged according to the students' class standing. The records for all the freshmen will be grouped together, the records for all the sophomores will be grouped together, and so on.

Select ORGANIZE

Select INDEX

Type: YEAR

Press <Enter>

Select A:

Difference Box: If you are using a computer with two floppy disk drives, select B:.

Type: CLASS

Press <Enter>

The message **100% indexed 15 Records indexed** appears.

Press any key

3. Now you want to view one of the indexed files.

Select SET UP

Select DATABASE FILE

Select A:

Difference Box: If you are using a computer with two floppy disk drives, select B:

Select STUDENT.DBF

Type: Y

Because you indicated that the file is indexed, a list of the indexed files appears. An indexed file is opened by selecting it from this list. The first file selected is the master index. Up to seven indexed files can be open at a time on a computer that has 384 K or more of memory. On a computer with 256 K, only two index files can be open at a time. You are going to open two of the indexed files.

> *Select ID_NUMBE.NDX*
>
> *Select MAILING.NDX*

Your screen should look like Figure 7-3.

> Press <Left arrow> to close the menu

4. Now you want to view one of the indexed files.

> *Select RETRIEVE*
>
> *Select DISPLAY*
>
> *Select SPECIFY SCOPE*
>
> *Select ALL*
>
> *Select CONSTRUCT A FIELD LIST*
>
> *Select NAME*
>
> *Select YEAR*
>
> *Select SSNUMBER*
>
> Press <Right arrow>
>
> *Select EXECUTE THE COMMAND*

Your screen should look like Figure 7-4. Notice that the ID_NUMBER index is displayed. You can tell it is the ID_NUMBER index because the records are listed in ascending order according to Social Security number. Of the two opened indexes, the ID_NUMBER index is displayed because it is the master index.

5. Next, look at the record numbers. Remember that the SORT option renumbered the records consecutively in ascending order. When a file is indexed, records maintain their original record numbers. The record numbers in Figure 7-4 are 6, 14, 3, 2, 1, 8 and so on.

FIGURE 7-3 Opening an Indexed File

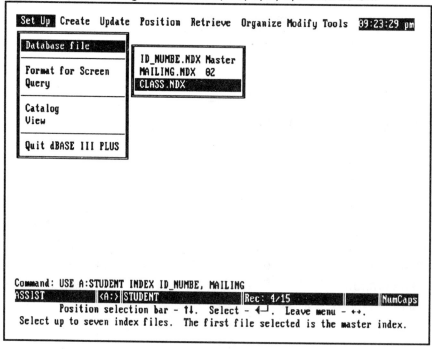

Application Software Manual

FIGURE 7-4 Displaying an Indexed File

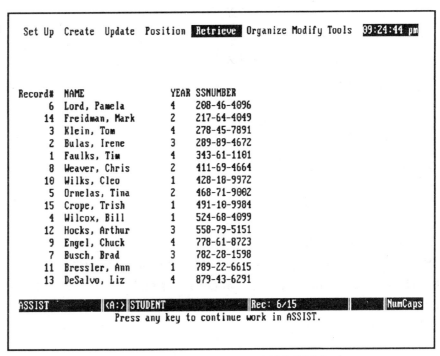

```
Set Up  Create  Update  Position  Retrieve  Organize Modify Tools   09:24:44 pm


Record#  NAME                YEAR SSNUMBER
      6  Lord, Pamela           4  208-46-4096
     14  Freidman, Mark         2  217-64-4049
      3  Klein, Tom             4  278-45-7891
      2  Bulas, Irene           3  289-89-4672
      1  Faulks, Tim            4  343-61-1101
      8  Weaver, Chris          2  411-69-4664
     10  Wilks, Cleo            1  428-18-9972
      5  Ornelas, Tina          2  468-71-9002
     15  Crope, Trish           1  491-10-9984
      4  Wilcox, Bill           1  524-68-4099
     12  Hocks, Arthur          3  558-79-5151
      9  Engel, Chuck           4  778-61-8723
      7  Busch, Brad            3  782-28-1598
     11  Bressler, Ann          1  789-22-6615
     13  DeSalvo, Liz           4  879-43-6291

ASSIST          <A:> STUDENT              Rec: 6/15            NumCaps
           Press any key to continue work in ASSIST.
```

6. Next, add a record to the file. The ID_NUMBER index and the MAILING index are open. Therefore, the added record will be incorporated into these two indexes automatically. Since the CLASS index is not open, the added record will not be incorporated into it.

> Press any key
>
> *Select UPDATE*
>
> *Select APPEND*

A data entry form for record 16 appears. Use the following information to fill in the form:

NAME:	Diaz, Kate
YEAR:	3
GPA:	3.6
BIRTHDATE:	09/27/59
SSNUMBER:	009-56-0983
ACCOUNT:	8.38
ADDRESS:	75 Hilltop Dr.
CITY:	Leominster
STATE:	MA
ZIP:	03402

Press <Enter> after the data is entered

7. Check to make sure the two indexes are updated.

> *Select RETRIEVE*
>
> *Select DISPLAY*

Select SPECIFY SCOPE

Select ALL

Select CONSTRUCT A FIELD LIST

Select NAME

Select ADDRESS

Select CITY

Select STATE

Select ZIP

Press <Right arrow>

Select EXECUTE THE COMMAND

Record 16, for Kate Diaz, is the first record listed. The ID_NUMBER index is still the active index, so the records are listed in ascending order according to Social Security numbers.

8. Now check to make sure that record 16 also is in the MAILING index. To do this, change the active index using the SET UP option.

Press any key

Select SET UP

Select DATABASE FILE

Select A:

Difference Box: If you are using a computer with two floppy disk drives, select B:.

Select STUDENT.DBF

Type: Y

Select MAILING.NDX

Press <Left arrow>

Select RETRIEVE

Select DISPLAY

Select SPECIFY SCOPE

Select ALL

Select CONSTRUCT A FIELD LIST

Select NAME

Select ADDRESS

Select CITY

Select STATE

Select ZIP

Press <Right arrow>

Select EXECUTE THE COMMAND

Again, record 16 is the first record listed, but this time it is first because it is the record with the lowest ZIP code number. Notice that the records are now listed in ascending order according to ZIP code. They are listed this way because the active index is now the Mailing index.

Press any key

9. You have finished with this Your Turn exercise. You can either leave your work on the screen while you read the following section, or you can exit from dBASE III PLUS.

Indexing on Multiple Fields

There are times when indexing on more than one field is useful. To index on more than one field, join the fields with plus signs when the prompt **Enter an index key expression** appears. This command can be used only on fields of the same type. It cannot be used to index on fields that are both character and numeric. All the fields must be either character or numeric.

The order in which the fields are listed in this command is significant. dBASE III PLUS first arranges all the records by the first field listed, then by the second field listed, and so on. When using this command, make sure the fields are listed in the order that produces the desired results.

YOUR TURN

Use the INDEX option on multiple fields to list the students alphabetically by class. If necessary, start the dBASE III PLUS program.

1. First, make the CLASS file the master index.

> *Select SET UP*
>
> *Select DATABASE FILE*
>
> *Select A:*

Difference Box: If you are using a computer with two floppy disk drives, select B:.

> *Select STUDENT.DBF*
>
> Type: Y
>
> *Select CLASS. NDX*
>
> Press <Left arrow>
>
> *Select RETRIEVE*
>
> *Select DISPLAY*
>
> *Select SPECIFY SCOPE*
>
> *Select ALL*
>
> *Select CONSTRUCT A FIELD LIST*
>
> *Select NAME*

Select YEAR

Press <Right arrow>

Select EXECUTE THE COMMAND

Notice that Kate Diaz is not on the list. She is not on the list because the CLASS index was closed when her record was added. Look at how the names are listed. They are grouped according to class standing, but the names are in no particular order. This index will be more useful if the students are listed alphabetically within each class. Indexing on multiple fields enables you to do this.

Press any key

2. You are now going to index both the YEAR and NAME fields.

Select ORGANIZE

Select INDEX

The prompt **Enter an index key expression** appears. You are going to enter two fields connected with a plus sign.

Type: Year + Name

Press <Enter>

Select A:

Difference Box: If you are using a computer with two floppy disk drives, select B:.

Type: CLASS

Because an index named CLASS was created previously, the message **A:CLASS.ndx already exists, overwrite it? (Y/N)** appears.

Type: Y

When the message **Press any key to continue working in ASSIST** appears, press any key.

3. Take another look at the CLASS index.

Select RETRIEVE

Select DISPLAY

Select SPECIFY SCOPE

Select ALL

Select CONSTRUCT A FIELD LIST

Select NAME

Select YEAR

Press <Right arrow>

Select EXECUTE THE COMMAND

Your screen should look like Figure 7-5. The records are still grouped by class, all the freshmen together, all the sophomores together, and so on, but now the names also are listed alphabetically within each class.

Press any key

4. You have finished with this Your Turn exercise. You can either leave your work on the screen while you read the following section, or you can exit from dBASE III PLUS.

❏ SEARCHING AN INDEXED DATABASE FILE

When database files become large, it can be a tedious chore to look for a particular record. That problem is eliminated with the SEEK option from the Position Menu. The SEEK option searches an indexed file for a particular alphanumeric string. dBASE III PLUS searches the indexed file for the first record containing the string specified. If the string for which you are searching is a character rather than numeric string, that string has to be enclosed in quotation marks when dBASE III PLUS prompts you to enter the string for which you are searching. When a record with the string is found, dBASE III PLUS places a record pointer on it. That record can then be displayed. The SEEK option works only on indexed files.

YOUR TURN

Create an index in which all the students are listed alphabetically. Then use that index to search for specific students. The STUDENT file should be active. If necessary, start the dBASE III PLUS program.

1. First create a new index file that lists the students in alphabetical order.

Select ORGANIZE

Select INDEX

FIGURE 7-5 Indexing on Multiple Fields

```
 Set Up  Create  Update  Position  Retrieve  Organize Modify Tools   08:56:01 am



 Record#  NAME                YEAR
     11  Bressler, Ann        1
     15  Crope, Trish         1
      4  Wilcox, Bill         1
     10  Wilks, Cleo          1
     14  Freidman, Mark       2
      5  Ornelas, Tina        2
      8  Weaver, Chris        2
      2  Bulas, Irene         3
      7  Busch, Brad          3
     16  Diaz, Kate           3
     12  Hocks, Arthur        3
     13  DeSalvo, Liz         4
      9  Engel, Chuck         4
      1  Faulks, Tim          4
      3  Klein, Tom           4
      6  Lord, Pamela         4

 ASSIST          <A:> STUDENT              Rec: 11/16              Num
           Press any key to continue work in ASSIST.
```

Type: Name

Press <Enter>

Select A:

Difference Box: If you are using a computer with two floppy disk drives, select B:.

Type: Alphaname

Press <Enter>

Press any key

Now open the Alphaname index.

Select SET UP

Select DATABASE FILE

Select A:

Difference Box: If you are using a computer with two floppy disk drives, select B:.

Select STUDENT.DBF

Type: Y

Select ALPHANAM.NDX

Press <Left arrow>

2. Next, use the SEEK option with the ALPHANAME index.

Select POSITION

Select SEEK

The prompt **Enter an expression** appears. Because the expression to be entered is a character string, it has to be enclosed in quotation marks.

Type: "Desalvo, Liz"

Press <Enter>

The message **No find** appears. There is a student whose last name is DeSalvo, and her name is in the database file, but dBASE III PLUS did not find the record because it distinguishes capital and lowercase letters. For dBASE III PLUS to find the record, the name must be typed exactly as it appears in the record.

Press any key

Select POSITION

Select SEEK

Type: "DeSalvo, Liz"

Press <Enter>

This time the record is found but does not appear on the screen. You know the record was found because the **No find** prompt did not appear.

Press any key

Next, display the record.

> *Select RETRIEVE*
>
> *Select DISPLAY*
>
> *Select CONSTRUCT A FIELD LIST*
>
> *Select NAME*
>
> *Select GPA*
>
> *Select ADDRESS*
>
> *Select CITY*
>
> *Select STATE*
>
> *Select ZIP*
>
> Press <Right arrow>
>
> *Select EXECUTE THE COMMAND*

The record for Liz DeSalvo appears.

> Press any key

3. Now you are going to look for the record of a student whose last name is Weaver.

> *Select POSITION*
>
> *Select SEEK*
>
> Type: `"Weaver"`
>
> Press <Enter>
>
> Press any key
>
> *Select RETRIEVE*
>
> *Select DISPLAY*
>
> *Select CONSTRUCT A FIELD LIST*
>
> *Select NAME*
>
> *Select GPA*
>
> *Select ADDRESS*
>
> *Select CITY*
>
> *Select STATE*
>
> *Select ZIP*
>
> Press <Right arrow>
>
> *Select EXECUTE THE COMMAND*

The record for Chris Weaver appears. Notice that although you entered only the student's last name as the string you wanted to find, dBASE III PLUS still found the record,

> Press any key

4. You have finished with this Your Turn exercise. You can either leave your work on the screen while you read the following section, or you can exit from dBASE III PLUS.

❏ CREATING A REPORT WITH dBASE III PLUS

Data stored in a database file can provide users with helpful information. Until the information can take the form of a report on paper, however, its usefulness is limited. The following section explains how to create a hard-copy report using dBASE III PLUS files.

A dBASE III PLUS report is created with the REPORT option from the Create Menu. After selecting REPORT from the Create Menu, dBASE III PLUS guides you through the creation of the report by displaying a series of screens and prompts.

YOUR TURN

Start dBASE III PLUS if necessary. The next several hands-on exercises take you through the creation of a report using the STUDENT file. The STUDENT file should be the active file.

1. Once the STUDENT file is active, you are ready to start the process of creating a report.

      Select CREATE

      Select REPORT

      Select A:

Difference Box: If you are using a computer with two floppy disk drives, select B:.

The prompt **Enter the name of the file** appears. Provide the report file with a name.

      Type: Student

      Press <Enter>

The name of the database file and report are the same: STUDENT. This does not cause a problem because dBASE III PLUS automatically adds the extension FRM to the report. The two files, STUDENT.DBF and STUDENT.FRM, are stored as two separate files. Using the same name for the database file and report can help to clarify the contents of the files. Your screen should look like Figure 7-6. Leave the report screen on your monitor while you read the next section.

Designing the Report

The dBASE III PLUS report screen has a menu with five options: OPTIONS, GROUPS, COLUMNS, LOCATE, and EXIT. The Options Menu enables users to design the format of a report, that is, how the report will look on paper. The first option in the Options Menu is PAGE TITLE. You can enter up to four lines of text that will be printed at the top of each report page. The rest of the options from the Options Menu already have default settings. You can change such things as the width of the page, left and right

FIGURE 7-6 Creating a Report

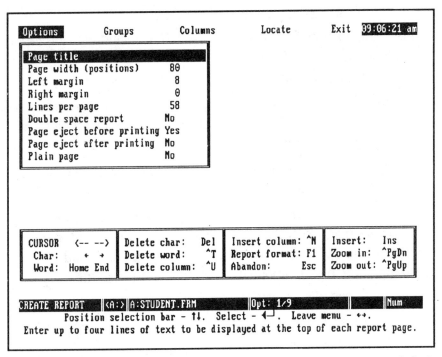

```
 Options        Groups      Columns      Locate      Exit  09:06:21 am
┌─────────────────────────────────────┐
│ Page title                          │
│ Page width (positions)    80        │
│ Left margin                8        │
│ Right margin               0        │
│ Lines per page            58        │
│ Double space report       No        │
│ Page eject before printing Yes      │
│ Page eject after printing  No        │
│ Plain page                No        │
│                                     │
│                                     │
│ ┌──────────┬────────────────┬──────────────────┬─────────────────┐ │
│ │ CURSOR  <-- -->│ Delete char:  Del │ Insert column: ^N │ Insert:   Ins │ │
│ │ Char:    ←  →  │ Delete word:   ^T │ Report format: F1 │ Zoom in:  ^PgDn│ │
│ │ Word:  Home End│ Delete column: ^U │ Abandon:      Esc │ Zoom out: ^PgUp│ │
│ └──────────┴────────────────┴──────────────────┴─────────────────┘ │
└─────────────────────────────────────┘
 CREATE REPORT   <A:> A:STUDENT.FRM        Opt: 1/9              Num
       Position selection bar - ↑↓.   Select - ◄┘.   Leave menu - ←→.
  Enter up to four lines of text to be displayed at the top of each report page.
```

margins, how many lines will print on the page, and so on. However, for most standard reports, the default settings will be acceptable.

The Groups Menu enables users to group together certain portions of the database file when it is printed. For example, if the database file is alphabetized by last name, a report can be printed with all the last names beginning with A grouped together, all the last names beginning with B grouped together, and so on.

The Columns Menu enables users to designate which fields will be included in a report. In addition, a heading for each column can be entered from the Columns Menu. The Locate Menu enables users to move to certain columns in a report. The Exit Menu enables users to save a report.

YOUR TURN

The STUDENT file should be active and the report screen should be on your monitor.

1. First, enter a page title for the report.

> *Select OPTIONS*
>
> Press <Enter> to select PAGE TITLE
>
> Type: STATE COLLEGE
>
> Press <Enter>
>
> Type: STUDENT NAME AND ADDRESS
>
> Press <Enter> three times

2. Next, indicate the columns to be included in the report.

> *Select COLUMNS*

Press <Enter> to select CONTENTS

At this point, you must designate the field to be included in the report. To see a list of the available fields, press <F10>.

Press <F10>

The fields from the STUDENT file appear at the left of the screen. You decide that the report will contain the name, address, city, state, and balance for all the students in the file.

Select NAME

The word NAME moves into the Columns Menu next to the CONTENTS option.

Press <Enter>

Notice that **20** now appears next to width. That is because the NAME field has a width of 20. Now you are going to enter a column heading to describe the contents of this column. The header can be up to four lines long and sixty characters wide. The field headers are printed at the top of each page above the corresponding columns.

Press <Down arrow>

Press <Enter> to select HEADING

Type: NAME

Press <Enter> four times

The first column has now been defined. To define the second column, you must press the <PgDn> key.

Press <PgDn>

The Columns Menu is once again empty.

Press <Enter> to select CONTENTS

Press <F10>

Select ADDRESS

Press <Enter>

Press <Down arrow>

Press <Enter> to select HEADING

Type: ADDRESS

Press <Enter> four times

Press <PgDn>

Press <Enter> to select CONTENTS

Press <F10>

Select CITY

Press <Enter>

Press <Down arrow>

Press <Enter> to select HEADING

Type: CITY

Press <Enter> four times

Press <PgDn>

Press <Enter> to select CONTENTS

Press <F10>

Select STATE

Press <Enter>

Press <Down arrow>

Press <Enter> to select HEADING

Type: STATE

Press <Enter> four times

Press <PgDn>

Press <Enter> to select CONTENTS

Press <F10>

Select ACCOUNT

Press <Enter>

Press <Down arrow>

Press <Enter> to select HEADING

Type: ACCOUNT

Press <Enter> four times

Because ACCOUNT is a numeric field, the option TOTAL THIS COLUMN from the Columns menu is available. The default setting is YES. Leave the default setting at YES.

Select EXIT

Press <Enter> to select SAVE

The Assistant Menu returns to the screen.

3. You have finished with this Your Turn exercise. You can either leave your work on the screen while you read the following section, or you can exit from dBASE III PLUS.

❑ MODIFYING A REPORT

When the report form has been designated and saved, it can be recalled for editing or modification if necessary. To edit a report, select REPORT from the Modify Menu. Next, select the disk drive where the report is located, and finally select the name of the report you want to edit. The report screen appears. The menu at the bottom of the screen lists the keys used for editing.

❑ PRINTING A REPORT

When a report is entered into a database file, a hard copy of the report can be printed. To print a report, select REPORT from the Retrieve Menu. Next, select the disk drive where the report is located. Select the report to be printed and the option EXECUTE THE COMMAND. The prompt, **Direct the output to the printer? [Y/N]** appears. Enter Y for yes and the report will be printed. When printing a report, dBASE III PLUS does not hold the last line of the report in a print buffer. The entire report is printed.

YOUR TURN

Print a copy of the STUDENT report. Make sure that your computer is hooked up to a printer and that the printer has plenty of paper and is online. If necessary, start the dBASE III PLUS program.

1. Check to make sure the STUDENT file is the active file.

> *Select RETRIEVE*
>
> *Select REPORT*
>
> *Select A:*

> **Difference Box:** If you are using a computer with two floppy disk drives, select B:.

> *Select STUDENT.FRM*
>
> *Select EXECUTE THE COMMAND*
>
> Type: Y

2. The report is both displayed on the screen and printed. Your printed report should look like Figure 7-7.

> Press any key

3. You are now finished working with the STUDENT file. Exit from dBASE III PLUS.

> *Select SET UP*
>
> *Select QUIT dBASE III PLUS*

When the system prompt appears, take your disks out of the computer. Turn the computer and monitor off.

❑ SUMMARY POINTS

- ■ There are two ways to rearrange the order of records within a dBASE III PLUS file: using the SORT option and using the INDEX option from the Organize Menu.
- ■ The SEEK option from the Position Menu searches indexed files for relevant data.
- ■ The REPORT option from the Create Menu enables the user to create a hard copy report using dBASE III PLUS files.

**FIGURE 7-7 Student
Account Balance Report**

```
Page No.       1
03/25/92
                              STATE COLLEGE
                         STUDENT NAME AND ADDRESS

NAME                   ADDRESS         CITY       STATE  ACCOUNT


Bressler, Ann          45 S. Luke St.  Pasadena   TX       0.00
Bulas, Irene           908 W. Summit   Oak Hill   TX    1203.87
Busch, Brad            32 Badner       Dallas     TX     803.52
Crope, Trish           67 Baldwin      Oak Hill   TX     175.50
DeSalvo, Liz           9. W. Second    Dallas     TX       0.00
Diaz, Kate             75 Hilltop Dr.  Leominster MA       8.38
Engel, Chuck           14 Indian Rd.   Houston    TX      12.18
Faulks, Tim            78 Main St.     Miami      FL     286.59
Freidman, Mark         3426 Little St. Pasadena   TX      33.68
Hocks, Arthur          90 Kellog Rd.   Lubbock    TX     446.29
Klein, Tom             12 Yong St.     Hampton    NC      96.95
Lord, Pamela           98 Pike St.     El Paso    TX     576.94
Ornelas, Tina          123 First St.   Amarillo   TX    2005.32
Weaver, Chris          909 Clough      Lubbock    TX      68.07
Wilcox, Bill           6 Williams Rd.  Anadale    TX       0.00
Wilks, Cleo            76 Gorrel       Laredo     TX    1096.20
*** Total ***
                                                         6813.49
```

❏ COMMAND SUMMARY

Main Menu	Secondary Menu	Description
Create	Query	Creates a new Query file.
Create	Report	Creates a new column-style report file.
Modify	Report	Allows you to edit or modify a report form.
Organize	Index	Creates an index file that dBASE uses to sort records in the database whenever it is opened.
Organize	Sort	Sorts a database in a specified order to be saved in a new file.
Position	Seek	Searches an indexed file for a particular alphanumeric string.
Retrieve	Report	Allows you to view or print a column-style report.

❏ dBASE III PLUS EXERCISES

In this exercise you are going to create a database file for the registrar's office at a state university. The file will be named ENROLL and will contain general information about students such as personal data, programs, and majors. If you need help answering any of the questions that follow, refer to "Indexing a File," "Creating a Report with dBASE III PLUS," and "Printing a Report" earlier in this chapter.

1. Start the dBASE III PLUS program. Make sure your work disk is in Drive A.

Difference Box: On a computer with two floppy disk drives, place the work disk in Drive B.

2. Use the CREATE option to start a new file, and name it ENROLL. The file should have the following structure:

Field Name	Type	Width
NUMBER	Character	2
LAST_NAME	Character	10
FIRST_NAME	Character	10
ADDRESS	Character	16
CITY	Character	15
STATE	Character	2
MAJOR	Character	10
DEGREE	Character	3

3.   At the prompt **Input data records now? (Y/N)**, enter Y and enter the following information:

No.	Last_Name	First_Name	Address	City	State	Major	Degree
1	Mansfield	Carolyn	190 Main St.	Los Angeles	CA	Education	BA
2	Magpoc	William	1200 Victory Rd.	Long Beach	CA	Business	BA
3	Rath	Alexis	221 Maple Ave.	Reno	NV	Business	BA
4	Byrtum	Laura	849 Napoleon Rd.	Los Angeles	CA	Health	BA
5	Burkett	Lynn	12 Central	Long Beach	CA	Music	MA
6	Catayee	Monique	110 Main St.	Phoeniz	AZ	Theater	MA
7	Marin	Bernard	12 King Rd.	Ventura	CA	Accounting	BA
8	Byler	Diane	Anderson Hall	Los Angeles	CA	Business	BA
9	Heil	Pascal	302 West Hall	Los Angeles	CA	Education	BA
10	Jaccoud	Lynn	120 S. Main St.	Stockton	CA	Finance	BA
11	Wegman	Nelly	430 Clough	Davis	CA	Accounting	BA
12	Pinkston	Mark	65 High St.	Fresno	CA	Statistics	MA
13	Burroughs	Beverly	26 S. Summit	Ventura	CA	Journalism	BA
14	King	Stephen	201 E. Wooster	Corvallis	OR	History	MA
15	Paulin	Jack	102 High	Ogden	UT	Math	MA
16	Proctor	Christine	34 Eighth St.	Portland	OR	Chemistry	MA
17	Priess	Ronald	120 Prout Hall	Los Angeles	CA	Marketing	BA
18	Atkins	Lee	12560 Euclid	San Jose	CA	Education	BA
19	Asik	Jennifer	22 Mercer	San Jose	CA	History	MA
20	Dowell	Gail	112 Ridge	Long Beach	CA	Business	MA
21	Wacker	Annick	320 East Merry	Stockton	CA	Economics	BA
22	Garrett	Lynda	39 Vine St.	Fresno	CA	Music	MA
23	McGovern	Alice	1200 Sand Ridge	Los Angeles	CA	Theater	PhD
24	McDonald	Francoise	210 Main St.	Taos	NM	Education	BA
25	Ausustin	Liliane	333 Jeffers Rd.	Davis	CA	Finance	BA

4. Use the BROWSE option to review the data; make sure that everything is accurate. If you find errors correct them.

5. Now index the file on the MAJOR field. How do you index a file? Index the ENROLL file on the MAJOR field. Name the indexed file DEPT.

6. How do you access an indexed file? Access the DEPT file.

7. Use the DISPLAY option to display the records in the DEPT file. Use the SPECIFY SCOPE option and select ALL to display all the records. Use the CONSTRUCT A FIELD LIST option and select LAST_NAME, FIRST_NAME, and MAJOR as the fields you want to display. Is there any difference in the order of the records? What is it?

8. Create a report and name it MAJOR. Type the following for a page title:

```
List of Students Grouped by Major
```

Use the LAST_NAME, FIRST_NAME, and MAJOR fields as the contents for three columns. Enter appropriate column headings. Group the report on the MAJOR field. Save the Report form.

9. Print the MAJOR.FRM report.

10. Access the ENROLL database file. Use the LIST option to list the student number, last name, major, and program for all students enrolled in a master's program. How many students are working toward earning their master's degrees? Repeat the listing option to find all of the students working toward earning their bachelor's degrees, and finally for all students studying for their doctorate degrees. Print a hard copy of each listing.

❑ dBASE III PLUS PROBLEMS   1-8

To complete the following problems, you need to use files on the Student File disk. In order to complete these exercises, you will need to be able to sort a database file, index a file, create a report with dBASE III PLUS, and print a report.

1. On the Student File disk there is a dBASE III PLUS file called PHOTOS. Start the dBASE III PLUS program and retrieve this file. Make a copy of this file and call the copy PHOTOS 1. That way, if you make a mistake, you will always have the original file.

2. The PHOTOS1 file keeps track of customers who have made an appointment at a photography studio. Retrieve a record from the PHOTOS1 file. Look it over carefully. The customer's first name, last name, and telephone number are stored in the file. In addition, the CATEGORY field stores data on what type of photograph is being taken. Options for the CATEGORY field are:

Individual:	The photograph is of one person only.
Couple:	The photograph is of two people.
Group:	The photograph is of more than two people.
Wedding:	The appointment is to shoot a wedding.

The DATE field stores the date of the appointment. The COST field stores the amount being charged for the appointment. The PAID category indicates whether or not the person has already paid for the appointment.

3.   Sort the database file so that it is in alphabetical order by last name. Name the sorted file PHOTOSRT. *(is sorted)*

4.   Create a report using the PHOTOSRT file. Name the report PHOTOS. The report should have the following title:

```
Appointments
```

Include all the fields in the report. Position the first two fields so that the LASTNAME field is the first column in the report and the FIRSTNAME field is the second column in the report. Provide appropriate titles for all the columns in the report. Save the report.

5.   Print the PHOTOS report.

6.   Now you want to create a report that includes only those customers who have not paid. Using the PHOTOS1 file, create a sorted file. Sort the file by the COST field first and the LASTNAME field second. That way, customers owing the same amount will be listed alphabetically by last name. Name the sorted file UNPAID. *paid = T unpaid = F*

Using the UNPAID file, create a query file. Name the query file UNPAID. The condition you want to designate in the query table is to find those records where the PAID field is false. Save the query file. *.QRY*

7.   Use the UNPAID file to create the report. The report should include the LASTNAME, FIRSTNAME, PHONE, CATEGORY, DATE, and COST fields, in that order. Provide appropriate titles for the columns. *NOTPAID* The report should print a total of the amounts listed in the COST column. Save the report.

8.   Print the UNPAID report.

❑ dBASE III PLUS CHALLENGE

Assume you work for a local museum. The director of public relations, who is in charge of all the museum's programs, wants you to create a dBASE III PLUS file to keep track of the museum's membership. She wants to be able to retrieve information easily in order to prepare for the mailing of the museum's publications. She also wants to keep track of the expiration date for membership in the museum's programs to help encourage membership renewal.

Assume the museum has two types of memberships. Membership in the Exhibition Program provides free parking, free access to all permanent and temporary exhibitions, free publications (a monthly arts newsletter and a quarterly magazine), and discounts at the gift shop. Membership in the Science Club provides free parking; free access to all permanent and temporary exhibitions; a free monthly science publication; discounts at the gift shop; and free admission to lectures by major scientists, in-house workshops, and field trips. A patron can belong to both the Exhibition Program and the Science Club.

There are five categories of memberships to both the Exhibition Program and the Science Club: Child, Student, Adult, Family, and Senior Citizen.

The database file needs to include the following fields:

Last Name	To store the member's last name
First Name	To store the member's first name
Address	To store the member's address
City	To store the city where the member lives
State	To store the state where the member lives
ZIP	To store the ZIP code
Phone	To store the member's telephone number
Type	To indicate whether the member belongs to the Exhibition Program, the Science Club, or both
Category	To indicate whether the membership is for a child, student, adult, family, or senior citizen
Expiration Date	Month and year when the current membership expires

The director wants to be able to easily print the following reports:

■ A report that lists the first name, last name, and full address of Exhibition Program members only. The data should be listed in order by zip code so that it can be used for mailing the monthly arts newsletter. Records that have the same ZIP code should be listed alphabetically by last name.

■ A report that lists the first name, last name, and full address of Science Club members only. The data should be listed in order by ZIP code so that it can be used for mailing the monthly science publication. Records that have the same ZIP code should be listed alphabetically by last name.

■ A report that lists the first name, last name, and full address of all memberships for children and families. The data should be listed in order by ZIP code so that it can be used for mailing information on museum programs that are of particular interest to children.

■ A report that lists the first name, last name, telephone number, type, category, and expiration date of all the members. The report should be listed in order by expiration date so it can be used to telephone people to remind them to renew their memberships.

1. Create a database file that is capable of storing the necessary data and printing the reports.

2. Enter fifteen records into your file. Be sure to vary the data stored in the fields. That is, make sure your file includes all types of members (Exhibition Program, Science Club, both); that it includes all categories of members (child, adult, family, student, senior citizen); that it includes a variety of expiration dates and a variety of ZIP codes.

3. Using the data from your data file, create and print the four reports required by the director. Make sure each report includes a title that easily identifies the information it provides. Include column titles.

CHAPTER 8

Introduction to dBASE IV

OUTLINE

❏ INTRODUCTION

Schools, hospitals, restaurants, and all types of businesses store data. The ability to retrieve, sort, and analyze data quickly and efficiently can make the difference between a company's success and failure. The types of data collected include employee records, bills, supply lists, budgets, and insurance information. Before microcomputers became standard business equipment, the most common way to organize data was to store the records in folders in file cabinets. File cabinets use a lot of space, however, and sometimes several departments may keep the same data. This duplication of data is a waste of time, effort, and space, and can lead to confusion or errors if one copy is changed. Database management software is a program that computerizes record-keeping tasks. The purpose of this chapter is to explain dBASE IV, a sophisticated and powerful data management tool.

❏ GUIDE TO dBASE IV

A data manager software package, like dBASE IV, is used to organize files and to store the type of data that is kept in folders in a manual filing system. Each data item that is stored, such as a first name, a last name, an address, an invoice amount, is called a field. A group of related fields forms a record. A business may key a personnel record on each employee. This record would contain fields such as the employee's name, address, salary, and so on. A file is a group of related records. All the personnel records could make up one file. The business might have other files for customers, vendors or inventory, for example. Fields, records and files can all be easily created using dBASE IV.

Each of the following sections introduces one or more features of dBASE IV. At the end of each section there is a hands-on activity marked with the symbol **Your Turn**. Do not try the hands-on activity until after you have carefully read the section preceding it.

dBASE IV refers to the key marked ⏎ as the <Enter> key. Throughout this chapter, when you are instructed to press the <Enter> key, press the key marked ⏎ .

The following symbols and typefaces are used throughout the chapter. This is what they mean:

Press <Alt>-T	A hyphen indicates two keys are pressed together. In this example, hold the <Alt> key while you press T once.
Save as **DOS utilities**	Boldface indicates words or phrases that appear on the computer screen. The text could be a prompt or a menu selection.
Type: Number	Typewriter font indicates text that is to be entered into a file.
The ADDRESS file	Capital letters indicate the name of a file.

There are two ways to enter commands in dBASE IV. One is by using the menu system which is called the Control Center. The second way is by typing commands at the dot prompt. For beginning users of dBASE IV, using the menu system is easier. Therefore, this chapter approaches learning the dBASE IV program by using the Control Center. Typing commands at the dot prompt is not covered.

Getting Started with dBASE IV

dBASE IV can only be used on a hard disk drive. Follow these steps to access dBASE IV from a hard drive on which it has been installed.

1. Turn on the computer and monitor.

2. A prompt may appear asking you to enter the date. If it does, type the current date using numbers and hyphens, for example 1-15-93. Press <Enter>.

3. A prompt may appear asking you to enter the time. If it does, you can either press <Enter> to bypass this prompt, or you can enter the time using a 24-hour format. For example, enter 16:30:00 if it is 4:30 p.m. Press <Enter> after entering the time.

4. When the system prompt C> appears on the screen, enter cd\ and the name of the directory in which dBASE IV is stored on the hard drive. For example, if the program is stored in a directory named DBPLUS, enter cd\dbplus and press <Enter>.

5. The system prompt C> appears again. Enter dbase and press <Enter>. When dBASE IV has been started properly, the Control Center appears on the screen.

  YOUR TURN

In this exercise, you are going to start dBASE IV on the computer. This exercise assumes that the dBASE IV program is stored in a directory named dbplus. If dBASE IV is stored in a different directory in the computer you are using, ask your instructor for directions.

1. Turn on the computer. If a prompt appears asking you to enter the date, type today's date using numbers and hyphens. For example, if the date is September 28, 1993, you would do the following:

> Type: 09-28-93
>
> Press <Enter>

If a prompt appears asking you to enter the time, either press <Enter> or enter the time in a 24-hour format and press <Enter>.

2. The system prompt C> should appear on the screen.

> Type: cd\dbplus
>
> Press <Enter>

The system prompt C> should appear on the screen again.

> Type: dbase
>
> Press <Enter>

After a moment, the Control Center appears on the screen. Your screen should look like Figure 8-1. Leave the Control Center on the screen while you read the following section.

❏ USING THE CONTROL CENTER

A menu is a list of choices or options shown on the display screen from which the user selects a command or option. The Control Center is a menu system which acts as a home base for the dBASE IV program.

FIGURE 8-1 The Control Center

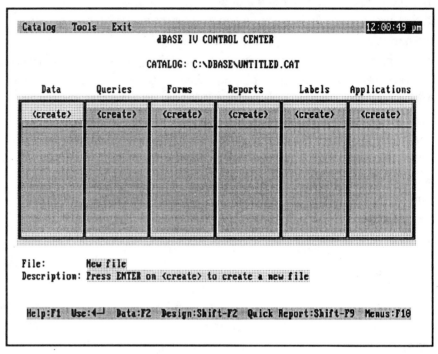

All the commands needed to create and maintain a database file are in the Control Center. Before creating database files, you must understand the components of the Control Center (refer to Figure 8-1).

At the top of the screen is the menu bar and clock. The menu bar displays the available menu options. There are two ways to activate the menus. One way is to press <F10> for **Menus**. A pull-down menu for the current menu option appears. Use <Left arrow> and <Right arrow> to select other menu options. Use <Up arrow> and <Down arrow> to make a selection from a pull-down menu. When the desired option from a pull-down menu is highlighted, press <Enter> to select it. In many cases, another pull-down menu will appear.

The second way to activate the menu bar is to hold down <Alt> and press the first letter of the menu to be opened. For example, you would press <Alt>-T to open the Tools menu.

The name of the active catalog appears in the center of the screen under the menu bar. A catalog may contain any number of related files. The files from the current catalog are listed in the six panels in the middle of the screen. In Figure 8-1, these panels are empty.

The majority of the Control Center is made up of the six panels in the middle of the screen. A database file may include several different types of files that are related. These related files would make up a catalog for a particular database file. For example, a database file may have its own report files and query files. There are six types of files available from the Control Center.

■ The **Data** panel displays database files which contain the records and fields.
■ The **Query** panel displays the names of query files. Query files allow the user to manipulate the data according to specific instructions. They also allow the user to selectively update files.
■ Form files are custom screen displays used for entering, editing, and viewing records.
■ Report files allow the user to print records in a specified format.
■ Label files enable the user to print customized labels using data from database files.
■ Applications files store programs that accomplish a variety of database management tasks.

There are two choices available in the panels. Either a new file can be created by selecting **<create>** or an existing file can be selected by highlighting the file name and pressing <Enter>. To move from panel to panel, use <Left arrow> and <Right arrow>. To move from file name to file name, use <Up arrow> and <Down arrow>. When the Control Center first appears, the cursor is on **<create>** in the Data panel.

If you choose an option from a menu and then decide you do not want it, press <Esc> to cancel the selection. Each time <Esc> is pressed, you are taken back one step. Continue to press <Esc> until you are back to the desired menu.

❏ GETTING HELP WITH dBASE IV

dBASE IV has a very useful Help feature. When using dBASE IV you can obtain information about the menu option currently selected by pressing <F1>. If you get lost or stuck while trying to perform an operation, try to solve the problem by pressing <F1> and reading the Help screen that appears. The Help feature provides information only on the menu option that is highlighted.

❏ QUITTING dBASE IV

The command to exit from dBASE IV is found in the **Exit** menu. To leave dBASE IV, press <F10> for **Menus** and move the highlight to the **Exit** menu. Press <Down arrow> to highlight **Quit to DOS** and press <Enter>. When the system prompt appears you can remove your disk from the disk drive and turn off the computer and monitor.

If you accidentally select **Exit to dot prompt** from the **Exit** menu, the entire screen goes blank except for the Status Bar and a dot at the bottom of the screen. It is called a dot prompt. If you were entering commands by typing them at the dot prompt rather than selecting them from the Control Center, you would want this dot prompt on your screen. However, in this section you will only be entering commands using the Control Center. If the dot prompt appears on the screen, type `assist` and press <Enter>. The Control Center will reappear.

YOUR TURN

In this exercise, you are going to practice moving around the Control Center, selecting menu options, using the Help feature, and quitting from dBASE IV. Before you begin, use the Copy command covered in Chapter 1 to copy a file named CLIENT.DBF from the Student File Disk onto your data disk. Once the file is copied onto your data disk, place the data disk in drive A.

1.   The Control Center should be on your screen from the previous exercise. First, practice moving along the menu bar.

> Press <F10>

Notice that the Catalog menu is now open.

> Press <Right arrow>

Now the Tools menu is open.

Press <Right arrow> two times

The Catalog menu is open again. Try making selections from the menu bar by pressing <Alt> and the first letter of the option.

Press <Alt>-E

The Exit menu is open.

Press <Alt>-T

The Tools Menu is open.

Press <Alt>-C

The Catalog Menu is open.

Press <Down arrow> two times

The highlighting moved down to the **Edit description of catalog**.

2. Next you want to practice making menu selections. You are going to change the default directory to drive A, the drive containing the Student File Disk.

Press <Right arrow>

The Tools menu should be open.

Press <Down arrow> three times

The option **DOS utilities** should be highlighted.

Press <Enter>

Press <Alt>-D to access the DOS menu

Press <Down arrow> twice to highlight **Set default drive:directory**

Your screen should look like Figure 8-2.

FIGURE 8-2 Setting the Default Directory

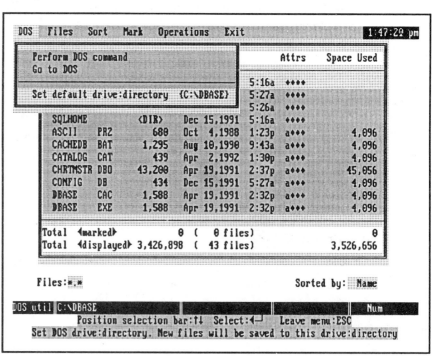

Press <Enter>

A window appears asking you to enter the default drive and directory.

Press <Ctrl>-Y to delete the current entry

Type: A:

Your screen should look like Figure 8-3.

Press <Enter>

Press <Alt>-E

Press <Enter>

After a few moments, the Control Center returns to the screen with a list of file names in the **Data** panel. The Control Center is on the screen. You are going to create a catalog and place the CLIENT file in it.

Press <Alt>-<C> for the Catalog menu

Press <Enter> to select **Use a different catalog**

Press <Enter> to select **<create>**

The prompt **Enter name for new catalog** appears.

Type: EXERCISES

Press <Enter>

Make sure the highlight is in the Data panel.

Press <Alt>-C for the Catalog menu

Highlight **Add file to catalog**

Press <Enter>

FIGURE 8-3 Changing the Default Drive

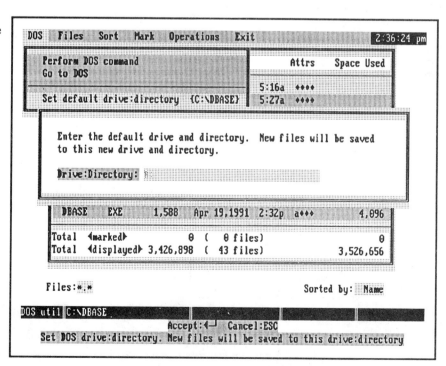

Highlight **CLIENT.DBF**

Press <Enter>

The prompt **Edit the description of this .dbf file** appears.

Type: `Sample database file`

Press <Enter>

The CLIENT file appears in the Data panel. The top of the screen says **CATALOG A:\EXER-CISE.CAT**. You want to select the CLIENT file.

Press <Down arrow> until **CLIENT** is highlighted

Press <Enter>

Press <Right arrow> twice to highlight **Display data**

Press <Enter>

Your screen should look like Figure 8-4. The screen is displaying all the records in the CLIENT file. The fields, **FIRST_NAME, LAST_NAME, ADDRESS, CITY, STATE,** and **ZIP** are listed across the top of the screen. The records are listed in rows running down the screen. At the bottom of the screen is the Status Bar. In the first box it says **Browse** because you are currently in the option that allows you to browse through all the records in the file. The second box which displays **A:\CLIENT** is showing the current drive and filename. **Rec: 1/12** appears in the third box. This box provides information on the status of the records in the current file. The first number tells you which record the program is currently accessing and the second number reports the total number of records in the current database file. Therefore, **Rec: 1/12** means that the computer is currently accessing record 1, and there are a total of twelve records in the CLIENT file. The last box, which is currently empty, indicates the status of <Ins> and <Caps Lock>. <Ins> the insert key, is used when editing a database file. If the

FIGURE 8-4 Displaying the CLIENT File

FIRST_NAME	LAST_NAME	ADDRESS	CITY	STATE	ZIP
Eileen	Shook	920 Conneaut Ave.	Bowling Green	Ohio	43402
Mark	McFee	431 Eberly	Bowling Green	Ohio	43402
Michelle	Ross	790 Willmington	Bowling Green	Ohio	43402
Daniel	Gray	9087 Main Apt #2	Bowling Green	Ohio	43402
Rachel	Sonnenburg	89 Bellamy	Bowling Green	Ohio	43402
Richard	Bacon	123 Crim	Bowling Green	Ohio	43402
Marcy	Vanderkamp	89 W. Wooster	Bowling Green	Ohio	43402
Bruce	Williamson	12 Court St.	Bowling Green	Ohio	43402
Fredique	Mitchell	78965 Ohio St.	Bowling Green	Ohio	43402
Carson	Thompson	134 W. Summit	Bowling Green	Ohio	43402
Amber	McDonald	71 Normandie	Bowling Green	Ohio	43402
Lawrence	Ireland	654 College Drive	Bowling Green	Ohio	43402

| Browse | A:\CLIENT | | Rec 1/12 | File | | Num |

insert key is on, **Ins** appears in this box. If the capitals lock key is on, **Caps** appears in this box.

Press <Caps Lock>

Caps should now appear in the box. Anything you type while **Caps** appears in the Status Bar will be in all capital letters.

Press <Caps Lock>

The last box in the Status Bar should be empty again. Both <Ins> and <Cap Lock> are toggle switchs, which means that if you press them once, the key is on. If pressed a second time, the key is off. Pressing it a third time turns it on again.

3. Next, practice moving around the CLIENT file. The CLIENT file keeps track of clients' names, addresses, and business-related numbers. Each record contains seven fields: First Name, Last Name, Address, City, State, ZIP, and Cnumber.

Press <Right arrow>

The cursor moves to the next character, the *i* in *Eileen*.

Press <Tab>

The cursor moves right to the next field, the LAST_NAME field.

Press <Tab> again

The cursor moves to the ADDRESS field.

Press <End>

The cursor moves to the last field in the file, CNUMBER. Previously you could not see this field on the screen.

Press <Home>

The cursor moves to the first field in the file, FIRST_NAME.

Press <Down arrow>

The cursor moves down one row to Record 2. The entry in the Status Bar reads **Rec 2/12**.

Press <Down arrow> again

The cursor moves to Record 3.

Press <Up arrow>

The cursor moves back to Record 2. Pressing <Up arrow> moves the cursor to the previous record. Pressing <Down arrow> moves the cursor to the next record. Pressing <Tab> moves the cursor to the next field in a record. Pressing <Shift>-<Tab> moves the cursor to the previous field in a record. Pressing <End> moves the cursor to the last field in a record. Pressing <Home> moves the cursor to the first field in a record.

Press <Alt>-E

Press <Enter>

The Control Center returns to the screen.

4. Next you are going to practice accessing the Help feature.

Press <F1>

A Help screen appears that explains how to use files from the Control Center. Read this screen. When you have finished, note the menu at the bottom of the Help window. It includes three options **CONTENTS, RELATED TOPICS,** and **PRINT. CONTENTS** is highlighted.

Press <Enter>

The Table of Contents for help regarding the Control Center appears.

Highlight **About the Control Center** and press <Enter>

Read the information about the Control Center, pressing <F4> for **MORE** as necessary. When you have finished reading press <Esc> and the Control Center returns to the screen.

5. Now you are going to exit from dBASE IV.

Press <Alt>-E

Press <Down arrow> to highlight **Quit to DOS**

Press <Enter>

The system prompt returns to the screen. Take the Student File Disk out of Drive A and turn off the computer and monitor.

❏ Designing a Database File

Designing a database file involves deciding what fields will be included in each record, the names of the fields, maximum number of characters each field is likely to contain, and whether the data to be stored in a field is alphanumeric, numeric, or logical. Although the design of a database file can be edited and changed after it has been created, prior planning can be a time-saver. Before entering the design on the computer, take some time to think about and organize the data to be stored in the database file you are creating.

To create a new database file from the Control Center, highlight the **<create>** marker in the **Data** panel and press <Enter> The database design screen appears. The database design screen allows you to define the fields to be included in the database file.

Defining Fields

Defining a field consists of establishing the field's name, type, and width. A field name identifies its contents. Common field names are LASTNAME, FIRSTNAME, CITY, STATE. Notice there are no spaces in LASTNAME or FIRSTNAME. Field names cannot contain any spaces. Underscores, in addition to letters and numbers, are permitted. Therefore, LAST_NAME or FIRST_NAME would be acceptable field names. A field name may include up to ten characters; the first character must be a letter.

The field type identifies the kind of data stored in the field. A field can be defined as one of the following types: character, date, logical, memo, numeric, and float. Character fields are used to store data composed of any of the letters, numbers, or special characters found on the keyboard. Date fields are used to store dates. Unless instructed to do otherwise, dBASE IV stores and displays dates in the mm/dd/yy format (m stands for month, d stands for day, and y for year).

Logical fields are used to store data based on the response to a true/false question. An example of a logical field might be PAID. If a customer had paid for an item, either a T, for true, or Y, for yes, would be the data entered into the PAID field. If the customer had not paid, F, for false, or N, for no, would be entered into the field.

Memo fields are used to store large blocks of text. They hold the same kind of data as that of character fields (letters, numbers, and special characters). However, memo fields can store 5,000 characters or more, while character fields can store only up to 254 characters. Memo fields, for example, might contain notes on the individual records.

Numeric fields are used to store numbers that are used in mathematical formulas. A numeric field can be either integer or decimal. An integer number is one that would never have a decimal place. The number of books checked out of a library is an example of an integer number.

Float fields are used to store floating point numbers, which are often used in scientific applications. A float field can be from 1 to 20 spaces wide.

Not all fields that store numbers are numeric. A field is defined as numeric only if the numbers stored in it are used in a computation. Fields that store Social Security numbers, telephone numbers, or employee numbers would be character rather than numeric fields because those numbers would not be used in a formula. Fields that store the quantity of an item ordered or the cost of an item would be numeric because those numbers could be used in a formula. Multiplying the number stored in the QUANTITY field by the number stored in the COST field would result in the total amount owed, for example.

The field width is the maximum number of characters required to store information in the field. For example, in a STATE field the width would be two because the maximum number of characters the field would have to hold is two (for example, OH for Ohio, MA for Massachusetts, CA for California). Because the field width that is defined for each field takes up memory space, it is a good idea to know as closely as possible how many storage characters are necessary for all fields. That is, if a database file contains a LASTNAME field, it is a waste of memory to define the field width as thirty if most of the last names stored in the file are going to be twenty characters or less.

Each type of field has a limit regarding how many characters it can store. Character fields have a maximum field width of 254. Date fields always have a field width of eight. The only possible width for a logical field is one, because the entry will always be one letter (T, F, Y, or N). dBASE IV automatically inserts a field width of eight whenever a date field is defined and a field width of one whenever a logical field is defined, since these are the only possible widths for these two fields. When defining the width of a numeric field, decimal points and negative signs must be considered because they count as digits. The maximum width of a numeric field is nineteen.

The last column in the database design screen is **Index**. If a field is indexed, you can order the database file by that field. Pressing the Space Bar changes the entry in the Index column to a Y for yes or an N for no.

To save the database file and exit from the design screen, press <Alt>-E for Exit and select the **Save changes and exit** option. When the database file is being saved for the first time, dBASE IV prompts you to name it.

File names can be up to eight characters long. The first character must be a letter, but the name can contain numbers and underscore characters. The file name cannot contain any blank spaces. The file name

MY DATA would not be acceptable because of the space. The file name would be acceptable if an underscore instead of a space were used: MY_DATA.

dBASE IV automatically adds a file extension to file names. A file extension is a period and three letters that follow the file name. File extensions help identify different types of files. When creating a database file, dBASE IV automatically adds the file extension dbf (for database file) after the file name. An example of another type of file that can be created with dBASE IV is a label form file, which is used for creating mailing labels. dBASE IV adds the file extension lbl (for label) after a label form file. By looking at the file extensions, a user can easily tell the difference between a database file and a file that contains a form for mailing labels.

 YOUR TURN

In this exercise you are going to boot your computer, load the dBASE IV program, name a database file, and define the fields for that file.

1. Turn on the computer and monitor.

2. A prompt may appear asking you to enter the date. If it does, type the current date using numbers and hyphens. For example if the date is September 28, you would do the following:

> Type: 09-28-93
>
> Press <Enter>

If a prompt appears asking you to enter the time, either press <Enter> or enter the time in a 24-hour format and press <Enter>.

3. The system prompt C> should appear on the screen.

> Type: cd\dbplus
>
> Press <Enter>

4. The system prompt C> appears again.

> Type: dbase
>
> Press <Enter>

The Control Center appears on the screen. Place the formatted disk that is your data disk in Drive A. Change the default drive to A.

> Press <Alt>-T for the Tools menu
>
> Highlight **DOS utilities** and press <Enter> to select it
>
> Press <Alt>-D for the DOS menu
>
> Highlight **Set default drive:directory** and press <Enter> to select it
>
> Press <Ctrl>-Y to delete the current entry
>
> Type: A:
>
> Press <Enter>
>
> Press <Alt>-E for the Exit menu

Press <Enter>

In the center at the top of the screen it should say **CATALOG: A:\ EXERCISE.CAT**.

5. You are ready to create the database file. The highlight should already be on the **<create>** option in the **Data** panel.

Press <Enter>

Your screen should look like Figure 8-5. This is the database design screen.

6. The purpose of the file you are creating is to keep track of books in a personal library. For each book, you are going to keep a record of the following information:

1. Number — Allocated sequentially to each new book
2. Title — Title of the book
3. Author — Author's last and first name
4. Date of purchase — Month and year when the book was purchased
5. Cost — Amount paid for the book
6. Use — School or personal use

7. Start defining the six fields in the database design screen. The blinking cursor should be under the heading **Field Name**.

Type: NUMBER

Press <Enter>

The cursor moves to the **Field Type** column. You want this field to be a character field, so press <Enter> to accept the character default setting. The cursor moves to the field width column. Choose 3 as the width for the NUMBER field, because it is doubtful that you will own more than 999 books:

FIGURE 8-5 The Database Design Screen

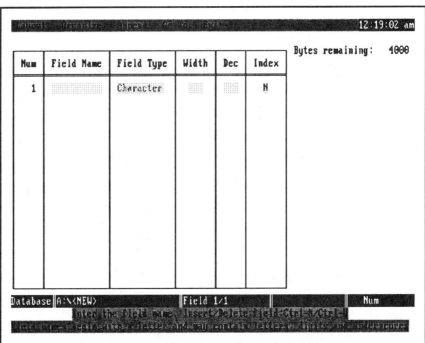

Type: 3

Press <Enter>

Because the field type is not numeric, the cursor automatically skips the decimal column and jumps to the index column. You do not want to index the NUMBER field. The default entry in the Index column is **N** for No.

Press <Enter>

The cursor moves down a row so that you can enter the information on the second field.

8. Enter the information on the remaining fields as follows. If you notice a typing mistake before you have pressed <Enter>, use <Backspace> to delete the characters and retype the entry. If you notice a typing mistake in a field that has already been entered, use the <Up arrow>, <Down arrow>, <Left arrow>, and <Right arrow> keys to move the cursor to the entry where the mistake occurred. Then use the <Del> key to delete characters and the <Ins> key to insert characters to help you correct the error.

Type: TITLE

Press <Enter>

Press <Enter> again

Type: 25

Press <Enter>

Press <Enter>

Type: LAST_NAME

Press <Enter>

Press <Enter> again

Type: 15

Press <Enter>

Press <Enter>

Type: FIRST_NAME

At this point, the computer beeps and the cursor automatically moves to the Field Type column. This happens because the field name FIRST_NAME is ten characters wide, which is the maximum width that a field name can be. dBASE does not accept more than ten characters for a field name, so it automatically moves the cursor to the next column. The beep alerts you to the fact that the cursor has moved to the next column so you do not have to press the <Enter> key. Again, accept the default setting for Field Type and enter the field width.

Press <Enter>

Type: 15

Press <Enter>

Press <Enter>

Type: PUR_MONTH

Press <Enter>

Press <Enter> again

Type: 2

Press <Enter>

Press <Enter>

Type: PUR_YEAR

Press <Enter>

Press <Enter> again

Type: 2

Press <Enter>

Press <Enter>

Type: COST

Press <Enter>

The COST field is not a character field. It is a numeric field with two decimal places. Notice what the prompt line at the bottom of the screen says: **Change field type:Spacebar**.

Press the Space Bar once

The word **Numeric** now appears in the Field Type column for the COST field.

Press <Enter>

Type: 8

Press <Enter>

This time the cursor moves to the decimal column, because the field type is numeric. Two decimal places are required.

Type: 2

Press <Enter>

Press <Enter>

Type: USE

Press <Enter>

You want the USE field to be a logical field. This time, instead of pressing the Space Bar to select the field type, use L for LOGICAL.

Type: L

dBASE IV immediately selects Logical for the field type, 1 for the field width, and moves the cursor to the next line. (You could also select LOGICAL by pressing the Space Bar several times or select NUMERIC by entering N.)

9. All the fields for this data file are now defined. Your screen should look like Figure 8-6. Look over all your entries to make sure there are no mistakes. If there are mistakes use the <Up arrow>, <Down arrow>, <Left arrow>, <Right arrow> and <Ins> keys to correct them.

Now end the field definition process.

FIGURE 8-6 Defining Fields

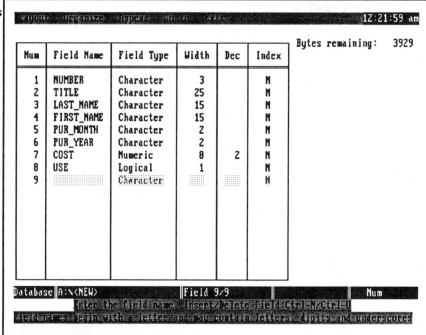

Num	Field Name	Field Type	Width	Dec	Index
1	NUMBER	Character	3		N
2	TITLE	Character	25		N
3	LAST_NAME	Character	15		N
4	FIRST_NAME	Character	15		N
5	PUR_MONTH	Character	2		N
6	PUR_YEAR	Character	2		N
7	COST	Numeric	8	2	N
8	USE	Logical	1		N
9		Character			N

Bytes remaining: 3929

12:21:59 am

Database A:\<NEW>   Field 9/9   Num

Enter the field name. Insert/Delete field:Ctrl-N/Ctrl-U
Field names begin with a letter and may contain letters, digits and underscores

Press <Alt>-E for the Exit menu

Press <Enter> to select **Save changes and exit**

The prompt **Save as** appears.

Type: BOOKS

The Control Center returns to the screen. Leave the Control Center on the screen while you read the following section.

Displaying the Structure of a Database File

After the design for a database file has been defined, the user can view the structure. By displaying the structure on the screen, a user can find out what fields are included in the file, its field names, widths, and field types.

Before the design of a database file can be displayed, however, the file has to be active. The file whose name appears next to the word **File** at the bottom of the Control Center is the active file. If you want to display the structure of a file other than the one whose name is displayed, or if there is no file name listed next to the word **File,** you must first access the database file. To access the database file, highlight the name of the file in the panel and press <Enter>.

To display the design of the active database file, press <Shift>-<F2> for Design. The database design screen appears. One of the pull-down menus is open. If you do not want to use this menu, press <Esc>. To exit from the display, press <Alt>-E and press <Enter>. The Control Center returns to the screen.

YOUR TURN

In this exercise you are going to display the design of the BOOKS database file. Look towards the bottom of the Control Center. Notice that the file name BOOKS.DBF appears next to the word **File**. Because the BOOKS file is currently active, you do not have to access it.

1. The Control Center should be on your screen.

>   Press <Shift>-<F2>

>   Press <Esc>

3. The design for the BOOKS database file appears.

4. Look the structure over carefully.

>   Press <Alt>-E

>   Highlight **Abandon changes and exit**

>   Press <Enter>

The Control Center returns to the screen. You can either exit from dBASE IV or leave the Control Center on the screen while you read the following section.

Editing the Design of a Database File

It is easy to make changes to the design of a database file. Fields can be added, deleted, or redefined; field names, widths, or types can be changed.

The database file to be edited must be active. That is, its name has to appear next to the word **File** at the bottom of the Control Center. If you want to edit the design of a file other than the one whose name is displayed, or if there is no file name displayed, access the database file by selecting it from the panel.

Once the database file to be edited is active, press <Shift>-<F2> for Design and press <Esc> to close the pull-down menu that is open. To edit the design of the database file, move the cursor to the field that is to be changed. Pressing <Up arrow> moves the cursor up a field; pressing <Down arrow> moves the cursor down a field. Pressing <Left arrow> and <Right arrow> moves the cursor one character to the left or right, respectively. Pressing <Tab> moves the cursor through the design category by category. That is, the cursor jumps from the field name, to the type, width, decimal (if there is an entry in that column), index, and then down to the field name of the following field, and so on.

To insert a character, position the cursor where the character is to be inserted, press <Ins> and enter the character or characters. To delete a character, position the cursor under the character to be deleted and press <Del>.

To insert a new field, position the cursor where the field is to be inserted and press <Ctrl>-N. A new field is inserted and all the fields following the new field move down one position. The field's name, type, width, and, if necessary, decimal places must then be entered. To delete a field, position the cursor on the field to be deleted and press <Ctrl>-U. The field is deleted and all the fields following the deleted field move up one position. If only a word, rather than an entire field, is to be deleted, place the cursor on that word and press <Ctrl>-Y. The word is deleted and a new entry can be made.

After all of the changes have been made, press <Alt>-E for the Exit menu and press <Enter> to select **Save changes and exit**. The prompt **Press ENTER key to confirm. Press any other key to resume** appears at the bottom of the screen. If all the editing changes have been made, press <Enter>. The changes are saved and the Control Center returns to the screen. If you want to cancel the option to save the database design, press any key other than <Enter>. You can then continue to make changes to the database design.

YOUR TURN

In this exercise, you are going to make changes to the BOOKS database.

1. The Control Center should be on your screen and the BOOKS file should be active. If necessary, start the dBASE IV program. Change the default drive to A. Check the bottom of the Control Center to make sure that the BOOKS.DBF file is active. If it is not, highlight BOOKS in the **Data** panel and press <Enter>. Press <Enter> to select **Use file.**

        Press <Shift>-<F2> for Design

        Press <Esc>

2. The database design screen appears. You want to add a new field to the file. Some of the books have more than one author, but only one author's name is stored in each database record. The field you are going to add is a logical field named CODE. If a book has more than one author, you will enter Y for Yes. If it has only one author, you enter N for No.

3. The cursor should be in field 1, the NUMBER field.

        Press <Down arrow> four times

The cursor is now in field 5. You want to insert a new field 5 so that the CODE field comes right after the author's first name.

        Press <Ctrl>-N

A new field 5 is added. You can now enter the new field name.

        Type: CODE

        Press <Enter>

        Type: L

4. You now want to switch the order in which the fields appear. You want the COST field to come right after the CODE field. To do this, delete the COST field from where it now appears and reinsert it in its new location. First you have to move the cursor to the COST field.

        Press <Down arrow> two times

The cursor should be in the COST field.

        Press <Ctrl>-U

The COST field is deleted and all the fields that came after it moved up one spot.

        Press <Up arrow> two times

The cursor should now be in field 6, the PUR_MONTH field.

Press <Ctrl>-N

There is now room to add a new field 6.

Type: COST

Press <Enter>

Press N to enter the Numeric field type

Type: 8

Press <Enter>

Type: 2

Press <Enter>

Press <Enter>

The COST field is inserted in its new location. Now, save the edited BOOKS database file.

Press <Alt>-E for Exit

Press <Enter> to select **Save changes and exit**

The prompt **You have made changes to the field structure of this database file. Are you sure you want to save these changes?** appears.

Press <Enter>

The Control Center returns to the screen. You can either exit from dBASE IV or you can leave the Control Center on the screen while you read the following section.

❏ ENTERING DATA INTO A DATABASE FILE

Once the structure for the database file has been completed, records can be entered into the file. Make sure the database file to which the records are to be added is the active file. The active file is the file whose file name appears at the bottom of the Control Center next to the word **File**. If the file to receive the records is not the active file, access that file by selecting it from the **Data** panel. To enter records into the active file, press <F2> for **Data**. A blank Edit screen appears.

The edit screen contains an empty data-entry form. The data is entered in the data-entry form in the space provided for each field. After typing the data for one field, press <Enter> and the cursor moves to the next field. If the data fills the field completely, you do not have to press <Enter>; the cursor automatically moves to the next field. After data for the last field in the record has been added, a blank data-entry form for the next record appears. dBASE IV saves the data that is entered record by record. That is, once the blank entry-form for the next record appears, the previous record is saved.

If you make a typing mistake while entering data into a field and have not pressed <Enter>, use <Backspace> to delete your mistake and type the entry again. If you notice a mistake that has already been entered into a field, use the up or down arrow keys to move the cursor to that field. Use either <Backspace> or <Del> to delete the error and enter the correction.

If you want to move back to check the entries in a previous record, press <PgUp>. Pressing <PgUp> moves to the previous record. To move to the next record in the file, press <PgDn>.

As you enter each record into the database file, dBASE IV assigns it a record number. The record number for the current record is displayed in the Status Bar at the bottom of the screen. dBASE IV displays two record numbers separated by a slash. The first is the number of the current record; that is, the record that appears on the screen. The second is the total number of records in the database file.

Remember, when creating the design for a database file, capitalization does not matter because dBASE IV automatically capitalizes all the field names. Capitalization does, however, make a difference when entering records into the database file. dBASE IV stores the data in the records exactly as you enter them, including whatever capitalization is used.

When all the records have been entered, end the data-entry process by pressing <Alt>-E for the Exit menu and pressing <Enter> to select **Exit**.

YOUR TURN

In this exercise you are going to enter fifteen records into the BOOKS file. Check to make sure the default drive is A and the BOOKS file is the active file. If the file name BOOKS does not appear next to the word **File** at the bottom of the Control Center, highlight the BOOKS file on the **Data** panel and press <Enter>.

1. When the BOOKS file is the active file, you are ready to access the data-entry form.

    Press <F2>

A blank data-entry form appears. Your screen should look like Figure 8-7.

2. The cursor is in the space next to NUMBER.

    Type: 1
    Press <Enter>
    Type: A Short Course in PL/C
    Press <Enter>
    Type: Clark
    Press <Enter>
    Type: Ann
    Press <Enter>
    Type: N

The computer beeps and the cursor automatically moves to the next field although you did not press <Enter>. This happens because the field width is one and you typed one character. The beep alerts you to the fact that the cursor is already in the next field. This also occurs with the rest of the entries in this record.

    Type: 25.00
    Type: 07
    Type: 93

FIGURE 8-7 Edit screen for the BOOKS File

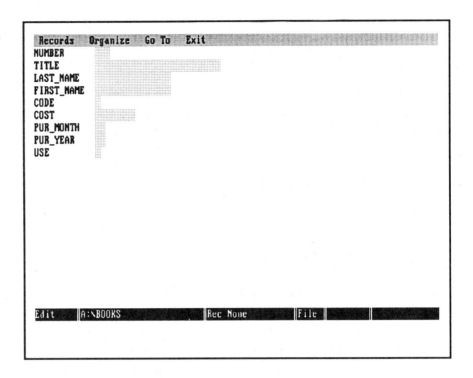

```
Records  Organize  Go To  Exit
NUMBER
TITLE
LAST_NAME
FIRST_NAME
CODE
COST
PUR_MONTH
PUR_YEAR
USE




Edit     A:\BOOKS              Rec None        File
```

Type: N

After you enter the last field, dBASE IV automatically advances to the next record.

3. You are now going to add fourteen more records to the LIBRARY file.

Enter the following information:

No.	Title	Last Name	First Name	Code	Cost	Mo	Year	Use
2	Accounting Today	Asman	Mark	Y	50.50	01	93	Y
3	Advanced Structured COBOL	Welburn	Tyler	N	35.00	10	91	N
4	Business Policies	Christensen	Roland	Y	45.00	01	90	Y
5	COBOL for the 90's	Spence	John	N	28.00	11	91	N
6	Computers are Fun	Rice	Jean	Y	34.00	02	90	N
7	Consumer Behavior	Williams	Terrel	N	40.00	01	91	N
8	Economics	McConnel	Campbell	N	65.00	12	90	N
9	International Marketing	Kramer	Roland	N	52.00	09	91	Y
10	Introduction to BASIC	Mandell	Steven	N	54.00	01	90	N
11	Using 1-2-3	Leblond	Geoffrey	Y	21.50	04	92	N
12	Discovering PC DOS	Worcester	Clark	N	18.50	07	92	N
13	Harbrace College Handbook	Hodges	John	N	16.75	10	90	Y
14	Facts from Figures	Morney	M	N	16.00	11	91	N
15	Financial Accounting	Eskew	Robert	Y	38.80	09	92	Y

4. When all the records are entered, number 16 appears on the screen. You are ready to exit.

Press <Alt>-E

Press <Enter> to select **Exit**

The Control Center returns to the screen.

5. You have finished with this Your Turn exercise. You can either leave your work on the screen while you read the following sections, or you can exit from dBASE IV.

❏ UPDATING A DATABASE FILE

Very rarely is a database file ever finalized. Typically, changes such as adding or deleting records and updating the data stored in the records are continually made to a database file. Editing a database file is a very easy operation using the Control Center.

The Browse Table and Edit Screen

There are two ways the data in a database file can be displayed. Data can be displayed using the Edit screen or using the Browse screen.

The Edit screen displays the data one record at a time. All the fields in the record are displayed running vertically down the screen. Only one record can be displayed at a time.

The Browse table displays as many records as will fit on the screen in a table format. The fields appear as columns going across the screen and the records appear as rows going down the screen.

Pressing <F2> for Data toggles between the Edit screen and the Browse Table. The data in a database file can be edited in either the Edit screen or the Browse table.

Editing a Record

To edit records in an active database file, press <F2> for Data. The Edit screen appears. Press <F2> again, and the Browse table appears. To switch back to the Edit screen, press <F2> a third time.

Using the Edit screen, if the record that is displayed is not the record needing to be edited, press <PgUp> or <PgDn> to browse through the records until the one you want to edit is displayed. Pressing <Up arrow> and <Down arrow> moves you through the record a field at a time as long as you do not go past the first or last field. For example, if the cursor is in the first field of the record and you press <Up arrow>, the previous record appears on the screen. If the cursor is in the last field of the record and you press <Down arrow> the next record appears on the screen.

Once the appropriate record is displayed, use <Up arrow> and <Down arrow> to move to the field to be edited. Use <Left arrow> and <Right arrow> to move through the characters in a particular field. Use <Backspace> or <Del> to delete characters. If you want to insert characters, press <Ins>. If you try to enter characters without pressing <Ins> first, the characters you enter will type over the characters that were already there. Typing over characters is, of course, another method for editing data.

After making editing changes to one record, you can edit other records by pressing <PgUp> or <PgDn>. As many data records can be edited as necessary.

Using the Browse table, if the record that is highlighted in the Browse table is not the record needing to be edited, press <Up arrow> or <Down arrow> until the one you want to edit is highlighted. Pressing <Tab> and <Shift>-<Tab> moves you through the record a field at a time as long as you do not go past the first or last field. For example, if the cursor is in the first field of the record and you press <Shift>-<Tab>, the previous record appears on the screen. If the cursor is in the last field of the record and you press <Tab> the next record appears on the screen.

Once the appropriate record is highlighted, use <Tab> and <Shift>-<Tab> to move to the field to be edited. Use <Left arrow> and <Right arrow> to move through the characters in a particular field. Use <Backspace> or <Del> to delete characters. If you want to insert characters, press <Ins>. If you try to enter characters without pressing <Ins> first, the characters you enter will type over the characters that were already there. Typing over characters is, of course, another method for editing data.

After making editing changes to one record, you can edit other records by pressing <Up arrow> or <Down arrow>. As many data records can be edited as necessary.

When the editing process is complete, exit from the editing process by pressing <Alt>-E for Exit and press <Enter> to select **Exit**.

 YOUR TURN

In this exercise you are going to edit several of the records in the BOOKS database file.

1. The Control Center should be on your screen and the BOOKS file should be active. If necessary, start the dBASE IV program and set the default drive to A:. Check the bottom of the Control Center to make sure that the BOOKS file is active. If it is not, highlight the BOOKS file in the Data panel and press <Enter> to select it. When the BOOKS file is active, start the process of editing the records.

>Press <F2> for Data

Either the Browse table or Edit screen appears. You want the Edit screen. If necessary, press <F2> to access the Edit screen. Once you are in the Edit screen, you want to display the first record. Press <PgUp> until record 1 is displayed. Notice the words **Edit** and **Rec: 1/15** in the Status Bar at the bottom of the screen. This means you are in the Edit screen, that record 1 is currently displayed, and there are a total of fifteen records in the BOOKS database file.

2. Now you want to switch to the Browse table.

>Press <F2>

The Browse table appears. Record 1 is displayed. Notice the first box of the Status Bar now says **Browse**.

>Press <F2>

The screen switches back to the Edit screen and Record 1 is displayed.

>Press <F2> again

You are now back in the Browse table. The Status Bar should say **Browse** and **Rec 1/15**.

3. The BOOKS file needs to be edited because you are now using three more of your books at school.

Press <Tab> until the cursor is in the USE field in record 1.

Type: Y

The computer beeps and the cursor jumps to the NUMBER field in record 2. The other two books you are now using at school are record 3, Advanced Structured COBOL, and record 12, Discovering PC DOS.

Edit those two records so that Y is entered into the USE field rather than N

4. The records have now all been edited. You are ready to exit from the editing procedure.

Press <Alt>-E for Exit

Press <Enter> to select Exit

5. You have finished with this Your Turn exercise. You can either leave your work on the screen while you read the following section, or you can exit from dBASE IV.

Adding a Record

Records can be added to an active database file through either the Browse table or the Edit screen. Since the Edit screen allows the user to concentrate on one records at a time, it is generally easier to add records using the Edit screen. To add a record, press <F2> for Data. If the Browse table appears, press <F2> again.

Once you are in the Edit screen, press <Alt>-R for the Records menu. Press <Enter> to select the option **Add new records**. A blank record appears on the screen. This blank record can be filled out using the same method as that for entering data into the database file for the first time. As many records as necessary can be added. Pressing <PgDn> or <Enter> after entering data into the last field in the file accesses another blank data-entry form. When all the records have been added, press <Alt>-E for Exit and press <Enter> to select **Exit**.

YOUR TURN

In this exercise, add five new records to the BOOKS file.

1. The Control Center should be on your screen and the BOOKS file should be active. If necessary, start the dBASE IV program, set the default drive to A:, and select the BOOKS file from the **Data** panel. When the BOOKS file is active, you can add records to the database file.

Press <F2> for Data

If the Browse table appears, press <F2> again. You should be in the Edit screen.

Press <Alt>-R for the Records menu

Press <Enter> to select **Add new records**

A blank record appears on the screen. In the Status Bar, the indicator **Rec: EOF/15** appears. This means that you are at the end of the file and there are a total of fifteen records in the BOOKS database file.

2. You are now ready to add the five new records. The cursor should be in the NUMBER field. Enter the following:

No.	Title	Last Name	First Name	Code	Cost	Month	Year	Use
16	Getting Things Done	Bliss	Edwin	N	23.60	02	91	N
17	Intermediate Algebra	Mangan	Frances	N	22.30	09	90	Y
18	Management	Glueck	William	N	28.45	07	02	N
19	Learning to Program in C	Plum	Thomas	N	48.90	07	92	N
20	Information Systems	Burch	John	Y	52.60	01	92	Y

When all the data is entered, save the records and end the process of adding records to a database file. A blank form for record 21 is on the screen.

> Press <Alt>-E for the Exit menu
>
> Press <Enter> to select **Exit**

The Control Center returns to the screen.

3. You have finished with this Your Turn exercise. You can either leave your work on the screen while you read the following section, or you can exit from dBASE IV.

Deleting a Record

Deleting records using dBASE IV is a two-step process. First, mark the records for deletion and then remove the marked records from the database file. By marking the records first, you have the option of retrieving the material before it is permanently removed from the database file. Once records are removed from the database file they are irretrievable, so be careful when deleting them. You do not want to lose data that you may need at a later point.

Records can be marked for deletion in either the Browse table or the Edit screen. The Browse table displays many records at once, so it may be easier to mark records for deletion using the Browse table. To mark records for deletion, press <F2> for Data and press <F2> again, if necessary to display the Browse table. Move the cursor to the record that is to be deleted. Press <Alt>-R for the Records menu, highlight **Mark record for deletion**, and press <Enter>. The word **Del** appears in the right corner of the Status Bar at the bottom of the screen indicating that the record has been marked for deletion.

To remove a mark from a record, move the cursor back to the record that is marked for deletion. Press <Alt>-R for the Record menu. This time the option says **Clear deletion mark**. Highlight the **Clear deletion mark** option and press <Enter>. The record is no longer marked for deletion.

When all the records to be deleted are marked, press <Alt>-E for the Exit menu and press <Enter> to select **Exit**. At this point, the records are only marked; they have not been removed from the database file. To delete marked records from the database file, highlight the name of the database file in the Data panel and press <Shift>-<F2> for Design. The database design appears and the Organize menu is displayed. Highlight the option **Erase marked records** and press <Enter> to select it. A prompt appears asking for confirmation to delete the records. Press Y to select yes and the records are permanently removed from the database file. A message appears displaying the current number of records in the database file. Press <Alt>-E for the Exit menu and press <Enter> to select **Exit** to return to the Control Center.

YOUR TURN

In this exercise you are going to delete a record from the BOOKS database file.

1. The Control Center should be on your screen, and the BOOKS file should be active. If necessary, start the dBASE IV program, change the default drive to A:, and select the BOOKS file from the Data panel. Check to make sure that the BOOKS file is active. When the BOOKS file is active, you can delete records.

> Press <F2> for Data
>
> If necessary, press <F2> again to display the Browse table
>
> Press <Up arrow> or <Down arrow> to move the pointer to record 17
>
> Press <Alt>-R for the Records menu
>
> Highlight **Mark record for deletion**
>
> Press <Enter>

Your screen should look like Figure 8-8. Notice that the word **Del** appears in the Status Bar.

> Press <Alt>-R again

Notice the option now says **Clear deletion mark**

> Press <Enter>

The word **Del** is no longer in the Status Bar and record 17 is no longer marked for deletion.

> Press <Alt>-R
>
> Press <Enter> to select **Mark record for deletion**

Again, record 17 is marked for deletion. Leave it marked. Look at the Status Bar. It should say **Rec: 17/20**, which means there are 20 records in the database file.

> Press <Alt>-E for the Exit menu
>
> Press <Enter> to select **Exit**

2. You are now ready to permanently remove record 17 from the BOOKS database file. Make sure the filename BOOKS is highlighted in the Data panel.

> Press <Shift>-<F2>
>
> Highlight **Erase marked records**
>
> Press <Enter>

The prompt **Are you sure you want to erase all marked records?** appears.

> Press Y for yes

The message **19 records packed** appears briefly on the screen.

FIGURE 8-8 Marking a Record for Deletion

Records	Organize	Fields	Go To	Exit

NUMBER	TITLE	LAST_NAME	FIRST_NAME	CODE	COST
░░	Intermediate Algebra	Mangan	Frances	N	22.30
18	Management	Glueck	William	N	28.45
19	Learning to Program in C	Plum	Thomas	N	48.90
20	Information Systems	Burch	John	Y	52.60

| Browse | A:\BOOKS | | Rec 17/20 | File | Del |

Press <Alt>-E for the Exit menu

Press <Enter> to select **Save changes and Exit**

Press <Enter> again

Press <F2> for Data

Now look at the Status Bar. Notice that there are now a total of nineteen records in the BOOKS database file. Check to make sure the record was deleted.

Press <Up arrow> until the Status Bar says **Rec 17/19**.

Record 17 is now the record for the book *Management* rather than *Intermediate Algebra.*

Press <Alt>-E and <Enter> to return to the Control Center

3. You have finished with this Your Turn exercise. You can either leave your work on the screen while you read the following section, or you can exit from dBASE IV.

❏ MANAGING FILES

After working with dBASE IV, you will begin to accumulate a lot of files on your data disk. Appropriate management of the files is extremely important. The **DOS utilities** option from the Tools menu includes several commands that enable users to maintain files that have been created and stored. The following sections explain these options.

Listing the File Directory

It is often very useful to be able to list the names of the files that are stored on a disk. After creating several files you might forget some of their names or need to know how much storage space you have on your disk. You can access this information by listing the file directory.

To list the file directory, press <Alt>-T for the Tools menu. Move the highlight to **DOS utilities** and press <Enter>. The DOS utilities screen appears. The screen displays the files on the current disk in a file list or it displays directories and subdirectories in a directory tree. Pressing <F9> switches you back and forth between a file list and a directory tree.

When a file list is dispalyed, a lot of information is provided about each file. The **Name\Extension** column lists the file name and extension. The **Size** column lists the amount of space the file takes up on the disk. The **Date & Time** column displays the last date and time the file was updated. The **Attrs** column shows whether an attribute has been set for the file. The **Space Used** column shows the space needed on the disk to store each file. The disk space needed depends on the cluster size for the current disk. The values in this column will always be equal to or greater than the values in the **Size** column. Pressing <Up arrow> and <Down arrow> moves the highlight through the list of files.

At the very bottom of the list are two rows that display the number and total size of all the files in the list and display the number and total size of all marked files. Marked files can be operated on as a group. For example, you could mark eight files and then copy or delete them all at the same time. To mark or unmark a file, move the highlight to it and press <Enter>.

Copying a File

Copying files is important for creating backups. You should always have a backup of your data in case the original file is lost or damaged.

To copy a file, press <Alt>-T for the Tools menu. Highlight the **DOS utilities** option and press <Enter>. The DOS utilities screen appears. The files on the current disk are displayed in a file list or directories and subdirectories are displayed in a directory tree. To copy files, you want the file list displayed. Pressing <F9> switches you back and forth between a file list and a directory tree.

Once a file list is displayed, move the highlight to the file you want to copy. Press <Alt>-O for the Operations menu, highlight the **Copy** option and press <Enter>. Press <Enter> again to select the option **Single File**. A window appears that displays the file name of the file you are copying. First you have to select the drive where the new file is to be stored. The default disk drive is displayed. If that is the drive where you want your backup copy, press <Enter>. If you want your backup copy in a different drive, enter the new drive and press <Enter>. Type a file name that is different from the original file name and press <Ctrl>-<End>. Ending the file name with the letters BK is a convenient way to easily identify the files on your disk that are backup copies.

Deleting a File

The command to erase a file is also found in the DOS utilities screen under the Operations menu. To delete a file, press <Alt>-T for the Tools menu, move the highlight to **DOS utilities** and press <Enter>. The DOS utilities screen appears. The files on the current disk are displayed in a file list or directories and subdirectories are displayed in a directory tree. To delete files, you want the file list displayed. If necessary, press <F9> to switch to a file list.

Once a file list is displayed, move the highlight to the file you want to delete. Press <Alt>-O for the Operations menu, highlight the **Delete** option and press <Enter>. Press <Enter> again to select the option **Single File**. A window appears with the name of the file that will be deleted. If this is correct, press <Enter> to select **Proceed**. If it is not correct, highlight **Cancel** and press <Enter>.

Renaming a File

If it is necessary to change the name of a file, it can be easily accomplished with the **Rename** option on the Operations menu. To rename a file, press <Alt>-T for the Tools menu, move the highlight to **DOS utilities** and press <Enter>. The DOS utilities screen appears. The files on the current disk are displayed in a file list or directories and subdirectories are displayed in a directory tree. To rename files, you want the file list displayed. If necessary, press <F9> to switch to a file list.

Once a file list is displayed, move the highlight to the file you want to rename. Press <Alt>-O for the Operations menu, highlight the **Rename** option and press <Enter>. Press <Enter> again to select the option **Single File**. A window appears with the name of the file that will be renamed. Type the new name for the file and press <Enter>.

YOUR TURN

In this hands-on exercise, you are going to practice making a copy of a file, renaming a file, and deleting a file.

1. The Control Center should be on your screen and the BOOKS file should be active. If necessary, start the program, set the default drive, and select the BOOKS file from the **Data** panel.

> Press <Alt>-T for the Tools menu
>
> Move the highlight to **DOS utilities**
>
> Press <Enter>

The DOS utilities screen appears. Your screen should look similar to Figure 8-9. All the files on the disk in drive A are listed in the window in the middle of the screen. Use the <Up arrow> and <Down arrow> to scroll through the file list.

> Highlight the **BOOKS.DBF** filename
>
> Press <Alt>-O for the Operations menu
>
> Highlight the **Copy** option
>
> Press <Enter>
>
> Press <Enter> to select **Single File**

A new window appears with the **BOOKS.DBF** listed as the file to be copied. **A:** is listed as the Drive.

> Press <Enter> to select **A:**

You need to type a new name for the file.

> Press <Ctrl>-Y to delete the current entry
>
> Type: BOOKSBK.DBF

Your screen should look like Figure 8-10

FIGURE 8-9 The DOS
Utilities Screen

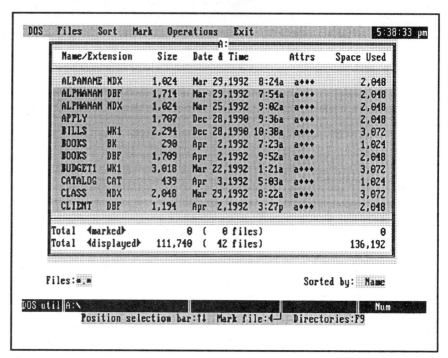

Press <Ctrl>-<End>

The DOS utilities screen returns.

2. Next you are going to rename the BOOKSBK.DBF.

  Move the highlight to **BOOKSBK.DBF**

  Press <ALt>-o for the Operations menu

  Highlight the **Rename** option

FIGURE 8-10 Copying a
File

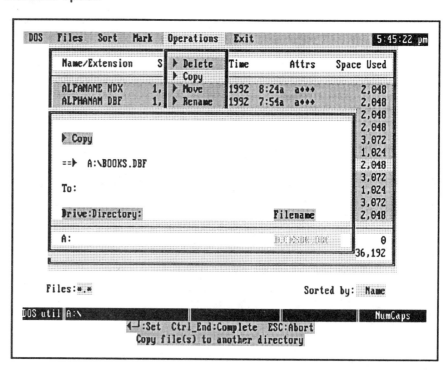

                  Chapter 8: Introduction to dBASE IV

Press <Enter>

Press <Enter> to select **Single File**

Press <Ctrl>-Y to delete the current entry

Type: BOOKS-BK.DBF

Press <Enter>

3. Now you are going to make another copy of the BOOKS.DBF file and then erase the copy.

Move the highlight to **BOOKS.DBF**

Press <Alt>-O for the Operations menu

Press <Enter>

Highlight the **Copy** option

Press <Enter>

Press <Enter> again to select **Single File**

Press <Enter> to select drive **A:**

Press <Ctrl>-Y to delete the current entry

Type: BOOKS-2.DBF

Press <Ctrl>-<End>

Now delete the BOOKS-2.DBF file.

Move the highlight to **BOOKS-2.DBF**

Press <Alt>-O for the Operations menu

Highlight the **Delete** option

Press <Enter>

Press <Enter> to select **Single File**

Make sure the BOOKS-2.DBF is the file that is going to be deleted.

Press <Enter> to select **Proceed**

The BOOKS-2.DBF is deleted.

Press <Alt>-E for the Exit menu

Press <Enter> to select **Exit to Control Center**

The Control Center returns to your screen.

4. You have finished with this Your Turn exercise. You can either leave your work on the screen while you read the following section, or you can exit from dBASE IV.

❏ QUERIES

The ability to create queries make dBASE IV a very powerful tool. A query is a set of instructions that specifies how dBASE IV will organize or change the data. A view query enables you to display only those records that meet a specific criterion. An update query enables you to make broad changes to a database file. View queries are discussed in this chapter.

To create a query, first make sure the file that will be the source from which the view is created is the active file. If necessary, select the file from the **Data** panel. Then, move the highlight to **<create>** in the **Query** panel and press <Enter>. The queries design screen appears. The screen includes a frame showing the name of the active file and then some field names. This frame is called the file skeleton. The cursor is under the name of the active database file. All the fields in that file appear in boxes at the bottom of the screen, in a frame called the view skeleton. Pressing <Tab> and <Shift>-<Tab> moves the cursor back and forth through the frame skeleton.

To include a field in a query, press <Tab> until the cursor is under that field name. Press <F5> for Field and that field is entered into the view skeleton. If all the fields are entered in the view skeleton, move the highlight to under the file name. Press <F5> for Field and all the fields are deleted from the view skeleton.

A field name can easily be removed from the view skeleton. In the file skeleton, place the highlight under the field name you want to delete from the view skeleton and press <F5> for Field. The field name is removed from the view skeleton.

To see the results of the view query, press <F2> for Data. The selected fields are displayed on the screen. To return to the queries design screen, press <Shift>-<F2>.

To save a query, press <Alt>-L for the Layout menu. Highlight the **Save this query** option and press <Enter>. Type in a name for the query and press <Enter>.

To return to the Control Center from the queries design screen, press <Alt>-E for the Exit menu, highlight either **Save changes and exit** or **Abandon changes and exit** and press <Return>. The queries you created are listed in the **Queries** panel.

❏ USING OPERATORS IN QUERIES

At times it is useful to be able to display specific records rather than displaying all the records in a file. For example, you might want to display only those records that meet certain conditions. Using the BOOKS file as an example, suppose you want to know which books cost more than $40. Relational operators enable the user to display only those records that meet certain conditions, such as "cost more than $40." Table 8-1 defines the relational operators available in dBASE IV.

TABLE 8-1 Relational Operators

Relational Operator	Relation
=	Equal to
<	Less than
>	Greater than
<=	Less than or equal to
>=	Greater than or equal to
<> or #	Not equal to

To display only those records that meet certain requirements, first access the queries design screen. In the file skeleton, move the cursor to the field name that must meet the condition and then type in the condition. For example, if you wanted to see only those books that cost more than $40, you would type 40 under the field name COST in the file skeleton.

You can use more than one condition at a time. If you place more than one condition in the same row of a file skeleton, all the conditions must be met for a record to be included in the results. This is known as an AND condition. If you place two or more conditions in different rows of a file skeleton, only one of the conditions has to be met in order for that record to be included in the results. This is know as an OR condition.

 YOUR TURN

In this hands-on exercise, you are going to practice creating queries.

1. The Control Center should be on your screen and the BOOKS file should be active. If necessary, start the dBASE IV program, set the default drive to A: and select **BOOKS** from the **Data** panel. First, you are going to create a query that displays all the books that cost more than $40.

Highlight **<create>** in the **Queries** panel

Press <Return>

Your screen should look like Figure 8-11. This is the queries design screen. At the top of the screen is the file skeleton. The view skeleton is displayed at the bottom of the screen. You want to delete all the field names out of the view skeleton. The highlight should be under **Books.dbf** in the file skeleton.

Press <F5> for Fields

All the field names should be gone from the bottom of the screen.

2. The fields you want to include in your query are TITLE and COST. Only those books that cost more than $40.00 are to be included in the results.

Press <Tab> twice to move the highlight to **TITLE**

Press <F5> for Fields

The field name TITLE now appears in the view skeleton.

Press <Tab> four times to move the highlight to **COST**

You are going to use a relational operator to find only the books costing more than $40.00.

Type: > 40

Press <F5> for Fields

The field name COST now appears in the view skeleton. You now want to view the results of the query.

Press <F2> for Data

**FIGURE 8-11 The Queries
Design Screen**

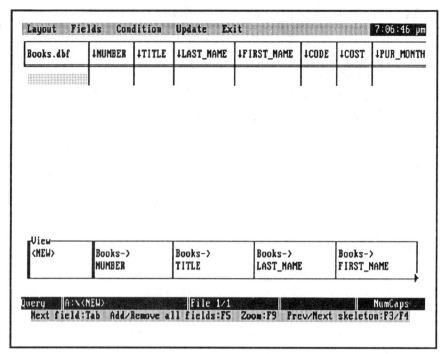

Your screen should look like Figure 8-12. Only those books costing more than $40.00 are
listed.

> Press <Shift>-<F2>

Now you want to save this query.

> Press <Alt>-L for the Layout menu

> Highlight **Save this query**

**FIGURE 8-12 Displaying
Query Reports**

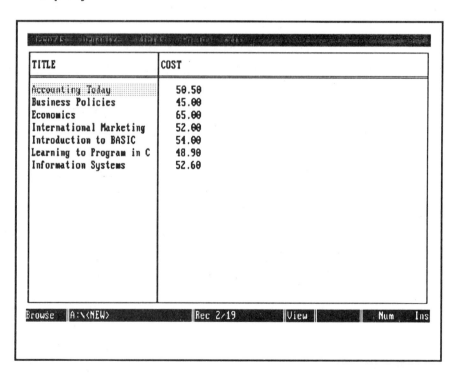

Press <Enter>

Type: OVER40

Press <Enter>

3.   Now display all books that were purchased after 1990.

If necessary move the higlight to **COST**

Press <Ctrl>-Y to delete the entry

Press <F5>

The field name COST is removed from the view skeleton.

Press <Tab> twice to move the highlight to **PUR_YEAR**

Type: > "90"

You must include the quotation marks around 90 because PUR_YEAR is a character field, not a numeric field. Without the quotation marks dBASE IV will read the 90 as a numeric entry and will give you a **data mismatch** error message. Now display the results.

Press <F2> for Data

The books that were purchased after 1990 are displayed.

Press <Shift>-<F2>

Press <Alt>-L for the Layout menu

Move the highlight to **Save this query**

Press <Enter>

Press <Backspace> and delete the OVER40.qbe filename.

Type: AFTER90

Press <Enter>

4.   Now you want to know how many books you have by the author Steven Mandell. The highlight should be under **PUR_YEAR**.

Press <Ctrl>-Y to delete the entry

Press <F5> for Data

Press <Shift>-<Tab> five times to move the highlight back to **LAST_NAME**

Type: "Mandell"

The character string must be entered between quotation marks and you must type it exactly as it appears in the record. For example, if you type *"mandell"* instead of *"Mandell"*, dBASE IV cannot find the record.

Press <F5> for Fields

Press <F2> for Data

The one book by Mandell in your personal library is displayed on the screen.

Press <Shift>-<F2>

5. Now suppose you want to combine the first two commands to display the titles of all the books purchased after 1990 that cost more than $40. The two conditions must be placed on the same row to create an AND condition.

> Press <Ctrl>-Y to delete the entry under **LAST_NAME**
>
> Press <F5>
>
> Press <Tab> three times to move the highlight to **COST**
>
> Type: > 40
>
> Press <F5> for Fields
>
> Press <Tab> twice to move the highlight to **PUR_YEAR**
>
> Type: > "90"
>
> Press <F5> for Fields
>
> Press <F2> for Data

dBASE IV displays the books that cost more than $40 and were purchased after 1990.

> Press <Shift>-<F2>
>
> Press <Alt>-E for the Exit menu
>
> Press <Enter> to select **Save changes and exit**

Notice the two query files you saved **OVER40** and **AFTER90** are now listed in the **Queries** panel.

6. You have finished with this Your Turn exercise. You can either leave your work on the screen while you read the following section, or you can exit from dBASE IV.

❏ PRINTING DATA

As a means to quickly print data, dBASE IV includes a Quick Report feature. To use this feature, move the highlight over the name of the file you want to print in either the **Data** panel or the **Queries** panel. Press <Shift>-<F9> for Quick Report. Press <Enter> to select **Begin Printing**. A Quick Report will begin printing. If you just want to view the report on the screen and not print it, move the highlight to **View report on screen** and press <Enter>. The Quick Report scrolls by on the screen.

 YOUR TURN

In this exercise you are going to print the **AFTER90** and **OVER40** query files.

1. The Control Center should be on your screen and the BOOKS file should be active. If necessary, start the dBASE IV program, change the default drive to A: and select the **BOOKS** file from the **Data** panel.

In order to print the files, your computer must be hooked up to a printer, and the printer must be loaded with paper and online. If your computer is not hooked up to a printer, you can display the records as instructed in this exercise.

>Move the highlight to **OVER40** in the **Queries** panel.

>Press <Shift>-<F9> for Quick Report

After a moment, your screen should look like Figure 8-13. If your computer is not hooked up to a printer, move the highlight to **View report on screen** and press <Enter>. If your computer is hooked up to a printer, press <Enter> to select **Begin printing**. The Quick Report is printed. If you displayed the Quick Report on the screen, press <Esc> to return to the Control Center.

2. Now you want to print the **AFTER90** query file.

>Move the highlight to **AFTER90** in the **Queries** panel.

>Press <Shift>-<F9> for Quick Report

After a moment the Quick Report menu appears. If your computer is not hooked up to a printer, move the highlight to **View report on screen** and press <Enter>. If your computer is hooked up to a printer, press <Enter> to select **Begin printing**. The Quick Report is printed. If you displayed the Quick Report on the screen, press <Esc> to return to the Control Center.

3. You have finished with this Your Turn exercise. You can either leave your work on the screen while you read the following section, or you can exit from dBASE IV.

**FIGURE 8-13 Printing a
Quick Report**

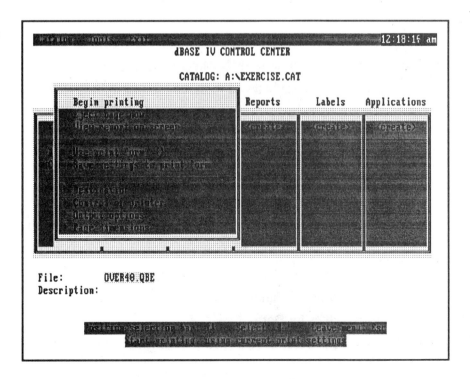

Thus far this section has introduced dBASE IV commands that enable users to create, edit, and display data files. When a file has been created, it can provide valuable information about a variety of subjects through the use of aggregate operators. The aggregate operators covered in this chapter are SUM, AVERAGE, and COUNT. Aggregate operators are used in the query design screen.

Count

The aggregate operator COUNT tallies the records in a file that meet the selection criteria. To use the aggregate operator COUNT, enter the word COUNT in the column of the field you want to count. Enter the selection criteria in the appropriate column. The selection criteria can either be in the same column as COUNT or in another column. If it is in the same column, a comma must separate the aggregate operator and the selection criteria. For example, you would enter COUNT, > 40 in the COST field to count the numbers of books that cost more than $40.00. When you press <F2> for Data, the number counted is displayed in the appropriate field column.

YOUR TURN

In this hands-on exercise, you are going to practice using the aggregate operator COUNT.

1. The Control Center should be on your screen and the BOOKS file should be active. If necessary, start the program, set the default drive to A:, and select the **BOOKS** file from the **Data** panel.

> Highlight **<create>** in the **Queries** panel
> Press <Enter>
> Press <F5> to delete all the field names from the view skeleton

2. You want to find out how many books you purchased in 1992.

> Press <Tab> eight times to move the highlight to **PUR_YEAR**
> Type: COUNT, = "92"
> Press <F5> for Fields
> Press <F2> for Data

The number of books purchased in 1992 is displayed.

> Press <Shift-<F2>

3. Now you want to know how many books you purchased in 1992 that cost $25 or more.

> Press <Shift>-<Tab> twice to move the highlight to **COST**
> Type: COUNT, >= 25
> Press <F5> for Fields
> Press <F2> for Data

The number of books purchased in 1992 costing $25 or more is displayed.

Press <Shift>-<F2>

Press <Alt>-E for the Exit menu

Move the highlight to **Abandon changes and exit**

Press <Enter>

Press Y for yes

4. You have finished with this Your Turn exercise. You can either leave your work on the screen while you read the following section, or you can exit from dBASE IV.

Sum

The contents of numeric fields can be added using the aggregate operator SUM. The aggregate operator SUM can only be used in fields where the field type is numeric or float. The unconditional SUM command calculates the sum of all the values in the specified data field. To use the unconditional SUM command, simply type SUM in the field's column.

The SUM command also can be used with relational operators. To use SUM with relational operators, enter the word SUM in the column of the field you want to total. Enter the selection criteria in the appropriate column. The selection criteria can either be in the same column as SUM or in another column. If it is in the same column, a comma must separate the aggregate operator and the selection criteria. When you press <F2> for Data, the calculated total is displayed in the appropriate field column.

YOUR TURN

In this hands-on exercise, you are going to practice using the SUM option.

1. The Control Center should be on your screen and the BOOKS file should be active. If necessary, start the program, set the default drive to A:, and select the **BOOKS** file from the **Data** panel.

Highlight **<create>** in the **Queries** panel

Press <Enter>

Press <F5> to delete all the field names from the view skeleton

Find the total cost of the books in your library by using the SUM command.

Press <Tab> six times to move the highlight to **COST**

Type: SUM

Press <F5> for Fields

Press <F2> for Data

The total cost of the all the records is displayed.

Press <Shift>-<F2>

2. Now you are going to find out how much money you spent on books in 1992.

Press <Tab> twice to move the highlight to **PUR_YEAR**

Type: = "92"

Press <F5> for Fields

Press <F2> for Data

The total cost of the books purchased in 1992 is displayed.

Press <Shift>-<F2>

3. You want to know how much money you spent in 1992 for books that cost $25 or more.

Press <Shift>-<Tab> twice to move the highlight back to **COST**

Type: SUM, >= 25

Press <F2> for Data

The total amount spent on books costing $25 or more in 1992 is displayed.

<Shift>-<F2>

Press <Alt>-E for the Exit menu

Move the highlight to **Abandon changes and exit**

Press <Enter>

Press Y for yes

4. You have finished with this Your Turn exercise. You can either leave your work on the screen while you read the following section, or you can exit from dBASE IV.

Average

The aggregate operator AVERAGE calculates an average value for the contents of a numeric field. The aggregate operator AVERAGE can only be used in fields where the field type is numeric or float. The unconditional AVERAGE command calculates the average of all the values in the specified data field. To use the unconditional AVERAGE command, simply type AVERAGE in the field's column.

The AVERAGE command also can be used with relational operators. To use the aggregate operator AVERAGE, with relational operators, enter the word AVERAGE in the column of the field you want to average. Enter the selection criteria in the appropriate column. The selection criteria can either be in the same column as AVERAGE or in another column. If it is in the same column, a comma must separate the aggregate operator and the selection criteria. When you press <F2> for Data, the calculated average is displayed in the appropriate field column.

YOUR TURN

In this hands-on exercise, you are going to practice using the aggregate operator AVERAGE.

1. The Control Center should be on your screen and the BOOKS file should be active. If necessary, start the program, set the default drive to A:, and select the **BOOKS** file from the **Data** panel. Find the average cost of all your books.

Highlight **<create>** in the **Queries** panel

Chapter 8: Introduction to dBASE IV

Press <Enter>

Press <F5> to delete all the field names from the view skeleton

Find the average cost of the books in your library by using the AVERAGE command.

Press <Tab> six times to move the highlight to **COST**

Type: AVERAGE

Press <F5> for Fields

Press <F2> for Data

The average cost of all the records is displayed.

Press <Shift>-<F2>

2. You have finished working with the BOOKS database file.

Press <Alt>-E for the Exit menu

Move the highlight to **Abandon changes and exit**

Press <Enter>

Press Y for yes

Press <Alt>-E for the Exit menu

Highlight **Quit to DOS**

Press <Return>

Take your disks out of the computer. Turn the computer and monitor off.

❏ SUMMARY POINTS

■ A data manager (data management package) can be used for the same purposes as a manual filing system: to record and file information.

■ Each data item stored, such as a first name, a last name, and address, or an invoice amount, is called a field.

■ A group of related fields forms a record.

■ A group of related records is a file.

■ Defining the structure of a database file involves deciding what fields will be included in each record, the name of each field, the width of the field and whether the data stored in a field is alphanumeric, numeric or logical.

■ Once data has been entered into a database file, the file can be updated, which includes editing records, adding records and deleting records.

Key	Description
<Ctrl>-N	Inserts a new line or field definition.
<Ctrl>-T	Erases one word to the right of the cursor position.
<Ctrl>-U	Marks a record for deletion in Browse or Edit mode; deletes a field definition.
<Ctrl>-Y	Erases to the end of the line in Append or Edit.
<F1> Help	Displays on-screen Help.
<F2> Data	In the Control Center, displays the records in a database file. When the records are displayed, shifts to Browse table or Edit screen.
<F5> Field	Adds a field to the view skeleton.
<F9> Zoom	In DOS utilities screen, switches display between a file list or a directory tree.
<F10> Menus	Accesses the menus for the current screen.
<Shift>-<F1> Pick	Displays a list of items available for the current fill-in.
<Shift-<F2> Design	Displays the Design screen; allows you to change the design of the database once it has been created.
<Shift>-<F8> Ditto	Copies data from the corresponding field of the previous record into the current record.
<Shift>-<F9> Quick Report	Prints a quick report of current database file.

THE CONTROL CENTER

Menu	Menu Option	Description
Catalog	Use a different catalog	Creates a new catalog.
Data	<create>	Displays the Database design screen for creating a new dabase file.
Queries	<create>	Displays the Query design screen for creating a new query.
Tools	DOS utilities DOS Set default drive:directory	Allows you to specify the drive and/or directory that data files are stored in.
Tools	DOS utilities Operations Copy	Allows you to copy one or more files.
Tools	DOS utilities Operations Delete	Allows you to delete one or more files.
Tools	DOS utilities Operations Rename	Allows you to rename a file.
Exit	Quit to DOS	Exits the program.

BROWSE TABLE/
EDIT SCREEN

Menu	Menu Option	Description
Records	Add new records	Allows you to add records to a database.
Records	Mark record for deletion/ Clear deletion mark	Allows you to mark a record for deletion or clear the deletion mark.
Organize	Erase marked records	Premanently removes records that have been marked for deletion from a database file.

QUERIES

Layout	Save this Query	Allows you to save a query file.

❏ dBASE IV EXERCISES

1. Assume that the computer is shut off. List all the necessary steps needed to start the dBASE IV program.

2. Start the dBASE IV program. Assume you have been hired by Kenneth Fretwell, D.D.S., to establish a database management system for his office. Use dBASE IV to create a database file named PATIENTS.

3. Your PATIENTS file has eight fields. For each field, enter the following into the database design screen.

Field Name	Type	Width	Dec
First_Name	Character	10	
Last_Name	Character	10	
Address	Character	15	
City	Character	10	
St	Character	2	
ZIP	Character	5	
Age	Character	2	
Balance	Numeric	6	2

4. Enter the following data in the PATIENTS file.

First_Name	Last_Name	Address	City	St	ZIP	Age	Balance
David	Busch	552 Wallace	Columbus	OH	43216	27	58.60
Patricia	Busch	552 Wallace	Columbus	OH	43216	28	0
Tom	Allen	67 Curtis	Columbus	OH	43216	78	8.90
Eileen	Spires	890 Pine	Columbus	OH	43216	56	120.00
Dave	Jenkins	10 W. Wooster	Columbus	OH	43216	13	93.50
Pamela	Weaver	16 Clough	Columbus	OH	43216	10	0
Bradley	Busch	552 Wallace	Columbus	OH	43216	7	25.00
William	Bentley	77 Palmer	Dayton	OH	45401	45	0

5. Proofread all the records you entered. Make any corrections necessary and save the changes.

6. Add the following records to the PATIENTS file.

First_Name	Last_Name	Address	City	St	ZIP	Age	Balance
Wilma	Lukes	909 Clough	Columbus	OH	43216	89	280.09
Douglas	Swartz	9 Main	Dayton	OH	45401	32	46.90
Linda	Plazer	12 Vine	Columbus	OH	43216	25	176.00
Ann	Bressler	25 Baldwin	Columbus	OH	43216	25	0

7. Tom Allen and William Bentley changed dentists. Delete their records from the file.

8. The Busch family moved. Their new address is 41 Normandie in Columbus. Update their records and assume their ZIP code is the same.

9. Dr. Fretwell is going to start a No Cavities Club for children under the age of 16. Create a query file that includes all of Dr. Fretwell's patients who are eligible for membership in the club. Save the Query file using the filename CLUB.

10. Use the aggregate operator SUM to find the total balance due from all of the patients.

11. Create a query file that includes only those patients who owe more than $35. Save the file using the filename OVER35. Create another query file that includes only those patients with a zero balance. Save the file using the filename ZERO.

11. Print a Quick Report of the CLUB, OVER35, and ZERO query files.

❑ dBASE IV PROBLEMS

To complete the following exercises, you need to use files on the Student File Disk. In order to complete these exercises, you will need to be able to design a database file, define fields, display the design of a database file, edit the design of a database file, enter data into a database file, add a record, copy a file, and calculate an average.

1.   On the Student File disk there is a dBASE IV file called SALARY. Start the dBASE IV program and access this file. Make a copy of this file and call the copy SALARY1. That way, if you make a mistake, you will always have the original file.

2.   Assume that you are working in the payroll department of a company. The company uses dBASE IV to keep information regarding employees' names, addresses, job names, and hourly salaries. Access the SALARY1 database file. How do you display a file's design? Display the design of the PAYROLL1 file. How many fields are there in the file? How many numeric fields? What is the width of the field JOBNAME? The field STATUS defines the personnel status (F for full-time and P for part-time). What is its type? How many data records are in the file?

3.   Now you want to see the records of the employees. Display all the records. What is the name of the employee corresponding to record 5? What is his job title? What is the name of the last employee?

4.   Now you want to create a query that includes only the last name, first name, and job title of all employees. Describe the steps necessary to obtain this information.

5.   Now display the same information for full-time employees only. How many full-time employees are employed by the company?

6.   Display the last name, first name, employee number, and job title for all part-time employees who are writers.

7.   What is the average hourly wage of all the employees? Which employees earn more than $9 an hour?

8.   The payroll department manager wants you to create a new database file that will store information about the employees who worked during March. The file should contain the following information:

Field Name	Field Type	Width	Dec
EMPLNUM	N	3	
MONTH	N	2	
ENDPER	C	6	
NORMHRS	N	5	2

The EMPLNUM field keeps track of the employee number; the MONTH field keeps track of the month of work; the ENDPER field keeps track of the ending period; and the NORMHRS field keeps track of the total hours of work. Create the new database file and name it MONTH3.

9.   Enter the structure of the new file using the information in step 8.

10.   The payroll department manager wants you to add a new field to the MONTH3 database file. This field is to keep track of the number of overtime hours an employee puts in. Add the following field:

Field Name	Field Type	Width	Dec
OVERTIME	N	6	2

11.   Edit the design of the MONTH3 database. Change the field width of the NORMHRS field to 6.

12.   When you are satisfied with the structure of the MONTH3 database file, use the appropriate command to save your modifications.

13.   What is the command to add records to a file? Using this command, enter the following data into the file:

EMPLNUM	MONTH	ENDPERIOD	NORMHRS	OVERTIME
0	3	033193	160.00	30.00
2	3	033193	160.00	40.00
3	3	033193	160.00	0.00
4	3	033193	140.00	0.00
6	3	033193	160.00	0.00
7	3	033193	160.00	20.00
8	3	033193	160.00	20.00
9	3	033193	160.00	0.00
10	3	033193	160.00	0.00
11	3	033193	100.00	0.00
13	3	033193	160.00	0.00
14	3	033193	80.00	0.00
15	3	033193	90.00	0.00

Save the data. Exit from dBASE IV.

❏ dBASE IV CHALLENGE

Assume a video rental store has asked you for help in setting up a dBASE IV file that will help them keep track of the rental of video cassettes. The video store would like you to create a file for them that includes the following data for each video tape:

Item number: This is a number the store assigns each tape. It is a five digit number preceded by a V. For example, V-78902.

Title: This would be the name of the movie. For example, *Out of Africa.*

Price: This would be what the video store charges to rent the movie overnight.

Status: This would keep track of whether the movie is currently in the store or is rented out. For example, a *Y* for Yes might indicate the movie is in the store available for rental and a *N* for No might indicate the movie is currently loaned out.

1.   Create a new database file named VIDEO.DBF that can keep track of the information required by the video store.

2.   Make up information on twelve movies and enter the data for those twelve movies into the VIDEO.DBF file. Select six of the movies as being rented out and the other six as being in the store available for rent. Vary the rental price of the movies. The video store charges more to rent new releases than it does to rent older movies.

3.   Now you want to demonstrate to the video store how the VIDEO file can be used. Print a list of all the movies that are currently out on loan.

4.   The video store wants to know on an average how much they charge to rent movies. Find the average rental cost of all the movies.

5.   Someone comes into the video store and wants to know if one of the movies in your database file is out on loan. Find and print the record of that one movie to see whether or not it is available.

CHAPTER 9

More dBASE IV Features

OUTLINE

❑ Introduction

The previous chapter presented all the commands needed to create a database file with dBASE IV. Once a file has been created, it can be manipulated in many useful ways. The purpose of this chapter is to introduce the more advanced dBASE IV commands that make it possible to efficiently arrange data stored in a database file so that it can be used to create a report.

❑ Finding Records

When a database is small, there is no problem with finding a particular record. Scrolling through all the records in a small database file is easy. Usually, however, database files are quite large, containing hundreds of records. Scrolling through all the records in such a large database file would take too much time. dBASE IV includes tools for quickly locating specific records.

When data is displayed in the Browse table, one way to quickly move through the records is by using <PgUp> and <PgDn>. Pressing <PgUp> or <PgDn> quickly moves you through records one screen at a time. Typically, there are 17 records displayed on the screen at one time in the Browse table.

When the data in a database file is displayed, either in the Browse table or the Edit screen, one of the menu options is Go To. The Go To menu has several options for finding records quickly. The first option, **Top record** displays the first record in a database file if you are in the Edit screen. In the Browse table, the record pointer is moved to the first record. The second option **Last record**, displays the last record in the database file if you are in the Edit screen. In the Browse table, the record pointer is moved to the last record.

The third option **Record number** allows you to move to a specific record. After selecting the **Record number** option, the prompt **Enter record number** appears. Enter the number of the record that you want to go to and press <Enter>. In the Edit screen, the record is displayed on the screen and in the Browse table, the record pointer is moved to the record.

The **Forward search** and **Backward search** options allow you to find records containing specific data. To use the search options, move the cursor to the field you want to search. Press <Alt>-G for the Go To menu. Select **Forward search** if you want to search from the current database file to the end of the file. Select **Backward search** if you want to search from the current file to the beginning of the database file. The prompt **Enter search string** appears. The **Match capitalization** option allows you to find the exact entry for which you are searching. For example, if the option says, **Match capitalization YES** and you entered *Black* (a last name), the program would not find *black* (a color). If the option says, **Match capitalization NO**, the program would find all occurrences of the word black, regardless of the capitalization. Highlighting the **Match capitalization** option and pressing <Enter> toggles the option back and forth between **NO** and **YES**.

At the **Enter search string** prompt, enter the data for which you want to search and press <Enter>. dBASE IV finds and displays the first record that contains the data you entered. If no records are found, the message **Not Found** is displayed. To find other records that include the search string, Press <Shift>-<F3> for Find Previous to find the previous occurrence or press <Shift>-<F4> to find the next occurrence.

Wildcard characters can be used in the search string. The question mark, *?*, is a wildcard for a single character. The asterisk, *, is a wildcard for any number of characters. A search for *b?g*, would find records containing *big, bog, bag, bug, beg*. A search for *b*g*, would expand the search to include records containing *bedbug, batting, backlog, bowling,* and *bumbling*, for example.

❏ SORTING A DATABASE FILE

As discussed in the previous chapter, a database file is made up of records that a user enters into the data-entry form. As each record is entered, dBASE IV automatically assigns a chronological record number to it. The data records are stored in the file in the order in which they are entered, but this may not be the order that provides the most useful information. For example, records in a payroll file are not entered in alphabetical order. They are added when employees are hired and deleted when workers leave a company. To be useful, a database program must be able to arrange a payroll file in alphabetical order. In dBASE IV, the **Sort database on field list** option found in the Organize menu enables users to rearrange data records according to the contents of a specified field, which is called the key field. In the example of a payroll file being sorted alphabetically by last name, the field containing the last names would be the key field.

Sorting physically rearranges the records in the active database file. To maintain the original database file, dBASE IV copies the sorted database file into what is called the target file. The user must designate a new file name for the target file. When the sorting procedure is complete, the data records in the target file are arranged by the key field as specified. That is, when you have completed a sort, you have two complete files instead of one. When sorting a file, you can include only those records that meet specific criteria.

To sort a database file, display the data in either the Edit screen or the Browse table. Select **Sort database on field list** from the Organize menu. A window appears in which you can enter the names of the fields on which you want to search. To display the complete field list, press <Shift>-<F1> for Pick. Move the highlight to the field name you want to pick and press <Enter>. You can select as many fields as you want on which to sort. Once the field is picked, you can specify whether the sort should be in ascending or descending order. The default response is ascending order. When you have finishing picking fields, press <Ctrl>-<End> to end the sort instructions. A prompt appears asking you to enter the name for the new, rewritten file. Enter a new file name and press <Enter>. To see the results of the sort, exit to the Control Center, select the filename for the sorted file and press <F2> for Data. The sorted file is displayed.

YOUR TURN

The Your Turn exercises in this chapter use a slightly different format than the Your Turn exercises in the previous chapter. By now, you should be familiar with how to select a menu option using dBASE IV. That is, you move the highlight bar to the option you wish to select and press <Enter>. Instead of including both steps in the instructions, the exercises in this chapter simply tell you to *Select* a particular option. For example, instead of telling you,

Press <Alt>-T for the Tools menu

> Move highligh to **DOS utilities**
>
> Press <Enter>

The instructions tell you to

> Select **DOS utilities** from the Tools menu

Whenever you see the instruction *Select*, it means both to move the highlight to that option and to press <Enter>.

You are going to sort a database file using the **Sort database on field list** option from the Organize menu. You will create a file called SCHOOL that contains the names, classifications, grade-point averages, birth dates, Social Security numbers, account balances, and addresses of students at a college. Numbers are used to designate a student's classification: 4 = senior, 3 = junior, 2 sophomore, and 1 = freshman.

1. Start the dBASE IV program. Your data disk with the EXERCISE catalog should be in drive A. Change the default drive to drive A:. *Select <create>* from the **Data** panel. You are going to create a database file named SCHOOL using the information below. Enter the following information in the field definition form:

Field	Field Name	Type	Width	Dec	Index
1	NAME	Character	20		N
2	YEAR	Character	1		N
3	GPA	Numeric	4	2	N
4	BIRTHDATE	Date	8		N
5	SSNUMBER	Character	11		N
6	ACCOUNT	Numeric	8	2	N
7	ADDRESS	Character	15		N
8	CITY	Character	10		N
9	STATE	Character	2		N
10	ZIP	Numeric	5	0	N

Look over the database design carefully and make sure the entries are all correct. Correct any mistakes you find. When the database design is correct, you are ready to save it.

> Select **Save changes and Exit** from the Exit menu

The prompt **Save as** appears.

> Type: SCHOOL
>
> Press <Enter>

2. You are now ready to input data.

> Press <F2> for Data

Enter the information contained in Table 9-1. Notice after the third record that all the entries in the State field are TX. dBASE IV includes a way to copy the entry from the previous record into the current record. With the cursor in the field, press <Shift>-<F8> for Ditto. dBASE IV copies the data from the same field in the previous record to the current record. When you get to the fifth record and following records, press <Shift>-<F8> when the cursor is in the State field and TX will be entered automatically.

TABLE 9-1 Records for the SCHOOL File

Name	Yr	GPA	BDate	SSNumber	Account	Address	City	St	ZIP
Faulks, Tim	4	3.20	03/01/71	343-61-1101	286.59	78 Main St.	Miami	FL	32109
Bulas, Irene	3	3.00	07/19/72	289-89-4672	1203.87	908 W. Summit	Oak Hill	TX	78746
Klein, Tom	4	2.55	10/20/71	278-45-7891	96.95	12 Yong St.	Hampton	NC	27710
Wilcox, Bill	1	2.00	06/08/74	524-68-4099	0.00	6 Williams Rd.	Anadale	TX	78756
Ornelas, Tina	2	3.12	03/05/73	468-71-9002	2005.32	123 First St.	Amarillo	TX	79107
Lord, Pamela	4	3.78	03/03/71	208-46-4096	576.94	98 Pike St.	El Paso	TX	79910
Busch, Brad	3	3.70	04/04/67	782-28-1598	803.52	32 Badner	Dallas	TX	75221
Weaver, Chris	2	2.15	10/10/73	411-69-4664	68.07	909 Clough	Lubbock	TX	79408
Engel, Chuck	4	2.34	10/10/66	778-61-8723	12.18	14 Indian Rd.	Houston	TX	77002
Wilks, Cleo	1	3.81	11/02/74	428-18-9972	1096.20	76 Gorrel	Laredo	TX	78040
Bressler, Ann	1	2.08	07/16/69	789-22-6615	0.00	45 S. Luke St.	Pasadena	TX	77501
Hocks, Arthur	3	2.89	03/12/72	558-79-5151	446.29	90 Kellog Rd.	Lubbock	TX	79408
DeSalvo, Liz	4	2.22	06/14/71	879-43-6291	0.00	9. W. Second	Dallas	TX	75221
Freidman, Mark	2	3.98	09/02/74	217-64-4049	33.68	3426 Little St	Pasadena	TX	77501
Crope, Trish	1	3.21	03/11/71	491-10-9984	175.50	67 Baldwin	Oak Hill	TX	78746

3. Once the records are entered, you are ready to use the sort feature. You should be in the Edit screen and there is a blank form on the screen. First, move to the top of the file.

> Select **Top record** from the Go To menu

You want to sort all the records alphabetically by name.

> Select **Sort database on field list** from the Organize menu

A window appears in which you can enter the sort information.

> Press <Shift>-<F1> for Pick

A list of all the field names appears at the right side of the screen.

> Select the field name **NAME**

Your screen should look like Figure 9-1.

> Press <Ctrl>-<End> to end the sort instructions

The prompt **Enter name of sorted file** appears.

> Type: Name
>
> Press <Enter>

NAME is the name of the file that now stores the records listed in alphabetical order by name. After pressing <Enter>, the message **100% Sorted 15 Records sorted** appears. A prompt appears asking you to enter a description of the file.

> Type: The SCHOOL file sorted in alphabetical order on the
>   Name field.
>
> Press <Enter>

FIGURE 9-1 Entering Sort Information

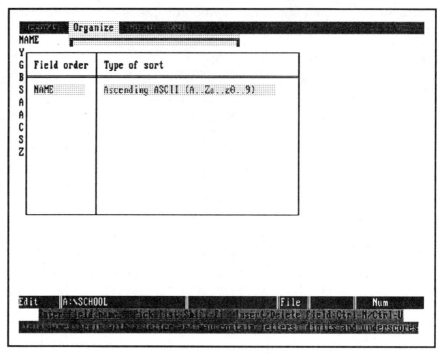

4. Now you want to view the new sorted file.

> *Select* ***Exit*** from the Exit menu
>
> *Select* ***NAME*** from the **Data** panel
>
> *Select* ***Use file***
>
> Press <F2> for Data
>
> Press <F2> again to switch to the Browse table

The names should appear on the screen listed in alphabetical order.

> *Select* ***Exit*** from the Exit menu

5. Now you are going to sort all the records by GPA in ascending order. The sorted file will be called GPA.

> *Select* ***SCHOOL*** from the **Data** panel
>
> *Select* ***Display data***
>
> *Select* ***Sort database on field list*** from the Organize menu
>
> Press <Shift>-<F1> for Pick
>
> *Select* ***GPA*** from the list of field names
>
> Press <Ctrl>-<End>
>
> Type: GPA
>
> Press <Enter>
>
> Type: The SCHOOL file sorted in ascending order by GPA field.
>
> Press <Enter>

The records are now sorted by grade-point average.

Chapter 9: More dBASE IV Features

*Select **Exit** from the Exit menu*

6. Now you want to look at the records sorted by grade-point average.

*Select **GPA** from the **Data** panel*

*Select **Display data***

The data should be displayed in the Browse table. If it is not, press <F2>. Look at the GPA column. The file should be listed in ascending order according to the GPA.

*Select **Exit** from the Exit menu*

7. You have finished with this Your Turn exercise. You can either leave your work on the screen while you read the following section, or you can exit from dBASE IV.

Conditional Sorts

A condition can be added to the dBASE IV SORT option dictating that only those records that satisfy the condition are included in the sort. dBASE IV tests each record for the condition and includes the record in the sort only if the condition is met.

To sort only a selected set of records, you must first create a query file that specifies the conditions for selecting records. To create a query file, select **<create>** from the **Queries** panel. The queries design screen appears where you can designate the conditions for the sort.

YOUR TURN

Use the SCHOOL file to perform a conditional sort. You want to know which students have a GPA of 3.5 or more. If necessary, start the dBASE IV program and select drive A: as the default drive. *Select **SCHOOL** from the **Data** panel and select **Use file.*** The SCHOOL file should be the active file.

1. Once the SCHOOL file is the active file, you are ready to create the query file.

*Select **<create>** from the **Queries** panel*

The queries design screen appears. If the file names appear in the view skeleton, press <F5>.

2. You are now ready to designate the condition for the sort. Remember, you want only grade-point averages that are equal to or greater than 3.5.

Press <Tab> to move the highlight to the NAME field

Press <F5>

The NAME field moves to the view skeleton.

Press <Tab> twice to move the highlight to GPA

Type: >= 3.5

Press <F5>

You now want to see the result of the query.

FIGURE 9-2 The
DEANLIST Query File

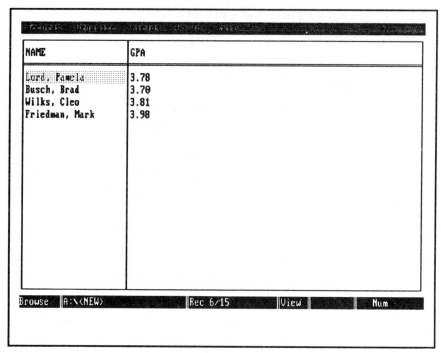

NAME	GPA
Lord, Pamela	3.78
Busch, Brad	3.70
Wilks, Cleo	3.81
Friedman, Mark	3.98

Browse A:\<NEW>   Rec 6/15   View   Num

Press <F2> for Data

Your screen should look like Figure 9-2. You have created the condition and are ready to exit from the queries design screen.

Press <Shift>-<F2>

Select **Save changes and exit** from the Exit menu

Type: DEANLIST

Press <Enter>

3. Next, sort the DEANLIST file. The DEANLIST file should be the active file.

Press <F2> for Data

Select **Sort database on field list** from the Organize menu

Press <Shift>-<F1>

Select **NAME**

Press <Ctrl>-<End>

Type: DEANLIST

Press <Enter>

Type: Alphabetical list of students with 3.5 or higher GPA

Press <Enter>

Select **Exit** from the Exit menu

Select **DEANLIST** from the **Data** panel

Select **Display data**

Only those records that have 3.5 or higher in the GPA are displayed and they are listed in alphabetical order by the Name field.

Select **Exit** from the Exit menu

The Control Center returns to the screen.

5. You have finished with this Your Turn exercise. You can either leave your work on the screen while you read the following section, or you can exit from dBASE IV.

❏ INDEXING A FILE

In some respects the INDEX option is similar to the SORT option. Both can arrange records in ascending order, alphabetically, chronologically or numerically. There are significant differences between sorting and indexing, however.

Sorting a file creates a new version of the entire file on the disk. Indexing is quicker and more efficient than sorting. dBASE can manipulate an index faster than it can sort the database file. An index in dBASE IV is similar to an index in a book. An index references items in a database according to certain criterion with a pointer to where the record is stored. Each indexed item refers to a field or fields rather than an entire record, so it takes up less space when it is saved. Logical and memo fields cannot be used for indexing. The index organizes the data to display it in the specified order, but the physical order of the records is not changed.

To create an index, highlight the file to be indexed on the **Data** panel. Press <F2> for Data. Select **Create new index** from the Organize menu. The **Create new index** submenu appears. First, select **Name of index**, type in a name and press <Enter>. Index names can be up to 10 characters long. They have the same restrictions as field names. To define the index select **Index expression**. Press <Shift>-<F1> for Pick and a list of all the field names is displayed. Select the field name that is to be used in the index expression. The item appears in the index expression line. The index expression can include one or more fields. The only restriction is that it cannot include logical or memo fields. Press <Enter> once the index expression is defined.

To index on a subset of the records in the database file, select **FOR clause**. Press <Shift>-<F1> for Pick and select the field name, operator, and functions that you would like to use. The **Order of index** option allows you to specify whether the index should be in ascending order or descending order. Press <Ctrl>-<End> to save the index.

When an index is created, it is automatically activated. To select a different index, press <Alt>-O for the Organize menu and select **Organize records by index**. A list of the active index tags appears. Select the index you want to use. Press <F2> for Data to look at the index.

YOUR TURN

You are going to create three indexes for fields SSNUMBER, ZIP, and YEAR. The students' Social Security numbers are used as their identification numbers. The index on the SSNUMBER field will list the students according to these identification numbers. The index on the

ZIP field will list the students according to ZIP code. The list could be used for a mass mailing. The index on the YEAR field will list the students according to their class; senior, junior, sophomore, or freshman. If necessary, start the dBASE IV program and change the default drive to A:.

1. You are ready to create the first index.

> Highlight SCHOOL on the **Data** panel
>
> Press <F2> for Data
>
> *Select* ***Create new index*** from the Organize menu

Your screen should look like Figure 9-3. This is the create new index submenu. The **Name of index** option is already highlighted.

> Press <Enter>
>
> Type: IDNUMBER
>
> Press <Enter>

The highlight moves to **Index expression**

> Press <Enter>
>
> Press <Shift>-<F1>
>
> Move the highlight to **SSNUMBER**
>
> Press <Enter>
>
> Press <Enter> again

You have finished defining this index.

> Press <Ctrl>-<End>

FIGURE 9-3 The Create New Index Submenu

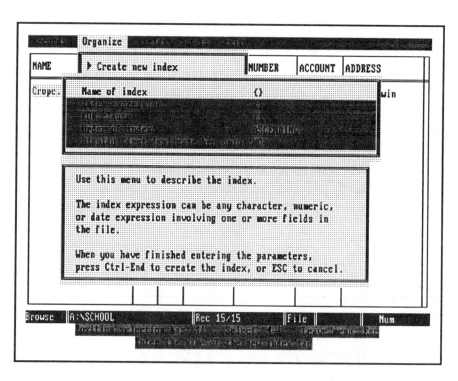

The message **100% indexed 15 Records indexed** appears.

2.   Next, index on the ZIP field to an index named MAIL_TX. That is, you are going to create an index called MAIL_TX in which the records are arranged in ascending order by ZIP code. Producing a mass mailing would be much easier with the records arranged by ZIP code. You are going to use the FOR clause in this index so that you can include only those ZIP codes for the state of Texas.

> *Select **Create new index*** from the Organize menu
>
> *Select **Name of Index***
>
> Type: MAIL_TX
>
> Press <Enter>
>
> *Select **Index expression***
>
> Press <Shift>-<F1>
>
> *Select **ZIP***
>
> Press <Enter>
>
> *Select **FOR Clause***

You are now going to create a clause that instructs dBASE IV to include ZIP codes that are greater than 69999 and less than 80000.

> Press <Shift>-<F1>
>
> *Select **ZIP***
>
> Type: >69999
>
> Press <Shift>-<F1>
>
> *Select **.AND.*** from the second column
>
> Press <Shift>-<F1>
>
> *Select **ZIP***
>
> Type: <80000
>
> Press <Enter>
>
> Press <F9> for Zoom

The FOR clause you just entered appears at the bottom of the screen. Your screen should look like Figure 9-4.

> Press <Enter>
>
> Press <Ctrl-<End>

The message **100% indexed 13 Records indexed** appears. Now you want to index on the YEAR field to an index named CLASS. That is, you are going to create an index called CLASS in which the records are arranged according to the students' class standing. The records for all the freshmen will be grouped together, the records for all the sophomores will be grouped together, and so on. In addition, you are going to index on more than one field so that the last names within each class are alphabetized.

FIGURE 9-4 Using the FOR Clause

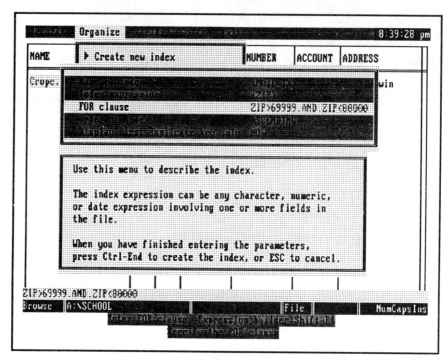

Select **Create new index** *from the Organize menu*

Select **Name of Index**

Type: CLASS

Press <Enter>

Select **Index expression**

Press <Shift>-<F1>

Select **YEAR**

Type: +

Press <Shift>-<F1>

Select **NAME**

Your screen should look like Figure 9-5. To index on more than one field, the field names must be joined by a plus sign. When the file is indexed, it will be sorted first by class and second by last name.

Press <Enter>

Press <Ctrl>-<End>

The message **100% indexed 15 Records indexed** appears.

3. Now you want to view each of the indexed files.

Select **Order records by index** *from the Organize menu*

Select **CLASS**

Look at the records closely. They are all grouped together by year (1, 2, 3, and 4) and within each year they are alphabetized by last name.

FIGURE 9-5 Indexing on Multiple Fields

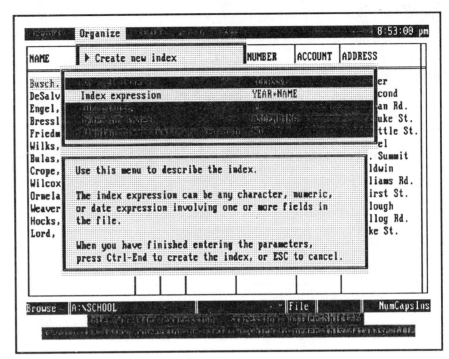

Select **Order records by index** from the Organize menu

Select **IDNUMBER**

Look at the records closely. They are listed in ascending order by social security number.

Select **Order records by index** from the Organize menu

Select **MAIL_TX**

Look at the records closely. Press <Tab> until you can see the STATE and ZIP fields. The ZIP codes are listed in ascending order (which consequently grouped the cities together) and only the ZIP codes in the 70000's are listed as a result of the FOR clause.

Select **Exit** from the Exit menu

9. You have finished with this Your Turn exercise. You can either leave your work on the screen while you read the following section, or you can exit from dBASE IV.

❑ CREATING A CUSTOM REPORT WITH dBASE IV

Data stored in a database file can provide users with helpful information. Until the information can take the form of a report on paper, however, its usefulness is limited. The following section explains how to create a customized report using dBASE IV files.

There are two types of reports in dBASE IV. In Chapter 8 you learned how to print a Quick Report. A Quick report is a fast and simple way to print all the data in a database file. The only thing a Quick Report adds is a page number and date at the top of each page. The column headers used in a Quick Report are the field names. A quick report cannot be formatted in any way.

The second type of report is the custom report, which you will learn how to create in this chapter. A custom report allows you to choose specific fields to be included in the report, include page headers and footers, arrange the columns in any order, add column headers that are different from those in the database file, and add lines and boxes to the report.

A custom report is created using the **Column layout** option on the Layout menu. The column layout displays all the fields in the database file. You can delete columns you do not want, you can rearrange the order of the column and you can arrange the data in groups, with totals printed for each group.

Modifying a Report Design

To modify a report design that has already been created, highlight the name of the report in the **Reports** panel and press <Shift>-<F2>. The reports design screen appears. Make the necessary changes. When all the changes have been made, select **Save changes and exit** from the Exit menu.

YOUR TURN

Start dBASE IV and change the default drive to A: if necessary. The next several hands-on exercises take you through the creation of a report using the NAME file. The NAME file should be the active file.

1. Once the NAME file is active, you are ready to start the process of creating a report.

   Select ***<create>*** *from the* **Reports** *panel*

The reports design screen appears with the Layout menu opened.

   Press <Esc>

Your screen should look like Figure 9-6. This is the reports design screen. The reports design screen uses report bands that divide the report into horizontal areas consisting of one or

FIGURE 9-6 The Reports Design Screen

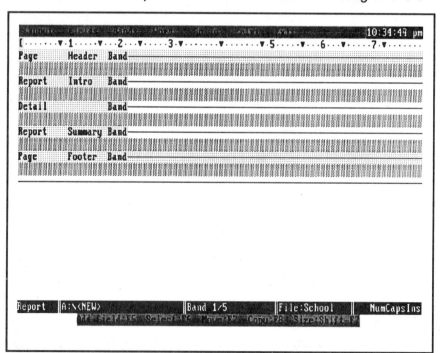

more lines. Five bands appear: Page Header Band, Report Intro Band, Detail Band, Report Summary Band, and Page Footer Band. Information entered into these bands prints at the specified location on the page. When a band is open, the information contained in the band prints on the page. When a band is closed, the information in the band does not print. To close a band place the cursor on the border of the band and press <Enter>. To open a closed band, place the cursor on the border of the band and press <Enter>.

The page header prints at the top of each page of the report. The Page Header Band often contains the column headings.

> Press <Down arrow>

The cursor should now be in the space under the Page Header Band

> Press <F5> for Add field
>
> Highlight **Date** from the Predefined column and press <Enter>
>
> Press <Ctrl>-<End>

Now the current date will automatically print at the top of the report.

> Press <Enter> three times
>
> Press the Space Bar 30 times
>
> Type: `STATE COLLEGE`
>
> Press <Enter>
>
> Press the Space Bar 25 times
>
> Type: `STUDENT ACCOUNT BALANCE`
>
> Press <Enter> twice

Now you want to add the column titles

> Type: `Student's Name`
>
> Press the Space Bar 11 times
>
> Type: `Address`
>
> Press the Space Bar 13 times
>
> Type: `City`
>
> Press Space Bar 10 times
>
> Type: `State`
>
> Press Space Bar 5 times
>
> Type: `Balance`
>
> Press <Enter>

Your screen should look like Figure 9-7.

2. You want to close the Report Intro Band

> Move the cursor into the Report Intro Band
>
> Press <Enter>

3. Next you want to enter the fields for the report in the Detail Band.

FIGURE 9-7 Entering
Information in the Page
Header Band

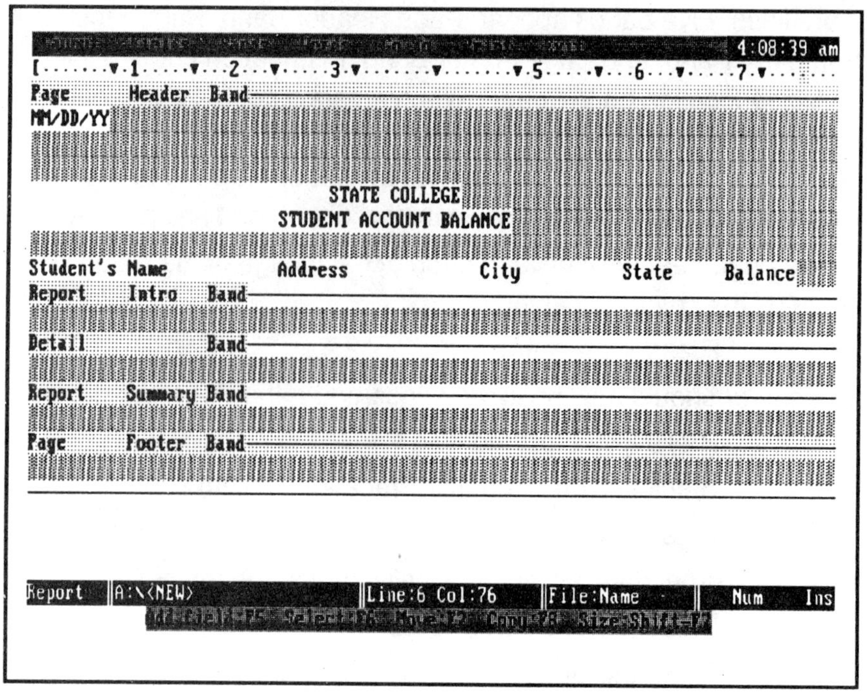

Move the cursor to the left edge of the line under the Detail Band

Press <F5> for Add field

Highlight **NAME** and press <Enter>

Press <Ctrl>-<End>

Xs appear in the line to indicate the amount of space needed for the Name field.

Press <Right arrow> five times

Press <F5> for Add field

Highlight **ADDRESS** and press <Enter>

Press <Ctrl>-<End>

Xs appear in the line to indicate the amount of space needed for the Address field.

Press <Right arrow> five times

Press <F5> for Add field

Highlight **CITY** and press <Enter>

Press <Ctrl>-<End>

Xs appear in the line to indicate the amount of space needed for the City field.

Press <Right arrow> five times

Press <F5> for Add field

Highlight **STATE** and press <Enter>

Press <Ctrl>-<End>

Xs appear in the line to indicate the amount of space needed for the State field.

Press <Right arrow> seven times

Press <F5> for Add field

Press <Enter> to select **ACCOUNT**

Press <Ctrl>-<End>

9s appear in the line to indicate the amount of space needed for the Account field.

4. Now you are going to make an entry in the Report Summary Band.

Press <Down arrow> two times

Press <Enter>

Press <Tab> 8 times

Press <Right arrow> three times

Press <F5> for Add field

Highlight **Sum** in the SUMMARY column and press <Enter> to select it

Highlight **Field to summarize on** and press <Enter> to select it

Press <Enter> to select **ACCOUNT**

Press <Ctrl>-<End>

Your screen should look like Figure 9-8.

*Select **Save changes and exit** from the Exit menu*

Type: Student

Press <Enter>

5. You have finished with this exercise. You can either leave the Control Center on the screen while you read the following section or you can exit dBASE IV.

FIGURE 9-8 Creating a Custom Report

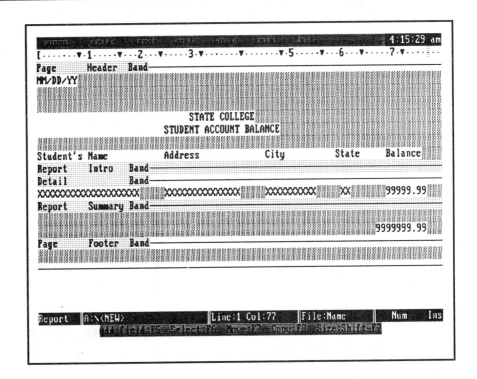

Once a report is entered into a database file, a hard copy of the report can be printed. To print a report, highlight the name of the report in the **Reports** panel and press <Enter>. Press <Enter> to select **Print report**. To view the report on the screen, select **View report on screen**. To print the report, select **Begin printing**.

YOUR TURN

Print a copy of the STUDENT report. Make sure that your computer is hooked up to a printer and that the printer has plenty of paper and is online. If necessary, start the dBASE IV program and change the default drive to A:.

1. You are ready to print the report.

> Highlight **STUDENT** in the **Report** panel
>
> Press <Enter>
>
> Press <Enter> to select **Print report**
>
> Select **View report on screen**

Your screen should look like Figure 9-9. Notice the Balance column includes a total.

> Press <Esc> twice
>
> Press any key

2. This time, print the report. **STUDENT** should be highlighted in the **Report** panel.

> Press <Enter>

FIGURE 9-9 The STUDENT Report

```
04/07/92


                        STATE COLLEGE
                   STUDENT ACCOUNT BALANCE

Student's Name       Address          City        State    Balance
Bressler, Ann        45 S. Luke St.   Pasadena    TX          0.00
Bulas, Irene         908 W. Summit    Oak Hill    TX       1203.87
Busch, Brad          32 Badner        Dallas      TX        803.52
Crope, Trish         67 Baldwin       Oak Hill    TX        175.50
DeSalvo, Liz         9 W. Second      Dallas      TX          0.00
Engel, Chuck         14 Indian Rd.    Houston     TX         12.18
Faulks, Tim          78 Main St.      Miami       FL        286.58
Freidman, Mark       3426 Little St   Pasadena    TX         33.68
Hocks, Arthur        98 Kellog Rd.    Lubbock     TX        446.29
Klein, Tom           12 Yong St.      Hampton     NC         96.95
Lord, Pamela         98 Pike St.      El Paso     TX        576.94
Ornelas, Tina        123 First St.    Amarillo    TX       2005.32
Weaver, Chris        909 Clough       Lubbock     TX         68.07
Wilcox, Bill         6 Williams Rd.   Anadale     TX          0.00
Wilks, Cleo          76 Gorrel        Laredo      TX       1096.20

                                                          6805.10
```

Press <Enter> to select **Print report**

Press <Enter> to select **Begin printing**

The report is printed.

3. You are now finished working with the SCHOOL file. Exit from dBASE IV.

*Select **Quit to DOS** from the Exit menu*

When the system prompt appears, take your disk out of the computer. Turn the computer and monitor off.

❑ SUMMARY POINTS

- ■ The options from the Go To menu allow you to quickly find a specific record.
- ■ There are two ways to rearrange the order of records within a dBASE IV file: using the SORT option and using the INDEX option from the Organize Menu.
- ■ The <create> option from the Reports panel enables the user to create a hard copy report using dBASE IV files.

❑ COMMAND SUMMARY

Key	Description
<Ctrl>-<End>	Save work and leave window
<F2> Data	In the Control Center, displays the records in a database file. When the records are displayed, shifts to Browse table or Edit screen.
<F5> Field	Adds a field to the report layout screen or view skeleton.
<Shift>-<F1> Pick	Displays a list of items available for the current fill-in.
<Shift>-<F2> Design	Displays the Design screen; allows you to change the design of the database file or report form.
<Shift>-<F3> Find Previous	Locates previous occurrence of search string.
<Shift>-<F4> Find Next	Locates next occurrence of search string.
<Shift>-<F8> Ditto	Copies data from the corresponding field of the previous record into the current record.

THE CONTROL CENTER

Menu	Menu Option	Description
Reports	<create>	Displays the Report design screen for creating a new report form.

REPORTS DESIGN SCREEN

Menu	Menu Option	Description
Print	Begin printing	Prints the current report.
Print	View report on screen	Displays the current report on the screen.
Exit	Save changes and exit	Save the report form.

COMMAND SUMMARY, continued

BROWSE TABLE/EDIT SCREEN

Menu	Menu Option	Description
Organize	Create new index	Creates a new index on the current database file.
Organize	Order records by index	Lists the records in the order specified by the selected index.
Organize	Sort database on field list	Sorts the database file by a particular field or fields.
Go To	Top record	In the Edit screen, displays the first record in the database file; in the Browse table, moves the pointer to the first record in the file.
Go To	Last Record	In the Edit screen, displays the last record in the database file; in the Browse table, moves the pointer to the last record.
Go To	Record Number	In Edit screen, displays the specified record; in the Browse table, moves the pointer to the specified record.
Go To	Forward search	Allows you to find records containing specific data
Go To	Backward search	Allows you to find records containing specific data

❏ dBASE IV Exercises

In this exercise you are going to create a database file for the registrar's office at a state university. The file will be named REGISTER and will contain general information about students such as personal data, programs, and majors. If you need help answering any of the questions that follow, refer to "Indexing a File," "Creating a Report with dBASE IV," and "Printing a Report" earlier in this chapter.

1. Start the dBASE IV program. Make sure your work disk is in Drive A.

2. Design a new database file named REGISTER. The file should have the following design:

Field Name	Type	Width
NUMBER	Character	2
LAST_NAME	Character	10
FIRST_NAME	Character	10
ADDRESS	Character	16
CITY	Character	15
STATE	Character	2
MAJOR	Character	10
DEGREE	Character	3

3. Enter the following information:

No.	Last_Name	First_Name	Address	City	State	Major	Degree
1	Mansfield	Carolyn	190 Main St.	Los Angeles	CA	Education	BA
2	Magpoc	William	1200 Victory Rd.	Long Beach	CA	Business	BA
3	Rath	Alexis	221 Maple Ave.	Reno	NV	Business	BA
4	Byrtum	Laura	849 Napoleon Rd.	Los Angeles	CA	Health	BA
5	Burkett	Lynn	12 Central	Long Beach	CA	Music	MA
6	Catayee	Monique	110 Main St.	Phoeniz	AZ	Theater	MA
7	Marin	Bernard	12 King Rd.	Ventura	CA	Accounting	BA
8	Byler	Diane	Anderson Hall	Los Angeles	CA	Business	BA
9	Heil	Pascal	302 West Hall	Los Angeles	CA	Education	BA
10	Jaccoud	Lynn	120 S. Main St.	Stockton	CA	Finance	BA
11	Wegman	Nelly	430 Clough	Davis	CA	Accounting	BA
12	Pinkston	Mark	65 High St.	Fresno	CA	Statistics	MA
13	Burroughs	Beverly	26 S. Summit	Ventura	CA	Journalism	BA
14	King	Stephen	201 E. Wooster	Corvallis	OR	History	MA
15	Paulin	Jack	102 High	Ogden	UT	Math	MA
16	Proctor	Christine	34 Eighth St.	Portland	OR	Chemistry	MA
17	Priess	Ronald	120 Prout Hall	Los Angeles	CA	Marketing	BA
18	Atkins	Lee	12560 Euclid	San Jose	CA	Education	BA
19	Asik	Jennifer	22 Mercer	San Jose	CA	History	MA
20	Dowell	Gail	112 Ridge	Long Beach	CA	Business	MA
21	Wacker	Annick	320 East Merry	Stockton	CA	Economics	BA
22	Garrett	Lynda	39 Vine St.	Fresno	CA	Music	MA
23	McGovern	Alice	1200 Sand Ridge	Los Angeles	CA	Theater	PhD
24	McDonald	Francoise	210 Main St.	Taos	NM	Education	BA
25	Ausustin	Liliane	333 Jeffers Rd.	Davis	CA	Finance	BA

4. Use the BROWSE table to review the data; make sure that everything is accurate. If you find errors correct them.

5. Now sort the file on the MAJOR field first and the LAST_NAME field second. Name the new file MAJOR.

6. Display the records in the MAJOR file. What is the order of the records?

7. Create a report and name it MAJOR . Use the MAJOR file for the report. Use the following for a page title:

```
List of Students Grouped by Major
```

Use the LAST_NAME, FIRST_NAME, and MAJOR fields as the contents for three columns. Enter appropriate column headings. Group the report on the MAJOR field. Save the Report form.

8. Print the MAJOR report.

9. Access the REGISTER database file. Create a query file that lists the student number, last name, major, and program for all students enrolled in a master's program. How many students are working toward earning their master's degrees? Create another query file to find all of the students working toward earning their bachelor's degrees, and finally for all students studying for their doctorate degrees. Print a quick report of each query file.

❑ dBASE IV Problems

To complete the following problems, you need to use files on the Student File Disk. In order to complete these exercises, you will need to be able to sort a database file, create a report with dBASE IV, and print a report.

1. On the Student File Disk there is a dBASE IV file called SHOOT. Start the dBASE IV program and retrieve this file. Make a copy of this file and call the copy SHOOT1. That way, if you make a mistake, you will always have the original file.

2. The SHOOT1 file keeps track of customers who have made an appointment at a photography studio. Retrieve a record from the SHOOT1 file. Look it over carefully. The customer's first name, last name, and telephone number are stored in the file. In addition, the CATEGORY field stores data on what type of photograph is being taken. Options for the CATEGORY field are:

Individual: The photograph is of one person only.
Couple: The photograph is of two people.
Group: The photograph is of more than two people.
Wedding: The appointment is to shoot a wedding.

The DATE field stores the date of the appointment. The COST field stores the amount being charged for the appointment. The PAID category indicates whether or not the person has already paid for the appointment.

3. Sort the database file so that it is in alphabetical order by last name. Name the sorted file LASTNAME.

4. Create a report using the LASTNAME file. Name the report PHOTOS. The report should have the following title:

Appointments

Include all the fields in the report. Position the first two fields so that the LASTNAME field is the first column in the report and the FIRSTNAME field is the second column in the report. Provide appropriate titles for all the columns in the report. Save the report.

5. Print the PHOTOS report.

6. Now you want to create a report that includes only those customers who have not paid. Using the SHOOT1 file, create a sorted file. Sort the file by the COST field first and the LASTNAME field second.

That way, customers owing the same amount will be listed alphabetically by last name. Name the sorted file UNPAID.

Using the UNPAID file, create a query file. Name the query file UNPAID. The condition you want to designate in the query table is to find those records where the PAID field is false. Save the query file.

7. Use the UNPAID file to create the report. The report should include the LASTNAME, FIRSTNAME, PHONE, CATEGORY, DATE, and COST fields, in that order. Provide appropriate titles for the columns. The report should print a total of the amounts listed in the COST column. Save the report.

8. Print the UNPAID report.

❏ dBASE IV CHALLENGE

Assume you work for a local museum. The director of public relations, who is in charge of all the museum's programs, wants you to create a dBASE IV file to keep track of the museum's membership. She wants to be able to retrieve information easily in order to prepare for the mailing of the museum's publications. She also wants to keep track of the expiration date for membership in the museum's programs to help encourage membership renewal.

Assume the museum has two types of memberships. Membership in the Exhibition Program provides free parking, free access to all permanent and temporary exhibitions, free publications (a monthly arts newsletter and a quarterly magazine), and discounts at the gift shop. Membership in the Science Club provides free parking; free access to all permanent and temporary exhibitions; a free monthly science publication; discounts at the gift shop; and free admission to lectures by major scientists, in-house workshops, and field trips. A patron can belong to both the Exhibition Program and the Science Club. There are five categories of memberships to both the Exhibition Program and the Science Club: Child, Student, Adult, Family, and Senior Citizen.

The database file needs to include the following fields:

Last Name	To store the member's last name
First Name	To store the member's first name
Address	To store the member's address
City	To store the city where the member lives
State	To store the state where the member lives
ZIP	To store the ZIP code
Phone	To store the member's telephone number
Type	To indicate whether the member belongs to the Exhibition Program, the Science Club, or both
Category	To indicate whether the membership is for a child, student, adult, family, or senior citizen
Expiration Date	Month and year when the current membership expires

The director wants to be able to easily print the following reports:

■ A report that lists the first name, last name, and full address of Exhibition Program members only. The data should be listed in order by zip code so that it can be used for mailing the monthly arts newsletter. Records that have the same ZIP code should be listed alphabetically by last name.

■ A report that lists the first name, last name, and full address of Science Club members only. The data should be listed in order by ZIP code so that it can be used for mailing the monthly science publication. Records that have the same ZIP code should be listed alphabetically by last name.

■ A report that lists the first name, last name, and full address of all memberships for children and families. The data should be listed in order by ZIP code so that it can be used for mailing information on museum programs that are of particular interest to children.

■ A report that lists the first name, last name, telephone number, type, category, and expiration date of all the members. The report should be listed in order by expiration date so it can be used to telephone people to remind them to renew their memberships.

1. Create a database file that is capable of storing the necessary data and printing the reports.

2. Enter fifteen records into your file. Be sure to vary the data stored in the fields. That is, make sure your file includes all types of members (Exhibition Program, Science Club, both); that it includes all categories of members (child, adult, family, student, senior citizen); that it includes a variety of expiration dates and a variety of ZIP codes.

3. Using the data from your data file, create and print the four reports required by the director. Make sure each report includes a title that easily identifies the information it provides. Include column titles.

CHAPTER 10

Introduction to VP-Expert

OUTLINE

❏ Introduction

Expert systems technology is a subfield of research in the area of artificial intelligence. Artificial intelligence is concerned with developing techniques whereby computers can be used to solve problems that appear to require imagination, intuition, or intelligence. Artificial intelligence is a very broad concept encompassing a number of applications, one of which is expert systems technology.

Expert systems technology is the development of computer software that simulates human problem-solving abilities. An expert system uses human knowledge that has been collected and stored in a computer to solve problems that ordinarily can be solved only by a human expert. Expert systems imitate the reasoning process experts go through to solve a specific problem.

The purpose of this chapter is to introduce the concept of expert systems. It provides instructions on how to get started using WordTech's VP-Expert, a rule-based expert system development tool.

❏ Understanding Expert Systems

The object of an expert system is to transfer the expertise of a human expert from that person to a computer and then from the computer to other humans who may not be expert in the field. When an end user accesses information from an expert system, it is called a consultation.

The first step in developing such a system is to gather as much information about the specific domain as possible. The domain is the field or area of activity. Examples of various domains are medicine, law, tax analysis, genealogy, and engineering. The domain knowledge, or the knowledge pertaining to a specific domain, could be gathered from books, manuals, human experts, data bases, special research reports, or a combination of all these sources.

The domain knowledge partly makes up the knowledge base. The knowledge base contains everything necessary for understanding, formulating, and solving the problem. In addition to the domain knowledge, the knowledge base contains a rule base that is the actual expertise of the system. The rules in the rule base are generally stated as IF/THEN propositions. The following is an example of a rule:

IF   temperature > 98.6 AND
              temperature < 102
THEN   fever = moderate

Such a rule could be used to help diagnose an illness. Basically this rule says if the body temperature is greater than 98.6 degrees but less than 102, then the person has a moderate fever.

The unique feature of an expert system is its ability to reason. The computer is programmed so that it can make inferences from data stored in the knowledge base. The "brain" of an expert system is the inference engine, the component where the reasoning is performed. The inference engine includes procedures regarding problem solving.

❏ Guide to VP-Expert

The remainder of this chapter focuses on how to use the educational version of VP-Expert 3.0. VP-Expert is a rule-based expert system development tool by WordTech that allows quick and easy expert system development.

Some of the directions for using VP-Expert vary depending on whether the computer has two floppy disk drives or a hard disk drive. The directions in this chapter are written for computers with a hard disk drive. Difference Boxes are included for computers with two floppy disk drives. VP-Expert will run on IBM PCs and compatibles with 384K or more RAM.

Each of the following sections introduces one or more features of VP-Expert. At the end of each section there is a hands-on activity called **Your Turn.** Do not try any of the hands-on activities until you have carefully read the section preceding it.

From now on the key marked ⏎ is referred to as <Enter>. Throughout this chapter, when instructed to press <Enter>, press the key marked ⏎ .

The following symbols and typefaces appear throughout the chapter. This is what they mean:

Choose a file? (prompt) **Error in line 15** (message) Select **Induce** (menu option)	Boldface text indicates words or phrases that appear on the computer screen. The text could be a prompt, message or name of a menu option.
Type: `IF color = red`	Typewriter font indicates text that is to be entered.
Press <Enter>	Angle brackets are used to signify a specific key on the keyboard. Press the key whose name is enclosed by the angle brackets.
ACTIONS	All capital letters indicate key words. Key words are commands to VP-Expert.

There are three ways to make a menu selection using VP-Expert. One way is to press the first letter of the option name. For example, if you wanted to select the **Induce** option from VP-Expert's Main Menu, you would press the letter `I`. The second method is to move the highlighted bar, using the <Left arrow> or the <Right arrow>, to the option you wish to select and press <Enter>. Finally, you can press the function key that corresponds to the selection you wish to make. For example, the number 2 appears in front of the **Induce** option on VP-Expert's Main Menu. You could select the **Induce** option by pressing the <F2> function key. When the directions in this and the following chapter instruct you to "Select" an option, use the method you prefer to make the appropriate selection.

❏ GETTING STARTED WITH VP-EXPERT

Before you can use VP-Expert on a computer system with a hard drive, you need to copy the program onto the hard drive. First, use the DISKCOPY command to make a backup copy of the VP-Expert program that came with this book. Refer to Chapter 1 if you need to review how to use the DISKCOPY command. Store the original program disk or disks in a safe place. Use your backup copy of the program and complete the following directions to copy the program onto the hard drive. If the program is on 5 1/4-inch disks, there are two disks. If the program is on a 3 1/2-inch disk, it is on one disk.

1. Turn on the computer and the monitor. The C prompt should be on the screen.

    Type: `MD vpx`
    Press <Enter>

2. Place the VP-Expert Program Disk into drive A. If you have 5 1/4-inch disks, place the VP-Expert Program Disk 1 of 2 into drive A.

Type: `copy A:*.* C:\vpx`

Press <Enter>

All the files on the VP-Expert Program Disk are copied into the VPX subdirectory. If you are using a 3 1/2-inch disk, go on to number 3. If you are using 5 1/4-inch disks, place the VP-Expert Program Disk 2 of 2 into drive A.

Type: `copy A:*.* c:\vpx`

Press <Enter>

All the files on the VP-Expert Program Disk 2 of 2 are copied into the VPX subdirectory.

3. To start VP-Expert, make sure the C prompt is on the screen.

Type: `CD vpx`

Press <Enter>

Type: `vpx`

Press <Enter>

The VP-Expert opening screen appears.

Difference Box: Starting VP-Expert on a System with Two Floppy Disk Drives

Before using VP-Expert on a computer system with two floppy disk drives, you need to make a backup copy of the VP-Expert program disk or disks that came with this book. Use the DISKCOPY command to make a backup copy of the VP-Expert program. Refer to Chapter 1 if you need to review how to use the DISKCOPY command. Store the original program disk or disks in a safe place. Use your backup copy when running the program. If the program is on a 3 1/2-inch disk, it is on one disk. If the program is on 5 1/4-inch disks, there are two disks. Disk 1 contains all the program files needed to run VP-Expert. Disk 2 contains the VP-Expert Help system and sample knowledge base files.

To start the program using 5 1/4-inch disks, place the backup copy of the VP-Expert Program Disk 1 of 2 in drive A. Place either the backup of the VP-Expert Program Disk 2 of 2 or your data disk in drive B.The A> prompt should be on the screen.

Type: `vpx`

Press <Enter>

Select **Path**

Type: `B:`

Press <Enter>

❏ GETTING HELP WITH VP-EXPERT

VP-Expert has a very useful Help System that provides help as to how to use the program. The Help System is itself a knowledge base. The Help System can be activated at any point by pressing the <F1> function key.

YOUR TURN

In this hands-on exercise, you are going to practice using the VP-Expert Help System. The exercise assumes you have already copied the VP-Expert program onto the hard drive. If the program is not on the hard drive, use the directions above to copy the program to the hard drive.

Difference Box: If you are using 5 1/4-inch disks on a system with two floppy disk drives, the VP-Expert Program Disk 2 of 2 must be in drive B in order to complete this exercise. When you have finished with the exercise, remove the Program Disk 2 of 2 from drive B and replace it with your data disk.

1. Turn on the computer and monitor.

> Type: `cd vpx`
>
> Press <Enter>
>
> Type: `vpx`
>
> Press any key

Your screen should look like Figure 10-1. Notice that the first option on the Menu is **Help**. Remember, there are three methods by which you can select the Help option: Press `H` for **Help**, press <Left arrow> to move the highlighted bar to **Help** and press <Enter>, or press the <F1> function key.

> Select **Help**

FIGURE 10-1 VP-Expert's Main Menu

```
                  ───────[ RULES ]───────        ───────[ FACTS ]───────




    1Help    2Induce   3Edit    4Consult  5Tree     6FileName 7Path     8Quit
    1Help 2Go 3Whatif 4Variable 5Rule 7Set 8Edit 9Quit
```

The Help Screen for VP-Expert's Main menu appears. The Help Screen explains each section from the Main Menu. Read this screen.

2.   Notice the menu at the bottom of the screen. The first option on the menu indicates you can scroll up a line at a time by pressing <Up arrow> or scroll down a line at a time by pressing <Down arrow>. The second option indicates you can scroll up a page at a time by pressing <PgUp> or scroll down a page at a time by pressing <PgDn>. The third and fourth options indicate that pressing <Home> takes you to the top of the current file and pressing <End> takes you to the bottom of the current file. The fifth option indicates that pressing <Esc> accesses more help topics. The sixth option indicates that pressing P enables you to print. The final option **F1** provides keystroke help.

>   Press <Esc>

3.   A list of VP-Expert's Help topics appears on the screen. You can move through the list either by pressing <Up arrow>, <Down arrow>, <Home>, or <End>.

>   Press <End>

The highlighted bar moves to the bottom of the list.

>   Press <Home>

The highlighted bar moves to the top of the list.

>   Press <Down arrow> until **CONFIDENCE_FACTORS** is highlighted.

>   Press <Return>

A Help Screen describing confidence factors appears. Read the screen. Notice at the end of the screen it says, **See also TRUTHTHRESH**.

>   Press <Esc>

>   Press <PgDn> until you see **TRUTHTHRESH**

>   Highlight **TRUTHTHRESH**

>   Press <Return>

Read the Help Screen that appears and then press <Esc>.

4.   Continue looking up topics on the Help System. When you have finished, press <Esc> to exit from the Help System and return to VP-Expert's Main Menu. Leave the Main Menu on the screen while you read the following section.

❏ CREATING A KNOWLEDGE BASE FROM AN INDUCTION TABLE

Perhaps the easiest way to create a knowledge base is to use VP-Expert's ability to automatically generate a knowledge base from an induction table. An induction table is a table that represents examples in the form of rows and columns. The following is an example of an induction table:

Age	Weight (lbs)	Calcium (mg.)
1	13	360
1	20	540
3	29	800
6	44	800
10	62	800
14	100	1200
16	130	1200

Look at this induction table closely. The purpose of the table is to recommend daily dietary allowances of calcium. The recommendation is based on the age and weight of the child. The table is made up of rows and columns. The top row provides column headings. These headings define the variables. The third column contains the goal variable, that is, the variable determined by the two preceding variables.

VP-Expert is a rule-based expert system. If this table were to be used as part of a knowledge base, it would have to be translated into rules. This table would be translated as follows:

If *Age* is 1 and *Weight* is 13 THEN
Calcium is 360 mg.

IF *Age* is 1 and *Weight* is 20 THEN
Calcium is 540 mg.

IF *Age* is 3 and *Weight* is 29 THEN
Calcium is 800 mg.

If *Age* is 6 and *Weight* is 44 THEN
Calcium is 800 mg.

If *Age* is 10 and *Weight* is 62 THEN
Calcium is 800 mg.

IF *Age* is 14 and *Weight* is 100 THEN
Calcium is 1200 mg.

IF *Age* is 16 and *Weight* is 130 THEN
Calcium is 1200 mg.

VP-Expert's Induce command automatically creates a knowledge base from an induction table. That is, it automatically interprets a table into a set of rules such as the ones above. The knowledge base created using the Induce command is limited in its complexity, but for some applications, the Induce command is the most efficient way to start a knowledge base.

An induction table can be created using several different methods. It can be created in the text editor that comes with VP-Expert, in a Lotus 1-2-3 spreadsheet or in a dBASE database file.

Creating an induction table using the text editor that comes with VP-Expert is not difficult. VP-Expert's Editor is similar to a word processor. Creating an induction table is simply a matter of entering text in columns. Table 10-1 lists the editing commands used in the VP-Expert Editor.

TABLE 10-1 VP-Expert Editing Commands

Key	Function
<Up arrow>, <Down arrow>	Moves the cursor down or up a line.
<Left arrow>, <Right arrow>	Moves the cursor left or right one character.
<Ctrl>-<Left arrow>	Moves the cursor left one word.
<Ctrl>-<Right arrow>	Moves the cursor right one word.
<PgUp>	Moves the cursor to the preceding screen.
<PgDn>	Moves the cursor to the following screen.
<Ctrl>-<PgUp>	Moves the cursor to the beginning of the file.
<Ctrl>-<PgDn>	Moves the cursor to the end of the file.
<Home>	Moves the cursor to the beginning of the line.
<End>	Moves the cursor to the end of the line.
<Ins>	Turns the insert mode on or off. The default setting is on.
<Tab>	Moves the cursor to the next tab stop.
<Shift>-<Tab>	Moves the cursor back one tab stop.
<Ctrl>-<Return>	Pressing these two keys together adds a blank line of space.
<Del>	Deletes the character at the cursor position.
<Ctrl>-<Y>	Deletes the entire line in which the cursor is located.
<Alt>-<F6>	Saves the file and exits from the Editor.
<Alt>-<F8>	Abandons the file without saving or updating it.
<Alt>-<F5>	Updates the file without exiting from the Editor.

 YOUR TURN

In this hands-on exercise you are going to create an induction table using VP-Expert's text editor. Before you begin, check to make sure your data disk is in drive A.

1. If necessary start the VP-Expert program. VP-Expert's Main Menu should be on your screen. First you are going to change the working directory to drive A.

> Select **Path**
>
> Type: A:
>
> Press <Enter>

VP Expert's Main Menu should return to the screen.

> Select **Induce**

The VP-Expert's Induce Menu appears.

> Select **Create**

The prompt **Choose a Text File** appears. You need to provide a file name for the induction table file.

> Type: `Media`
>
> Press <Enter>

The VP-Expert Editor appears. Your screen should look like Figure 10-2.

2. VP-Expert's text editor works much like a word processor. The blank space is the editing window into which you will enter text. The flashing box in the upper left corner is the cursor. The name of the file is in the upper right corner. Notice that VP-Expert automatically added the extension **tbl** to the file name **Media**. The triangles at the bottom of the screen indicate tab stops, which are set for every five spaces.

You are going to type in an induction table to help someone decide the best advertising media to be used based on the following criteria:

Audience to be reached: a small, selective audience (for example, people who fall within a certain age group), or a broad, mass audience.

Budget: Small, under $10,000; Medium, $10,000-$50,000; Large, over $50,000

> Type: `Audience`
>
> Press <Tab> twice
>
> Type: `Budget`
>
> Press <Tab> once
>
> Type: `Media`
>
> Press <Enter>

FIGURE 10-2 Creating an Induction Table

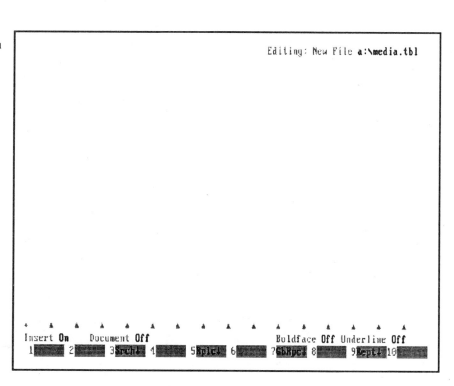

A left triangle appears at the end of the line, and the cursor moves to the next line. The left triangle indicates that the <Enter> key was pressed.

3.   You have now entered the column headings. Complete the induction table by typing the following under each column heading. When typing in two-word entries, such as Mass_Market, be sure to include the underscore between the two words. The underscore or underline is found on top of the hyphen on the right side of the first row of keys on the keyboard. When finished, your screen should look like Figure 10-3.

Audience	Budget	Media
Selective	Small	Direct_Mail
Selective	Medium	Radio
Selective	Large	Magazine
Mass_Market	Small	Newspaper
Mass_Market	Medium	Outdoor_Billboards
Mass_Market	Large	Television

When you have finished, look over your induction table carefully and make sure it looks like Figure 10-3. The entries must be correct and lined up in the proper columns. Make sure there are no spelling mistakes and that you included the underscore in Mass_Market, Direct_Mail and Outdoor_Billboards. Make any necessary corrections. When you are satisfied with your induction table, you must save it.

> Press <Alt>-<F6>

The prompt **Save as "a:\ media.tbl" (Y or N)?** appears.

> Type: Y

FIGURE 10-3 The MEDIA Induction Table

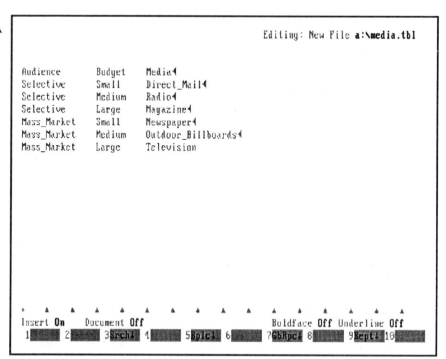

4. The Induce Menu appears. You now want to create a knowledge base from your MEDIA induction table.

      Select **Text**

The prompt **Choose a Text File** appears. The MEDIA file should be listed and highlighted on the screen.

      Press <Enter> to select the MEDIA file

Next, the prompt **Choose a file** appears.

      Type: `Media.KBS`

      Press <Enter>

5. The Induce Menu returns to the screen.

      Select **Quit**

The VP-Expert Main Menu returns to the screen. Now you are going to run a consultation using the MEDIA.KBS knowledge base.

      Select **FileName**

      Press <Enter> to select **MEDIA.KBS**

      Select **Consult**

Three boxes are on the screen. The top box is called the **consultation window**. This is where the actual consultation will take place. Right now, the prompt **Select GO to begin consultation** is in the consultation window. The window in the lower left corner is called the **rules window**. This is where the actual consultation will take place. The window in the lower right corner is called the **facts window**. The facts window displays conclusions reached during the consultation.

      Press `G` for **Go**

Your screen should look like Figure 10-4. The system is asking if the advertising is for the mass market or for a selective audience. There are three steps required to select an option. First, use the left and right arrow keys to highlight the desired response. Next, press <Enter> to select the highlighted response and, finally, press <End> to move on to the next question.

      Press <Right arrow> to select **Mass_Market**

      Press <Enter>

      Press <End>

The next question, regarding the size of the budget, appears.

      Press <Right arrow> twice to select **Large**

      Press <Enter>

      Press <End>

The consultation is complete, but flashed off the screen before you could read it. To see the result of the consultation, do the following:

      Select **Variable**

FIGURE 10-4 Running a
Consultation

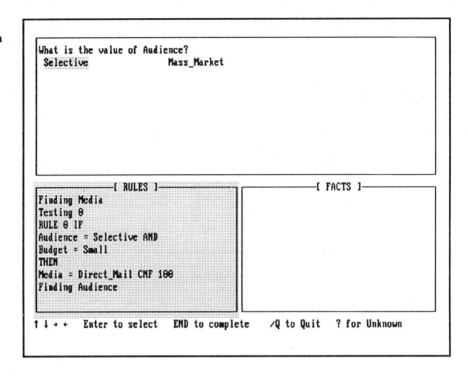

```
What is the value of Audience?
  Selective                Mass_Market




┌─────────────────[ RULES ]─────────────────┐  ┌──────[ FACTS ]──────┐
│ Finding Media                              │  │                     │
│ Testing 0                                  │  │                     │
│ RULE 0 IF                                  │  │                     │
│ Audience = Selective AND                   │  │                     │
│ Budget = Small                             │  │                     │
│ THEN                                       │  │                     │
│ Media = Direct_Mail CNF 100                │  │                     │
│ Finding Audience                           │  │                     │
└────────────────────────────────────────────┘  └─────────────────────┘
 ↑ ↓ → ←   Enter to select   END to complete   /Q to Quit   ? for Unknown
```

The prompt, **Name of variable you want to see** appears.

> Press <Right arrow> to select Media
>
> Press <Enter>

The result of the consultation, **Media = Television CNF 100** appears in the consultation window. **CNF 100** indicates the confidence factor. In this case the confidence factor is 100%. Try another consultation.

> Press <Enter> to start the consultation again
>
> Press <Enter> to select **Selective**
>
> Press <End>
>
> Press <Right arrow> to select **Medium**
>
> Press <Enter>
>
> Press <End>
>
> Select **Variable**
>
> Press <Right arrow> twice to highlight **Media**
>
> Press <Enter> to select **Media**

This time the system advised using radio as the advertising media. Continue experimenting with making consultations. When you have finished, press <F8> to quit. The VP-Expert Main Menu should return to your screen. If you want to quit at this point, select **Quit** from the VP-Expert Main Menu.

A knowledge base created with VP-Expert consists of three parts: the ACTIONS block, rules, and statements. In addition, a fourth element, called clauses, is found in the ACTIONS block, as well as in rules. Each of these knowledge base elements are explained in the following sections.

The ACTIONS Block

The ACTIONS block defines the problems of the consultation. That is, it tells the inference engine what it needs to find out. This information is conveyed to the inference engine in FIND clauses. FIND clauses instruct VP-Expert to find the value or values for one or more variables. The FIND clause actually sets up the "goal" that is to be achieved by the consultation. For this reason, the variable listed in the FIND clause is called the goal variable. The ACTIONS block also determines the order in which the variables are to be found.

The ACTIONS block is made up of three elements:
- the key word ACTIONS
- clauses
- a semicolon

The ACTIONS block must begin with the key word "ACTIONS." After the key word "ACTIONS" comes one or more clauses, one of which must be a FIND clause. Finally, the ACTIONS block must end with a semicolon.

Rules

Rules are always stated as IF/THEN propositions. The actual knowledge of an expert system is contained within the rules. Rules enable the system to make decisions; they are made up of four elements:
- the rule name
- the rule premise
- the rule conclusion
- a semicolon

Each rule must begin with the key word "RULE," followed by a label or rule name. Each rule in a knowledge base has to have a different name. The name can be made up of letters, numbers, and the symbols _, $, %, ^, and |. Often, it is easier to use numbers (0, 1, 2, 3, and so on) as rule names.

Following the rule name is the rule premise. The rule premise, which is always introduced with the key word "IF," states one or more conditions that compare the contents of a variable to a value. The following six comparisons can be made:

=	is equal to
<	is less than
<=	is less than or equal to
>	is greater than
>=	is greater than or equal to
<>	is not equal to

An example of a rule premise is, IF gpa >= 3.3.

A rule premise can contain up to ten conditions. Conditions are added to the rule premise by using the logical operators AND and OR. The following conditions could be added to the previous example of a rule premise:

IF gpa >= 3.3 AND
income < 12000 OR
family > 4

When the AND condition is used, both statements must be true; when the OR statement is used, one or both conditions must be true. Therefore, in order for this rule premise to "pass," that is, to be considered as true, either the value for the "gpa" variable must be greater than or equal to 3.3 and either the value for the "income" variable must be less than 12000, or the value for the "family" variable must be greater than 4, or both.

Every rule premise must be followed by a rule conclusion. Rule conclusions begin with the key word THEN and must contain at least one equation, the purpose of which is to assign a value to a variable when the IF premise is true. For example, in the following rule:

RULE 1

IF gpa >= 3.3 AND
income < 12000 OR
family > 4
THEN scholarship = eligible

The value "eligible" is to be assigned to the variable "scholarship" when the premise "IF gpa >= 3.3 AND income < 12000 OR family > 4" is evaluated as true.

Statements

Statements provide further directions to the expert system. The purpose of most VP-Expert statements is to assign specific characteristics to variables. Three examples of statements are ASK statements, CHOICES statements, and PLURAL statements. The purpose of these three types of statements is explained in this section. A list of all of VP-Expert's statements appears at the end of Chapter 12.

The ASK statement assigns a value to all the variables the user must define. The following ASK statement

ASK gpa: "What is your grade point average?";

assigns to the variable "gpa" whatever value the user enters in response to this question.

CHOICES statements accompany ASK statements. When the question from an ASK statement is displayed during a consultation, values from the corresponding CHOICES statement are displayed as a menu. Look at the following example:

ASK gpa: "What is your grade point average?";
CHOICES gpa: under_3.3, 3.3_to_3.6, over_3.6;

Notice that both the ASK statement and the CHOICES statement include the same variable "gpa." A CHOICES statement must include a variable that is named in an ASK statement. In this example, when the consultation is run, the question "What is your grade point average?" will be displayed with the three options listed: under 3.3, 3.3 to 3.6, over 3.6. The end user selects an option by moving the highlighted bar over his or her choice and pressing <Enter>. When the end user selects an option, that value is assigned to the appropriate variable. In this example, if the end user selected 3.3 to 3.6, the value for the variable gpa would become 3.3 to 3.6.

The PLURAL statement enables more than one value to be assigned to a variable. Look at the following example:

ASK Quarter: "What quarter will you be attending school?";
CHOICES Quarter: Fall, Winter, Spring, Summer;
PLURAL Quarter;

During the consultation the question "What quarter will you be attending school?" would appear on the screen with the options, Fall, Winter, Spring, and Summer listed below it. In this example, the end user could select more than one option because the PLURAL statement enables the variable "Quarter" to be assigned more than one value.

 YOUR TURN

In this exercise, you are going to look at the knowledge base that VP-Expert created from the MEDIA induction table.

1. If necessary, start the VP-Expert program. Remember to change the path to drive A:.
The VP-Expert Main Menu should be on your screen.

> Select **FileName**

The prompt **Choose a file** appears. The file name **MEDIA.KBS** appears and is highlighted.

> Press <Enter>

> The VP-Expert Main Menu returns to the screen.

> Select **Edit**

The MEDIA knowledge base appears. Your screen should look like Figure 10-5.

2. You are now going to look over the MEDIA knowledge base carefully to familiarize yourself with the three parts of a knowledge base. Notice the first word in the knowledge base is the key word **ACTIONS**. This introduces the ACTIONS block which, you will remember, leads the consultation, telling the inference engine what to do. Here, the ACTIONS block is directing the consultation to **FIND Media**, that is, find a value for the Media variable. Remember that the FIND clause establishes the goal of the consultation. In this example **Media** is the goal variable. The semicolon following the word **Media** indicates the end of the ACTIONS block.

The rules follow the ACTIONS block. Remember, the rules are the IF/THEN propositions that enable the system to make decisions. Each rule statement has a name, which is in this case a number. The first rule, **RULE 0**, states, if the value for Audience is equal to Mass_Market and the value for Budget is equal to Large, then the value for Media is equal to television.

FIGURE 10-5 Displaying the MEDIA Knowledge Base

```
                                                    Editing: Old File a:\media.kbs

ACTIONS◄
        FIND Media◄
        DISPLAY "The value of Media is {Media}";◄
◄
RULE 0◄
IF      Audience = Selective AND◄
        Budget = Small◄
THEN    Media = Direct_Mail;◄
◄
RULE 1◄
IF      Audience = Selective AND◄
        Budget = Medium◄
THEN    Media = Radio;◄
◄
RULE 2◄
IF      Audience = Selective AND◄
        Budget = Large◄
THEN    Media = Magazine;◄


↑  ▲   ▲   ▲   ▲   ▲   ▲   ▲   ▲   ▲   ▲   ▲   ▲   ▲   ▲   ▲
Insert On    Document Off                    Boldface Off Underline Off
   1    2    3    4    5    6    7    8    9    10
```

Use <Down arrow> to scroll down through the entire knowledge base and read all five rules. Notice that each rule is introduced with a rule name, **RULE 0, RULE 1, RULE 2**, and so on, and that each rule ends with a semicolon. The semicolon has to be present to indicate to the system that the end of that particular rule has been reached.

3.   After RULE 5 there is an ASK statement, followed by a CHOICE statement. Remember, statements provide further directions to the system. The statements say:

ASK Audience: "What is the value of Audience?";

CHOICES Audience: Selective, Mass_Market,;

Remember when you ran the MEDIA consultation, the first question to appear in the consultation window was "What is the value of Audience?" This ASK statement directed the system to display that question in the consultation window. The CHOICES statement directed the system to list the options Mass Market and Selective. Whenever you made a selection of either Mass market or Selective, that value was assigned to the variable "Audience."

If necessary, press <Down arrow> to read the second ASK and CHOICES statements. The second ASK statement directs the system to display the question, "What is the value of Budget?" so that a value for the variable "Budget" can be established. The choices are Small, Medium, and Large. Based on the option selected by the end user, the system assigns a value to the Media variable.

4. Using the up and down arrow keys, read over the MEDIA knowledge base carefully. Make sure you understand the three parts of the knowledge base: the ACTIONS block, rules, and statements. When you are finished, press <Alt>-<F8> and Y to quit without making any changes to the knowledge base. The VP-Expert Main Menu returns to the screen.

When using an induction table to create a knowledge base, the knowledge base that is created has an arbitrary format that is not particularly user friendly. For example, in the current MEDIA consultation, the end user is asked **What is the value of Audience?** and **What is the value of Budget?** In addition, at the end of the consultation it was not readily apparent exactly what or where the result was. Someone not familiar with the knowledge base would have no idea of the meaning of such a question as "What is the value of audience?" nor would they know where to look to find the result of the consultation.

A knowledge base created with the Induce command can easily be edited to make it more user friendly. Before editing a knowledge base, however, you must be familiar with VP-Expert's formatting rules. Table 10-2 describes these rules.

TABLE 10-2 Rules for Formatting a VP-Expert Knowledge Base

- The ACTIONS block must begin with the word ACTIONS.
- Rule statements must begin with the key word RULE. The key word RULE must be followed by a label that cannot be longer than 20 characters.
- Rule labels, variable names, and values cannot contain spaces. The underline character can be used to indicate a space. VP-Expert will replace the underline character with a space in display text during a consultation.
- Rule labels and variable names may contain numbers, letters, and the special characters ___, $, %, ^, and |. Variable names must begin with a letter.
- In statements that create onscreen messages, such as ASK and DISPLAY, the text that is to appear onscreen must be in double quotes.
- The ACTIONS block must end with a semicolon. Every rule and every statement must end with a semicolon. The only other place a semicolon can appear in a knowledge base is inside the double quotes surrounding display text.
- VP-Expert key words cannot be used as variable names. A complete list of VP-Expert Key words is given at the end of Chapter 11.
- Comment lines, which are notes that are to be ignored by the inference engine, can be included by beginning each comment line with an exclamation mark (!). Syntax errors will occur if the exclamation point is left out.

YOUR TURN

In this hands-on exercise you are going to refine the MEDIA knowledge base to make it more user friendly.

1. The VP-Expert Main Menu should be on your screen.

    Select **Edit**

If necessary, highlight **Media** as the name of the knowledge base you want to use and press <Enter>. The MEDIA knowledge base should be on your screen.

2. First you are going to edit the ASK statements so that they are easier to understand.

Press <Down arrow> until it is in the line that begins "**ASK Audience...**"

Currently, the question that is displayed is "What is the value of Audience?" You can change this question to "Is the advertising to appeal to a mass market or a selective audience?"

Press <Right arrow> until the cursor is on the **W** in **What**

Press <Ctrl>-<T>

The word **What** is deleted.

Press <Ctrl>-<T> twice

The word **is** is deleted. Continue pressing <Ctrl>-<T> until the entire sentence is deleted. The opening double quotation mark should still be on the screen. If it is not, enter a double quotation mark.

Type: `Is the advertising to appeal to a mass market or`

Press <Ctrl>-<Enter>

You have to press <Ctrl>-<Enter> together, rather than just <Enter> to create a new line for the additional text to be entered.

Type: `a selective audience?";`

Your screen should look like Figure 10-6. Check to make sure the question that is to be displayed on the screen is contained within double quotation marks and that there is a semicolon after the last quotation mark.

3. Using the arrow keys, move the cursor so that it is on the **W** in **What** in the sentence "What is the value of Budget?"

Press <Ctrl>-<T> until the whole sentence is deleted

FIGURE 10-6 Editing the MEDIA Knowledge Base

```
                                              Editing: Old File a:\media.kbs

◀
RULE 4◀
IF      Audience = Mass_Market AND◀
        Budget = Medium◀
THEN    Media = Outdoor_Billboards;◀
◀
RULE 5◀
IF      Audience = Mass_Market AND◀
        Budget = Large◀
THEN    Media = Television;◀
◀
ASK Audience: "Is the advertising to appeal to a mass market or◀
a selective audience?";◀
CHOICES Audience: Selective,Mass_Market;◀
◀
ASK Budget: "What is the value of Budget?";◀
CHOICES Budget: Small,Medium,Large;◀
◀

+   ▲   ▲   ▲   ▲   ▲   ▲   ▲   ▲   ▲   ▲   ▲   ▲   ▲   ▲
Insert On    Document Off                     Boldface Off Underline Off
  1     2     3     4     5     6     7     8     9     10
```

The opening double quotation mark should still be on the screen. If it is not, enter a double quotation mark.

> Type: `Is your advertising budget small (under $10,000),`
>
> Press <Ctrl>-<Enter>
>
> Type: `medium (between $10,000 and $50,000) or large (over`
> `$50,000)?";`

Again, check to make sure the question to be displayed on the screen is between quotation marks and that there is a semicolon after the last quotation mark.

> Press <Alt>-<F6> to save the revised knowledge base

The prompt **Save as "a:\media.kbs" (Y or N)?** appears

> Press Y

The VP-Expert Main Menu returns to the screen. Leave the Main Menu on the screen while you read the following section.

❑ CHECKING FOR ERRORS IN THE KNOWLEDGE BASE

If anything is entered incorrectly in the knowledge base, an error message will appear when you try to run a consultation. Following is an example of a typical error message:

Missing ';'

(Press any key to go on)

Error in line 15

This message indicates that line 15 in the knowledge base is missing a mandatory semicolon. When you press any key to continue, the knowledge base will appear on your screen with the cursor in the line indicated in the error message. In this example, the cursor would appear in line 15. A summary of common VP-Expert error messages is found at the end of Chapter 11. Refer to this summary to help you correct your mistakes.

VP-Expert can only make an educated guess at the line number where the error occurs. Look over the line where the cursor appears, carefully. If you cannot find the error in that line, check previous lines for errors. Table 10-3 will help you find some common knowledge base mistakes. Once the knowledge base is entered correctly, the three consultation windows appear and the message **File loaded** is displayed.

YOUR TURN

You are going to check your edited MEDIA knowledge base to make sure there are no errors in it.

TABLE 10-3 Checklist for Finding Errors within a Knowledge Base

- ■ The ACTIONS block ends with a semicolon.
- ■ Each rule ends with a semicolon.
- ■ Each statement ends with a semicolon.
- ■ A semicolon does not appear anywhere in the knowledge base other than at the end of an ACTIONS block, at the end of a rule, at the end of a statement, or within the double quotation marks surrounding text that is to be displayed during a consultation, that is, text in an ASK statement, DISPLAY clause, etc.
- ■ All VP-Expert key words must be spelled correctly.
- ■ Rule labels, variable names, and values can only contain letters, numbers, and the characters _, $, %, ^, and l. There can be no spaces in rule labels, variable names, or values.
- ■ VP-Expert key words cannot be used as variable names.

1. The VP-Expert Main Menu should be on your screen.

    Select **Consult**

If you made the editing changes correctly, the prompt **Select GO to begin consultation** appears. If you get an error message, read the error message carefully, press any key, and see if you can correct your error. Refer to the Summary of Common VP-Expert Error Messages at the end of Chapter 11 for help.

2. Once your knowledge base is loaded, run a consultation to see the changes you made to the file.

    Select **Go**

Now the question in the consultation window reads, **Is the advertising to appeal to a mass market or a selective audience?**

    Press <Enter> to select **Selective**

    Press <End>

Your edited second question appears.

    Press <Enter> to select **Small**

    Press <End>

    Select **Variable**

    Press <Right arrow> twice to highlight **Media**

    Press <Enter>

The result of the consultation, **Direct_Mail,** still is not very easy to find. In the next section, you will learn how to insert a DISPLAY clause to display the result of the consultation in a more user-friendly fashion.

    Select **Quit**

The VP-Expert Main Menu returns to the screen. Leave the Main Menu on the screen while you read the following section.

In the discussion on the elements that comprise a knowledge base, it was mentioned that the fourth element, clauses, appears in the ACTIONS block and in the rules of the knowledge base. Clauses provide further instructions to the knowledge base.

The DISPLAY Clause

The DISPLAY clause can be used both in the ACTIONS block and in rules. The DISPLAY key word introduces text that is to appear on the screen during a consultation. DISPLAY clauses that occur in the ACTIONS block will always appear in the order that they occur in the block. When used in rules, DISPLAY clauses appear only if the rule with which they are associated is evaluated as true. In the following example,

> RULE 1 IF gpa >= 3.3 AND
> income < 1200 OR
> family > 4
> THEN scholarship = eligible
> DISPLAY "The candidate is eligible for a scholarship.";

If Rule 1 evaluates as true, then the sentence that appears in quotes after the key word DISPLAY will appear on the screen during the consultation. The text to be displayed must always appear between double quotation marks in the knowledge base.

 YOUR TURN

In this exercise you are going to add two DISPLAY clauses to the ACTIONS block.

1.   The VP-Expert Main Menu should be on your screen.

>   Select **Edit**

If necessary, select **Media** in response to the prompt **What is the name of the knowledge base you want to use?** The MEDIA knowledge base appears.

2.   First you want to add a DISPLAY clause that will help to introduce the consultation.

>   Press <Right arrow> until the cursor is on the triangle that follows the S in ACTIONS
>
>   Press <Ctrl>-<Enter>

There should now be a line of space between the key word **ACTIONS** and the **FIND** clause.

>   Press <Tab>
>
>   Type: DISPLAY "What is the best advertising media for your product?
>
>   Press <Ctrl>-<Enter>
>
>   Type: To find out, press any key to begin the consultation.~"

Make sure you enter the ~ symbol after the period and before the quotation mark. When used in a DISPLAY clause this symbol causes the program to pause until a key has been pressed.

3. Notice the DISPLAY clause that follows the FIND clause. It says:

    DISPLAY "The value of Media is {Media}";

You are going to edit this clause so it is more user friendly.

> Move the cursor to the **T** in the word **The**
>
> Press <Ctrl>-<T> eleven times
>
> Type: An appropriate advertising media for your product is {Media}
>
> Press <Ctrl>-<Enter>
>
> Type: Press any key to continue.~";

Make sure the variable **Media** is contained within the curly brackets. When the consultation is run, the value for **Media** will appear in place of {Media}.

4. You have now added the two DISPLAY clauses. Your screen should look like Figure 10-7. Check to make sure you entered the DISPLAY clauses correctly.

> Press <Alt>-<F6> to save the edited knowledge base

The prompt **Save as "a:\ media.kbs" (Y or N)?** appears.

> Press Y

The VP-Main menu appears.

5. Run another consultation to see what changes the DISPLAY clauses made.

**FIGURE 10-7 The
DISPLAY Clause**

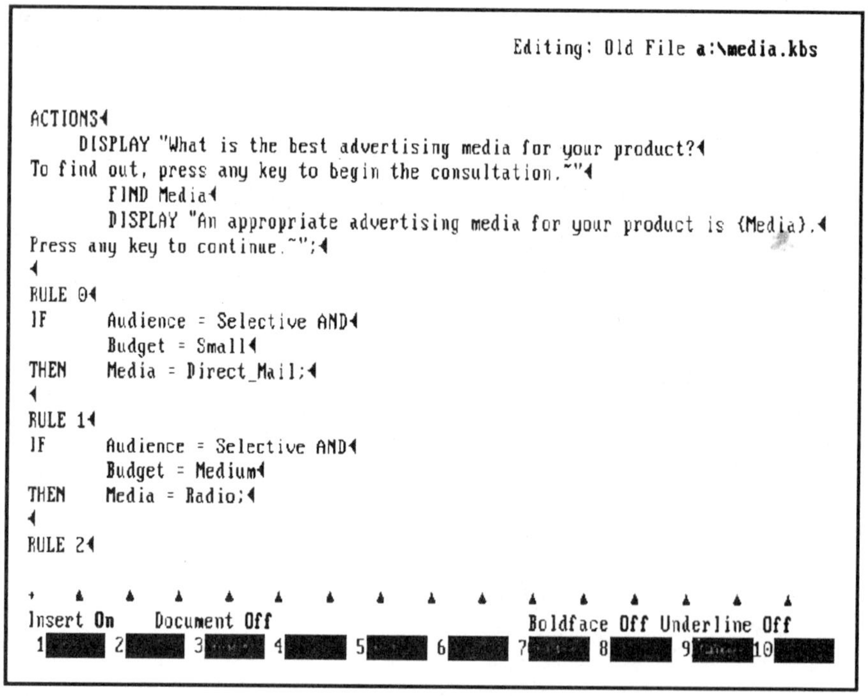

```
                                         Editing: Old File a:\media.kbs

ACTIONS◀
        DISPLAY "What is the best advertising media for your product?◀
To find out, press any key to begin the consultation.~"◀
        FIND Media◀
        DISPLAY "An appropriate advertising media for your product is {Media}.◀
Press any key to continue.~";◀
◀
RULE 0◀
IF      Audience = Selective AND◀
        Budget = Small◀
THEN    Media = Direct_Mail;◀
◀
RULE 1◀
IF      Audience = Selective AND◀
        Budget = Medium◀
THEN    Media = Radio;◀
◀
RULE 2◀


Insert On    Document Off                    Boldface Off Underline Off
   1    2     3     4     5     6     7     8     9    10
```

Chapter 10: Introduction to VP-Expert

Select **Consult**

Select **Go**

Your DISPLAY clause, **"What is the best advertising media for your product? To find out, press any key to begin the consultation"** should appear on the screen.

Press any key

The first consultation question appears.

Highlight **Mass_Market**

Press <Enter>

Press End

The second consultation question appears.

Press <Enter> to select **Small**

Press <Enter>

Press <End>

The second DISPLAY clause appears with the value "Newspaper" inserted in place of {Media}. If you wish, run a few more consultations to see the effect the DISPLAY clauses have. When you are finished, exit from the consultation and return to VP-Expert's Main Menu.

❏ ADDING VARIABLES TO THE KNOWLEDGE BASE

The more variables a knowledge base contains, the greater is the breadth of information the knowledge base can impart. When variables are added to a knowledge base, the original knowledge base has to be edited, ASK and CHOICES statements must be added, and the number of rules increases.

Block commands help to make the process of adding variables to the knowledge base easier. Table 10-4 lists the block commands that can be used with VP-Expert's text editor.

TABLE 10-4 VP-Expert Block Commands

Keys	Function
<Ctrl>-<F3>	Pressing <Ctrl>-<F3> marks the beginning of the block.
<Ctrl>-<F4>	Pressing <Ctrl>-<F4> marks the end of the block.
<Ctrl>-<F7>	Pressing <Ctrl>-<F7> copies a marked block.
<Ctrl>-<F5>	Pressing <Ctrl>-<F5> cancels a marked block.

YOUR TURN

In this exercise you are going to add a variable to the MEDIA knowledge base. Adding the variable is going to double the number of rules.

1. The VP-Expert Main Menu should be on your screen.

Select **Edit**

If necessary, select **Media** as the name of the file you wish to edit. The MEDIA knowledge base appears on your screen.

2. You want to add a variable to the MEDIA knowledge base that allows the end user to identify the stage of the advertising campaign. That is, is this a new product just being introduced, or is it a product that has been on the market for awhile?

> Move the cursor to the very end of the knowledge base
>
> Type: `ASK Stage: "At what stage is the product in its life`
> `cycle?";`
>
> Press <Enter>
>
> Type: `CHOICES Stage: Introduction, Market_Maturity;`

3. Next, you need to edit the rules and add new rules. Move the cursor to Rule 0. Currently, Rule 0 states:

RULE 0

IF

> **Audience = Selective AND**
>
> **Budget = Small**

THEN Media=Direct_Mail

You need to add a condition for the Stage variable. Move the cursor so that it is on the triangle following the word **Small** in Rule 0.

> Press the Space Bar once
>
> Type: `AND`
>
> Press <Ctrl>-<Enter>

The cursor should move into a blank line of space created by pressing <Ctrl>-<Enter>.

> Press <Right arrow> until the cursor is beneath the **B** in **Budget**
>
> Type: `Stage = Introduction`

Your screen should look like Figure 10-8.

4. Next, edit RULE 0.

> Move the cursor to the **D** in **Direct_Mail**
>
> Press <Ctrl>-<T>
>
> Type: `Circulars;`

Do not forget the semicolon after **Circulars**.

5. Now you want to copy Rule 0 by blocking it.

> Move the cursor to the beginning of the blank line of space between Rule 0 and
> Rule 1
>
> Press <Ctrl>-<Enter> two times to create space

FIGURE 10-8 Adding
Variables to the MEDIA
Knowledge Base

```
                                          Editing: Old File a:\media.kbs


ACTIONS◄
        DISPLAY "What is the best advertising media for your product?◄
To find out, press any key to begin the consultation.~"◄
        FIND Media◄
        DISPLAY "An appropriate advertising media for your product is {Media}.◄
Press any key to continue.~";◄
◄
RULE 0◄
IF      Audience = Selective AND◄
        Budget = Small AND◄
        Stage=Introduction
THEN    Media = Direct_Mail;◄
◄
RULE 1◄
IF      Audience = Selective AND◄
        Budget = Medium◄
THEN    Media = Radio;◄
◄


 ↑  ▲  ▲  ▲  ▲  ▲  ▲  ▲  ▲  ▲  ▲  ▲  ▲  ▲  ▲  ▲
Insert On   Document Off                    Boldface Off Underline Off
  1      2      3      4      5      6      7      8      9      10
```

Move the cursor to the **R** in **Rule 0**

Press <Ctrl>-<F3> to begin marking the block

Move the cursor to the end of Rule 0

All of Rule 0 should be highlighted.

Press <Ctrl>-<F4> to end marking the block

Move the cursor to the beginning of the second line of space beneath the marked block

Press <Ctrl>-<F7> to copy the block

A copy of Rule 0 should appear underneath the original Rule 0.

Press <Ctrl>-<F5> to cancel the block

6. Now you want to edit this rule you just copied. First you must give it a new rule name.

Move the cursor to the triangle following Rule 0 of the copied block

Type: A

Now you want to replace the value **Introduction** with the value **Market_Maturity**.

Move the cursor to the **I** in **Introduction** in Rule 0A

Press <Ctrl>-<T> to delete the word

Type: Market_Maturity

Move the cursor to the **C** in **Circulars** in Rule 0A

Press <Ctrl>-<T>

Type: Direct_Mail;

Do not forget to type the semicolon to end the new RULE 0A

7. You should now be familiar with the editing process. Remember, if you are inserting an entire line, you must press <Ctrl>-<Enter> to insert a blank line of space for the new line. Edit Rule 1 so it looks like the following (the changes you have to make appear in boldface):

```
RULE 1
IF         Audience = Selective AND
           Budget = Medium AND
           Stage = Introduction
THEN       Media = Promotional_Novelties;
```

Create a few lines of blank space after Rule 1 and copy Rule 1. Edit the copy of Rule 1 to look like the following:

```
RULE 1A
IF         Audience = Selective AND
           Budget = Medium AND
           Stage = Market_Maturity
THEN       Media =  Radio;
```

Do not forget the semicolon after Radio.

8. Edit the remainder of the MEDIA knowledge base as follows. Use the Copy function to help you in your editing:

```
RULE 2
IF         Audience = Selective AND
           Budget = Large AND
           STAGE = Introduction
THEN       Media= Monthly_Magazine;

RULE 2A
IF         Audience = Selective AND
           Budget = Large AND
           Stage = Market_Maturity
THEN       Media = Catalogs;

RULE 3
IF         Audience = Mass_Market AND
           Budget= Small AND
           Stage = Introduction
THEN       Media = Local_Newspaper;

RULE 3A
IF         Audience = Mass_Market AND
           Budget = Small AND
           Stage = Market_Maturity
THEN       Media = Bus&Train_Cards;
```

```
RULE 4
IF        Audience = Mass_Market AND
          Budget = Medium AND
          Stage = Introduction
THEN      Media=Outdoor_Billboards;

RULE 4A
IF        Audience = Mass_Market AND
          Budget = Medium AND
          Stage = Market_Maturity
THEN      Media = Weekly_Magazine;

RULE 5
IF        Audience = Mass_Market AND
          Budget = Large AND
          Stage = Introduction
THEN      Media = Television;

RULE 5A
IF        Audience = Mass_Market AND
          Budget = Large AND
          Stage = Market_Maturity
THEN      Media = National_Newspaper;
```

Look over the **MEDIA** knowledge base carefully. Make sure you included a semicolon after each rule. Check for spelling mistakes. When you are satisfied the MEDIA knowledge base has been edited correctly, press <Alt>-<F6> to save it.

9. Run a new consultation to see the changes made by adding the new variables. If you get an error message, read it carefully and correct the error. Run a few consultations with the edited knowledge base. You will notice it takes longer to run the consultation because there is more information the knowledge base has to sort through. When you have finished running consultations, leave the knowledge base and select **Quit** from VP-Expert's Main Menu to exit from the program.

- Expert systems technology, the development of computer software that simulates human problem-solving abilities, is an area of research in the field of artificial intelligence.
- A consultation takes place when an end user accesses information from an expert system.
- The knowledge base of an expert system is made up of the domain knowledge and the rule base.
- The "brain" of an expert system is the inference engine. The inference engine is the component where reasoning is performed.
- Some of the areas in which expert systems are used include law, medicine, engineering, business, geology, financial analysis and tax analysis.
- An induction table is a table that represents examples in the form of rows and columns. VP-Expert's Induce command converts an induction table into a workable knowledge base.
- There are four elements to a knowledge base: The ACTIONS block, rules, statements, and clauses. The ACTIONS block is made up of the key word ACTIONS, clauses, and a semicolon. Rules are made up of the rule name, the rule premise, the rule conclusion, and a semicolon. Statements and clauses are always introduced with a VP-Expert key word.

❏ VP-EXPERT EXERCISES

1. Start the VP-Expert program. The VP-Expert Main Menu should be on the screen. Set the path to A:.

2. You are going to create an expert system to help someone decide what kind of a car to purchase. The end user will be able to specify whether he or she is interested in a small, sporty, or compact car. In addition the end user will specify a price range he or she can afford: under $6,000, between $6,000 and $10,000, or over $10,000. You will create the knowledge base from an induction table.

> Select **Induce**
> Select **Create**
> Type: CAR
> Press <Enter>

A blank editing window appears for you to enter the induction table. Key in the induction table as follows:

```
Style        Cost            Car
Small        Under_8000      Geo_Metro
Small        8000-12000      Ford_Escort
Small        Over_12000      Toyota_Corolla
Sporty       Under_8000      None
Sporty       8000-12000      Pontiac_Fiero
Sporty       Over_12000      Mazda_RX-7
Compact      Under_8000      Dodge_Aries
Compact      8000-12000      Toyota_Camry
Compact      Over_12000      Volkswagen_Quantum
```

Look over your induction table carefully, checking for spelling mistakes. Make sure you included all the necessary underscores between words. When you are ready to save the induction table, press <Alt>-<F6>. At the prompt **Save as "a:\ car.tbl"(Y or N)?** press Y.

3. The Induce Menu should appear on your screen.
   Select **Text**
The prompt **Choose a Text File** appears.
   Select **CARS.TBL**
The prompt **Choose a file** appears.
   Type: CARS.KBS
   Press <Enter>
   Select **Quit**

4. You are now ready to run a consultation. The Induce Menu should be on your screen.
   Select **Consult**
   Select **Go** to begin the consultation
Run a couple of consultations. When you have finished, select **Quit**.

5. Now you want to edit the knowledge base so that it is more user friendly.
   Select **Edit**
The CAR knowledge base appears. Move the cursor to the end of the knowledge base. Edit the two ASK statements to the following:

```
ASK Style: "What style of car do you prefer?";
ASK Cost: "Within which price range would you like the car to
fall?";
```

Next edit the ACTIONS block so that it looks like this:

```
    ACTIONS
    DISPLAY "Interested in buying a new car?
Press any key to help you pick one out.~"
    FIND Car
    DISPLAY "You might consider test driving a {Car}.
    Press any key to continue.~";
```

Save your edited CAR knowledge base and run another consultation to make sure all your changes are correct. When you are sure your knowledge base is working correctly, exit from VP-Expert.

❏ VP-EXPERT PROBLEMS

To complete the following exercises you will need a DOS disk, the VP-Expert 3.0 program disk, and the Student File Disk that comes with this book.

1. Start the VP-Expert program. The VP-Expert Main Menu should be on your screen.

2. On the Student File Disk is a knowledge base named CAREER. It's purpose is to help people select a career in which they might be interested. Run a consultation using the CAREER knowledge base to become familiar with it.

3. Edit the ACTION block to the following. All the DISPLAY clauses must appear exactly as they do here, including where one line ends and the next line begins. For example, in the first DISPLAY clause, press <Ctrl>-<Enter> after typing *"...to enter as a"* in order to insert a blank line and to move the cursor to the next line so you can type, *"career, press any key..."* and so on.

```
ACTIONS
DISPLAY "If you're beginning to consider what field to enter as a
career, press any key to receive some suggestions.~"
FIND job
DISPLAY "You may want to further explore the job occupation of
{job} as a possible career option. Press any key to continue.~";
```

4. Edit the ASK statements as follows:

```
ASK environment: "Is your preference to work in an office, work
outdoors, or work at a job that includes a lot of travel?";
ASK salary: "What is the range of salary you expect to receive?";
```

5. You want to add a variable to the CAREER knowledge base. You want to give the end user the option of selecting law or medicine as an area of interest. This requires extensive editing of the CAREER knowledge base. First add the following ASK and CHOICES statement to the end of the CAREER knowledge base:

```
ASK field: "In which one of the following fields are you
interested?";
CHOICES field: law, medicine;
```

6. Edit the rules in the CAREER knowledge base to look like the following. Use VP-Expert's block commands:

```
RULE 0
IF    environment=office AND
      salary=15000-20000 AND
      field=law
THEN  job=legal_secretary;

RULE 1
IF    environment=office AND
      salary=20000-25000 AND
      field=law
THEN  job=paralegal;

RULE 2
IF    environment=office AND
      salary=25000-30000 AND
      field=law
THEN  job=paralegal;
```

```
RULE 2A
IF    environment=office AND
      salary=15000-20000 AND
      field=medicine
THEN  job=medical_secretary;


RULE 2B
IF    environment=office AND
      salary=20000-25000 AND
      field=medicine
THEN  job=medical_assistant;


RULE 2C
IF    environment=office AND
      salary=25000-30000 AND
      field=medicine
THEN  job=physical_therapist;


RULE 3
IF    environment=outdoors AND
      salary=15000-20000 AND
      field=law
THEN  job=security_guard;


RULE 4
IF    environment=outdoors AND
      salary=20000-25000 AND
      field=law
THEN  job=park_ranger;


RULE 5
IF    environment=outdoors AND
      salary=25000-30000 AND
      field=law
THEN  job=conservationist;


RULE 5A
IF    environment=outdoors AND
      salary=15000-20000 AND
      field=medicine
THEN  job=emergency_medical_technician;
```

```
RULE 5B
IF    environment=outdoors AND
      salary=25000-30000 AND
      field=medicine
THEN  job=zoologist;


RULE 5C
IF    environment=outdoors AND
      salary=25000-30000 AND
      field=medicine
THEN  job=veterinarian;


RULE 6
IF    environment=travel AND
      salary=15000-20000 AND
      field=law
THEN  job=reporter;


RULE 7
IF    environment=travel AND
      salary=20000-25000 AND
      field=law
THEN  job=labor_relations_specialist;


RULE 8
IF    environment=travel AND
      salary=25000-30000 AND
      field=law
THEN  job=attorney;


RULE 8A
IF    environment=travel AND
      salary=15000-20000 AND
      field=medicine
THEN  job=medicine;


RULE 8B
IF    environment=travel AND
      salary=20000-25000 AND
      field=medicine
THEN  job=speech_pathologist;
```

```
RULE 8C
IF     environment=travel AND
       salary=20000-25000 AND
       field=medicine
THEN   job=hospital_administration;
```

7. When you have finished keying in the changes to the knowledge base, proofread your knowledge base carefully. Check for spelling mistakes. Check to make sure there is a semicolon at the end of each rule. Check to make sure all the necessary underscores between words are keyed in. After proofreading the knowledge base, correct any mistakes you find. When your consultation runs without any problems, exit from VP-Expert.

CHAPTER 11

More VP-Expert Features

OUTLINE

❑ INTRODUCTION

In Chapter 10, you learned the basics of creating an expert system by using an induction table. This chapter introduces VP-Expert's more advanced capabilities, such as computing the confidence factor and using mathematical calculations in a knowledge base. In addition, you will be introduced to more formatting commands that enable you to create a professional looking, user-friendly consultation.

❑ USING CONFIDENCE FACTORS

In VP-Expert, confidence factors are numbers that indicate the level of certainty of a value. These numbers can be input into the knowledge base itself. That is, the developer can assign a confidence factor to the conclusion drawn by a rule. For example, in the following rule

RULE 1

IF   climate=humid AND

        moisture=high

THEN   crop=rice CNF 80;

The number 80 indicates that this conclusion was drawn with 80% certainty. The letters *CNF* are used to identify the confidence factor in the rule.

Confidence factors can also be entered by the end user during a consultation. That is, the end user can input his or her level of certainty in an answer being provided during a consultation. To enter a confidence factor during a consultation, highlight the option to be selected, press <Home>, enter a number between 0 and 100 as a confidence factor, press <Enter>, and press <End>.

If the end user enters a confidence factor of less than 50, that selection is negated. VP-Expert includes a truth threshold which requires the confidence factor to be above a certain number in order for the rule to evaluate as true. The default setting for the truth threshold is 50. If no confidence factor is entered by the end user, VP-Expert assumes the confidence factor is 100%.

 YOUR TURN

In the hands-on exercises in this section you will be creating a knowledge base to help businesses decide on an appropriate area of the country to relocate, based upon criteria such as climate, health care, and available transportation. In this exercise you are going to begin the knowledge base by entering an induction table.

1.   Turn on the computer and start the VP-Expert program. Make sure your data disk is in drive A. The VP-Expert Main Menu should be on your screen.

> **Difference box:** On a system with two floopy disk drives, place your data disk in drive B. Select **Path**, type B: and press <Enter>. Use these directions for changing the path to B: throughout this chapter.

Select **Path**

Type: A:

Press <Enter>

Select **Induce**

Select **Create**

The prompt **Choose a text File** appears.

Type: Locate

Press <Enter>

2. You are now ready to type the induction table. To begin, you are going to enter data concerning climate, housing, and health care. When a consultation is run, the end user will be able to identify if a warm or cool climate is preferred; if housing costs in the area run between $75,000-$125,000 or between $125,000-$175,000; and, if the number of hospitals and physicians in the area is a primary concern. Based on the user input, the expert system suggests an area for relocation.

Carefully enter the following:

Climate	Housing	Health	Location
Warm	$75000-125000	Yes	Albuquerque_NM
Warm	$75000-125000	No	Winter_Haven_FL
Warm	$125000-175000	Yes	Portland_OR
Warm	$125000-175000	No	Austin_TX
Cool	$75000-125000	Yes	St_Louis_MO
Cool	$75000-125000	No	Pittsfield_MA
Cool	$125000-175000	Yes	Minneapolis_MN
Cool	$125000-175000	No	Billings_MT

FIGURE 11-1 Entering the Location Induction Table

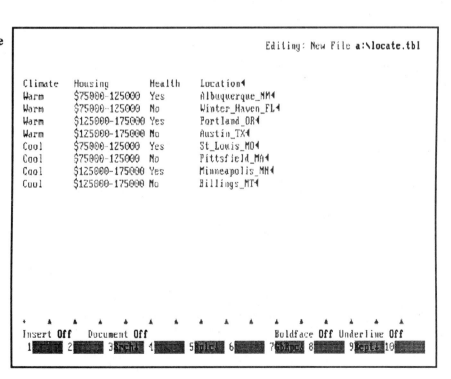

When you have finished, your screen should look like Figure 11-1. Look over your induction table carefully. Check for spelling mistakes. Make sure there is an underscore between words wherever necessary. When you are certain the induction table is entered correctly, press <Alt>-<F6> to save it. The prompt **Save as "a:\locate.tbl" (Y or N)?** appears.

> Press Y

Difference Box: If you are using a system with two floppy disk drives, the prompt will read **Save as "b:\locate.tbl" Y or N)?**

---

3. Next you want to create the knowledge base from the induction table you just created and then run a consultation to make sure there are no errors.

> Select **Text**

The prompt **Choose a Text File** appears.

> Select **LOCATE**

The prompt **Choose a file** appears.

> Type: LOCATE.KBS
>
> Select **Quit**

When the VP-Expert Main menu appears, you are ready to run a consultation.

> Select **FileName**
>
> Select **LOCATE.KBS**
>
> Select **Consult**
>
> Select **Go**

If you get an error message, correct your error. Run a few consultations to make sure the system is working properly.

4. Next, you want to edit the knowledge base.

> Select **Quit** to exit from the consultation
>
> Select **Edit**

The LOCATE knowledge base appears on the screen. Edit the ACTIONS block so it appears exactly as it does here. Press <Ctrl>-<Enter> at the end of each line to move the cursor to the next line of space.

```
ACTIONS
DISPLAY "This relocation planner will help you to select an
appropriate location for your company based upon your specific
requirements. Press any key to begin the consultation.~"
FIND Location
DISPLAY "You should consider {Location} as a location for your
company. Press any key to continue.~";
```

5. Edit the ASK and CHOICES statements at the end of the knowledge base so they appear exactly as they do here. Press <Ctrl>-<Enter> at the end of each line to move the cursor to the next line of space.

```
ASK Climate: "Would you like your company to be located in a
warm climate or a cool climate?";
CHOICES Climate: Warm, Cool;
ASK Housing: "Would you prefer that the cost of housing in the area
be between $75,000 and $125,000 or between $125,000 and $175,000?";
CHOICES Housing: $75000-125000, $125000-175000;
ASK Health: "Is the number of health care facilities and physicians
in the area a prime consideration in your location selection?";
CHOICES Health: Yes, No;
```

When you have finished editing the knowledge base, save it and run another consultation to make sure there are no errors.

6. Next, enter confidence factors. In order to do this, you must edit the knowledge base in two ways. You must enter a confidence factor next to each city, and enter instructions to the end user on how to enter confidence factors. Exit from the consultation and access the LOCATE knowledge base. Edit the ACTIONS block to look like the following (boldface type indicates the changes). Remember to press <Ctrl>-<Enter> at the end of each line.

```
ACTIONS
DISPLAY "This relocation planner will help you to select an
appropriate location for you company based upon your specific
requirements. Press any key to begin the consultation.~"
DISPLAY "If you wish, for each question asked during the
consultation you can enter your degree of certainty in your answer.
For example, entering 80 would indicate you are 80% confident in
your response to the question. To enter your confidence level, move
the highlighting to your selection, press the HOME key, type a
number between 0 and 100, press ENTER and press END. If you do not
enter a number, the system assumes you are 100% confident in your
response. Press any key to continue with this consultation.~"
FIND Location
DISPLAY "You should consider {Location} as a location for your
company.";
```

7. Next, add confidence factors into the knowledge base itself. In each of the rule's THEN statements add *CNF 90;* at the end of the statement. For example, the THEN statement in RULE 0 should be edited to look like the following (boldface text indicates the change):

```
THEN Location=Albuquerque_NM CNF 90;
```

In other words, enter a confidence factor of 90 by each of the cities in the knowledge base. Be sure to leave a space between the state and "CNF" and between "CNF" and "90;".

8. Finally, you want to edit the knowledge base so that the final confidence factor is displayed. The final confidence factor takes into consideration the confidence factor the user enters together with the confidence factor already in the knowledge base next to each city. In order for the final confidence factor to be displayed, edit the third DISPLAY statement in the knowledge base as follows (boldface text indicates the change):

```
DISPLAY "You should consider {# Location} as a location for your
company.";
```

When a consultation is run, the confidence factor will display in place of the number symbol. Save the edited knowledge base and run a few consultations to make sure the program is working properly. Be sure to enter confidence factors as you run the consultations. Notice how the confidence factors entered by the end user affect the final confidence factor that is displayed at the end of the consultation. After running a few consultations, exit from the consultation and return to VP-Expert's Main menu.

❑ ASSIGNING MULTIPLE VALUES TO A VARIABLE

In the knowledge bases you have created so far, all the variables have been assigned only one value. During a consultation, a user can select more than one option by moving the highlighting to his or her first choice, pressing <Enter>, moving the highlighting to the second choice, pressing <Enter>, and finally pressing <End>. That is, the user can make as many selections as desired by highlighting the choice and pressing <Enter>. The selection process is not ended until the <End> key is pressed.

If a variable is going to be assigned more than one value, that variable has to be designated as a plural variable in the knowledge base. A PLURAL statement in the knowledge base enables a variable to be assigned more than one value. In the following example,

ASK Season: "During what season will you be planting?";
CHOICES Season: Fall, Winter, Spring, Summer;
PLURAL: Season;

the PLURAL statement makes it possible for the end user to select more than one season.

❑ USING THE LOGICAL OPERATOR OR

In addition to the keyword AND, the keyword OR is used to combine conditions in a rule. If a rule contains the logical operator OR, either one or the other of the conditions must be true in order for the rule to evaluate as true. Look over the following example:

RULE 1
IF soil_temp >= 45 AND
    season = spring OR
    season = fall OR
    rainfall = 2
THEN planting = okay;

To translate this rule, if the soil temperature is greater than or equal to 45 degrees *and* either the season is spring *or* the season is fall *or* rainfall is equal to 2 inches, then planting is equal to okay. That is, in order for this rule to evaluate as true, both the soil temperature has to be equal to or greater than 45 and one of the following three statements (season = spring; season = fall; rainfall = 2) have to be true.

Sometimes it helps to understand rules that use both the AND and OR logical operators to imagine a set of parentheses surrounding the expressions separated by OR. To use the rule above as an example:

RULE 1
IF   soil_temp >= 45 AND
     (season = spring OR
     season = fall OR
     rainfall = 2)
THEN   planting = okay;

This helps you to visualize the necessary requirements for the rule to pass as true—that is, the first condition must be true and at least one of the following conditions must be true. Do not use parentheses when creating your knowledge base, however, as this will result in a syntax error.

YOUR TURN

In this exercise you are going to introduce another variable, transportation, into the LOCATE knowledge base. The transportation variable is going to be defined as plural so the end user can select more than one option. The VP-Expert program should be loaded, the path should be set to A:, the LOCATE knowledge base should be active, and the Main Menu should be on your screen.

1. The first step is to edit the existing LOCATE knowledge base.

        Select **Edit**

The LOCATE knowledge base should appear on your screen. It is a good idea to copy the LOCATE knowledge base and work with the copy in case you make some mistakes and want to start over with this Your Turn exercise. Do the following to make a copy of the LOCATE knowledge base:

        Press <Alt>-<F6> to save the LOCATE knowledge base

The prompt **Save as "locate.kbs" (Y or N)** appears.

        Press N for no

The prompt **Please enter the file where you want to save your text** appears.

        Type: a:\Locate2
        Press <Enter>

Difference Box: If you are using a computer with two floppy disk drives, type `b:\Locate2` and press <Enter>.

Now you want to access your backup copy of the LOCATE knowledge base.

> Select **Quit**
> Select **FileName**
> Select **Locate2.KBS**
> Select **Edit**

The LOCATE2 knowledge base should appear on your screen. Check the upper right corner to make sure the file name says **locate2.** You are now ready to edit the knowledge base.

2. Move the cursor to the end of the knowledge base. Add the following statements at the very end of the knowledge base (remember to press <Ctrl>-<Enter> at the end of each line):

```
ASK Transportation: "Which of the following modes of transportation
need to be readily accessible? Up to three options can be
selected.";
CHOICES: Transportation: Public, Air, Amtrack;
PLURAL: Transportation;
```

3. Next, each of the rules have to be edited to account for the new variable. In editing the rules, you are going to use the logical operator OR. Edit Rule 0 to look like the following (boldface text indicates the changes):

```
RULE 0
IF    Climate = Warm AND
      Housing = $750000-125000 AND
      Health = Yes AND
      Transportation = Public OR
      Transportation = Air OR
      Transportation = Amtrack
THEN  Location = Albuquerque-NM CNF 90;
```

4. Next you are going to block from Rule 0 the new lines pertaining to the transportation variable and copy them into all the remaining rules in the knowledge base. To begin, place the cursor on the A in AND in the line **Health = Yes AND** in Rule 0.

> Press <Ctrl>-<F3> to start the block
> Move the cursor to the triangle following the *k* in *Amtrack*
> Press <Ctrl>-<F4> to end the block

Your screen should look like Figure 11-2. Move the cursor so that it is on the triangle following the line **Health = No** in Rule 1.

> Press the Space Bar once
> Press <Ctrl>-<F7> to copy the block

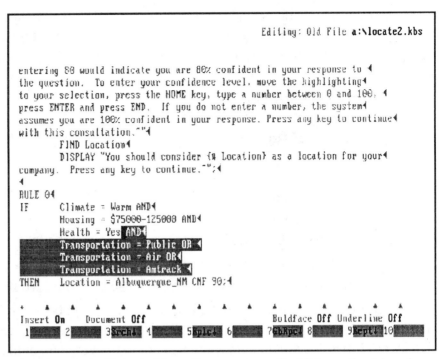

FIGURE 11-2 Copying a Block in the LOCATE2 Knowledge Base

entering 80 would indicate you are 80% confident in your response to ◄
the question. To enter your confidence level, move the highlighting◄
to your selection, press the HOME key, type a number between 0 and 100, ◄
press ENTER and press END. If you do not enter a number, the system◄
assumes you are 100% confident in your response. Press any key to continue◄
with this consultation."◄
    FIND Location◄
    DISPLAY "You should consider {# Location} as a location for your◄
company. Press any key to continue.";◄
◄
RULE 0◄
IF   Climate = Warm AND◄
      Housing = $75000-125000 AND◄
      Health = Yes AND◄
      Transportation = Public OR ◄
      Transportation = Air OR◄
      Transportation = Amtrack ◄
THEN   Location = Albuquerque_NM CNF 90;◄

Insert **On**   Document **Off**   Boldface **Off** Underline **Off**
 1   2   3   4   5   6   7   8   9   10

The transportation block now appears in Rule 1. Move the cursor so that it is on the triangle following the line **Health = Yes** in Rule 2.

> Press the Space Bar once
>
> Press <Ctrl>-<F7> to copy the block

The transportation block now appears in Rule 2. Continue copying this block into Rules 3 through 7. When this new segment of text is properly inserted into all the rules, press <Ctrl>-<F5> to cancel the block.

5.   Not all of the cities have Amtrack service, so further editing is needed. Move the cursor to Rule 3. Austin, Texas, does not have Amtrack service. First, you are going to insert a new rule that provides for a city that does have Amtrack service. Block Rule 3 and copy it so that it comes immediately before Rule 4. Edit the new Rule 3 so that it looks like the following:

```
RULE 3A
IF    Climate = Warm AND
      Housing = $75000-125000 AND
      Health = No AND
      Transportation = Public OR
      Transportation = Air OR
      Transportation = Amtrack
THEN  Location = Charlottesville- VA CNF 90;
```

After editing the new Rule 3A, go back to Rule 3 and make the following changes:

> Delete the entire line that reads **Transportation = Amtrack**
>
> Delete the word **OR** from the line that reads **Transportation = Air OR**

6. Billings, Montana, does not have Amtrack service. Move the cursor to RULE 7. Insert a new rule that provides for a city that does have Amtrack service by blocking Rule 7 and copying it so that it follows the original Rule 7. Edit the new Rule 7 to look like the following:

```
RULE 7A
IF    Climate = Cool AND
      Housing = $75000-125000 AND
      Health = No AND
      Transportation = Public OR
      Transportation = Air OR
      Transportation = Amtrack
THEN  Location=Provo_UT CNF 90;
```

After editing the new Rule 7A, go back to Rule 7 and make the following changes:

> Delete the entire line that reads **Transportation = Amtrack**

> Delete the word OR from the line that reads **Transportation = Air OR**

7. The changes you just made to the LOCATE knowledge base made it possible for more than one city to meet the end user's specifications; therefore, you have to insert another variable in the PLURAL statement. Move the cursor to the very end of the knowledge base. Edit the PLURAL statement as follows:

```
PLURAL: Transportation, Location;
```

8. Save the edited knowledge base and run a consultation. If you get an error message, figure out your mistake and fix it. Use the Summary of Common VP-Expert Error Messages at the end of this chapter to help you. Once you have corrected all errors, run a few consultations. Be sure to try out **all** the options. That is, enter confidence factors and select more than one mode of transportation. Remember, the way to select more than one option is to move the highlighting to your first selection, press <Enter>, move the highlighting to the next selection, press <Enter> and so on. When all the options have been selected, press <End>. If more than one city meets the criterion, they both will be listed in the final clause. After running several consultations, select **Quit.** The VP-Expert Main Menu returns to the screen.

❏ USING THE WHY? AND HOW? COMMANDS

At any point in a consultation being performed with VP-Expert, the end user can select the Why? or How? command to find out why a certain question is being asked or how a particular value was determined. To use the Why? and How? commands during a consultation, when a prompt appears asking the end user to make a selection, press the slash key </>. The Go Menu then appears at the bottom of the screen. Select **Why?** to find out why that particular question is being asked. One of two things will happen. Either the rule that caused that question to be asked is displayed, or text is displayed that explains why the question is being asked. In order for text to be displayed, BECAUSE text has to be included in the knowledge base. If there is no BECAUSE text in the knowledge base, then the rule that caused the question to be asked is displayed.

Adding a BECAUSE Statement to a Knowledge Base

In order for explanatory text to appear in response to the Why? command, BECAUSE text has to be added to the rules. BECAUSE text must come at the end of the rule, and it must end with a semicolon. The text that is to appear during the consultation has to be enclosed in quotation marks. The following example illustrates how BECAUSE text is incorporated into a rule:

RULE 1
IF   soil_temp >= 45 AND
     season = spring OR
     season = fall OR
     rainfall = 2
THEN   planting = okay

BECAUSE "The soil temperature, season, and amount of rainfall are needed to determine whether or not planting is appropriate.";

 YOUR TURN

In this exercise you are going to use the Why? command without BECAUSE text in the LOCATE knowledge base. Then, you will add BECAUSE text to each of the rules.

1.   The VP-Expert Main Menu should be on your screen, the path should be set to A:, and the LOCATE2.kbs file should be active.

> Select **Consult**
>
> Select **Go**

Begin the consultation, pressing any key as necessary. The first prompt, **Would you like your company to be located In a warm climate or a cool climate?** appears.

> Press the slash key </> to access the Go Menu
>
> Select **Why?**

Your screen should look like Figure 11-3. Since there is no BECAUSE text, the rule that caused the prompt to appear is displayed in a box in the center of the screen.

2.   Next, you are going to use the How? command. The prompt **Would you like your company to be located in a warm climate or a cool climate?** should still be active.

> Select **Warm**

The housing prompt appears.

> Select **$75000-125000**

The health care facilities prompt appears.

> Select **No**

You now want to use the How? command.

**FIGURE 11-3 Using the
Why? Command**

```
you can enter your degree of certainty in your answer.  For example,
entering 80 would indicate you are 80% confident in your response to
the question.  To enter your confidence level, move the highlighting
to your selection, press the HOME key, type a number between 0 and 100,
press ENTER and press END.  If you do not enter a number, the system
assumes you are 100% confident in your response. Press any key to continue
with this consultation.
Would you like your company to be located in a-
                              -[ WHY ]-
RULE 0 IF
Climate = Warm AND
Housing = $75000-125000 AND
Health = Yes AND
Transportation = Public OR
Transportation = Air OR
Transportation = Amtrack
THEN
Location = Albuquerque_NM CNF 90

(Press Any Key To Continue)


1Help     2How?      3Why?      4Slow     5Fast      6Quit
Ask why a question was asked
```

Press the slash key </>

The highlighting is already on **How?**

Press <Enter>

You have to select **How?** by pressing <Enter>. If you try to select it by typing **H** for **How,** you will get the Help Menu. Your screen should look like Figure 11-4.The purpose of the How? command is to tell the end user how a value was assigned to a variable. The prompt that appears is asking the end user to indicate which variable he or she wants to know about.

Press <Right arrow> to highlight **Housing**

Press <Enter>

The prompt that appears states:

Housing was set because:

You said so.

(Press any key to continue)

That is, the end user selected the value for the housing variable. If the value had been assigned in a rule, the rule would have appeared. In the LOCATE2 knowledge base, all the values are determined by the end user, so this same prompt would appear no matter which variable was selected. The How? command is only available during a consultation. That is, you can never execute the How? command after an option for the final prompt has been made, because at that point, VP-Expert finds a value for the goal variable and the consultation is ended. For example, you cannot use the How? command in a consultation using the LOCATE2 knowledge base after selecting options to the modes of transportation prompt.

Press any key and complete the consultation

FIGURE 11-4 Using the
How? Command

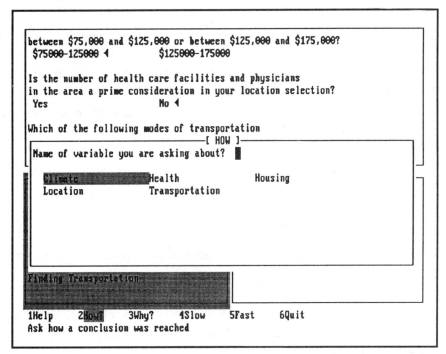

3. Now you want to add BECAUSE text to the LOCATE2 knowledge base. Quit the consultation and select **Edit.** The LOCATE2 knowledge base appears on your screen. Edit Rule 0 to look like the following (boldface text indicates the changes). Remember to press <Ctrl>-<Enter> at the end of each line when entering the BECAUSE text:

```
RULE 0
IF   Climate = Warm AND
     Housing = $75000-125000 AND
     Health = Yes AND
     Transportation = Public OR
     Transportation = Air OR
     Transportation=Amtrack
THEN Location = Albuquerque-NM CNF 90
```

BECAUSE "Your preference in climate, cost of housing, number of
health care facilities, and types of transportation are needed to
help determine a location site.";

Do not forget to delete the semicolon after the THEN clause and insert the new semicolon after the BECAUSE text.

4. Block the BECAUSE text and copy it into its proper location in all of the rules. Again, do not forget to delete the semicolon at the end of the THEN clauses. When the BECAUSE text has been copied into all of the rules, save the edited LOCATE2 knowledge base. Run a consultation. If an error message appears, fix your mistake. During the consultation, be sure to select the Why? command to see the results. When you have finished, quit the consultation. The VP-Expert Main Menu appears on your screen.

You may have noticed by now that the consultation screen seems slightly crowded. In addition, the constant display of the inference engine in the rules window can be distracting. To an end user who has no interest in the workings of the inference engine, it can be confusing. The CLS clause and the RUNTIME statement are VP-Expert commands that help make a consultation a little more user friendly.

Using the CLS Clause

The purpose of the CLS clause is to clear the consultation window so that DISPLAY text does not build up on the screen. CLS is inserted in the knowledge base at the point where the screen is to be cleared. The following example illustrates how the CLS clause can be used:

```
ACTIONS
DISPLAY "The purpose of this consultation is to help you determine the appropriateness of planting
various crops. Press any key to continue.~"
CLS
DISPLAY "A series of questions will follow. To make a selection, highlight your choice using the arrow
keys, press <Enter>, and then press <End>. To continue with this consultation, press any key.~"
CLS
DISPLAY "......
```

The CLS clauses in this example clear the screen of each DISPLAY text before the next DISPLAY text appears.

Using The RUNTIME Statement

The purpose of the RUNTIME statement is to eliminate the rules and results windows from the screen during a consultation. The following example illustrates how the RUNTIME statement can be used:

```
RUNTIME;
EXECUTE;
ACTIONS

DISPLAY "The purpose of this consultation is to help you determine the appropriateness of planting
various crops. Press any key to continue.~"
```

In this example, when a consultation is run, the only thing that will appear on the screen is the DISPLAY text. A RUNTIME statement can appear anywhere within the knowledge base.

 YOUR TURN

In this exercise you are going to edit the LOCATE2 knowledge base by inserting two CLS clauses and a RUNTIME statement. If necessary, start the VP-Expert program, change the path to A:, and load the LOCATE2 knowledge base.

1.   The VP-Expert Main Menu should be on your screen.

Select **Edit**

The LOCATE2 knowledge base should appear on your screen. Edit the beginning of the knowledge base so that it looks like the following (boldface text indicates the changes):

```
RUNTIME;
ACTIONS
DISPLAY "This relocation planner will help you to select an
appropriate location for your company based upon your specific
requirements. Press any key to begin the consultation.~"
CLS
DISPLAY "If you wish, for each question asked during the
consultation you can enter your degree of certainty in your answer.
For example, entering 80 would indicate you are 80% confident in
your response to the question. To enter your confidence level, move
the highlighting to your selection, press the HOME key, type a
number between 0 and 100, press RETURN and press END. If you do not
enter a number, the system assumes you are 100% confident in your
response. Press any key to continue with this consultation.~"
CLS
FIND LOCATION
```

Save the edited LOCATE2 knowledge base

2. You now want to run a consultation to see the effect of the changes.

Select **Consult**

Select **Go**

If an error message appears, fix your mistake. Once your additions have been made correctly, your screen should look like Figure11-5. The results window and rules window are no longer displayed.

Press any key

The first DISPLAY text disappears and the second DISPLAY text appears.

Press any key

The climate prompt is displayed. Complete the consultation. To run another consultation, the end user would select **Go**. Press Quit to return to VP-Expert's Main Menu.

❑ PRINTING A HARD COPY OF DISPLAY TEXT

In some cases it would be useful to the end user for a hard copy of certain text that is displayed during a consultation to be printed. The PRINTON and PRINTOFF clauses together with the EJECT clause enable the developer of the knowledge base to indicate text that should be printed during the run of a consultation.

FIGURE 11-5 Running a
User-Friendly Consultation

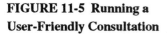

```
This relocation planner will help you to select an appropriate
location for your company based upon your specific requirements. Press
any key to begin the consultation.
```

Using the PRINTON and PRINTOFF Clauses

The PRINTON and PRINTOFF clauses are used in conjunction with DISPLAY clauses. Their purpose is to enable the DISPLAY text to be not only displayed on the screen, but sent to the printer as well. The following example illustrates how the PRINTON and PRINTOFF clauses can be used.

```
ACTIONS
DISPLAY "The purpose of this consultation is to help you determine the appropriateness of planting
various crops. Press any key to continue.~"
CLS
DISPLAY "A series of questions will follow. To make a selection, highlight your choice using the arrow
keys, press <Enter>, and then press <End>. To continue with this consultation, press any key.~"
CLS
FIND Crop
PRINTON
DISPLAY "You should consider {crop} as an appropriate crop to plant."
PRINTOFF;
```

In this example, during the consultation the text in the first two DISPLAY clauses will not print because they are not included within the PRINTON and PRINTOFF clauses. However, the text to the third DISPLAY clause will be both displayed on the screen and printed. In order for the PRINTON and PRINTOFF clauses to work, the computer has to be hooked up to a printer and the printer has to be loaded with paper and be online during the consultation.

Using the EJECT Clause

The EJECT clause is used with a DISPLAY clause. The purpose of the EJECT clause is to tell the printer to eject the remainder of the current page and go to the top of the next page. The EJECT clause is only necessary if the PRINTON and PRINTOFF clauses are being used. The following example illustrates how the EJECT clause can be used.

PRINTON
DISPLAY "You should consider {crop} as an appropriate crop to plant.";
PRINTOFF
EJECT

In this example, the EJECT clause causes the printer to eject the page upon which "You should consider . . ." was printed and move the printer head to the top of the next page. The clause is useful only with continuous-feed paper.

 YOUR TURN

In this exercise you are going to insert PRINTON, PRINTOFF, and EJECT clauses into the LOCATE2 knowledge base. Before you start this exercise, make sure the computer you are using is connected to a printer and that the printer is loaded with paper and is online.

1.   The VP-Expert Main Menu should be on your screen. The LOCATE2 knowledge base should be active.

        Select **Edit**

The LOCATE2 knowledge base appears. Edit the ACTIONS block so it looks like the following (boldface text indicates the changes):

```
FIND LOCATION
```
PRINTON
```
DISPLAY "You should consider {#Location} as a location for your
company. Press any key to continue.~"
```
PRINTOFF

EJECT;
```
RULE 0
```

Since the PRINTOFF and EJECT clauses are being added at the end of the ACTIONS block, the semicolon has to be deleted from the end of the DISPLAY text, which was the original end of the ACTIONS block, and inserted following EJECT, which is the new end of the ACTIONS block. Save the edited LOCATE2 knowledge base.

2.   Run a consultation. The text in the final DISPLAY clause should both appear on the screen and print out on the printer. Select Quit to return to the Main Menu.

❏ USING MATHEMATICAL OPERATIONS

There are two ways in which mathematical operations can be used in a knowledge base. First, they can be used to indicate a value in a rule condition. For example, in the following rule

RULE 1

IF   total_rainfall <= (.1 * average_rainfall)

THEN   conditions = drought

if the value for the total_rainfall variable is less than or equal to the value of the average_rainfall variable multiplied by .1, then the value for the conditions variable equals drought.

The second way mathematical operations can be used is to assign a value to a variable. For example, if the following rule passes

RULE 1

IF   crop = corn

THEN   herbicide = (acres * 5)

then five times the value of the acres variable is assigned to the herbicide variable.

VP-Expert uses the following symbols to represent mathematical operations:

- +   Addition
- -   Subtraction
- *   Multiplication
- /   Division

The math operations must be enclosed in parentheses. Notice in the above two examples, (.1 * average_rainfall) and (acres * 5) are enclosed by parentheses.

❏ ASSIGNING VALUES TO VARIABLES WITH END USER INPUT

In all the examples used so far, values for variables were assigned by having the end user select an option or options provided in a menu. Instead of selecting an option from a menu, it is possible for the end user to key in the answer to a prompt. If the end user is to key in a response to a prompt, the ASK statement that generates that prompt does not have a corresponding CHOICES statement. When the end user keys in his or her response and presses <Enter>, the entry made by the end user is assigned as the value for the variable in the ASK statement.

YOUR TURN

In this exercise you are going to create a new knowledge base called TAXES that can be used in conjunction with the LOCATE2 knowledge base. The purpose of the TAXES knowledge base is to compute the local taxes for any of the locations included in the LOCATE2 knowledge base. In creating the TAXES knowledge base you will use a mathematical operator, and you will have the end user input a response to a prompt.

1. The VP-Expert Main Menu should be on your screen. The path should be set for A: and the LOCATE2 knowledge base should be active. This time, you are going to enter the knowledge base directly rather than using an induction table.

> Select **FileName**
>
> Type: Taxes
>
> Press <Enter>
>
> Select **Edit**

A blank text editing window appears. Key in the TAXES knowledge base as follows. Remember to press <Ctrl>-<Enter> at the end of each line:

```
RUNTIME;
ACTIONS
DISPLAY "This consultation is to be used in conjunction with the
relocation planner. Its purpose is to compute the local taxes for
the location identified by the relocation planner. Press any key to
begin the consultation.~"
CLS
FIND Taxes
DISPLAY "The taxes taken out of this salary would amount to {Taxes}.
Press any key to continue~";

RULE 0
IF    Location = Albuquerque_NM OR
      Location = Winter_Haven_FL OR
      Location = Austin_TX AND
      Salary>0
THEN  Taxes=(Salary * .01);

RULE 1
IF    Location = St_Louis_MO OR
      Location = Billings_MT AND
      Salary>0
THEN  Taxes=(Salary * .03);

RULE 2
IF    Location = Charlottesville_VA OR
      Location = Pittsfield_MA AND
      Salary>0
THEN  Taxes=(Salary * .04);
```

```
RULE 3
IF     Location = Portland_OR OR
       Location = Minneapolis_MN OR
       Location = Provo_UT AND
       Salary>O
THEN Taxes = (Salary * .05);
```

ASK Location: "For which one of the following locations would you like to compute the local taxes?";
CHOICES Location: Albuquerque_NM, Winter_Haven-FL, Portland_OR, Austin_TX, Charlottesville_VA, St_Louis_MO, Pittsfield_MA, Minneapolis_MN, Provo_UT, Billings_MT;
ASK Salary: "Enter the salary upon which the tax computation should be based. Do not use a dollar sign or commas. For example, type 25000 for a $25,000 salary. Type the salary, press RETURN.";

Read over your knowledge base carefully. When you think it is entered correctly, save the TAXES knowledge base.

2. Run a consultation. If there are any errors, find your mistakes and fix them. Run several consultations to make sure the program works properly. When you are sure the program works, exit from VP-Expert.

❏ SUMMARY POINTS

- A confidence factor is a number that indicates the level of certainty of a value.
- During a consultation, a variable can be assigned more than one value if an appropriate PLURAL statement is included in the knowledge base.
- If a rule contains the logical operator OR, either one or the other of the conditions connected by the OR operator must be true in order for the rule to pass.
- The Why? command enables the end user to find out why a particular question is being asked. The How? command enables the end user to find out how a particular value was determined.
- The CLS clause clears the consultation window during a consultation. The RUNTIME statement deletes the rules window and the results window from the screen during a consultation.
- The PRINTON and PRINTOFF clauses enable designated DISPLAY text to be printed as well as displayed on the screen.
- The mathematical operations of addition (+), subtraction (-), multiplication (*), and division (/) can be included in a knowledge base.

❏ SUMMARY OF VP-EXPERT KEY WORDS

@ABS	BECAUSE	FORMAT	RECEIVE
@ACOS	BKCOLOR	GET	RECORD_NUM
@ASIN	CALL	IF	RESET
@ATAN	CCALL	INDEX	ROW
@COS	CHAIN	LOADFACTS	RULE
@EXP	CHOICES	MENU	RUNTIME
@LOG	CLOSE	MENU_SIZE	SAVEFACTS
@SIN	CLS	MRESET	SHIP
@SQT	COLOR	NAMED	SHOWTEXT
@TAN	COLUMN	OR	SORT
ACTIONS	DISPLAY	PDISPLAY	THEN
ALL	EJECT	PLURAL	TRUTHTHRESH
AND	ELSE	POP	UNKNOWN
APPEND	END	PRINTOFF	WHILEKNOWN
ASK	ENDOFF	PRINTON	WKS
AUTOQUERY	EXECUTE	PUT	WORKON
BCALL	FIND	PWKS	

❏ SUMMARY OF VP-EXPERT STATEMENTS

ACTIONS	BKCOLOR	EXECUTE	RUNTIME
ASK	CHOICES	PLURAL	
AUTOQUERY	ENDOFF	RULE	

❏ SUMMARY OF VP-EXPERT CLAUSES

APPEND	EJECT	PDISPLAY	SAVEFACTS
BCALL	END	POP	SHIP
CALL	FIND	PRINTOFF	SHOWTEXT
CCALL	FORMAT	PRINTON	SORT
CHAIN	GET	PUT	TRUTHTHRESH
CLOSE	INDEX	PWKS	WHILEKNOWN
CLS	LOADFACTS	RECEIVE	WKS
COLOR	MENU	RESET	WORKON
DISPLAY	RESET		

❑ SUMMARY OF COMMON VP-EXPERT ERROR MESSAGES

Error in math expression	A number of parentheses may be missing; the formula might be illogical.
Illegal confidence factor	Confidence factors must be within the range of 0 to 100.
Illegal statement	There is an invalid statement in the knowledge base. Check to make sure all key words are spelled correctly; check statement syntax.
Math expression too long	A math expression cannot be longer than 256 characters.
Missing comma	Variables in ASK, CHOICES, and PLURAL statements must be separated by commas.
Out of memory error	The memory limit has been exceeded.
Premature end of file	Check to make sure that the last character in the knowledge base is a semicolon (;).
Syntax error	There is a syntax error in a clause or a statement.
Text string too long	ASK, BECAUSE, and DISPLAY text is limited to 1,000 characters.
Too many columns	Induction tables cannot contain more than 11 columns.
Too many examples	Induction tables cannot contain more than 150 rows.
Word too long	Rule names and most variables and values cannot exceed 20 characters.

❑ SUMMARY OF VP-EXPERT FUNCTION KEY COMMANDS

On-Screen Formatting: The Function Keys Used Alone

Keys	Function	Description
<F1>	Help	Pressing <F1> provides on-screen Help.
<F2>	Reformat	Pressing <F2> enables a paragraph to be reformatted. Paragraphs are readjusted to margin settings after editing has altered line lengths.
<F3>	Tab Set	Pressing <F3> places a tab set or deletes an existing tab set at the cursor's current location.
<F4>	Margins/Justify	Pressing <F4> displays a screen that enables you to change the left and right margins as well as to turn justification on or off.
<F5>	Center	Pressing <F5> centers the line where the cursor is currently located.
<F7>	Bold	Pressing <F7> turns boldfacing on and off.
<F8>	Underline	Pressing <F8> turns underlining on and off.
<F9>	Document	Pressing <F9> turns the Document Mode on and off. The default setting is off. When the Document Mode is off, word wrap, justify, centering, and reformatting are inoperable.
<F10>	Print	Pressing <F10> activates the Print menu, from which you can print a file.

File Saving, Listing and Reformatting: The Functions Keys Used with the ALT Key

Keys	Function	Description
<Alt>-<F2>	Global Reformat	Pressing <Alt>-<F2> reformats the entire document from the cursor's current location forward. Document Mode must be on to use this command.
<Alt>-<F4>	Insert File	Pressing <Alt>-<F4> inserts an existing file at the cursor's current location.
<Alt>-<F5>	Update File	Pressing <Alt>-<F5> saves your document without exiting from the text editor.
<Alt>-<F6>	Save File	Pressing <Alt>-<F6> saves your file and exits from the text editor.
<Alt>-<F7>	Disk Directory	Pressing <Alt>-<F7> lists the files on the disk in the current directory or in a designated directory.
<Alt>-<F8>	Abandon Edit	Pressing <Alt>-<F8> exits from the text editor without saving changes made since the last save.

Manipulating Blocks of Text: The Functions Keys Used with the CTRL Key

Keys	Function	Description
<Ctrl>-<F3>	Start Block	Pressing <Ctrl>-<F3> marks the cursor's current location as the beginning of a block of text.
<Ctrl>-<F4>	End Block	Pressing <Ctrl>-<F4> marks the cursor's current location as the end of a block of text.
<Ctrl>-<F5>	Cancel Block	Pressing <Ctrl>-<F5> cancels a block of text that has been marked.
<Ctrl>-<F6>	Move Block	Pressing <Ctrl>-<F6> moves a block of text that has been marked to the cursor's current location. The block of text is deleted from its original position.
<Ctrl>-<F7>	Copy Block	Pressing <Ctrl>-<F7> copies a block of text that has been marked to the cursor's current location. The block of text remains in its original position.
<Ctrl>-<F8>	Delete Block	Pressing <Ctrl>-<F8> deletes a block of text that has been marked.
<Ctrl>-<F9>	Change Attributes	Pressing <Ctrl>-<F9> accesses a list of attributes such as normal, underline, boldface, or combined (underline and boldface). Typing the first letter of one of these attributes causes the block of text that has been marked to take on that attribute.
<Ctrl>-<F10>	Recall Block	Pressing <Ctrl>-<F10> recalls the most recently deleted word, line, or block to the cursor's current location.

Search and Replace: The Function Keys used with the SHIFT Key

Keys	Function	Description
<Shift>-<F3>	Search Forward	Pressing <Shift>-<F3> moves the cursor forward to the first instance of a designated text string.
<Shift>-<F5>	Replace Forward	Pressing <Shift>-<F5> replaces the next instance of a designated text string with a new text string.
<Shift>-<F7>	Global Replace	Pressing <Shift>-<F7> replaces every instance of a designated text string with a new string.
<Shift>-<F9>	Repeat Search	Pressing <Shift>-<F9> repeats the most recent Search, Search and Replace, or Global Replace command.

❏ VP-EXPERT EXERCISES

To complete the following exercises you will need the VP-Expert 3.0 program disk, and your data disk.

1. Start the VP-Expert program. Change the working directory to drive A. The VP-Expert Main Menu should be on your screen.

2. You are going to create a knowledge base that will help a student determine if he or she has met a college's general English Composition, Foreign Language, and Social Sciences requirements for graduation. The requirements are as follows:

English Composition	English 110
	English 112
Foreign Language (FL stands for the particular language: French, Spanish, etc.)	FL 101 or FL 111
	FL 201
Social Studies	A variety of classes can be taken, but the student must take a total of six classes.

Create the knowledge base directly from the text editor. Name the knowledge base REQUIRE. Key in the knowledge base as follows:

```
ACTIONS
DISPLAY "This consultation will help you determine what courses you
have left to take to complete your English Composition, Foreign
Language, and Social Sciences requirements for graduation.
Press any key to continue.~"
FIND Require
DISPLAY "You have the following requirements left to fulfill (the
first number indicates the number of Social Science courses you
have left to take):
{Require}
```

```
     Press any key to continue.~";

RULE 0
IF    Eng=Both_110_&_112
THEN  Require=English_Comp_None;

RULE 1
IF    Eng=ENG112_only
THEN  Require=ENG11O;

RULE 2
IF    Eng=ENG11O_only
THEN  Require=ENG112;

RULE 3
IF    FL=Both_101_&_201 OR
      FL=Both_111_&_201 OR
      FL=All_3_classes
THEN  Require=Foreign_Lang_None;

RULE 4
IF    FL= FL101_only OR
      FL=FL111_only
THEN  Require=FL201;

RULE 5
IF    FL=FL201_only
THEN  Require=FL101_or_FL111;

RULE 6
IF    SS=6
THEN  Require=zero;

RULE 7
IF    SS<6
THEN  Require=(6 - SS);
```

ASK Eng: "Which of the following English Composition classes have
you taken (select one option)?";

CHOICES ENG: ENG110_only, ENG112_only, Both_110_&_112;

ASK FL: "Which of the following Foreign Language classes have you
taken (select one option)?";
CHOICES FL: FL101_only, FL111_only, FL_201_only, Both_101_&_201,
Both_111_&_201, All 3_classes;

ASK SS: "How many Social Science classes you have taken? Enter a
number between 0 and 6 and press RETURN.";

Look over your work carefully. When you are sure your REQUIRE knowledge base is entered correctly, save it.

3. Before you run a consultation, there are some editing changes you need to make. Access the REQUIRE knowledge base so that you can edit it. The REQUIRE variable has to be designated as a PLURAL variable. Add the appropriate PLURAL statement.

4. You want to eliminate the rules window and results window from the screen during the consultation. Add the appropriate statement to the REQUIRE knowledge base that accomplishes this.

5. You want the DISPLAY clause to be cleared from the screen during a consultation. Add the appropriate clause to the REQUIRE knowledge base that accomplishes this.

6. Save the edited REQUIRE knowledge base and run a consultation. If you receive an error message, locate your mistake and fix it. Once the knowledge base is working correctly, run several consultations making various selections.

7. You want to edit the REQUIRE knowledge base further. Quit from the consultation and access the REQUIRE knowledge base. You want the final DISPLAY text to remain on the screen until the end user presses a key, and you want this final DISPLAY text to be printed. Make the needed changes to the REQUIRE knowledge base. Save the edited REQUIRE knowledge base and run some consultations to make sure the knowledge base is working properly. Be sure to run the consultations on a terminal that is connected to a printer to make sure the DISPLAY text prints as it should.

8. You need to add another value for the Eng and FL variables. As the REQUIRE knowledge base stands now, the student can enter 0 if he or she has not taken a Social Science class, but if the student has not taken an English Composition or Foreign Language class, there is no appropriate option to select. You want to edit the knowledge base so that the option None appears with both the English Composition and Foreign Language prompts. You must edit the rules so that if the student selects None at either of these prompts, the appropriate answer is listed with the goal variable during the final display. That is, if the student selects None at the English Composition prompt, then the student has to take both ENG110 and ENG112. If the student selects None at the Foreign Language prompt, then the student has to take either FL101 or FL111 and FL201. Remember, you have to keep the names of the values to twenty characters or less. It is a good idea to make a backup copy of the REQUIRE knowledge base and make the necessary editing changes to the backup. That way if you make a mistake and want to start over, you will still have your original REQUIRE knowledge base. Make the necessary changes. Save the edited knowledge base. Run several consultations to make sure it is working properly.

❏ VP-EXPERT PROBLEMS

To complete the following exercises you will need the VP-Expert 3.0 program disk, and the Student File Disk that comes with this book.

1. Start the VP-Expert program. The VP-Expert Main Menu should be on your screen.

2. On the Student File Disk is a knowledge base named INVEST. It's purpose is to suggest some investment alternatives to first-time investors with $500 to $1000 to invest. Run through a couple of consultations using the INVEST knowledge base to become familiar with it.

3. Edit the INVEST knowledge base as follows in order to make it more user-friendly:
- ■ Add the appropriate clause to the knowledge base to clear the screen of the opening DISPLAY text.
- ■ Add the appropriate statement to remove the results window and the rules window from the screen during the consultation.
- ■ Edit the final display text that identifies the goal variable in order to have it remain on the screen until the end user presses any key.

After making these changes, save the revised INVEST knowledge base and run a few consultations to make sure it is working properly.

4. Next you want to add confidence factors to the INVEST knowledge base. Edit the INVEST knowledge base so that the following confidence factors are assigned to each goal variable:

Goal Variable	Confidence Factor
Mutual Funds	90
Life Insurance	85
NOW Account	95
Certificate of Deposit	90
REITs	80
Common Stock	80

In addition, add a second DISPLAY clause in the ACTIONS block that instructs the end user as to how he or she can enter confidence factors during the consultation. Include a clause that will clear this DISPLAY text as well from the screen before the consultation begins. Edit the DISPLAY text, identifying the goal variable so that the final confidence factor will be displayed on the screen with the goal variable. Save the edited INVEST knowledge base. Run a few consultations to make sure the program is working properly. Be sure to enter confidence factors as you run your consultations.

5. Next, add BECAUSE statements to the knowledge base. Edit the INVEST knowledge base so that the following will be displayed when the end user selects the Why? command during a consultation:

```
The time frame of the investment and the risk level of the
investment help to determine where the money should be invested.
```

Edit the DISPLAY text that instructs the end user how to enter confidence factors, to include instructions on how to use the Why? command. Save the revised INVEST knowledge base. Run a few consultations using the Why? command to make sure the program is working properly.

6. You now want to create a new knowledge base to be used along with the INVEST knowledge base. It is for the end user who does not have any money to invest, but would like to begin setting aside some money so that eventually he or she will be able to make an investment. This new knowledge base is to compute how much money will have to be set aside each month, based upon amount of money the end user eventually wants to have to invest and how soon the end user wants to have the investment money. Name the new knowledge base INVEST2.

The INVEST2 knowledge base has to enable the end user to input the values for two variables:

Amount-the total amount of money the end user wants to have to invest

Time-the number of months the end user is willing to save

For example, if the end user wanted to have $1000 within one year, he or she enters 1000 for the amount of money they want to have to invest and 12 for how soon they want the investment money to be available (the number of months). The program should then compute and display the amount of money that needs to be set aside each month in order for the end user to have $1000 in 12 months.

Mathematical operations have to be included in the knowledge base. Keep the computation simple. That is, take the value the user assigns to the amount variable and divide it by the value the user assigns to the time variable. (In the above example, 1000 would be divided by 12.) Have the goal variable be displayed in a message that informs the end user how much money they will have to save each month in order to reach their goal. Include in this message a statement informing the end user that this calculation does not take into account any interest they may earn on the monthly savings. Obviously, if interest is included, they will reach their goal sooner.

CHAPTER 12

Desktop Publishing with WordPerfect 5.1

Outline

❑ INTRODUCTION

Prior to 1984, publishing was an expensive procedure carried out by trained, professional typographers. An event that significantly changed the publishing industry was the arrival of a reasonably-priced laser printer. In 1984 Hewlett Packard came out with the LaserJet printer priced at $3,495. For the first time, an important tool was available that enabled people to print word-processing documents that approached typeset quality. Software developers soon came out with software packages for the microcomputer that took advantage of the laser printer's quality and flexibility to help create professional-looking documents. Thus, desktop publishing was born. In 1986 approximately 53,000 software packages for desktop publishing were sold. This figure jumped to approximately 600,000 desktop publishing packages in 1990.

Desktop publishing is one of the fastest-growing, most popular application software programs available today. This chapter explains some of the terminology used in desktop publishing. In addition, it introduces basic desktop publishing techniques using WordPerfect.

❑ DEFINITIONS

Desktop publishing utilizes a personal computer, special software, and a printer to allow an organization or an individual to produce professional-looking documents suitable for publication. Documents created using desktop publishing can combine graphics and text. With desktop publishing, the user is no longer dependent on a typesetter to prepare materials for printing. The same person who writes the text can typeset it and design the final pages, complete with graphics.

Desktop publishing borrows much of its terminology from the field of typesetting. Many of these words are unfamiliar to people who know nothing about publishing or typesetting. It is important to learn this terminology before trying to design a document using desktop publishing.

Much of the terminology used in desktop publishing refers to type. These special words are used to describe the appearance of text on a page. For example, typeface is the style or shape of the letters. Two examples of typefaces are Helvetica and Bodoni (see Figure 12-1). Type size refers to the size of a letter measured by a standard system that uses points. A point is a unit of type measure. One point equals 1/72 of an inch; 72 points equal 1 inch. Type style is the way each typeface can be modified to add contrast or emphasis. Two examples of type style options are bold and italics.

FIGURE 12-1 Examples of Helvetica and Bodini Type

Helvetica family	Bodini family
Helvetica	Bodini
Helvetica italic	*Bodini italic*
Helvetica bold	**Bodini bold**
Helvetica bold italic	***Bodini bold italic***
Helvetica narrow	**Bodini Poster**
Helvetica narrow italic	
Helvetica narrow bold	
Helvetica narrow bold italic	

FIGURE 12-2 Examples of
Serif and Sans Serif Type

Serif type   **Sans serif type**

Bookman   **Avant Garde**
New Century Schoolbook **Helvetica**
Palatino

A font is a complete set of characters in a particular typeface, type size, and type style. *Font* comes from the French word fondre ("to melt"), and it originally referred to the process of melting and casting type. Before the advent of computer typesetting, printers used trays of cast metal letters to create documents. Each tray, or font, included all the letters of the alphabet for a specific typeface, type style, and type size. For example, one tray held only 10-point Times italic type, and another tray held only 10-point Times bold type. This is how font came to mean all the characters in a particular combination of typeface, type style, and type size.

A laser printer can access different typefaces in three ways. First, internal fonts are stored in the printer's ROM. These typefaces are always available and are easy to use. Second, font cartridges are circuit boards that plug into the laser printer. Each cartridge contains a limited selection of typefaces, sizes, and styles. Third, soft fonts, or downloadable fonts, are typefaces stored on disks. These typefaces must be copied (or downloaded) from the computer into the laser printer's memory each time the printer is turned on. Information about what the typeface should look like is stored on the disk and sent to the RAM of a printer. Cartridge fonts and soft fonts are loaded as they are needed.

A typeface can be either serif or sans serif. Serifs are small lines that decorate the edges of type. Typefaces that use serifs include Times Roman, Courier, and New Century Schoolbook. A sans serif typeface is a typeface that does not use serifs to embellish the letters (see Figure 12-2). Sans serif typefaces include Helvetica, Avant Garde, and Geneva.

The baseline is the invisible line on which type rests. The height of a lowercase letter is called the x height. The x height does not include ascenders or descenders.

The ascender is the portion of a letter that extends above the x height, such as the top of the letter *d* or *h*. The descender is the portion of the letter that extends below the baseline, such as the tail of the letter *p* or *y* (see Figure 12-3). The point size is measured from the top of the ascender to the bottom of the descender.

FIGURE 12-3 Parts of Type

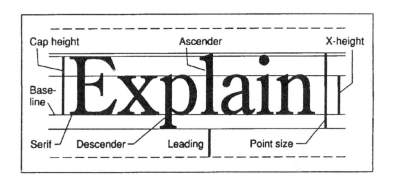

The vertical distance between two lines of type is called the leading (pronounced "ledding"). This term comes from the early days of printing, when letter blocks were made out of lead alloy. Printers inserted lead strips between lines to add space. Leading is measured from one baseline of text to the next baseline of text.

Adjusting the space between a pair of letters is called kerning. Certain letter combinations must be brought closer together to make the spacing between them look consistent with the rest of the spacing in the document. For example, the letters AW will appear further apart than the letters *MN*. (see Figure 12-4).

The determination of where a word should break at the end of a line is called hyphenation. Some desktop publishing software packages come with a hyphenation program. This program automatically breaks words that are too long to fit at the end of a line. Using hyphenation cuts down on the amount of variation in the spaces between words. In desktop publishing, hyphenation and justification are referred to as the H & J process.

There are a few general rules to follow when designing the page layout for a document. First, do not use more than two typefaces in a document. One typeface should be a serif and one a sans serif. Generally, the typeface used for the text in the body of the document should be serif. The small lines on the edges of the letters lead the eye from letter to letter, making the document easier to read. Headlines or titles should be in a sans serif type. Sans serif typefaces slow down eye movement, forcing the reader to pay closer attention to a few key words.

The second principle of good design is to be conservative. Different typefaces affect the reader in different ways. For example, squared-off sans serif typefaces give the reader a feeling of authority. Serif typefaces provide a friendlier feeling. If the effect that a certain typeface has on a reader is unknown, it is better to stick with a traditional typeface such as Times Roman or Helvetica. The use of unusual typefaces should be limited.

A third principle of good design is to use the same typeface for all headings. Different heading levels can be distinguished by varying the size and style of one typeface rather than by using several different typefaces.

A fourth principle of good design is to avoid cluttering the page with fancy borders, symbols, or type that is too small to read easily. It is tempting to use all the decorative and ornamental elements provided by page composition software simply because they are available. A cluttered page that is difficult to read, however, is not well designed.

In all the principles of good design, simplicity is the rule. It is particularly important for people who are novices in desktop publishing to keep their designs simple. Winning page designs are always simple and clear.

FIGURE 12-4 Kerning and Leading

As word processors continue to become more sophisticated, they are able to perform more desktop publishing tasks. More and more businesses are using word processors such as WordPerfect to publish their own newsletters, brochures, reports, and catalogs. Schools, churches, civic organizations, and clubs all circulate newsletters, bulletins, or reports that can be produced using word processors such as WordPerfect. The remainder of the chapter explains how to use some desktop publishing features with WordPerfect.

Selecting Fonts

Most printers are capable of printing in more than one typeface and type size. Depending on the printer being used, several typefaces and type sizes can be incorporated into a WordPerfect document. Pressing <Ctrl>-<F8> for FONT and 4 for BASE FONT enables you to see a list of the typefaces and type sizes available for the printer that has been installed to work with the WordPerfect program.

To view available typefaces, press <Ctrl>-<F8> and 4. A list of the typefaces and type sizes that are available with your printer appears. Move the highlight to the desired typeface and type size and press <Enter>.

If you change the type size, the display on the screen does not change. That is, you may select an 8-point type size and a 14-point type size to appear on the same page, but the screen displays the text as the same size. To see what the text will look like when printed, use the VIEW option by pressing <Shift>-<F7> for PRINT and 6 for VIEW DOCUMENT.

Creating Newspaper-Style Columns

Newspaper-style columns are columns that flow or "snake" up and down the page. That is, the text at the bottom of one column continues on the top of another column. Newspaper-style columns can be read quickly and easily, which is why they are used for documents such as newsletters. WordPerfect was the first wordprocessing program to display multiple columns side by side on the screen. Version 5.0 allows you to create up to twenty-four columns; however, you would rarely want to choose more than three or four columns. Text can either be entered directly in column format, or the column codes can be inserted after it has been typed.

Once you have defined your columns, you can turn them on and off again whenever you like. You can change the number of columns within the document, and even on a single page. For example you could have two columns at the top of a page and three columns at the bottom. Columns do not have to be the same width. You can have a wide column and a narrow column on the same page.

The first step in defining columns is to press <Alt>-<F7> for COLUMNS/TABLE. Next, press 1 for COLUMNS and then press 3 for COLUMN DEFINE. The full-screen menu shown in Figure 12-5 will appear. You can change the type of columns, the number of columns, the space between columns, and the actual column margins using this menu. The default settings are for two 3-inch wide newspaper-style columns with 1/2 inch of space between them.

FIGURE 12-5 The Text
Column Definition Menu

```
Text Column Definition

    1 - Type                                Newspaper

    2 - Number of Columns                   2

    3 - Distance Between Columns

    4 - Margins

    Column   Left    Right   Column   Left    Right
    1:       1"      4"      13:
    2:       4.5"    7.5"    14:
    3:                       15:
    4:                       16:
    5:                       17:
    6:                       18:
    7:                       19:
    8:                       20:
    9:                       21:
    10:                      22:
    11:                      23:
    12:                      24:

Selection: 0
```

Difference Box WordPerfect 5.0: To define columns in WordPerfect 5.0, press <Alt>-<F7> for MATH/COLUMNS. Press 4 for COLUMN DEFINE. The Text Column Definition menu appears.

After you have finished with the Text Column Definition menu, the main Math/Columns menu reappears, giving you a chance to turn columns on. With columns turned on, the hard page code, entered by pressing <Ctrl>-<Enter>, creates a hard column break. This enables you to force the columns to wrap where you want them and helps to even columns up.

Moving around the screen in column mode can be tricky. Text automatically wraps within a column, flowing to the next column after the first column is filled. The left and right arrow keys move the cursor only to the beginning or end of the line within the current column. Pressing <End> moves the cursor only to the end of the current line within the current column.

To move the cursor from column to column use the GOTO command. Press <Ctrl>-<Home> and then press either the left or right arrow key to move the cursor to the column to the left or right.

Adding a Headline

A headline that runs across all the columns can be included in a document. Lines can also be included above and below the headline. Vertical lines can also be placed between columns.

To insert a line, press <Alt>-<F9> for GRAPHICS. Next press 5   for LINE. To create a horizontal line, press 1 . To create a vertical line, press 2. You can then select the position of the line, the length of the line, and the width of the line.

YOUR TURN

In this exercise you are going to create a simple newsletter using WordPerfect.

1. Start WordPerfect. A blank text window should be on your screen. First you are going to enter the headline for the newsletter. The headline is going to have a ruler line above and below it.

>Press <Alt>-<F9> for GRAPHICS
>
>Press 5 for LINE
>
>Press 1 for HORIZONTAL

Your screen should look like Figure 12-6. This is the Horizontal Line Definition menu. The position of the line, FULL and BASELINE, is acceptable. The line will extend from the left margin to the right margin. You are going to change the width of the line to make it slightly wider.

>Press 4 for WIDTH OF LINE
>
>Type: .06
>
>Press <Enter>
>
>Press <F7> to return to the document screen

The horizontal line does not appear on the screen, but revealing codes will show you that the code for inserting a horizontal line is now included in the document.

>Press <Alt>-<F3> for REVEAL CODES

FIGURE 12-6 The Horizontal Line Definition Menu

```
Graphics: Horizontal Line

    1 - Horizontal Position        Full

    2 - Vertical Position          Baseline

    3 - Length of Line

    4 - Width of Line              0.013"

    5 - Gray Shading (% of black) 100%












Selection: 0
```

The code **[Hline:Full,Baseline, 6.5", 0.06",100%]** should appear in the Reveal Codes screen. Leave REVEAL CODES on.

Difference Box WordPerfect 5.0: The position of the horizontal line will be LEFT and RIGHT. To change the width of the line, press 3 for WIDTH OF LINE.

---

2. Next you want to select a typeface and type size for the headline.

> Press <Enter> two times
>
> Press <Ctrl>-<F8> for FONT
>
> Press 4 for BASE FONT

A list of the typefaces and the type sizes available for your printer appears. If possible, select a sans serif typeface, such as Helvetica, in a larger type size, such as 14 point. Move the highlight to your selection and press <Enter>. The typeface you selected appears in the Reveal Codes screen.

> Press <Shift>-<F6> for CENTER
>
> Type: THE HI-TECH TATTLER

Now you are going to add the ruler line underneath the headline.

> Press <Enter> two times
>
> Press <Alt>-<F9> for GRAPHICS
>
> Press 5 for LINE
>
> Press 1 for HORIZONTAL
>
> Press 4 for WIDTH OF LINE
>
> Enter: 0.06
>
> Press <Enter>
>
> Press <F7> to return to the document screen
>
> Press <Enter> three times

3. Now you are ready to define your columns.

> Press <Alt>-<F7> for COLUMNS/TABLE
>
> Press 1 for COLUMNS
>
> Press 3 for COLUMN DEFINE

The Text Column Definition menu appears. You do not need to change any of the settings.

> Press 0
>
> Press 1 for ON

Your screen should look like Figure 12-7. The column definition code and the column on code are now entered into your document.

**FIGURE 12-7 Defining
Newspaper Columns**

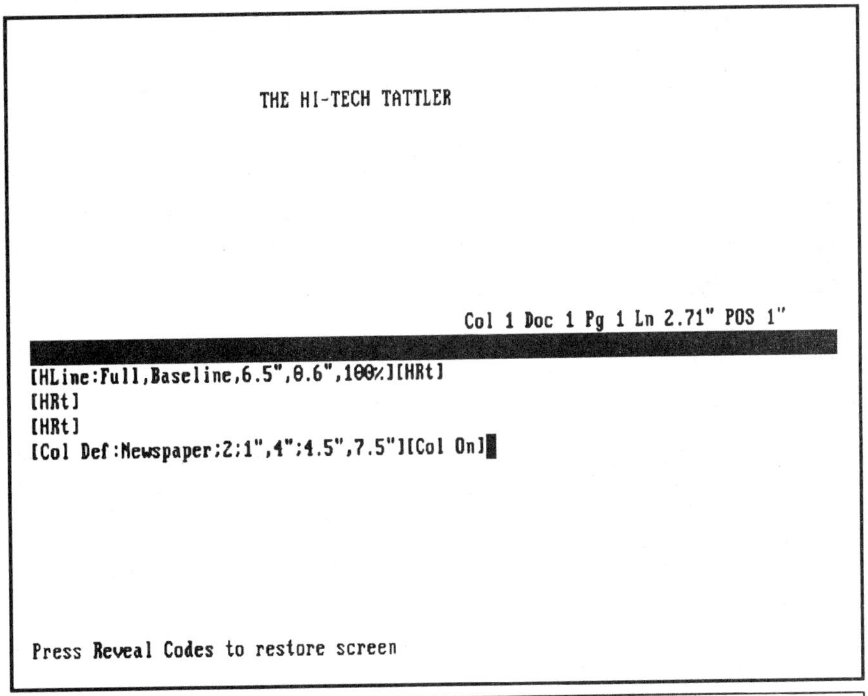

```
                        THE HI-TECH TATTLER




                                          Col 1 Doc 1 Pg 1 Ln 2.71" POS 1"
▬▬▬▬▬▬▬▬▬▬▬▬▬▬▬▬▬▬▬▬▬▬▬▬▬▬▬▬▬▬▬▬▬▬▬▬▬▬▬
[HLine:Full,Baseline,6.5",0.6",100%][HRt]
[HRt]
[HRt]
[Col Def:Newspaper;2;1",4";4.5",7.5"][Col On]█




Press Reveal Codes to restore screen
```

Difference Box WordPerfect 5.0: To define the columns, press <Alt>-<F7> for MATH/COLUMNS
and press 4 for COLUMN DEFINE. The Text Column Definition menu appears. Press 0 and press
3 for COLUMN ON/OFF.

4.   Before you enter the text for the newsletter, change the typeface.

Press <Ctrl>-<F8> for FONT

Press 4 for BASE FONT

A list of the typefaces and the type sizes available for your printer appears. If possible, select
a serif typeface, such as Times Roman, in a smaller type size, such as 12 points or 10
points. Move the highlight to your selection and press <Enter>. The font you selected appears in the Reveal Codes screen. Type the following text as it appears here. Press the
<Space Bar> three times to indent paragraphs. Use boldface where indicated:

Picnic a Success

```
Once again, great fun was had by all who attended the annual
Hi-Tech Manufacturing company picnic. The weather certainly
cooperated as it was a perfect day for swimming, softball, and, of
course, eating, which we all did plenty of!
   Congratulations go out to the winners of the annual softball game.
Phil Jarvis should be commended for his three home runs that helped
move the team from behind to win the game.
   A new attraction at this year's picnic proved to be very popular.
The dunking booth had long lines of not only children, but adults
as well, waiting to dunk their "favorite" Hi-Tech employee. A
```

special thanks goes out to the president of our company for being a good sport and volunteering to be the first person "dunked." Money that was raised from the dunking booth is going to be donated to the Sunshine Children's Home. A hearty thanks to all of you who sat in the dunking booth. You helped to raise money for a good cause. Everyone did an excellent job at helping to keep the park clean, which was appreciated. Thanks go out to everyone for making the picnic such a great success.

TWINS!

Congratulations go out to Michael Eicher and his wife Pamela on the birth of their twin daughters, Rhonda and Stephanie. The twins were a May Day surprise for the Eicher's. Mother and girls are doing great, but Michael says he "has his hands full."

A Message from the President

The month of April was very busy for Hi-Tech Manufacturing. Of course there was the company picnic which was, as always, a fun event that provided us with the opportunity of getting to know our coworkers and their families better. It also gave us a chance to relax from what can be stressful jobs.

During April, productivity in the warehouse also increased, as can be seen from the graph below. The installation of the new inventory system seems to have helped a great deal. I thank everyone for making the move to this new system such a smooth one.

Casual Day

Don't forget this Friday is casual day. Blue jeans are the acceptable attire for the day.

Vacation Days

Requests for vacation days must be turned in at least two weeks in advance of the days you want to take off. Don't forget to turn in your requests, in writing, to the personnel department.

4. Use the VIEW option to see how the text will look when printed.

> Press <Shift>-<F7> for PRINT

> Press 6 for VIEW DOCUMENT

You should see the document as a two-column newsletter.

> Press the <Space Bar> twice

The document screen returns.

Application Software Manual

5. You are now ready to save the newsletter.

    Press <F7> for Exit

    Press Y for Yes

    Enter: `a:newsletr`

Difference Box: If you are using a computer with two floppy disk drives, enter `b:newsletr`.

    Press <Enter>

The EXIT WP? prompt appears

    Press Y for Yes

You have finished with this Your Turn exercise.

❏ INSERTING A GRAPHIC IMAGE INTO TEXT

Illustrations and special text boxes can be inserted into WordPerfect documents. Graphic elements can be drawn or painted with PC graphics programs such as DrawPerfect, PC Paintbrush, or Corel Draw, or they can be digitized with an image scanner. In addition, there are collections of clip art on disk. A number of clipart graphics are supplied with the WordPerfect program. In order to print graphics, you must have a laser, ink-jet, or dot-matrix printer.

Several types of graphics boxes can be created: figures, tables, text boxes, and user-defined boxes. Options are available to create a distinct style for each type of box. Graphics boxes can have borders or not, and each border can be defined individually. You can attach a caption to an illustration so that it will stay with it even if you decide to move the illustration. You can shade graphics boxes for emphasis.

To insert an illustration or text box, press <Alt>-<F9> for GRAPHICS. The first menu lists the types of graphics that can be inserted. Once you select a graphic type, a second menu allows you to create, edit, renumber, or change the style options. A single Graphics Definition menu is used whenever you create or edit graphics. To insert a graphic, enter the name of the graphic to be included, and the file is converted automatically. Captions are also entered from the Graphics Definition menu.

Graphics can be positioned in a specific location on the page, regardless of any text that appears on the same page, or in relation to a particular paragraph. You can even treat a graphic image as a single character, so that it flows with the text. The text outside the graphics box can automatically wrap around the graphic, or you can let text and graphics overprint each other for special effects.

If your monitor is capable of displaying graphics, you can view the graphic in a special graphic editing screen. The editing screen allows you to resize and rotate your graphic and create other special effects.

Changing the Size of a Graphic Image

Once a graphic image has been inserted into the text, you can easily change its size. To change the size of a graphic image, you press 7 for SIZE from the Graphics Definition menu and enter the image's height and width.

> **Difference Box WordPerfect 5.0:** To change the size of a graphic image, press 6 for SIZE from the Graphics Definition menu and enter the image's height and width.

WordPerfect automatically places any graphic image you insert into a frame. A frame is the space into which a graphic image is inserted. The default horizontal position for the frame WordPerfect creates is for the right. The horizontal position of the frame can be changed to align at the left of the document, to be centered, or to extend from the left to the right margin.

Adding Borders to a Graphic Image

To add or change the border style of a graphic image, you first must make sure the cursor is in front of the code corresponding to the graphic to which you want it to apply. Once the cursor is positioned properly, press <Alt>-<F9> for GRAPHICS, the number that corresponds to the type of graphics box it is whose borders you want to change, and press 4 for OPTIONS. The Graphics Options menu appears.

From the Graphics Options menu you can select the border style of each side (left, right, top, bottom) of the image. The border style can be NONE, for no lines, a single line, a double line, a dashed line, a dotted line, a thick line, or an extra thick line. From this menu you can also set whether or not there should be gray shading in the box.

YOUR TURN

In this exercise, you are going to create a simple graph using Lotus 1-2-3 and then import it as a graphic image into your NEWSLETR file.

1.   Start the Lotus 1-2-3 program. Enter the following data into the cells indicated:

Cell	Labels and Values
AI	WAREHOUSE SHIPMENTS FOR APRIL
A3	2569
B3	2890
C3	3108
D3	3233
A4	Week 1
B4	Week 2
C4	Week 3
D4	Week 4

Save the file on your data disk as NEWSLETR.

2.   Create a simple bar graph. The first title for the bar graph should be WAREHOUSE SHIPMENTS. The second title for the bar graph should be Month of April. The title for the Y axis should be Orders Processed. The X range is cells A4 through D4 and the A range is cells A3 through D3. Save the graph as NEWSLETR. Lotus 1-2-3 automatically adds the

.PIC extension to the file name for the graph. View the bar graph to make sure it is correct. Once you are satisfied with the graph, save it again if you made any changes to it. Replace the old NEWSLETR.PIC file.

3. You are ready to exit from Lotus 1-2-3. Before you do, save the worksheet file again, replacing the old NEWSLETR.WK1 file. Exit from Lotus and load the WordPerfect program. Retrieve the NEWSLETR file. Place the cursor in the blank line of space above the title Casual Day.

> Press <Alt>-<F9> for GRAPHICS

> Press 1 for FIGURE

> Press 1 for CREATE

The Figure Definition menu appears.

> Press 1 for FILENAME

The prompt ENTER FILENAME appears at the bottom of the screen. You want to enter the name of the Lotus graph.

> Enter: `a:newsletr.pic`

Difference Box: If you are using a computer with two floppy disk drives, enter `b:newsletr.pic`.

> Press <Enter>

After a moment, the file name NEWSLETR.PIC appears next to the FILENAME option on the menu. Next, you want to change the horizontal position of the frame. Currently it is set for RIGHT. You want to set it for FULL so that it will extend the width of the column.

FIGURE 12-8 Importing a Lotus Graph into a WordPerfect File

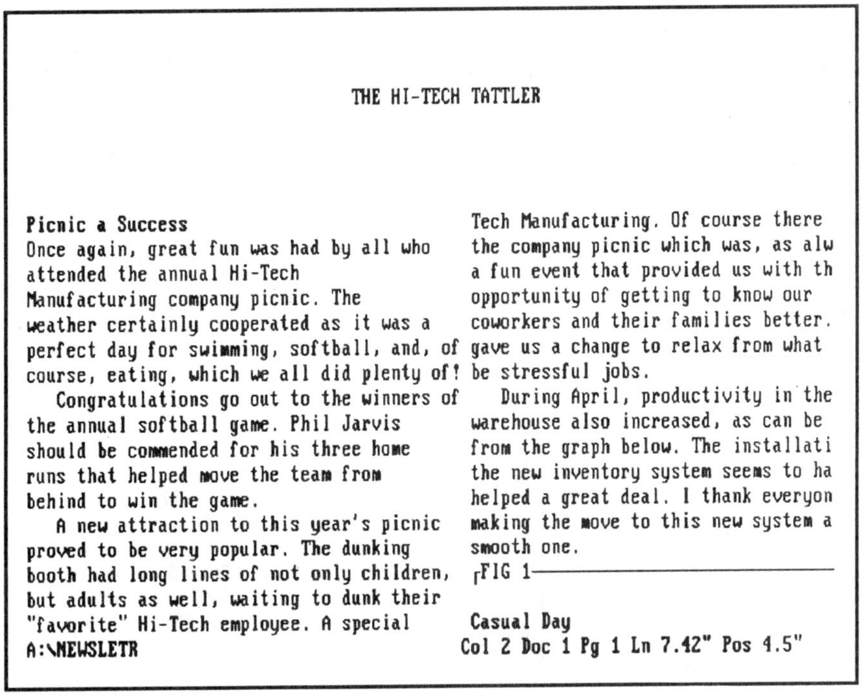

```
                        THE HI-TECH TATTLER


Picnic a Success                      Tech Manufacturing. Of course there
Once again, great fun was had by all who  the company picnic which was, as alw
attended the annual Hi-Tech           a fun event that provided us with th
Manufacturing company picnic. The     opportunity of getting to know our
weather certainly cooperated as it was a  coworkers and their families better.
perfect day for swimming, softball, and, of  gave us a change to relax from what
course, eating, which we all did plenty of!  be stressful jobs.
   Congratulations go out to the winners of    During April, productivity in the
the annual softball game. Phil Jarvis  warehouse also increased, as can be
should be commended for his three home  from the graph below. The installati
runs that helped move the team from   the new inventory system seems to ha
behind to win the game.               helped a great deal. I thank everyon
   A new attraction to this year's picnic  making the move to this new system a
proved to be very popular. The dunking  smooth one.
booth had long lines of not only children,  ┌FIG 1─────────────────────
but adults as well, waiting to dunk their
"favorite" Hi-Tech employee. A special  Casual Day
A:\NEWSLETR                           Col 2 Doc 1 Pg 1 Ln 7.42" Pos 4.5"
```

Press 6 for HORIZONTAL POSITION

Press 4 for FULL

Press <F7> to return to the document screen.

Your screen should look similar to Figure 12-8. WordPerfect automatically adds a line where the graphic will appear when the document is printed.

4.   Next you want to add a border around the graph. First you must position the cursor.

Press <Alt>-<F3> for REVEAL CODES

Find the figure code **[Fig Box:1;NEWSLETR.PIC;].** Move the cursor in the Reveal Codes screen so that it is highlighting this code.

Press <Alt>-<F9> for GRAPHICS

Press 1 for FIGURE

Press 4 for OPTIONS

Your screen should look like Figure 12-9. This is the Graphics Options screen.

Press 1 for BORDER STYLE

A menu listing the border style options appears at the bottom of the screen. You are going to select a double line to go around the entire image.

Press 3 for DOUBLE four times

Press <F7> to return to the document screen

Notice in the Reveal Codes screen that the **[Fig Opt]** code comes *before* the **[Fig Box:1;NEWSLETR.PIC;]** code.

5.   Now you want to view the newsletter so you can see what it will look like when printed.

Press <Shift>-<F7> for PRINT

FIGURE 12-9 The Graphics Options Screen

```
Options: Figure

       1 - Border Style
               Left                        Single
               Right                       Single
               Top                         Single
               Bottom                      Single
       2 - Outside Border Space
               Left                        0.167"
               Right                       0.167"
               Top                         0.167"
               Bottom                      0.167"
       3 - Inside Border Space
               Left                        0"
               Right                       0"
               Top                         0"
               Bottom                      0"
       4 - First Level Numbering Method    Numbers
       5 - Second Level Numbering Method   Off
       6 - Caption Number Style            [BOLD]Figure 1[bold]
       7 - Position of Caption             Below box, Outside borders
       8 - Minimum Offset from Paragraph   0"
       9 - Gray Shading (% of black)       0%

Selection: 0
```

Press 6 for VIEW

If your monitor displays graphics, the newsletter should be displayed in two columns and the bar graph should appear in the second column. Take a good look at the spacing in the newsletter. You may need to add a line of space above and below the bar graph. When you have finished viewing the newsletter, press the <Space Bar> to exit from the VIEW mode. Add space above and below the graph, if necessary. Save and print the NEWSLETR file.

6. You have finished with this Your Turn exercise. Exit from the WordPerfect program. Turn off the computer and monitor. Carefully store your disks.

❏ SUMMARY POINTS

■ Desktop publishing uses a personal computer, page composition software, and a printer to create professional-looking documents that combine text and graphics.

■ Businesses use desktop publishing to create newsletters, instructional materials, internal communications, marketing materials, and reports.

■ Desktop publishing borrows much of its terminology from typesetting. Many of the terms, such as *typeface, type style, point, type size,* and *font,* describe how the text looks on the page.

■ A typeface is either serif or sans serif. Serifs are small lines that decorate the edges of type. Sans serif typefaces do not use serifs to decorate the edges of letters.

■ Leading and kerning are ways to control the spacing of lines of text and the spacing between individual letters, respectively.

■ Page composition software places text and graphic images together on a page according to the user's specifications.

■ In order for a document to be effective, it must be well designed. The basic principle of all good design is to keep the design simple.

❏ COMMAND SUMMARY

Command	Keystroke	Function
Columns	<Alt>-<F7>	Use the Columns/Table key to define columns, then to turn them on or off as often as needed within a document.
Font	<Ctrl>-<F8>	This key gives the user access to all of the typefaces and sizes available on your printer.
Graphics	<Alt>-<F9>	The Graphics command can be used to insert several types of graphics or text boxes in a WordPerfect document. Graphics can be sized, cropped, and rotated.
Hyphenation	<Shift>-<F8>	In the Line Format menu; hyphenates the document either automatically or manually, using a set of hyphenation rules.
Italics	<Ctrl>-<F8>	In the Appearance submenu; turns italics on and off. Use italics instead of underlining for emphasis in most desktop-published documents.
Lines	<Alt>-<F9>	Allows the user to create either horizontal or parallel graphic lines of any width and of any shade of gray or black that can be positioned anywhere on the page.

Print Preview	\<Shift>-\<F7>	In the Print menu; allows the user to see what the finished document will look like without printing it out.
Setup	\<Shift>-\<F1>	Allows the user to customize WordPerfect for the way he or she works. Side-by-side column display is turned on or off in the Display submenu.
Soft Hyphen	\<Ctrl>-\< - >	Inserts a hyphen that allows the word to split automatically at the end of a line but disappears when the word no longer needs to be divied. (Make sure you use the hyphen key, not the \<Minus> key in the numeric/cursor keypad.)
Type Size	\<Ctrl>-\<F8>	The first submenu under Fonts allows the user to select type sizes so that they will resize automatically if the initial font or base font is changed.
Type Style	\<Ctrl>-\<F8>	In the Appearance submenu; allows the user to select from a number of print enhancements such as italics, double underline, small capitals, redline, strikeout, outline, shadow, boldface, and single underline. (Not all enhancements are available on all printers.)

❑ DESKTOP PUBLISHING EXERCISES

In this exercise you are going to create a newsletter that incorporates a graph image included in the WordPerfect program. In order to complete this exercise you need the WordPerfect Fonts/Graphics disk. If you need help with the exercise, review "Desktop Publishing with WordPerfect" Selecting Fonts," "Creating Newspaper-Style Columns," "Adding a Headline," "Inserting a Graphic Image into Text," and "Adding Borders to a Graphic Image" earlier in this chapter. The directions for the exercise are written for WordPerfect 5.1 and assume the program is stored on a hard disk drive. If you are using WordPerfect 5.0, refer to the difference boxes in the chapter.

1. Start the WordPerfect program. A blank text window should be on your screen. First select the typeface for the newsletter.
    Press \<Ctrl>-\<F8> for FONT
    Press 4 for BASE FONT
A list of available typefaces and sizes appears. Select a serif typeface, such as Times Roman in a point size of 10 points or 12 points, if possible. Once you have selected the typeface and type size for the newsletter, enter the headline as follows:
    Press \<Shift>-\<F6> for CENTER
    Press \<Ctrl>-\<F8> for FONT
The Font menu appears.
    Press 1 for SIZE
    Press 7 for EXTRA LARGE
    Type: Computer News
    Press \<Ctrl>-\<F8> for FONT
    Press 3 for NORMAL to return the font to its normal size
    Press \<Enter>

2. Now you are going to add two graphic lines below the headline to set it off from the body of the newsletter.

    Press <Alt>-<F9> for GRAPHICS

    Press 5 for LINE

    Press 1 for HORIZONTAL

You do not need to change anything in the menu; the defaults are all acceptable.

    Press <F7>

You want to place a second line below the first one, with a small amount of space between the two lines. Instead of pressing <Enter>, which would insert too much space, you are going to use the ADVANCE feature.

    Press <Shift>-<F8> for FORMAT

    Press 4 for OTHER

    Press 1 for ADVANCE

    Press 2 for DOWN

    Enter: .05

    Press <Enter>

    Press <F7> to return to the document screen

Now insert the second line.

    Press <Alt>-<F9> for GRAPHICS

    Press 5 for LINE

    Press 1 for HORIZONTAL

    Press <F7>

    Press <Enter> three times

3. Now you are ready to define the columns.

    Press <Alt>-<F7> for COLUMNS/TABLE

    Press 1 for COLUMNS

    Press 3 for DEFINE

The Text Column Definition menu appears. You are going to change the space between margins.

    Press 3 for DISTANCE BETWEEN COLUMNS

    Enter: 1

    Press <Enter>

The column margins automatically change to give you two margins of equal width. The rest of the default settings are acceptable so you can exit this menu.

    Press <Enter>

    Press 1 for ON

The columns are now turned on. Enter the text for the newsletter as follows. Press the <Space Bar> three times to indent paragraphs. The three subheadings, **Computers of the Future**, **An Optimistic Viewpoint**, and **A Pessimistic Viewpoint** should all be boldface and in a large type size. To set the type size, press <Ctrl>-<F8> for FONT, 1 for SIZE, and 5 for LARGE before keying in the subtitle. Once you have entered the subtitle, press <Ctrl>-<F8> for FONT and 3 for NORMAL to return the text to its normal size.

Computers of the Future

The year 2000 is just around the corner, and no matter whose crystal ball you look into, all of them predict that computers will be a significant factor in twenty-first century living. Some futurists say advances in computer technology will be so great that we cannot begin to predict what computers will be like-even in the next twenty years. These developments will affect the way we live, work, and play. The futurists see the effects with either optimism or pessimism.

An Optimistic Viewpoint

Optimists describe a society in which education becomes an interactive, self-motivating experience. The drudgery of maintaining a home will be eliminated. Human intelligence itself may be increased.

Home computer users will be able to display data, graphics, and moving video images on anything from walls to tiny screens worn on their wrists. Input will be spoken rather than typed. Through improved telecommunications, we will be able to access any television show or film from a huge library or contact anyone, anywhere in the world. We will stay in contact with our home computers via voice-operated controllers as small as a wristwatch. And of course, the home computer of the future will control robots that cook, clean, do the wash, and cut the grass in response to voice commands.

A Pessimistic Viewpoint

Pessimists, however, describe a world filled with functional illiterates glued to video screens and lethargic family members waited on by domestic robots. Perhaps people of this future civilization will cease to interact with their own families, preferring instead robots programmed with ideal and glamorous personalities. Databases will be so large that no one will have control over their contents, and individuals, no matter where they are, will be monitored by telepathic computer systems.

Save the file as COMPNEWS. Use the Spell checker to check the spelling.

4. You now want to insert a graphic image. You are going to insert the graphic in the center of the page.
   Press <Alt>-<F3> for REVEAL CODES

Move the cursor in the Reveal Codes screen to the very beginning of the file so that it is highlighting the **[Col Def:Newspaper;2;1",3.75";4.75",7.5]** code.

Press <Alt>-<F9> for GRAPHICS

Press 1 for FIGURE

Press 4 for OPTIONS

Press 1 for BORDER STYLE

Press 3 for DOUBLE four times

You want to add some inside border space to the graphics box.

Press 3 for INSIDE BORDER SPACE

Enter: .08

Press <Enter>

The cursor moves to the RIGHT option. Enter .08 three more times, next to the RIGHT, TOP, and BOTTOM options. Once the inside border space has been set, press <F7> to return to the document screen.

5.   You are going to access one of the clip art images that comes with WordPerfect. Check with your instructor to make sure these graphic images are stored on the hard drive and and find out the name of the directory in which they are stored.

Press <Alt>-<F9> for GRAPHICS

Press 1 for FIGURE

Press 1 for CREATE

You want to use a graphic image named PC-1.WPG. You need to enter the directory where this image is located. For example, if the PC-1.WPG file is stored in a subdirectory called GRAPHIC off the WP51 directory, you would enter the following:

Press 1 for FILENAME

The prompt **Enter filename** appears at the bottom of the screen.

Enter: c:\WP51\GRAPHIC\PC-1.WPG

Press <Enter>

Next, you need to select the anchor type. There are three anchor types: page, paragraph, and character. Page anchors insert the graphic in a fixed location on the page on which the code appears. Paragraph anchors position the graphic in relation to the paragraph, and will move along with the paragraph during editing. The third type of anchor is a character anchor. Character anchors position the graphic in the line of text at the position of the graphic code. They move along the line as you edit, just like a letter or any other character. For this exercise you want a page anchor.

Press 4 for ANCHOR TYPE

Press 2 for PAGE

Press <Enter>

Now you need to position the graphic on the page.

Press 5 for VERTICAL POSITION

Press 3 for CENTER

Press 6 for HORIZONTAL POSITION

Press 1 for MARGINS

Press 3 for CENTER

Next you want to set the size of the graphic.

Press 7 for SIZE

Press 1 for SET WIDTH /AUTO HEIGHT

This option allows you to set the width of the graphic and WordPerfect automatically adjusts its height according to the width you enter.

Enter: 3

Press <Enter>

You have finished with the Graphics Definition screen.

Press <F7> to return to the document screen

Save the COMPNEWS file again.

6. Now you are ready to view and print your newsletter.

Press <Shift>-<F7> for PRINT

Press 6 for VIEW DOCUMENT

If you do not have a graphics monitor, you will not be able to see the graphic. Instead, you will see a box showing approximately where the graphic will appear. When you have finished previewing your newsletter, return to the document screen.

Press <F7>

Print the COMPNEWS file. When you have printed your newsletter, you have finished with this exercise.

❏ DESKTOP PUBLISHING PROBLEMS

To complete the following exercise, you need to use a file on the Student File disk.

1. On the Student File disk there is a WordPerfect file called HRDWARE. Start the WordPerfect program and retrieve this file. Save this file and rename it HRDWARE2. You want to maintain the original HRDWARE file on your disk.

2. Read the text of the HRDWARE2 file. First, you want to add a headline to the document. Add the headline NEWSLETTER FOR DESKTOP PUBLISHERS to the top of the document. Include a ruler line above and below the headline. The headline should be in a sans serif typeface and a type size of 14 points, if possible.

3. Define the columns for the newsletter. You want the newsletter to have two columns. Format the newsletter into two columns.

4. Select the typeface and size for each of the subheadings in the newsletter along with the main text of the newsletter. The subheadings should be a larger type size and a sans serif typeface. The text should be a smaller type size and a serif typeface. You must first block the text and then set the typeface.

5. Save the newsletter and exit from WordPerfect. Now you need to create the graph to insert into the newsletter. Start the Lotus 1-2-3 program. Enter the following data into the cells indicated:

Cell	Labels and Values
A1	DESKTOP PUBLISHING HARDWARE
A3	800
B3	2200
C3	2400
A4	Monitor
B4	Scanner
C4	Printer

Save the file on your data disk as HRDWARE.

6.   Create a pie chart. The first title for the pie chart should be DESKTOP PUBLISHING HARDWARE. The second title should be Price Comparison. The X range is cells A4 through C4 and the A range is cells A3 through C3. Explode the wedge that corresponds to the printer. Save the graph as HRDWARE. Lotus 1-2-3 automatically adds the PIC extension to the file name for the graph. View the pie chart to make sure it is correct. Once you are satisfied with the graph, save it again if you made any changes to it. Replace the old HRDWARE.PIC file.

7.   You are ready to exit from Lotus 1-2-3. Before you do, save the worksheet file again, replacing the old HRDWARE.WK1 file. Exit from Lotus and load the WordPerfect program. Retrieve the HRDWARE2 file. Insert a graphics box in the blank line of space in the last section of the document under Cost. Import the HRDWARE.PIC Lotus graph into the graphics box. Select a border for the graphics box.

8.   View the newsletter so you can see what it will look like when printed. The newsletter should be in two columns and the pie chart should appear in the second column. Take a good look at the spacing in the newsletter. You may need to add a line of space above and below the pie chart. When you have finished viewing the newsletter, exit from the VIEW mode. Make any necessary adjustments to the newsletter. Save and print the HRDWARE2 file. Exit from the WordPerfect program. Turn off the computer and monitor. Carefully store your disks.

❏ DESKTOP PUBLISHING CHALLENGE

Write, design, and print a newsletter for a club or organization to which you belong. Design a two- or three-column layout. Include a headline with ruler lines and an appropriate graphic image from the clip art that comes with the WordPerfect program. You may want to experiment with other desktop publishing features. For example, if your newsletter is more than one page long, try adding a headline to the second page. You could also try moving columns so that text beginning on the first page continues on later pages.